AMAZING FACTS

The Indispensable Collection Of True Life Facts and Feats

AMAZING FACTS

The Indispensable Collection Of True Life Facts and Feats

Richard B. Manchester

Galahad Books
New York

PUBLISHED IN 1987 BY
GALAHAD BOOKS
166 FIFTH AVENUE
NEW YORK, NY 10010

ABRIDGED FROM THE MAMMOTH BOOK OF FASCINATING INFORMATION, THE MAMMOTH BOOK OF TRIVIA, AND THE SECOND MAMMOTH BOOK OF TRIVIA
BY ARRANGEMENT WITH HART ASSOCIATES

LIBRARY OF CONGRESS CATALOG CARD NUMBER: 87-80174
ISBN: 0-88365-717-1

PRINTED IN THE UNITED STATES OF AMERICA

Contents

The Advertising Art of Yesteryear

The products, the hopes, the interests, the worldly goods of a bygone day are mirrored in this album of advertising art of the late 19th and early 20th century. Some of these products have survived. Some of the stores which sold some of these things still exist; others are celebrated in legend, and history.

The pages which follow will awaken nostalgia, excite wonderment, and will interest folks of this generation who would like to cast an eye on what animated our forebears.

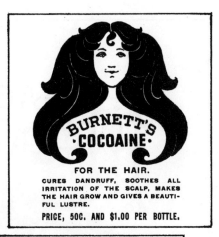

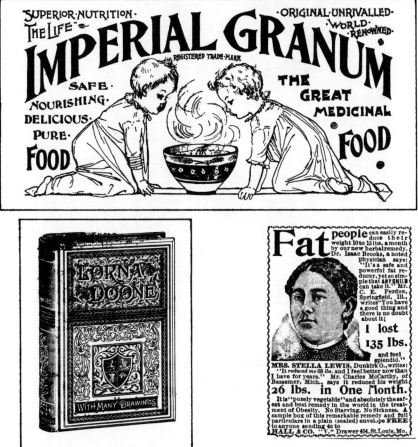

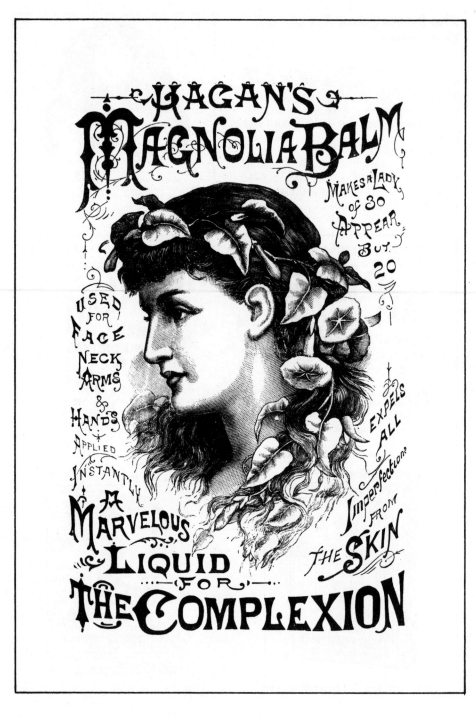

"Remington"

to the Front

'96 MODELS.

Remington Bicycles, like Remington firearms, are Standards of Excellence.

Highest reputation for best quality has brought the

"Remington" to the Front.

They are the finest cycles that experience can produce, that money can purchase. Our 1896 Catalog is very attractive and brim full of information. Mailed free on request. Order early to obtain one of first edition.

Agencies arranged in unoccupied territory. Are you handling the right line of wheels? 80 years of success in high class manufacturing is of great assistance to agents.

REMINGTON ARMS CO., 313-315 Broadway, New York City.

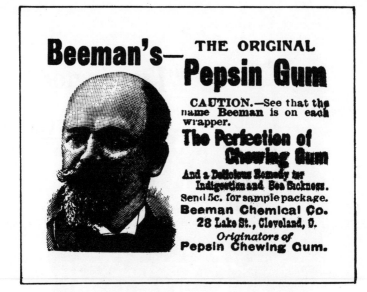

5

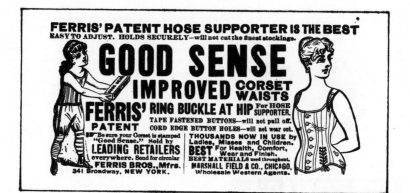

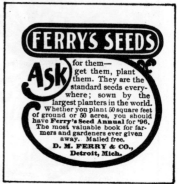
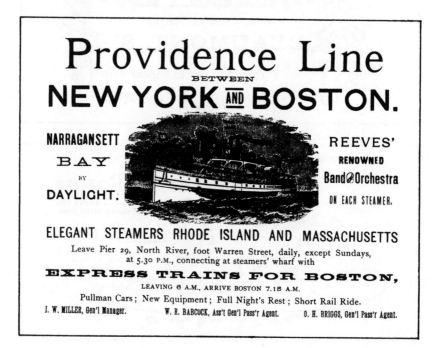

RÉCAMIER TOILET PREPARATIONS

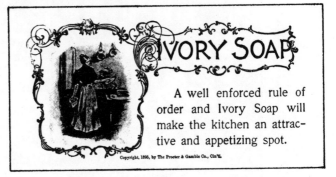

IVORY SOAP

A well enforced rule of order and Ivory Soap will make the kitchen an attractive and appetizing spot.

Copyright, 1896, by The Procter & Gamble Co., Cin'ti.

Millions Use PEARLINE for House Cleaning

Why? Because PEARLINE takes the drudgery right out of house-cleaning—does the work better—quicker and with less labor than anything known. Saves the worst of the wear by doing away with the rubbing. Cleans furniture—paint—carpets, without taking them up—pictures—glass—marble—bath tubs—everything—nothing too coarse, nothing too fine for PEARLINE. You'll appreciate this fact best by giving it a fair trial. House-cleaning time will pass so smoothly the men folks will not suspect its presence.   120   Manufactured only by JAMES PYLE, New York.

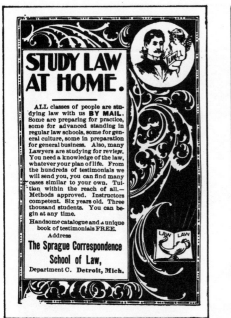

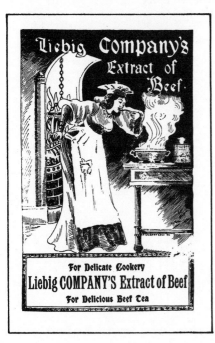

11

The Pianola, the Simplest Means of Playing the Piano

There are Just Two Means of Playing the Piano

Either by training one's own fingers to strike the piano-keys — an occupation of a lifetime — or by utilizing a modern invention and have the keys struck by perfectly adjusted felt-covered fingers, operated automatically, yet controlled *absolutely* by the player.

The success of the Pianola is possibly the strongest proof of the universal appreciation of the time and drudgery saved.

These two are the only means open to any one to produce music. Another's fingers may be hired to play, but only when one directs the fingers that strike the notes does he himself produce music and have thrown open to him the inexhaustible resources of the piano and the rich legacy of all the famous composers as well as the newer music of the present day.

Inconceivable as it may seem, *the Pianola-player controls the Pianola's fingers as they strike the piano with so great delicacy and sensitiveness as to make the playing indistinguishable from that of the human fingers.*

MOSZKOWSKI says: "Any one hidden in a room near by who will hear the Pianola for the first time will surely think that it is a great virtuoso that plays."

SAUER says: "I can freely say the Pianola gives me more pleasure than I have had from thousands of so-called treats of pianistic effort."

The Pianola has taken a prominent place in the history of musical development. At first looked upon as a clever mechanical toy, it has aroused an outburst of enthusiasm from the entire musical world as the realization of its technical and artistic possibilities has forced itself upon these critics. *Every musician of prominence in this country and in Europe has accepted the Pianola.*

"The Pianola must inevitably revolutionize the whole present pianistic situation."— *Musical Courier*.

The important position the Pianola is to occupy in the future of music makes it an object of interest to every one.

Visitors welcome. The price of the Pianola is but $250, yet it gives you the full value of your piano. Can be bought on instalments. Catalogue W sent upon request.

THE AEOLIAN CO.

18 WEST TWENTY-THIRD STREET, NEW YORK
500 FULTON STREET, BROOKLYN, N. Y.
124 EAST FOURTH STREET, CINCINNATI, O.

Chicago, Lyon & Healy	Pittsburg, C. C. Mellor Co.	Toronto, Mason & Risch P. Co.	Omaha, Schmoller & Mueller	Salt Lake City, Daynes M. Co.
Phila., C. J. Heppe & Son	New Orleans, Ph. Werlein, Ltd.	Providence, Steinert & Sons Co.	Los Angeles, South'n Cal. M. Cn.	Duluth, Duluth Music Co.
St. Louis, Bollman Bros. Co.	Detroit, Grinnell Bros.	Kas. City, Jenkins' Sons M. Co.	Albany, Cluett & Sons	Fort Wayne, The Packard Co.
Boston, M. Steinert & Sons Co.	Milwaukee, W. Rohlfing & Sons	St. Paul, W. J. Dyer & Bro.	Portland, Morris B. Wells	Dallas, Will A. Watkin M. Co.
Baltimore, Wm. Knabe & Co.	Washington, Wm. Knabe & Co.	Rochester, H. Tracy Balcom	Atlanta, Phillips & Crew Co.	Augusta, Thomas & Barton Co.
Cleveland, B. Dreher's Sons Co.	Newark, Lauter Co.	Denver, Denver Music Co.	Richmond, W. D. Moses & Co	Wheeling, F. W. Baumer Co.
Buffalo, H. Tracy Balcom	Montreal, L. E. N. Pratte & Co.	Toledo, Whitney & Currier Co.	Troy, Cluett & Sons	Montgomery, E. E. Forbes
San Francisco, Kohler & Chase	Minneapolis, Metrop'tan M. Co.	Syracuse, Chase & Smith Co.	Charleston, Henry Siegling	Helena, Reeves & Co.

(Fleming & Carnrick Press, New York)

12

13

Good morning

HAVE YOU USED **PEARS'** Soap?

15

16

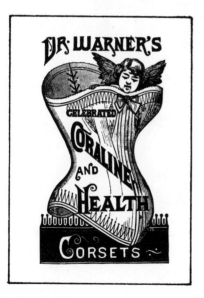

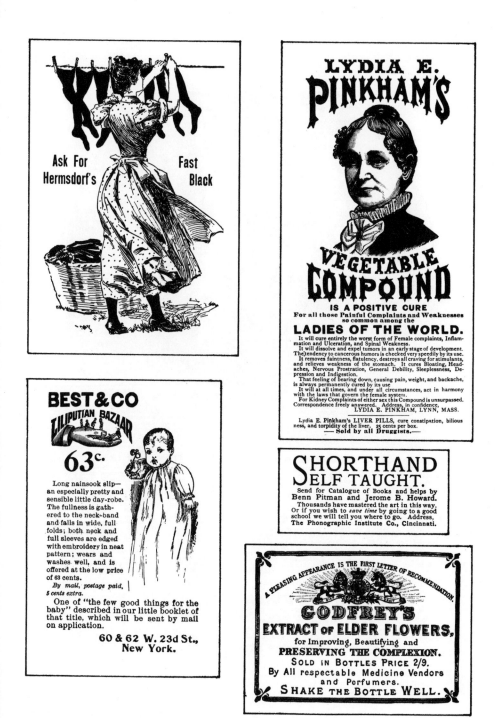

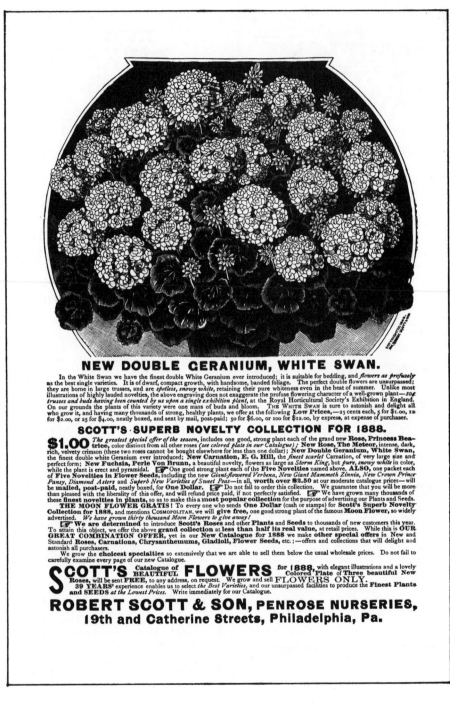
22

ALPHABETS

If one man could be credited with the invention of the alphabet, he would probably stand as the greatest inventor of all human history. For its long-reaching importance, the alphabet is the most significant of all cultural inventions. Writing would be possible without an alphabet, but hardly as accessible as it is today, and hardly as precise. The effects of widespread literacy and precise written languages have touched in some way on almost every other invention and cultural advance.

An alphabet is a code, a shorthand for human speech sounds. The alphabets of the world range from 11 letters to 72 letters, with the average in the 20s. Those letters cover the entire range of sounds in a language, yet are simple enough to be learned by a first-grader.

But the alphabet was not, of course, the invention of a single person. The alphabet was produced by a gradual evolution of written language from primitive picture drawings. Despite the invention of printing and typing, that alphabet has undergone relatively few important changes in 3,000 years.

There are three fundamental kinds of writing systems: logographic, syllabic, and alphabetic. They differ from one another in the kinds of units their symbols represent. Basically, the three systems evolved one from the other in that order, but all three are still in use.

In a *logographic* writing system, each symbol represents a word. Logographic writing systems developed directly from the oldest form of written communication: pictures representing objects or actions. Unlike a letter of the alphabet, a logographic symbol has no phonetic value, though the word it represents has a pronunciation. Our symbol 3, for instance, has no phonetic value, in itself, but does stand for a word pronounced *three*.

Chinese is the most familiar example of a contemporary logographic writing system. For the most part, each Chinese character stands for a single word rather than a sound. Learning to write Chinese requires memorizing many thousands of characters, a skill well beyond any first-grader. And the number of characters makes Chinese a difficult language to reproduce with a printing press.

But Chinese does have one advantage: the written language can be understood by people all over China, even though they speak dialects that are not mutually intelligible. The sign for "house," for instance, is understood by all Chinese to mean a dwelling, no matter how the word for "house" is pronounced in the speaker's dialect.

In a *syllabic* writing system, each symbol stands for a single syllable. A syllabic transcription of our word *alphabet* would require three signs: one for *al*, one for *pha*, and one for *bet*. Since the number of different syllabic sounds in any language is often less than a hundred, a syllabic written language is much easier to learn than a logographic system with its thousands of characters.

Japanese is an example of a written language that is basically syllabic. In the fifth century, the Japanese adopted Chinese script and selected 47 Chinese characters to represent 47 syllabic sounds of the Japanese language.

In one corner of the world, the neighboring countries of China, Japan, and Korea, we find all .hree kinds of writing systems in current use: the Chinese logographic, the Japanese syllabic, and the Korean alphabetic—the Koreans adopted an alphabet from Sanskrit forms.

By far the most common form of writing system around the world is the *alphabetic*, in which each symbol represents a single sound element. The number of single sound elements in a language is lower than the number of syllabic sounds, and so an alphabetic system can be learned easily at a young age. Our own alphabet makes do with just 26 letters; other alphabets have fewer.

The development of our alphabet—the Roman—follows an evolution from logographic to syllabic to alphabetic writing systems. Writing systems developed independently in the Far East and the Americas, but writing as we know it took shape in the Near East, beginning with the cuneiform writing of the Sumerians and the hieroglyphics of the ancient Egyptians—which may have themselves evolved from Sumerian writing.

The cuneiform writing of the Sumerians and Babylonians was in use by 3,000 B.C. Originally, Mesopotamian tongues were represented by pictures carved in stone. But the picture forms evolved into a syllabic shorthand of some 150 symbols, consisting of lines ending in the wedge-shaped marks that gave cuneiform its name. (The word comes from *cuneus*, Latin for "wedge.") The change may have been due in part to a move from the stone tablet to the clay tablet as a writing surface. Carving intricate pictures with a stylus is difficult with clay; pressing in wedge-shaped marks is far easier.

The hieroglyphic writing system of ancient Egypt originally consisted of word signs alone. Gradually, some of these symbols came to represent word sounds instead. A symbol standing for the word *ray*, for instance, could come to stand for the sound "ray," and thus could be joined with the sign for the word *sing* to produce *racing*.

With only word sounds to represent rather than the individual words, the Egyptian written language was reduced to a system of about 80 characters. Since each symbol no longer had to look something like the object or action it represented, and was less likely to be confused with another sign, writing could be executed much more quickly and carelessly. These hieroglyphic symbols, as written hastily by ordinary Egyptians, became the hieratic and demotic scripts of Egypt, and perhaps the syllabic symbols of other Near Eastern languages, such as Aramaic, Phoenician, and Early Hebrew.

We know that the Greek alphabet was derived from one or more of the Semitic alphabets, for the Greek and Semitic alphabets employed similar names for the letters, and listed the letters of their alphabets in basically the same order. Also, the names of the Semitic letters had some meaning in the Semitic tongues—*aleph*, the first letter, meant "ox," while *beth*, the second letter, meant "house"; the Greek names for those two letters, *alpha* and *beta*, had no meaning in Greek. Our word *alphabet*

This is one of the pages of a book published in Magdeburg, Germany in 1689. Four alphabets are presented: UPPER LEFT, *Black letter;* BOTTOM LEFT, *Roman;* UPPER RIGHT, *Hebrew;* BOTTOM RIGHT, *Greek.*

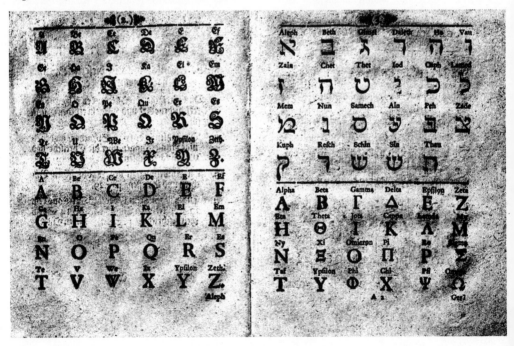

is formed from the names of the first two letters of the Greek alphabet, though it was the Romans who coined the word, not the Greeks.

But the exact origins of the Greek alphabet are still open to question. According to one theory, simplified Egyptian hieroglyphics evolved into an alphabet used in the Sinai Peninsula around 1,500 B.C., which later evolved into the various Semitic alphabets that fathered the Greek. Another theory holds that these Semitic alphabets developed independently of the Egyptian writing system somewhere in the Near East. Two alphabets in this area during the first millenium B.C. were those of the Phoenician language and those of the Aramaic, the region's most common language of the time. The Greek alphabet probably evolved from one or both of these scripts.

It's possible that the Greeks first came in contact with a form of the Aramaic alphabet that was used by Semitic peoples in Asia Minor before 1,000 B.C. A second borrowing of a Semitic alphabet may have come through Phoenician traders who roamed the Mediterranean in the earliest days of Greece. The Phoenician writing system was used in ancient Carthage, and formed the basis of the modern Berber alphabet. By the fourth century B.C., a number of Greek scripts had merged into a uniform Greek alphabet.

The earliest surviving Greek writing dates from the eighth century B.C., and was written right-to-left, as are Semitic tongues, or with alternating rows of right-to-left and left-to-right. All Greek writing wasn't left-to-right until the fifth century B.C. The Greeks directly borrowed some signs of the Semitic alphabet and adopted some of the unused symbols for use as vowels, since the Semitic scripts did not have vowel forms.

It was the Greeks, then, who first employed a truly alphabetic writing system like the one we use today. Originally, the Greek letters, like the Semitic, stood for syllable sounds: the letter *t*, for example, stood for either *te*, *ti*, or *ta*. To distinguish between the syllable sounds, the Greeks added vowel symbols after the *t*, and these vowel signs came to represent the vowel sound itself; the *t* then came to represent the consonant alone.

The Roman alphabet was derived directly from the Greek. It may have reached Italy with the Etruscans who settled there in the ninth century B.C., bringing with them a Greek alphabet from Asia Minor, or with Greeks who settled in southern Italy a century later. A number of languages and alphabets were in use in Italy for a time. But as the Romans gained predominance, their alphabet and language, called Latin, replaced all others. The oldest surviving example of Latin writing dates from the sixth century B.C., and was written right-to-left.

The Romans borrowed 16 of the 24 letters of the Greek alphabet, discarded other Greek letters that stood for sounds absent in Latin, and invented or adapted other letters for Latin sounds that did not exist in Greek. For instance, the Romans developed both the *c* and the *g* from the Greek letter *gamma*, and changed the Greek symbol for a long *a* to our *h*.

The Romans had no use for the sixth letter of the Greek alphabet, the *z*, since that sound did not exist in the language. It was reinstated in the first century B.C., along with the *y*, to transcribe Greek words, and placed at the end of the alphabet. The Romans introduced the letter *f*, taking the form from an old Greek symbol for a *w* sound. Initially, the *f* sound was represented in Latin by the letter combination *fh*. The Romans also used the letter *v* to stand for three sounds: the *u*, the *v*, and the *w*.

Three Greek symbols that the Romans did not incorporate into their alphabet were adopted for use as numerals. The Greek *theta* became the C, standing for 100; the Greek *phi* became the M, standing for mille, or 1,000; the Greek *chi* became the L, standing for 50.

Thus Latin was written with an alphabet of 23 letters. Around the 10th century, the *v* split into two letters, *u* and *v*. Soon after, the letter *w* entered the alphabet. The last of our 26 letters, the *j*, didn't appear until the 15th century; previously the *i* had stood for both the *i* and the *j* sound. The oldest letter in our alphabet is the *o*, which has remained unchanged since its use in the Semitic alphabets.

The Semitic scripts that evolved into our Roman alphabet also produced many of the world's other alphabets. Semitic traders brought an alphabet to India that was to become the Brahmi script, the parent of all Indian alphabets. The Aramaic alphabet became Persian script. The Aramaic alphabet as used by peoples in Arabia also evolved into the modern Arabic script, now the second most common in the world, after the Roman. Looking at a page of modern Arabic, it's hard to believe these symbols evolved from the same source that produced our own alphabet!

The Runic alphabet, used by Teutonic peoples in Northern Europe during the Roman Empire, was probably derived from either the Greek alphabet employed in the area close to the Black Sea, or the

Some characters from the Runic alphabet.

Latin alphabet of the Romans who colonized the area. The Slavic alphabets used today by many people in Eastern Europe were invented by the ninth-century missionary Cyril to transcribe the Slavic tongues; the forms were adopted from a Greek alphabet of the time. Two scripts developed, the Glagolithic and the Cyrillic, but since the 17th century only the Cyrillic has been used.

Not all Slavic languages use the Cyrillic alphabet, however. Missionaries who worked among the Poles and Czechs introduced the Roman alphabet instead of the Greek. In Yugoslavia today, we find two alphabets in use to transcribe the same language: the Serbians use a Cyrillic alphabet for Serbo-Croatian, while the Croatians use a Roman alphabet.

There are now about 65 alphabets in use around the world. The alphabet with the most letters is Cambodian, which has 72. Naturally, the logographic Chinese system has many more characters than there are letters in any alphabet: one Chinese dictionary listed almost 50,000 signs, including 92 for a single sound! And the most complex Chinese character has 52 individual strokes!

The alphabet with the least letters is Rotokas, a South Pacific tongue, which has 11 letters and only six consonants. Two Caucasian alphabets include just two vowels, while another Caucasian tongue, Ubyx, has 80 consonant sounds, the most of any language on earth. A Vietnamese language called Sedang can claim the most vowel sounds, 55.

Our alphabet has 26 letters, of course, but if you examine modern script you'll find that we really have two different alphabets: the lower case and the capitals. Look, for instance, at the upper and lower case forms A and a, or G and g, D and d, or R and r. You'd have little reason to guess that these symbols are different forms of the same letters!

The Roman alphabet consisted solely of capitals for many centuries. But the large, angular Latin letters that were suitable for carving in stone were less suitable for quick everyday writing. By the fourth century, scribes had adopted a set of letters, called *uncials*, that were developed from the capital

forms, but were more rounded and easier to write quickly. These uncials later contributed to the formation of the *minuscule* alphabet, forerunner of our lower case letters. Minuscules were far easier and quicker to write with a pen than the older majuscules, or capital forms.

By the eighth century, a "perfect minuscule" alphabet had been developed in Western Europe. This script, called the Carolingian, later became the model for the modern lower case alphabet. At the time of Gutenberg, around 1450, the Gothic or black letter script was the most common in Europe. Black letter remained in use through much of Europe until the 17th century—and in Germany, into the 20th century.

Early in the renaissance period, scribes in Florence developed a script, based on the earlier Carolingian minuscule, that was more sloping and cursive than black letter. This writing gradually became the modern Italian script you undoubtedly use today, as well as the modern *italic* type.

Our alphabet hasn't necessarily seen its last change, either. Many people are eager to see a reform of English orthography, or spelling, that would bring the written language more into line with the spoken language. In some modern tongues—Spanish, Italian, and German, for instance—the spoken language is fairly accurately transcribed by the written language. But in English, due to the retention of archaic forms, there is often no correlation between the way a word is spelled and the way it is pronounced—which makes the spelling bee a distinctly English or American activity.

The English words *cite*, *site*, and *sight* are all pronounced the same, but spelled differently. And the letter combination *ough* has a different pronunciation in each of the words *through*, *bough*, *cough*, *rough*, *brought*, *hiccough*, and *dough*. It's not that far-fetched to think that, a few centuries from now, those words might be spelled *thru*, *bow*, *cawf*, *ruff*, *brawt*, *hikup*, and *doe*—or perhaps with letters that aren't even in our alphabet today.

George Bernard Shaw, for one, proposed an alphabet of 40 symbols, in which each sound in our language would be represented by one letter. As Shaw pointed out, according to contemporary orthography, the word *fish* might be spelled *ghoti*—taking the *gh* from *enough*, the *o* from *women*, and the *ti* from words such as *nation*.

Our spelling is not, after all, as simple as *abc*.

Apples

An old-fashioned apple peeler and corer.

Nothing may be as American as apple pie, but there's really nothing American about the apple at all. This familiar fruit is now grown in every state, and eaten in some form by almost all of us. Yet when Columbus set foot in the New World, there wasn't a single apple tree on this side of the Atlantic!

The apple is actually native to parts of Europe and western Asia, and may have originated in the area of present-day Iran. The fruit has been eaten by man since earliest times. How early? No, it wasn't necessarily the apple that Adam and Eve tasted in the Garden of Eden.

The Bible tells us only that Adam and Eve sinned by eating the fruit of the "tree of knowledge of good and evil." The word *fruit* came into our language as *apple*, which was formerly used to mean any fruit. Nowhere does the Bible claim that the forbidden fruit was actually what we now call the apple. In similar legends from the East, the forbidden fruit was the *banana!*

The word *apple* was also used in past centuries for the pupil of the eye, a translation of the Latin *pupillam*. The Latin phrase "apple of the eye" thus meant simply the pupil of the eye. But the phrase has been used to refer to something precious.

The Apple of Discord in Greek mythology also was not necessarily an apple. According to the myth, Eris, sister of Ares, was angered at a group of wedding guests, and tossed an apple among them, intended for the most beautiful woman in the group. There were three claimants: Hera, Athena, and Aphrodite. The Trojan prince Paris was chosen as the judge. To win his favor, Hera offered him power; Athena promised him wisdom; Aphrodite promised him the most beautiful woman in the world. Paris chose Aphrodite, and she assisted him in carrying off Helen, beginning the Trojan War.

But it was surely the real apple that was flourishing in Europe by the third century B.C., when Roman censor Cato described seven varieties. The Romans did a great deal to spread the apple through the Empire, although certain species were probably growing earlier in Europe. The Druids of Britain, for instance, venerated the apple prior to the arrival of the Romans. Perhaps they knew that, centuries later, one of the fruits was to fall on the head of Isaac Newton and help man gain his first insight into gravity.

Apples were cultivated largely in monasteries until the 16th century, and thereafter in small private orchards. Over 100 varieties of apple were known in medieval Europe. The fruit continued to spread, to North America, to South America, to Australia, even to the Orient: Japan is currently one of the top apple-producing nations! And the apple in all its varieties is now the most widely cultivated tree fruit of the temperate climes.

The first apples to reach America arrived from England in 1629, along with seeds and propagating wood. Ten years later, the first apples grown in the United States were plucked from trees planted on Beacon Hill, Boston. By 1741, New England was producing apples for export, and apple cultivation was sweeping westward across America.

One of the men we might thank for spreading the apple tree in America was Jonathan Chapman, better known as Johnny Appleseed. Many people think Johnny was merely a legendary figure, but he lived, indeed. Born in Massachusetts around 1775, Chapman set out alone into the unexplored wilderness that is now Ohio, Indiana, and western Pennsylvania, with a sack of apple seeds he'd collected from cider mills. Wherever he went, he planted apple seeds, and retraced his paths to prune the trees he'd planted. Before he died in 1846, he covered more than 100,000 square miles with apple trees!

The fruit that gave Jonathan Chapman his nickname is known in botanical circles as *Malus pumila*. The apple is a pome, or fleshy fruit, like the pear and

27

quince. The *Malus* genus, which includes about 25 species, owes its name to the Latin word for "evil," due to its Biblical reputation.

The only apple we might dub truly "evil" is an apple with a worm in it. These pesky critters do not crawl inside the apple that provides their home—they're born there. Fruit flies stab holes in the skin of a ripening apple and release eggs into the fruit. The eggs hatch into white worms, which feed on the apple tissue as they grow. When the apple falls to the ground, the worms crawl out and burrow into the earth; the following summer, they emerge as fruit flies and begin searching for a likely apple for their eggs.

Another apple that might deserve the name *malus* is the crab apple—which owes its name not to a crustacean, but most likely to a Scottish word for a wild apple. Crab apples comprise a number of *Malus* species, whose high acid content and sour taste make them unsuitable for eating. Crab apple trees are often used as ornamental plants, and some of the fruits find their way into jelly or apple cider.

In the United States, we use the word *cider* for both the fermented and the unfermented juice of the apple. But in France, *cidre* always packs a punch of at least 3.2 percent alcohol. More than three-quarters of all French apples are used for cider—France produces over 40 million gallons a year! Most cider comes from Normandy and Brittany, from apples that would make poor eating fruits.

Some 900 million bushels of apples are currently harvested around the world each year, and more than a quarter of them find their way into cider. Worldwide apple production has almost doubled in the last 40 years. The largest apple growers are France and the United States, both of whom harvest more than 100 million bushels a year. Apples are grown in quantity in all of Western Europe, and in Japan, Australia, Argentina, and Canada.

In America, apples are grown from coast to coast, but the Pacific Northwest accounts for about 35 percent of the annual apple harvest, and the Northeast about 25 percent. Washington is the number-one apple growing state. New York, Virginia, Michigan, Pennsylvania, Oregon, and California are also large producers. Perhaps some of those Pennsylvania apples are relatives of the trees Johnny Appleseed planted!

Over 7,000 varieties of apple have been recorded in the United States, only a handful of which have become commercially important. Apple trees do not grow true to type by seed, and therefore are propagated by budding and grafting. Most varieties arose from chance seedlings that produced trees with good qualities, including resistance and high yield. A good tree can produce over 30 bushels of fruit each harvest. That means that when an Oregonian set the current world's record for apple picking—270 bushels in eight hours—he must have stripped the fruit from at least nine trees!

The *Delicious*, grown largely in the Northwest, is the most common variety of apple in the United States, accounting for about 20 percent of the annual production. The *McIntosh*, widely grown in the Northeast and in western Canada, accounts for about 10 percent. Other popular varieties are the *Winesap*, grown largely in the Northwest; the *Jonathan*, popular in the Midwest; the *Rome Beauty*, another Midwestern favorite; the *Baldwin*, grown in the Northeast and especially suited for apple juice; the *Northern Spy*, *York Imperial*, *Stayman Winesap*, and *Grimes Golden*.

More than half of the apples grown in the United States are eaten fresh, while about one-fifth are used for vinegar, juice, jelly, and apple butter, and one-fifth for canned pie stock and applesauce. In Europe, a far higher percentage of the apple production is used for cider. The average American consumes from 20 to 25 pounds of apples a year, in one form or another.

How much of the American apple harvest is currently used for good old-fashioned American apple pie is unknown. Also unknown is the origin of the phrase "apple pie order," for there's nothing particularly orderly about the apples in an apple pie. Some etymologists have suggested the phrase may have originated in the French *cap-à-pie*—"head to foot"—or *nappes-pliées*— "folded linen."

Other popular apple phrases include "apple polisher," a person who curries favor with gifts—like a student who brings his teacher an apple. "To upset the apple cart" requires no explanation. "Applesauce" connotes nonsense.

Then there's "an apple a day keeps the doctor away"—it might also keep the dentist at bay—and of course, the "Big Apple," one of the more kindly epithets for America's largest city, New York.

But the most profound comment on *Malus pumila* can be credited to William Shakespeare. "There's small choice," the bard wrote, "in rotten apples."

Asparagus

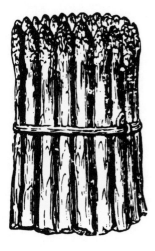

Today, asparagus may well be considered the "prince of vegetables," for the delicious green shoots—even the canned variety—are higher in price per pound than almost any other common vegetable. The high price and peculiar appearance of asparagus might suggest an exotic origin for the vegetable, but the fact is, asparagus is grown and eaten today, as always, almost exclusively in Europe and the United States.

Botanically, asparagus is a genus of the lily family, comprising some 120 species growing widely in the temperate zones of Europe and America. *Asparagus officinalis*, the popular edible variety, is a native of the temperate zones of the Old World, and grows naturally in southern England and the Russian steppes. Though the plant produces a flower and a small whitish berry, we eat only the stem, or shoot, of the plant.

Asparagus has been cultivated around the Mediterranean for many centuries, and there is evidence of the vegetable in Egypt as long ago as 3000 B.C. The Greeks and Romans were both fond of asparagus, and by the second century B.C. the green shoots were already considered a luxury food. The Romans cultivated asparagus in trenches, vying for the biggest shoots, and

served it often in pureed form at banquets. We know that Cleopatra entertained Marc Antony with asparagus at such a feast. The Roman expression "You can do it in less time than it takes to cook asparagus" was the Latin equivalent of "two shakes of a lamb's tail."

Asparagus cultivation lapsed for centuries, then reappeared in the 16th and 17th centuries in France and England. French monarch Louis XIV took great pride in serving his guests forced-grown asparagus in January.

"Asparagus" is a second-century Latin word based on the Greek word for "sprout" or "shoot." In 18th-century England the vegetable was known as "sparagus," "sparage," or "sparagrass," and later—somewhat tongue in cheek, perhaps—as "sparrow-grass."

Thomas Jefferson was one of the first farmers to cultivate asparagus in the United States, growing the vegetable in his greenhouse with seeds imported from Europe. Cultivation on a large scale began here in the 1850s. Today asparagus is grown in 15 states from Maine to Virginia; from California, well over 120,000 tons reach the market each year. In some places the plant has escaped cultivation and can be found growing naturally in salt marshes and along roadsides.

There are four basic varieties of asparagus in widespread cultivation today. The French *Argen-*

Asparagus steamer. In this upright copper pot with brass handles, asparagus may be cooked to perfection. This 10-inch high contraption is lined with tin.

teuil has a thick stem and a purple head. The English *Green* is, not surprisingly, green, smaller, thinner, and more flavorful than the Argenteuil. The Genoa variety—called *asperge violette* in France is, as you might have guessed, purple. (Mildly flavored white asparagus is also grown in Europe, chiefly for canning.) The most popular edible variety is the *Lauris*, a French hybrid developed from the English Green and now grown extensively in south-

ern France. And other species— mainly African climbing variet- ies—are used as decorative plants.

The asparagus spears we eat are actually shoots growing out of the soil from submerged roots, and if not picked before maturity, would eventually blossom into flowers and fruits. Each plant formerly produced less than a dozen shoots, but with modern cultivation techniques one plant can now furnish as many as 70. They're in season, by the way, from January through September—don't expect anything but canned spears at most other times.

Asparagus presents a problem in cooking, since the tender tips will cook much sooner than the fibrous stem bottoms. Chefs recommend that you cook the spears upright in a pan, with water reaching slightly more than halfway up the spears, so that the submerged bottoms are boiled, and the tips merely steamed. They also suggest that undercooked asparagus is preferable to overcooked spears, and warn against using strongly flavored sauces or wine with asparagus, since the vegetable contains high amounts of sulfur that can ruin a wine.

Well, now that you know where "sparrow-grass" comes from, the available varieties, and the best way to prepare it, the only question remaining is: how can you afford it?

Asparagus is higher in price per pound than almost any other common vegetable.

Backgammon

Backgammon is much older than craps, ranking as the oldest dice game still widely played.

Just 20 years ago, most Americans probably regarded backgammon—if they knew the game at all—as an exotic, unfamiliar game whose board often turned up, quite uselessly, on the back of checkerboards. Times have changed, and the games we play have changed as well. While checkers has lost a good deal of its popularity, "exotic" backgammon is now the fastest-growing game in America, with millions of dedicated players, hundreds of backgammon clubs, and an international circuit of major tournaments. Today, backgammon experts command lesson fees of up to $150 an hour!

But the current backgammon craze is hardly a phenomenon unique to our age. The popularity of backgammon has not risen steadily to its present peak, but rather has surged and ebbed through the ages. After a period of obscurity, backgammon is now riding the crest of a new wave of interest. Who knows? If backgammon continues to grow at the present rate, it might even become as popular as it was 2,000 years ago!

Historians have traced the origins of backgammon to many sources. The fact is, the game was never "invented." Instead, backgammon evolved from a number of old games, including the earliest known board games enjoyed by man.

In the 1920s, during British archaeologist Sir Leonard Woolley's excavation of the ancient Sumerian city of Ur, he found five game boards in the royal cemetery that bore a resemblance to early backgammon boards. The 5,000-year-old Sumerian game was played on a board of 20 squares, with six dice and seven pieces for each player.

A game board similar to those unearthed at Ur was found among the treasures in the tomb of the Egyptian king Tutankhamen, dating from 1500 B.C. Egyptian wall paintings show that the board game, called *senet,* was popular among the common people as well as among royalty. The Egyptians even had a sort of mechanical dice cup, a machine that shook and threw the dice to protect against dice cheats, who seem to be as ancient as dice themselves.

Oddly enough, the Spanish explorer Ferdinand Pizarro found the Aztecs in Mexico playing a game, *patolli,* that bore a remarkable similarity to the games enjoyed by the ancient Egyptians. Nobles in the court of Montezuma played *patolli* for high stakes, using semiprecious stones as game pieces. Some anthropologists view the similarity between the Aztec and Egyptian games as proof that the people of the Americas migrated to the Western Hemisphere from Africa or Asia.

The still popular Persian game of *parcheesi* may have been a remote ancestor of backgammon. In parcheesi, as in backgammon, the object of the game is to remove all of one's pieces from the board. Single pieces left on the parcheesi board may be "hit" by an opponent and sent back to the beginning of the board. Two or more of a player's pieces on a single square, or point, capture the point in parcheesi as well as in backgammon. Parcheesi also includes bonus provisions for a player rolling doubles.

Games far closer to modern backgammon were widely enjoyed by the ancient Greeks and Romans.

Plato commented on the popularity of these games, and Homer mentions them in the *Odyssey.* The Greeks, by the way, had names for various dice throws reminiscent of our *snake eyes.* A six was known as *aphrodite;* a one was called a *dog.*

In ancient Rome, we find the first game board featuring 12 points on each side, like the backgammon board. The Romans' *ludus duodecim scriptorum,* or "12-line game," is thought to have been adapted from earlier board games similar to the one found in Tutankhamen's tomb. But the Roman game board included *three* rows of 12 points. A later Roman game, called *tabulae,* reduced the number of points to 24, with 12 on each side, as in the modern game. The Romans played both games with three dice rather than two.

Tabulae was very popular among the Roman aristocracy. In the ruins of Pompeii, we find a *tabulae*-board table top in the courtyard of almost every villa. Nero was known to play the "sport of emperors" for as much as $15,000 a point, and the Emperor Commodus sometimes dipped into the royal treasury to pay off his *tabulae* gambling debts. But Roman paintings tell us that the game was popular among plebians as well. One painting depicts a fight

A Dutch backgammon set of the 17th century.

in an inn arising from a game of *tabulae*. Another suggests that the Romans used *tabulae* to play a form of classical "strip poker."

The beginning of the Christian era did little to stamp out *tabulae* in Europe. A marble slab game board dating from the early days of Christian Rome bears a cross and the inscription: "Christ grants aid and victory to dicers if they write His Name when they roll, Amen." Modern backgammon gamblers have been known to utter the name of the diety in a slightly different vein.

Roman legionnaires spread *tabulae* throughout the Empire. In England, the game became known as *tables*, a term which persisted well into the 17th century. But *tabulae* and similar games gradually waned in popularity in Europe until revived by Crusaders returning from the Mideast.

At the time of the Crusades, the Saracens enjoyed a game called *nard* that they'd learned from the Persians. The Persians, in turn, may have developed *nard* from earlier Mesopotamian or Indian games, or from parcheesi, or from the board games of Greece and Rome. *Nard* employed black and white pieces on a checkered game board with 12 divisions, and unlike *tabulae*, was played with two dice. By the time of the Third Crusade in the 12th century, backgammon-like games were so popular among the Crusaders that Kings Richard I of England and Philip II of France issued a joint edict prohibiting all gambling games among their troops.

A number of games similar to backgammon have been enjoyed for centuries in the Orient. The Chinese play *shwan-liu*, the Japanese enjoy *sunoroku*, the Koreans *ssang-ryouk*, and the Thais, *len sake*. But most historians believe that these Oriental equivalents of backgammon were imported from the West, and therefore played no part in the development of backgammon itself.

Tables, which included elements from both *tabulae* and *nard*, was widely played by the aristocracy through the Middle Ages, and the game eventually found its way to the lower classes as well. Medieval innkeepers customarily kept boards and dice on hand for their patrons. The Church opposed the game, as it did all gambling pastimes. In 1254, Louis IX outlawed it in France. Suppression of the game continued right up into the 16th century, forcing diehard players to disguise their boards as books, the hinged game board masquerading as the book cover and the dice and pieces hidden inside.

As many as 25 different versions of tables existed in medieval Europe. The modern backgammon board has existed since at least the 14th century, when the game was already quite popular in England. Chaucer mentions tables in the *Canterbury Tales*, with the line "They daucen, and they play-en at ches and tables." James I of Scotland was said to have spent the night before his murder in 1437 "playing at Chess and Tables." A psalter dating from 1499, considered one of the earliest illustrated books ever printed, contains a picture of a man and a woman playing tables. Shakespeare acknowledged the game in *Love's Labour Lost*, when the character Biron says:

This is the ape of the form, Monsieur the Nice,
That, when he plays at tables, chides the dice
In honourable terms.

A story is told that the Duke of Albany, the brother of James III of Scotland, used tables to win far more than cold cash. While imprisoned in Edinburgh castle in the 1480s, the Duke invited the captain of the guard into his cell one night to play tables. In the morning, the captain was found dead in the cell, and the Duke had made good his escape.

The 17th century saw the first wide use of the word *backgammon* in place of *tables*, along with a number of other innovations. For the first time, doubles entitled the roller to play the roll twice, as in the modern game. The concept of the *backgammon* victory was also introduced, although as used at the time a *backgammon* was actually the modern *gammon*—a victory in which the winner succeeds in bearing off all his men from the board before his opponent can remove any of his men.

The word *backgammon* itself has been traced to a number of sources. Some etymologists point to the Welsh *bach cammaun*, "small battle." But most favor the Middle English *baec gamen*, or "back game," traced by some to the medieval custom of constructing a backgammon board on the back of a chessboard, as is often done today. Thus, tables became known as the "game on the back" of the chessboard, and later, "back game."

On the Continent, the game was known as *tavole reale* in Italy, *tablas reales* in Spain, and *trictrac* in France. The French term is thought to owe its origin to the sound made by tumbling dice on a wooden board. A number of *trictrac* boards were

The game of backgammon was a favorite during the 18th century.

34

used by the French court at Versailles. One elaborately decorated board belonging to Marie Antoinette was reputed to have cost over a quarter-million francs.

For some reason, backgammon became very popular among 18th-century clergymen. During the same era, physicians also seem to have favored the pastime. One doctor wrote that backgammon was "an anodyne to the gout, the rheumatism, the azure devils, or the yellow spleen." Even Thomas Jefferson was a backgammon fancier, playing the game in his off hours, while drafting the Declaration of Independence.

Edmond Hoyle has been credited with formulating the rules to many popular games, but actually Hoyle never heard of most of the games for which he is supposed to have codified the rules. In the case of backgammon, however, Hoyle rightly deserves recognition. In 1743, Hoyle wrote a treatise on the game laying down many of the rules we follow today.

Backgammon waned in popularity during the 19th century, although Mississippi riverboat gamblers frequently included a backgammon board in their bag of tricks. Then, in the 1920s, interest in the game was suddenly revived when an unknown American player devised the concept of "doubling"—a rule by which a player can double the stakes in an attempt to force his opponent to concede the game. Doubling did away with long games that had to be played to a finish even after the eventual winner was already fairly obvious.

The concept of redoubling was added shortly thereafter, by another unknown genius. After a few thousand years of evolution, backgammon had become the game we know today. But the modern rules weren't completely codified until 1931, when Wheaton Vaughan of the New York Racquet and Tennis Club prepared the first universally recognized rulebook for the modern game. Backgammon has undergone few changes since then.

The most recent backgammon rage had its beginnings in 1964, when Russian Prince Alexis Obolensky of Palm Beach, Florida, founded an international tournament in the Bahamas for jet-set backgammon buffs. The tournament has been held there every year since then. The maiden 1964 tourney included just 32 players; by 1968, the number had swelled to 128, with additional tournaments for beginners and "consolation flights" for first-round drop-outs. The number of backgammon players in the United States, meanwhile, soared from about 200,000 in 1969 to over two million today. In 1973, game board producers sold more backgammon sets than they had sold in the previous 20 years combined!

Prince Obolensky went on to found similar tournaments in Las Vegas and other places. Since 1966, an annual international backgammon tournament has been held in the London Clermont Club. The 1978 tourney included 100 players competing for $100,000 in prizes. And private gambling matches, played for up to $25 a point, have been known to cost unlucky participants as much as $100,000!

Despite the current backgammon boom, there are certainly millions of Americans without the slightest notion of how the game is played. Though a great deal of strategy and calculation go into an expert game of backgammon, the basic rules of the game are not complex.

The backgammon board contains 24 triangular segments, called *points*, with 12 points on each side. Two players each begin with 15 pieces, arranged on the board as shown in the accompanying diagram. Each player moves his pieces in the direction indicated, according to the throw of two dice. The object of the game is to bring all of one's pieces into the appropriate home board, and then to *bear off* or remove the pieces with suitable throws of the dice.

A player with two or more of his pieces on a point is said to have *made* that point. His opponent's pieces may not come to rest on that point. A single piece remaining on a point is a *blot*. If an opponent's piece comes to rest on a point occupied by a blot, that blot is *hit* and placed on the *bar*, the line between the two halves of the board. A hit blot must then re-enter the game in the opponent's home board, and continue around the board toward the player's own home board.

In each turn, a player rolls two dice. He may move one piece a number of points corresponding to the number rolled on one die, then move a second piece a number of points corresponding to the second die. Or he may use both moves to advance just one piece. A throw of doubles entitles a player to four moves, each the number of points corresponding to the number shown on one die. For example, a pair of three's allows the roller to make four moves of three points each.

The first player to bear off all his pieces wins the game. A player who bears off all his pieces before his opponent can bear off any of his pieces wins a *gammon*. If he succeeds in bearing off all his men

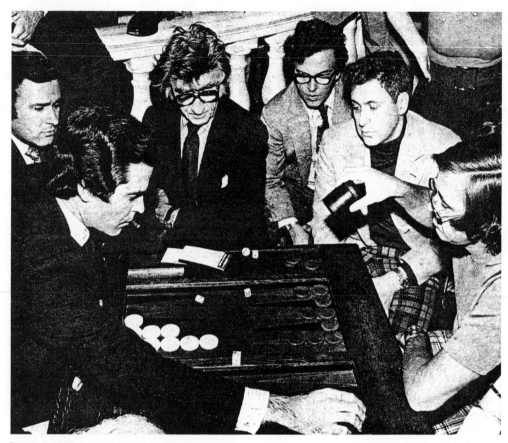

Seagram's 1974 American Championship Tournament of Backgammon at the Plaza Hotel in New York City. Prince *Alexis Obolensky, the doyen and arch promoter of back-gammon, is seated in the center with arms folded.*

while his opponent still has one or more pieces in the winner's home board, the player wins a *back-gammon*. Gammon winners collect double the stakes; backgammon winners collect triple.

No one can be expected to play a game of back-gammon using only the rules sketched above. But if you've never played before, you might have some idea now what all the fuss is about. Backgammon is far more than a simple racing game in which both players move their pieces around the board as quickly as possible. Backgammon players attempt to make points to hinder their opponent's play, and to move their pieces forward without leaving a blot that can be hit by the opponent. Backgammon strategy is intricate enough so that some newspapers, including the *New York Times*, now carry a backgammon column, as has been traditional for bridge or chess.

Backgammon can be played easily enough with just a pair of dice, a makeshift board drawn on a piece of cardboard, and a few checkers. But that hasn't stopped some buffs from shelling out hun-dreds, or even thousands, of dollars for more elabo-rate equipment. Stores devoted exclusively to back-gammon equipment display such luxurious equip-ment as a pearl-and-onyx inlaid board rimmed with gold, with pieces made of jade or ivory. Backgam-mon fanciers have coughed up over $600 for sets that include elephant-hide boards and sterling silver doubling cubes. And one backgammon board, made from batik leather, sells for well over $2,000!

36

One of the incarnations of Chiquita Banana.

Bananas

A recent survey disclosed that about half of all American shoppers buy bananas at least once a week.

"Yes, we have bananas" may not be as humorous nor as rhythmic as "Yes, we have no bananas," the well-known words to the once-popular song, but it's certainly closer to the truth. Americans do have bananas—billions of them! Our ever-growing taste for the fruit has made the United States the world's largest consumer of this yellow-skinned wonder. If Americans continue to consume bananas at the present rate, this country may soon earn the sobriquet of "banana republic."

The banana is now America's favorite fresh fruit. More apples and oranges are consumed here than bananas, but both these fruits are frequently enjoyed in juices and other processed products. Bananas are almost always eaten fresh. Americans now devour over 12 billion bananas each year—close to 19 pounds per person. Yet, virtually no bananas are grown within this country—and the fruit was almost unknown here until just a century or so ago!

A recent survey disclosed that about half of all American shoppers buy bananas at least once a week. And with good reason, for the banana is one of the most compact, inexpensive, and nutritious foods available. Bananas are high in potassium, iron, and various vitamins; and low in sodium. They are 99.8 percent fat free, and devoid of cholesterol. The fruit is so easily digestible that it's often the first solid food fed to babies. But most important, bananas are delicious. It's hard to disagree with British statesman Benjamin Disraeli who, writing from Cairo in 1831, called the banana "the most delicious thing in the world."

The banana has also been called the most ancient fruit on earth. Most botanists believe bananas first grew in southeast Asia, perhaps on the Malay Peninsula. Primitive people there considered the fruit so important that they took banana rootstocks with them wherever they migrated.

The fruit undoubtedly reached India and China at a very early date. The Chinese scholar Yang Fu, in a second-century work called *Record of Strange Things*, extolled the banana as having "a very sweet-tasting pulp, like honey or sugar. Four or five of these fruits are enough for a meal," he noted, "and after eating, the flavor lingers on among the teeth." The neighboring Koreans, however, considered the banana, rather than the apple, the forbidden fruit of the Garden of Eden.

Alexander the Great and his conquering Macedonians were probably the first Europeans to savor bananas in India during the fourth century B.C. We are told by the Roman historian Pliny that the Macedonians found wise men in India sitting in the shade of a banana tree, eating the fruit and discussing philosophy. Many centuries later, when the Swedish botanist Linnaeus classified the plant kingdom, he called the banana *Musa sapientum,* "fruit of the wise men."

The first banana recipe in history appears in the writings of the 10th-century Arab poet Masudi. He described a dish of bananas, almonds, honey, and nut oil that was all the rage in Damascus, Cairo, Constantinople, and other eastern cities. By the year 1000, the banana plant was a familiar sight throughout much of the Mideast.

During the 15th century, the Portuguese brought bananas from the Guinea Coast of Africa to the Canary Islands. It was the Portuguese who coined the word we use today to identify the fruit. The Indians of Alexander's time called the fruit *pala;* while in Africa, it was termed in various languages *banna, abana, gbana,* and *funana.* The Portuguese combined a number of these African words into the easily pronounceable *banana.*

Bananas first arrived in the New World in 1516, just 24 years after Columbus's first journey. A Spanish priest named Fra Tomas de Berlanga brought dry rootstocks from the Canary Islands to Santo Domingo, the first colonial city in the Americas. Bananas were found to grow well in the American tropics, and were soon placed under cultivation in South and Central America, Cuba, Jamaica, and "all other islands peopled by Christians."

One story has it that Puritan settlers in North America sampled bananas during the 1690s, and found them unpalatable—probably because they boiled them, skin and all. But the first recorded

appearance of the banana in this country dates from 1804, when a ship brought 30 bunches of the slender fruits from Cuba. Bananas remained rare and expensive items here through most of the 19th century.

Many Americans caught their first glimpse of the banana at the 1876 Centennial Exposition in Philadelphia. Bananas were still so unfamiliar to most Americans that the fruit and the telephone became the two most popular exhibits at the Exposition. The fruits sold for 10¢ apiece, a high price at the time. Each banana was wrapped in tin foil, although the fruit was naturally protected by its thick skin.

The high price of the fruit was perhaps due to the fact that up to half of each banana cargo was lost to spoilage en route. Then, in 1899, the plantations of Minor Keith, the ships of Lorenzo Baker, and the sales network of Andrew Preston were combined to form the United Fruit Company, which soon became the largest importer of bananas to America. Using modern farming techniques and refrigerated ships, the firm set up a network that

Banana tree.

brought fresh bananas to market within a month of harvest. This process eliminated the large-scale spoilage that had plagued earlier importers.

It was the United Fruit Company (now the United Brands Company) that devised the advertising campaign featuring the now familiar Chiquita banana. Beginning in the early 1940s, the lively banana with high-heeled shoes, ruffled dress, and fruit-bowl hat served as spokeswoman for the firm's principal product. Chiquita sang clever calypso jingles on radio, and later appeared in animated form on television. Chiquita is the official logo and trademark for bananas sold by United Brands.

The most prolific of all food plants, the banana "tree" is actually not a tree at all, but a giant herb—the largest plant on earth without a woody stem. The "trunk" of the banana plant is not a trunk at all, but is made up of thick leaves furled one upon another in overlapping layers, combining to form a shoot that can reach heights of up to 30 feet. And the palmlike leaves themselves often grow up to 10 feet long!

A banana plant will bear fruit only once, but each rootstock of the plant can, in turn, produce an unending series of plants, assuring a continuous crop. Cultivators allow one plant from each rootstock, or rhizome, to mature and bear fruit. Then, they cut down the plant and nurture another shoot from the rhizome.

Each plant bears about 10 bunches of fruit, called *hands,* and each hand contains from 10 to 20 bananas, or *fingers.* Thus, one banana plant will produce an average of 150 bananas, weighing about 85 pounds altogether.

A new banana plant sprouts quickly, producing leaves in

A banana plantation.

the bananas are washed, cut into clusters, labeled, boxed, and sent by rail to port.

The boxed bananas are loaded quickly aboard refrigerated ships—banana boats are often in and out of port within 12 hours—and delivered to ports in the United States. Before being shipped to markets, the fruit is stored in ripening rooms for a few days until the green color changes to a golden yellow. The entire trip from plantation to consumer's shopping cart can take as little as 10 days!

Bananas undergo their final ripening in the home. For best results, the fruits should be stored at room temperature until fully ripe, then placed in the refrigerator. Many Americans are reluctant to store bananas in the refrigerator, lessoned by an earlier Chiquita banana song that warned:

Bananas like the climate of the
very, very tropical equator,
So you should never put bananas
in the refrigerator.

Actually, however, refrigeration will cause the skin to turn brown, but the fruit itself will remain unspoiled for a few days inside its natural shell. The browner the banana's skin, the sweeter the fruit. As Chiquita banana sang:

When they are flecked with
brown and of a golden hue
That's when bananas are the
best for you.

There are over 100 varieties of banana now in cultivation. The two most common varieties are the Gros Michel and the Cavendish. The Gros Michel, grown in large quantities in Jamaica, Panama, and Costa Rica, was for

as little as three weeks. Some old-time banana plantation workers claim they can "hear" the plants growing in the dark. After about eight months, a single bud pushes through the center of a leaf cluster. Small flower clusters then appear, which eventually bend outward and upward as they turn into the hands. Thus the fruits actually grow upside-down. As soon as the fruits begin to form, plantation workers place plastic bags over each hand to protect the bananas from insects, birds, and scarring by wind-battered leaves.

Within a year, the bananas are ready for harvest. Unlike most other fruits, bananas are picked green and ripen later. If the fruits were allowed to ripen on the plant, they would split open and lose much of their sweet flavor.

At harvest time, the fruits are cut from the plants in their plastic bags, then sent by overhead cable or truck to nearby boxing stations. At the boxing station, many years the overwhelming favorite in this country. But the tall Gros Michel is particularly susceptible to wind storms. Winds of just 20 to 30 miles per hour can devastate an entire plantation in minutes. The shorter, sturdier Cavendish has therefore become the most popular variety on most plantations.

The *plantain*, a short, green banana is usually cooked, since its fruit is starchy rather then sweet. Many Caribbean and Central American dishes use the plantain in much the same way that we use the potato.

Incidentally, banana oil does not come from the banana, for banana plants produce no commercial oil of any kind. Banana oil is actually a synthetic compound, so-named because its aroma was thought to resemble the banana's.

The soft, sweet fruit of the banana is usually eaten raw in this country, but bananas can be broiled, baked, sauteed, grilled, or even frozen. Bananas make a delicious ingredient in dips, drinks, salads, breads, pancakes, fritters, and a variety of desserts. Innumerable recipes derive their special flavor by using the banana as a major ingredient. Bananas are cheap as well as versatile, costing no more today than they cost 20 years ago.

For a quick, nutritious drink, try a banana shake: mix a cup of milk, a banana, and a teaspoon of vanilla in an electric blender, turn on the switch, and enjoy.

If you prefer a more potent banana beverage, there's always the frozen banana daiquiri. You can make a banana daiquiri in your blender, too: just fill the container with a jigger of rum, an envelope of daiquiri mix, ice cubes, and a ripe banana. Then turn on the machine, and let the blender do the rest.

For those who really love bananas, there's even a "banana-wich," made with sliced bananas and peanut butter, with or without ham.

The ubiquitous banana split is surely one of this country's most popular dishes. A classic recipe calls for a banana sliced lengthwise and topped with vanilla, chocolate, and strawberry ice cream, whipped cream, nuts, and marshmallow, chocolate, and pineapple or strawberry sauce. A special dieter's banana split substitutes cottage cheese for ice cream—and, of course, omits the whipped cream and sauce. Presumably, few dieters could be found in the vicinity of the largest banana split in history, a mile-long feast concocted in St. Paul, Minnesota, in 1973. That record-breaker included 10,580 bananas, and 33,000 scoops of ice cream!

Fetish banana trees near the river Ogowe, Gabon.

40

BATHTUBS

This is a gullibility test:

The bathtub was introduced in England in 1828. The first tub in America was used by a Cincinnati resident named Thompson in 1842. After an argument among medical authorities concerning the benefits and hazards of bathing, the bathtub was banned in Boston in 1845. Six years later, the first bathtub was installed in the White House for Millard Fillmore.

Believe it? Well, this capsulized history of the bathtub appeared in the *New York Evening Mail* in 1917, and was immediately accepted as fact by many readers. But the article was actually the devious work of humorist H.L. Mencken, and was—as Mencken readily admitted—a "tissue of absurdities, all of them deliberate and most of them obvious." Yet, much to Mencken's amazement, more than one lazy writer subsequently published this information as the gospel truth.

Although the porcelain tub is now indispensable in every home, it is a rather recent innovation. However, the institution of bathing is much older than Mencken facetiously suggested. The fact is, regular bathing has periodically gone in and out of fashion over the centuries.

From time immemorial, the act of bathing has been regarded as a sacred rite in many cultures. The ancient Egyptians bathed before worship, in the belief that both the body and soul should be pure in the presence of the gods. Christian baptism is a bathing rite, symbolizing the washing away of original sin. To the devout Hindu, a bath is a once-yearly rite, taken only in the sacred waters of the Ganges.

The ancient Greeks are thought to have introduced the bathtub, or at least the wash basin. The Greek vessels were used to hold water for rinsing, but were too small to accommodate a bather. The ruins of the palace at Knossos, Crete, reveal a number of bathrooms that were apparently supplied by a relatively advanced plumbing system. Vase paintings suggest that the Greeks used some form of shower as well. Most early Greeks, by the way, washed only with cold water —warm water was considered effeminate.

In later periods, the Greeks built public baths; but it was the Romans who made the bathhouse the center of their social lives. In the early days of the Roman Republic, wealthy citizens often installed private baths in their homes, similar to the modern Turkish bath.

Later, the public bath came into vogue in almost all cities and towns of the Empire. Huge baths, or *thermae*, became the recreation centers of the Imperial City itself, providing not only bathing

Queen Elizabeth I of England reportedly bathed once a month, "whether she needed it or not."

facilities but gyms, libraries, theaters, gardens, and assembly halls.

The Roman baths were masterpieces of architecture and engineering, and the epitome of imperial luxury. The walls were usually covered with marble; the high, vaulted ceilings were decorated with colorful mosaics. The water taps were made of silver. Statues were everywhere, with small cubical lockers set in the niches between them. Hot water, provided by furnaces, was piped into the bath. The rooms were kept warm by smoke and by hot air circulating under the floors and in the hollow walls.

The first large Roman public bath was built by Agrippa in 27 B.C. Others were constructed by Nero (65 A.D.), Titus (81 A.D.), Domitian (95 A.D.), Trajan (100 A.D.), and Commodus (185 A.D.). Diocletian built baths in the year 302 that were large enough to accommodate 3,200 bathers at one time!

The Roman's bathing ritual consisted of a series of baths, each taken in a different room. The bather began in the undressing room, then moved to another room where he was anointed with oil, then to the gym for exercise. After the gym came the *calidarium*, or hot bath; then the steam room, the *tepidarium*, or lukewarm bath; and finally, the *frigidarium*, or cold bath which was usually a sort of swimming pool. Sounds much like our modern health spa, doesn't it?

Until the second century, men and women bathed together in Rome. Then emperor Hadrian ordered segregated bathing. However, Hadrian's decree was frequently overlooked during the more decadent eras of the Empire. In most cities outside Rome, men and women used the bathing facilities at different hours, but it was always considered immoral for a woman to bathe at night.

The Roman baths were the social centers of the time, combining the modern barroom, health spa, and community center. They were open continually except for religious holidays and times of national crisis. Customarily, a Roman would bathe before the principal meal of the day, but some of the more idle—and cleaner—citizens went through the entire bathing ritual as many as six times a day.

As the Empire waned and barbarian invaders destroyed the Roman aqueduct systems, most baths were shut down. But the public bath lived on in the Eastern Empire, and was eventually adopted by the Arabs, who liked vapor baths. The Turkish bath is a direct descendant of the Roman bath, via Constantinople.

The Teutonic tribesmen who overran Europe bathed for the most part in cold rivers or streams. During the Middle Ages, among some communities, bathing was considered a sin and an act of pride. Probably, the Church's opposition to bathing stemmed from the excesses of the Roman public bath.

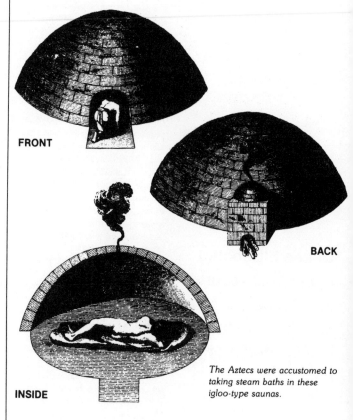

FRONT

BACK

INSIDE

The Aztecs were accustomed to taking steam baths in these igloo-type saunas.

42

43

Among the medieval landed classes, the lack of a need to bathe was considered a sign of wealth and leisure. Many an aristocrat bragged of never having taken a bath. Consequently, the demand for perfume and aromatic oils was very high, and the need for spices helped spur the explorations of the 15th century which led to the discovery of America. By the way, Queen Elizabeth of England reportedly bathed once a month, "whether she needed it or not."

After the institution of bathing was revived by the Crusaders' contact with Eastern bathhouses, the common people took frequent public baths. Public baths were common in France as early as the 12th century, and were reputedly as notorious for their promiscuous activities as had been their Roman precursors. By the 17th century, no decent citizen would consider entering a public bath, and the Church frequently decried the excesses of the institution.

Because of the aristocracy's aversion to bathing, many of the more famous palaces surviving today are completely without sanitation facilities. Although many people dispute it—and others refuse to believe it—there were evidently no toilets of any kind in either the Louvre or in the palace at Versailles. Members of the court were expected to relieve themselves before they entered the palace; the rows of statues that lined the garden promenades provided convenient niches for an undisturbed tinkle.

The Meshlakh, or cooling room, was one of the features of the Jermyn Street baths.

In Europe, the medicinal spring bath has been popular for centuries. During the 18th century, the English city of Bath—so named after an ancient Roman spa built there—became the most fashionable resort in all Europe, thanks chiefly to the restorative work of Beau Nash. Such luminaries as Pitt, Nelson, Gainsborough, Garrick, Gay, Pope, Steele, and Fielding came to enjoy the social life and the hot, radioactive waters of the natural spring. Like earlier baths, however, the resort at Bath eventually became associated with debauchery and the spread of disease.

The word "spa," incidentally, comes to us from the Belgian town of Spa. A mineral spring discovered in 1326 helped make the town a very fashionable resort during the 18th century. Today, the most famous spas in the world are at Baden-Baden in Germany (*bad* means "bath" in German), Carlsbad in Czechoslovakia, Vichy in France, and Hot Springs in Arkansas.

The earliest bathtubs in America were simple wooden tubs, lined with metal and the water was poured in by hand. The first public bath was opened here in 1852. An 1895 law ordered all municipalities in New York State to provide free public baths for their citizens, many of whom had no other means of washing.

In the early decades of this century, many apartments in American cities were equipped with a bathtub in the kitchen. When European immigrants arrived here, many considered the bathtub an unnecessary luxury, and used the tub as a planter for flowers and vegetables.

Traditionally, in Japan, the bath was a large wooden tub placed outside in the garden and filled with very hot water. The entire family bathed together at the same time. In Japanese baths, both public and private, there is rarely an attempt to achieve privacy. Public baths often have large unprotected openings through which people passing in the street can observe the bathers. But nowadays, bathing in Japan—especially in the cities—is becoming westernized.

America easily leads the world today in bathtubs per capita. Many American homes are equipped with two or three or even four tubs. The shower has recently replaced the bath as the preferred washing ritual. A shower, by the way, uses up only about half as much water as a tub bath.

This vinyl fold-up steam bath is billed as the "poor girl's sauna."

Beds

Of all the common objects examined in this book, there is none you're more likely to use on a day to day basis, or take more for granted, than the bed. You might drive your automobile for an hour or two a day, you might watch television for as many as four or five hours daily, but you probably spend about one-third of your life stretched out on a mattress of some kind. Yet we devote a woefully small part of our budget to bedtime comfort. A recent poll disclosed that the average American spends 120 times more money each year on tobacco products than on beds and bedding!

Eight hours of sleep daily may be considered the average, but side by side with the proverb "Early to bed, early to rise, makes a man healthy, wealthy, and wise," we must mention: "Six hours of sleep for a man, seven for a woman, and eight for a fool." Naturally, some people spend a good deal more time in bed than others—for sleeping as well as for sundry other pastimes. Noted authors who often worked in bed include Cicero, Horace, Milton, Voltaire, Jonathan Swift, Alexander Pope, Mark Twain,

and Marcel Proust. And speaking of bona fide lovers, British writer Max Beerbohm once declared that his ideal of happiness was "a four-poster in a field of poppies."

Considering the length of time man has been sleeping, the bed, as we know it, is a rather recent development. The first bed in history was a patch of earth where a tired caveman laid himself down to rest. We know little of the sleeping gear of primitive man, since all wooden objects from prehistoric times have vanished—not to mention piles of leaves, grass, moss, or feathers. The simple stone slab beds that do remain cannot be regarded as proof that all primitive peoples slept on stone. Our ancient ancestors probably slept much the way people in India, Africa, and other places do today, for the bed as an item of furniture is primarily a Western predilection.

Beds are virtually unknown in much of India, though one Indian maharajah of recent times boasted a one-ton bed complete with four life-sized nudes that automatically began fanning and playing music the moment the monarch put his weight on the mattress. Wealthy Arabs sometimes sleep on elaborate tentlike beds, but most people in the Mideast still slumber on simple piles of rugs. The Japanese customarily catch their shuteye on a mat, called a *tatami*, spread over the floor. Many Japanese do not even have a bedroom—in the morning, they roll up their *tatami* and their *futon*, or quilt, and use the sleeping quarters as a dining room.

The Chinese, on the other hand, have a long tradition of

bed slumber. Wooden beds similar to those made in ancient Egypt were in use in China as early as 2,000 years ago. Even the four-poster bed is not unknown in China. But, by our standards, old Chinese beds would not be very comfortable, with matting substituting for a mattress, and pillows made of wood or stone, carved to fit the head or neck.

In the West, the history of the bed begins in ancient Egypt. To our eyes, Egyptian beds look more like couches. And well they should, for Egyptians made no distinction between a day bed, or couch, and a night bed; they used the same item for both lounging and sleeping. The earliest known models were made of palm sticks or palm leaf wicker, lashed together with pieces of cord or rawhide. Later, Egyptian bed-makers introduced mortise-and-tenon constuction and wood bed frames veneered with ivory or ebony. In the royal household, beds made from naturally curved timbers were sometimes sheathed in gold. Most mattresses were made of woven cord, interlaced like the modern chaise lounge or beach chair.

The Egyptian bed was equipped with a footboard, but not with a headboard. Egyptian pillows would seem appallingly uncomfortable by modern standards: most were raised headrests, curved to fit the head or neck, made of wood, ivory, or alabaster, and sometimes inlaid with ivory or colored stones. Many beds, especially those in the poorer quarters, were fitted with a canopy of some kind from which mosquito netting could be hung. The Greek historian Herodotus claimed that contemporary Egyptians used the nets by day to catch fish.

Even in wealthier households, the Egyptian bedroom was starkly furnished, with just a bed and perhaps a chair and a small table. In many houses, there was but one bedroom, for the master of the house; the servants slept in the hall. The ruins of one aristocratic Egyptian home suggest that younger children sometimes slept in their parents' bedroom.

Most ancient peoples of the Mideast slept on beds similar to those in Egypt. Phoenician beds often sported foot panels with erotic ivory carvings—the Bible, you'll recall, equated "beds of ivory" with sinful luxury. Sardanapalus, the last great king of Assyria, evidently had quite a thing for beds, right to the end. According to an aprocryphal Greek fable, the Assyrian king committed suicide, along with his wives and concubines, on a pyre fueled by his 150 beds.

Since almost all the beds of ancient Greece were made of wood, none survive today. But artwork from the period shows that the Greeks slept on beds very similar to those of Egypt. The earliest models consisted of a wood frame and a mattress of lashed rawhide bands. Later, the wood frames were veneered with ivory, bronze, or silver. For some reason, the Greeks dropped the footboard in favor of the headboard.

As described in *The Odyssey*, Penelope's couch was fitted with a stuffed mattress, a purple linen sheet, and blankets made from fleeces and rugs. Considerably less fortunate, and less comfortable, were the men of Sparta, who were required to sleep in a tent along with 15 other compatriots, while their wives remained at home. Even married men were not permitted to sleep away from their tents until the age of 30!

The Greek sleeping chamber, called a *thalamos,* was small and windowless, with light reaching the room only through the large doorway. The master bedroom, which was often in the women's quarters, usually contained a bed and perhaps a few coffers and chairs. The Greek's idea of bedroom luxury was a bed of roses with "no rooster within earshot."

Although the bedrooms in most large Roman homes were arranged around an open central court, the average bedroom, or *cubiculum,* was as small and dark as the Greek *thalamos,* with glassless windows shuttered during sleeping hours to keep in heat and shut off light. A *cubiculum* customarily contained a bed, or *lectus,* along with a chair, chest, floor mat, and chamber pot. Although the Romans used both single and double beds, only in the poorest homes would you find two beds in the same room. In larger homes, curtains divided the bedroom into a space for attendants, a dressing room, and the sleeping area proper. Some of the homes found in the ruins of Pompeii contained sleeping alcoves set in wall niches behind curtains or sliding partitions.

Roman bedsteads were often mounted on a platform, and many were fitted with a canopy from which curtains or mosquito netting was hung.

The Romans, like the Greeks, customarily went to their tomb on their bed. Many *lecti* also doubled as couches for dining, and some could hold as many as six people. Wealthy Romans were evidently quite proud of their elegant bedding. The author Martial wrote of a rich man who feigned illness so that he could show off his bed coverings to visiting well-wishers. The poor, on the other hand, usually slept on masonry shelves along the walls of their *insulae,* or tenements. Others had to make do with a simple wood plank covered with a bug-ridden pallet.

This bedstead of English metal work was constructed during the 19th century.

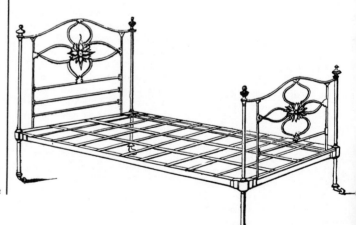

No matter what their social class, Romans rarely owned special sleepwear. Men removed their toga and climbed into bed in their undergarments, while women went to bed laden with their *capitium, mamillare,* and *strophium*—corset, bra, and panties. Bedtime was usually between seven and nine o'clock, and the dawn crowing of the rooster provided the only alarm clock. A breakfast of more than plain water was rare, as was a morning wash-up, since most Romans included a trip to the public baths as part of their daily routine.

Like many other luxuries, the comforts of the Roman boudoir, vanished with the end of the Empire. The Germanic tribes that overran Europe were accustomed to sleeping on the ground, atop piles of leaves or skins. During the early Middle Ages, many peasants slept in the barn along with their animals, or on the earth floor, or on a wooden bench in the hall, the only room in the house with a fireplace. Some enjoyed the luxury of mattresses stuffed with feathers, wool, hair, or straw. The Old English expression for "make a bed" literally meant "prepare straw."

In England, the earliest medieval bedroom, called a *bower,* was no more than a simple lean-to set against the outside wall of the house, or against a fence, with no passageway joining it to the house itself. Waking up on a winter morning was certainly a chilling experience. Perhaps that's why most people slept fully dressed, or swaddled in linen sheets. Bedtime comfort was evidently neither sought nor particu-larly missed, for the 10th-century English ruler Edgar banned "warm baths and soft beds" as effeminate.

In feudal days, only the lord and lady of the house were afforded the luxury of a bedroom. The servants still slept in the hall on piles of straw. Most bedrooms contained a bed, chest, chair, bench, and a clothes rack called a perch, with walls whitewashed or covered with curtains. The bed was usually made of wood fitted together with nails or pieces of iron, with a headboard or footboard decorated with crude carvings. Many beds were fitted with bolsters that raised sleepers to a nearly sitting position.

Aristocratic Europeans of the period moved frequently from one manor to another, carrying their furniture with them rather than furnishing each home. Therefore, many beds and couches were portable. The French word for furniture, *meubles,* and the German word *Mobel* are both derived from words meaning *movable.* And since a family's belongings had to be continually transported from house to house, furniture was kept at a minimum. A single chair was usually reserved for the lord of the house—from this tradition came our word *chairman,* to signify the predominant member of a group.

The heavy wood bedstead was left behind in the bedroom, however, while the lord carried along only his mattress, blankets, and other bedding from home to home. Bedding was considered a possession valuable enough to be included in wills. Ransacking soldiers usually headed straight for the bedroom when they entered a home, claiming bedding as booty. And it was not uncommon for a man to name his bed, as he would a pet!

Among his other idiosyncracies, English monarch Richard III carried along his heavy wooden bedstead when touring his domain. After King Richard's death, the bedstead remained in the inn where he'd last slept. A century later, the landlord of the inn took apart the bedstead and found a double bottom filled with Richard's stash of gold coins.

In wealthier homes, the simple bed of the early Middle Ages gradually gave way to a curtain-enclosed bed so large that it formed a room within a room. A canopy, called a *tester,* was suspended over the bed on rods or chains to form the ceiling. Beneath the canopy hung curtains, which completely enclosed the bed, holding in heat. The warm space between the bed and the wall, called the *ruelle,* was sometimes used to receive intimate guests. Bedding now included silk or leather-covered cushions, and velvet, silk, and—ouch!—pearl-studded pillows. By the end of the Middle Ages, bedrooms were roomy and well-lit, with glass windows, fireplaces, and hand-crafted beds and bedding. Gradually, the comforts worked their way down to the common man.

Elizabethans attached great ceremony to the marriage bed. Often, an entire wedding party accompanied the bride and groom to their bedroom for music, games, and the official blessing of the bed by a cleric. When the bride began to remove her wedding dress, she customarily tossed one of her stockings to the revelers, and the person who caught the garment was deemed the next in the room to marry—thus, our wedding custom of "tossing the garter."

Speaking of the nuptial bower, the marriage bed of Philip, Duke of Burgundy, and Princess Isabella of Portugal was probably the largest bed of all time, measuring 19 feet by 12½ feet. Constructed in 1430, in Bruges, Belgium, the bed has long since been dismantled. The largest bed still in existence is the Great Bed of Ware, built around 1580 for the Crow Inn in Ware, England. Now on exhibit at the Victoria and Albert Museum in London, this ponderous bed measured about 11 feet square and close to nine feet tall. Compare that with the largest bed now on the market, the nine- by-nine foot Super Size Diplomat, which sells for well over $2,000.

Camp beds were in use as early as the 15th century for traveling gentry. The camp beds of the era were hardly cots, though, and some of the heavier four-posters must surely have required a wagon all their own for transport. The trundle bed also appeared during the era, originally for servants who slept in their master's room. (Queen Elizabeth herself had a bedroom guard of 18 persons.) By day, the beds were rolled under the master's four-poster.

The familiar lullabye "Rock-a-bye Baby" is at least as old as the Elizabethan period. The lyrics may harken back to an earlier epoch when a mother might place baby's cradle in the branches of a tree to be rocked gently by the wind.

In France, the king's bed—known as the "Bed of State"—was treated with a reverence that sometimes surpassed that accorded the throne. Persons entering the king's chamber were expected to genuflect in front of the bed, even if the king was not in the room. A railing separating the sleeping area from the rest of the

An ornate bed, 19th century, exhibited at the London Crystal Palace show.

room was originally intended to keep dogs from the bed. The king's bed was also known as the "Bed of Justice," where from the period of Louis XI on, *le roi* customarily reclined while parliament was in session.

The age-old custom of laying a deceased relative to rest in his or her bed through the mourning period prompted the families of many beheaded aristocrats to have their dear ones' heads sewn back on, so that the body could

be more decorously displayed. A nobleman fortunate enough to keep his head, and perhaps a bit wary of losing it, often ordered servants to remain in his bedroom for as long as he might nap. One English duke insisted that his two daughters stand beside his bed during his afternoon nap. When he awoke one day to discover that one of the young women had had the audacity to sit down, he promptly sliced 20,000 pounds off her legacy.

The 17th century is sometimes known as "the century of magnificent beds," in tribute to the elaborate furniture of the

48

period. In England, most beds retained the full tester, though in France the half-tester became more popular. Beds of the time were large enough to serve as mini-parlors, where the lord or lady of the house could grant audiences without surrendering the warmth of the blankets. Women at the Palace of Versailles regularly received visitors—male and female alike—in bed, without raising eyebrows, for the bed was deemed the proper place to accept congratulations or condolences. In fact, the idea that sitting on another person's bed was somehow improper did not occur to anyone until the mid-17th century.

Louis XIV owned an estimated 413 beds in his various palaces. Louis's favorite bed at Versailles was fitted with crimson velvet curtains so heavily embroidered with gold that the crimson was scarcely visible. A ribald painting called "The Triumph of Venus" originally adorned the king's bed, but his second wife, a woman of a more religious bent, had it replaced with "The Sacrifice of Abraham."

The 18th century saw the appearance of the first metal bed-

steads since the days of ancient Rome. Metal beds had one large advantage over wooden beds: they were less likely to be infested with "sleep's foe, the flea, that proud insulting elf." Feather pillows became common during the era.

Across the ocean in America, simple wood beds and straw mattresses were still the rule in all but the wealthiest homes. American inns of the period offered little more in the way of comfort—an innkeeper would think nothing of asking a guest to share his bed with a stranger when accommodations became scarce.

Speaking of cheap accommodations, Parisian flophouses of the 19th century offered their more indigent guest a place at the "two-penny leanover," a long bench with a rope stretched in front of it, which the sleeper could lean over during his sit-up slumber. In the morning, an inappropriately named "valet" rudely awoke the guests by cutting the rope.

During the 19th century, Eng-

lish manufacturers began to turn out cast-iron bedsteads in quantity. Gradually, mattresses stuffed with feathers, leaves, hair, moss, wool, or seaweed gave way to the spring mattress, which had been patented in the late 18th century. The first spiral mattress—similar to the one you may sleep on—appeared first in 1826, intended for use aboard ship as an aid against seasickness. In 1857, the first box springs, one foot deep, reached the shores of America from France.

Victorian publications never dared show a bed in any of their advertisements. When illustrations of the bedroom were required, the bed itself was decorously hidden by curtains. At the same time, advertisers began to peddle inventions we now call alarm clocks, but which the class-conscious Victorians preferred to call "servant regulators."

Victoria herself could boast a few peculiar bedtime habits. Even after the death of her husband, Prince Albert, the queen always slept in a double bed, and had her servants lay out the deceased Prince's bedclothes each night. A picture of Albert's corpse hung continually above her bed.

With sturdy bedsteads and spring mattresses at their disposal, 19th-century Europeans began to turn their attention to the amenities of bedroom comfort. Tin hot-water bottles had been in use since the 17th century, but the rubber models were surely a vast improvement. Belly-warmers were also popular for a time, complete with a concave depression for the stomach. Electric blankets have made such devices obsolete, although the earliest warming blankets were a

This Spanish bedstead was made during the 19th century.

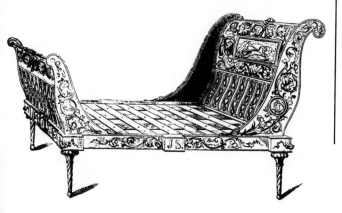

A four-poster bedstead of the Renaissance style.

dangerous proposition—electric blankets caused an estimated 2,600 fires during the first three years of their sale here.

The first railroad sleeping car in this country appeared in 1836, on the Cumberland Valley Railroad. In 1858, George Pullman introduced the sleeping car that was to make his name synonymous with railroad comfort. When introduced on the Chicago and Alton Railroad, Pullman's simple, practical vehicle cost but $1,000. By 1865, luxury Pullmans including everything *and* the kitchen sink were selling for 20 times that amount.

The first Murphy bed appeared in 1909, manufactured by the Murphy Door Bed Company of San Francisco. Initially called "in-a-door beds," the Murphy's were designed to fold back on a pivot behind a door or closet.

The foam rubber mattress is the most familiar slumbertime development of the 20th century, but the water bed is probably the most controversial. Some people now maintain that the water bed is unequaled for a slumber par excellence, while others warn that the watery bower leads only to seasickness, cold feet, and the threat of a bedroom deluge.

In 1975, a furniture company and a chemical engineer combined to bring out a new kind of water bed that might eliminate most critics' objections. Called a Gel-bed, the bed is filled with a plastic substance called Flo-lok that can't leak in quantity from the bed, doesn't make waves, and remains warm enough to eliminate the need for the heater found on other water beds. A Gel-bed mattress can presently be purchased for under $200—and a frame is not required!

The phrase "bedtime sports" may have illicit connotations, but there are indeed a number of athletic contests involving the bed. The Australian Bedmaking Championships are one example. The record time for bedmaking under the stringent rules of the tournament is 35.7 seconds, but we're not sure what kind of bed, or bedding, was used in that monumental performance. Since 1966, the annual Knaresborough Bed Race has thrilled participants in Yorkshire, England, with the record time for the two-and-a-half-mile course now standing at just over 14 minutes.

The record distance for bed pushing was achieved in 1975, by 12 young people in Greensburg, Pennsylvania, who wheeled a hospital bed a total of 1,776 miles in 17 days. A group of students attempting to match that feat once fitted a wheeled bed with a 197-cc. engine—and accumulated 52 traffic summonses during their maiden voyage.

Speaking of motorized beds, the late billionaire Howard Hughes designed a bed for himself that employed 30 electric motors, to move himself and various parts of the bed. The bed was also equipped with piped-in music and hot and cold running water!

The weirdest of all bed sportsmen are surely those human beings who subject their tender flesh to a bed of nails. The record for nonstop endurance of such an inhospitable bower was set in 1971, in Wooster, Ohio, when Vernon E. Craig lay atop a bed of nails for 25 hours, 20 minutes. And unverified claims for bed-of-nails endurance range as high as 111 days!

Some bed of roses!

Billiards

Billiards at a fashionable gathering during the 1890s.

Games such as croquet, archery, and lawn bowling are usually considered pastimes of the upper classes, while many gambling and team games find their most avid players at the other end of the social scale. Billiards has historically been one of the few games to find its greatest popularity at *both* ends of the social spectrum.

The first professional billiards championships were played by English gentlemen dressed in black tie and tails. Even today, the game is sometimes referred to as the "aristocrat of sports." Yet for many years, the pool hall was considered a house of ill fame, the hangout of juvenile delinquents, hustlers, and petty criminals. Politicians and clergymen decried the game, blaming the pool hall for everything from truancy to alcoholism.

Today, billiards and pool seem to find their fans closer to the middle of the social spectrum. Experts predicted that the advent of television would spell the doom of billiards in this country, but middle-class Americans are now taking up the game in increasing numbers. An estimated 20 million Americans play pool each year. Over a half-million homes in North America are now equipped with a billiard table of some kind. The game is booming in many other countries, too. During the 1960s, close to 9,000 new billiard parlors were built in Japan each year!

The Japanese learned billiards when they captured Singapore from the British during World War II. Shorter in stature than the British, the Japanese found the billiard tables too high for comfortable play. So they cut off six inches from each table leg, and took to billiards with a passion.

We don't know what the Japanese call the games, but Americans often use the words *billiards* and *pool* interchangeably. Actually, the terms refer to two entirely different games. Let's have a look at both, and a few of their cousins.

Billiards—sometimes known as English billiards in this country—is played on a table measuring 12 feet by six-and-a-half feet, with six pockets. Only three balls are used: a red ball, a white ball, and a spotted white ball. A line, called the balk line, is drawn across the table 29 inches from one of the shorter cushions. A semicircle 11½ inches in radius is drawn around the midpoint of the balk line.

Each white ball serves as the "cue" ball for one of the players—one player must always strike the plain white ball with his stick, the other the spotted white ball. A player continues to shoot as long as he makes a scoring play. His opponent takes over when he fails to make a score.

There are three scoring plays in billiards: the winning hazard, the losing hazard, and the cannon.

The word *hazard* originally referred to a pocket, possibly because the pockets were themselves descendants of the hoops and other obstacles used on the earliest billiard tables. *Cannon* is a corruption of *carom*, from the French equivalent, *carambole*.

A player scores a winning hazard when his ball drives either his opponent's ball or the red ball into a pocket. Two points are awarded for pocketing the opponent's ball, and three points for pocketing the red ball.

A player scores an ineptly-named losing hazard when his ball is pocketed after striking either his opponent's ball or the red ball. He scores two points for pocketing his ball after it has struck his opponent's ball, and three points for pocketing his ball off the red.

A cannon is scored when the striker's ball hits both his opponent's ball and the red ball, either simultaneously or successively. If no balls are pocketed, the cannon scores two points. If the striker's ball is pocketed after scoring a cannon, the striker gains an additional two or three points, depending on which ball, opponent's or red, was struck first by the striker's ball.

There's much more to billiards than the rules we've briefly outlined. Special regulations govern balls lying in the balk area. A player can score points when his opponent is the striker. But it should be clear that the game of billiards is much different from the game Americans usually enjoy on a billiard table: pool.

As every red-blooded American should know, pool, or pocket billiards, is played with 15 numbered balls and one white cue ball. The table measures five feet by 10 feet, significantly smaller than the table used for billiards. Players score by pocketing one of the numbered balls after contact with the cue ball, the only ball the player may strike with his stick. The striker must indicate before the shot which ball he intends to pocket, and which pocket he is aiming at.

There are many variations of pocket billiards. One of the most popular is *Eight Ball*. In this game, the first player to pocket one of the striped or solid-colored numbered balls must then attempt to pocket the other six similar balls, and then the eight ball. His opponent must pocket the other seven balls, striped or solid-colored as the case may be, and then the eight ball. A player pocketing the eight ball prematurely loses the game. Thus, if the eight ball is between the cue ball and the next ball that the striker must pocket, the striker is in a very difficult position—"behind the eight ball."

In the game of *Rotation*, the balls must be played in numerical order, with points awarded to the striker according to the numerical value of the pocketed ball. Since the 15 balls add up to 120 points, 61 points are required to win a game. 15-ball pocket billiards is similar to *Rotation* in that points are awarded for pocketing a ball according to its number. But in this game, the balls need not be pocketed in numerical order.

Nine Ball is played with—you guessed it—nine balls, the first eight of which must be pocketed in numerical order. A player wins the game by pocketing the nine ball after the first eight balls have been pocketed, or off a combination shot with the "on" ball—the ball that must be pocketed next. In *One-Pocket*, each player chooses a pocket and scores a point only for a ball sunk in that pocket, either by himself or by his opponent.

Snooker, which is now more popular in Britain than billiards itself, combines elements of both billiards and pool. The snooker table is identical in size to the large English billiard table, and includes a balk line and semicircle, as in billiards. In America, the game is sometimes played on the smaller pool table. Twenty-two balls in all are used: a cue ball, fifteen red balls, and six colored balls.

During each turn, the player must first pocket one of the red balls, then one of the non-red balls, then a red-ball, and so on. Pocketed red balls remain off the table; pocketed non-red balls are replaced on the table. When all red balls have been pocketed, the players must then attempt to pocket the non-red balls in ascending order of value: the yellow, green, brown, blue, pink, and black balls are worth two, three, four, five, six, and seven points, respectively. Players are awarded the appropriate points for a non-red ball whenever one is pocketed, and receive one point for each red ball pocketed.

The term *snooker* refers to a lie in which the "on" ball—the non-red ball that must be pocketed next—is obstructed by another ball. The cue ball must not strike any ball without first hitting the "on" ball. So a snookered player must attempt a carom shot that takes the cue ball around the obstructing ball or balls and into contact with the "on" ball. The term comes from either a slang word applied to first-year cadets at an English military school, or another word meaning "to ambush" in parts of England.

Snooker was developed from pool and billiards late in the 19th century. One story has it that the game originated among English troops in India. Tiring of ordinary billiards, the soldiers added a

black ball from a set of pool balls to spice up their game. Then they added a pink ball, then a blue, and eventually all seven of the solid-colored balls. But the game may well have originated instead from *Pyramids*, a game similar to pool that some historians claim was played in Persia as long ago as the 12th century. In any case, by the 1880s, snooker had reached England. In 1916, the first official champion was crowned.

Carom billiards in its various forms is played on a pool table without pockets, with a red ball, a white ball, and a spotted white ball. To score in simple carom billiards, a player must drive his cue ball against both of the other balls. In three-cushion carom billiards, a scoring player's ball must strike the cushions three times, as well as both of the other balls.

There are dozens of other billiard games, some widely known, others common only in a particular area. But all are offspring of the age-old game we now call English billiards.

The exact origin of billiards itself is obscure. The Scythian philosopher Anacharsis wrote of a game similar to billiards that he observed being played in Greece during the sixth century B.C. The English, French, Chinese, Irish, Italians, and Spanish have all claimed credit for inventing the game. But most historians conclude that billiards evolved from a variety of old games played with balls and a stick of some kind.

It may be that billiards evolved from the game of bowls, or lawn bowling, which was quite popular in England during the late Middle Ages. According to some accounts, avid English bowlers became so fed up with rainy weather and wet grass that they took their game indoors. But the size of the indoor bowling "alley" was limited by the size of the rooms in which the game was played. The smaller courts were less challenging. To make the game more difficult, bowlers began propelling their bowls with sticks instead of rolling them. Gradually, hoops and other obstacles were added to the alley. Then, at some unknown date, the court was raised to a table top, and *viola*—billiards was born.

Another interesting, though apocryphal, tale traces the origin of the game in England to a 16th-century London pawnbroker named William Kew. The Englishman allegedly took down the three balls identifying his pawnbroker's shop and used a yardstick to push the balls around in the street. Eventually, young canons from nearby St. Paul's Cathedral joined in the game. *Bill's yard*-stick became *billiard stick,* and later, *billiard cue,* from Kew. Of course, the clergymen invented the *cannon* shot.

We don't know for sure where billiards was invented, but it was in France that the game first achieved widespread popularity. The 15th-century monarch Louis XI played some form of the game. A century later, Henri III installed a primitive billiard table in his residence at Blois. Disregarding the tale of William Kew, the word *billiards* itself is probably French in origin, perhaps from *bille,* (stick or ball), or from *billart* (curved stick). By the 16th century, the word billiards was in use in both France and England.

Like their French counterparts, English monarchs seem to have taken a shine to billiards. During her captivity in 1576, Mary Queen of Scots complained that her billiard table had been removed. Thirty years later, James I ordered a "billiarde bourde, twelve foote longe and fower foote broade."

Shakespeare would have us believe that the ancient Romans enjoyed billiards. But the line, "Let us to billiards," which appears in *Antony and Cleopatra* is surely anachronistic. Oddly enough, the game had already appeared in America by the time the Bard composed the line! In 1565, Spanish settlers in St. Augustine, Florida, listed billiard equipment among their baggage, and presumably played the first game of billiards on this side of the Atlantic.

Early billard games employed only two balls. A third—the "neutral red ball"—was added to the French game during the reign of Louis XIV, who played the billiards on the advice of his physicians. The cannon shot, which requires three balls, did not become part of the game in England until late in the 18th century. By 1800, the game was played basically as it is today.

French drawings of early billiard players show a table with a hoop near each end, and cues resem-

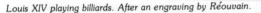

Louis XIV playing billiards. After an engraving by Réouvain.

54

bling short hockey sticks. At some point, the hoops gave way to pockets, one at each end. Later, the pockets were moved to the corners and side pockets were added. Slender cues began to replace thicker maces. In 1807, a French political prisoner named Captain Migaud invented the round leather cue tip, which provided considerably more ball control than earlier cue tips. But leather tips slide easily off the ball. An abrasive of some kind was needed.

For a time, players roughened the cue tip by rubbing it against a whitewashed ceiling. Then, an Englishman named Jack Carr discovered the chalk would fill the bill nicely. Carr toured Europe and demonstrated a billiards dexterity previously unknown, using his chalked cue tip to put spin on the ball. Thus the *masse* shot entered billiards, and the word *English* entered billiard terminology, referring to backspin placed on any kind of ball. Carr peddled a "special-formula twisting chalk" that he credited for his great skill, but actually Carr's magic substance was chalk, pure and simple.

To one John Thurston we owe the invention of the rubber table cushion, which replaced the crude felt-stuffed cushions previously in use. In 1845, Thurston patented the use of vulcanized rubber for billiard cushions. A year later, he patented the slate table bed that replaced the wood bed.

A billiard room was considered *de riguer* in fashionable Victorian homes. Architects of the era took great pains to design the room so that persons entering or sitting in the raised spectator section would not disturb the players. Even the fireplace was carefully positioned to avoid distraction. A billiards etiquette book from the period advised that persons about to enter a billiard room should listen through the door until they heard the balls click, so that their entrance would not disturb a player about to shoot.

During the 19th century, billiard balls made of ivory were in vogue. Since the billiard cue strikes its ball with the smallest surface area of any implement used in ball games, billiard balls have long demanded delicate manufacture. Traditionally, the finest tusks were reserved for billiard balls.

In 1880, crystalate balls made of nitrocellulose, camphor, and alcohol began to appear. In 1926, they were made obligatory by the Billiards Association and Control Council, the London-based governing body. Billiard equipment had now evolved basically into modern form. But the game itself was fast being superceded by its cousins: in the United States, by pocket and carom billiards; and in England, by snooker.

The term, *U.S. billiards* is sometimes used to designate the games of carom billiards and pocket billiards, or pool. Forms of pocket billiards were probably played on billiard tables from the time these tables first began to sport six pockets. Authorities date the real start of U.S. billiards from the year 1859, when the first American championship match was played in Detroit. The game was carom billiards, and the table measured six feet by 12 feet.

Within 10 years of that match, U.S. billiards championships were being played on a table measuring five-and-a-half feet by 11 feet. By 1876, the now standard five-by-ten-foot table was the rule. Four-ball and three-ball carom billiards in their varied forms remained the predominant billiard games here until well into the 20th century, when pocket billiards began its rise to eventual domination.

When the rules of pocket billiards were standardized around the turn of the century, Thomas Hueston and Alfredo DeOro were the premier players in this country. Ralph Greenleaf, called by many the greatest pocket billiards player of all time, dominated the game in the 1920s and early 30s. Until 1945, Walker Cochran was the premier three-cushion billiards player. By that time, carom billiards maestro Willie Hoppe had already become a legend.

Hoppe was an accomplished billiards player by the age of five. In 1906, he won the world title from Frenchman Maurice Vignaux at the age of 16—still wearing kneepants. Hoppe went on to dominate championship play for 46 years, capturing 51 titles in four different carom billiards games.

During World War II, Hoppe and pocket billiards ace Willie Mosconi exhibited their skills for the American armed forces. Mosconi first won his pocket billiards world title in 1941. He went on to 12 more championship victories until his retirement from title play 16 years later.

Willie's prowess with the pool cue has long been legendary. In 1956, Mosconi was matched against Jimmy Moore in a world championship tournament match in Kingston, North Carolina. Moore took the table for the break and played a safety. That was a mistake—Moore's *last* mistake. Mosconi took the table and proceeded to pocket 150 consecutive balls for the victory. Moore never got a chance to shoot again.

Noted pool sharp Luther Lassiter was another victim of Mosconi's selfish control of the green baize table. In a 1953 world championship match in San Francisco, Willie won the crown by running the

Welker Cochrane (left) posing before a match with Willie Hoppe.

game in only two innings. One year later, Willie set the world record for consecutively pocketed balls by running 526 balls in an exhibition match in Springfield, Ohio. That's better than 37 racks without a single miss!

Consecutive runs in English billiards are considerably easier to accomplish, as the world records for the longest billiards runs—or "highest breaks"—can attest. In 1907, an Englishman named Cook set the official record by racking up 42,746 points without a non-scoring shot. The same year, English billiards champ Tom Reece accomplished an amazing break of 499,135 during a London match. But, alas, the mark was not recognized as official, because no member of the press or public bothered to remain on hand for the 85 hours it took Reece to accomplish his feat.

Modern pool parlors are a far cry from the seedy, crime-ridden establishments of earlier notoriety. Today's pool parlors are often air-conditioned, with thick rugs, excellent lighting, and the finest pool equipment available. But pool has now become most popular as a bar game in the U.S.. Many taverns devote more of their space to the pursuit of pool pleasure than to the enjoyment of the grape. Though exact figures are unavailable, the prevalence of pool as a bar game has probably made *Eight Ball*, the most commonly played bar game, the reigning favorite of all pool games in this country.

Whether a championship match played under the glare of television lights or a friendly game in a local tavern, the age-old game of billiards remains one of man's most diverting pastimes. And pool-table banter must rank as one of the game's most appealing features, as this ditty from a decades-old issue of *Punch* suggests:

Oh! the man of the cue has but little to do,
If you listen to popular rumour;
From daylight to dark, he's as blithe as a lark,
And he sparkles with wit and good humour!

Cattle

The dog may be man's best friend, but from a strictly utilitarian point of view, the most important of man's allies in the animal kingdom is without doubt a group of large, docile creatures known collectively as cattle. The single genus to which these animals belong, *Bos,* provides man with his number-one draught animal, supplies half of his meat, 95 percent of his milk, and 80 percent of his leather. Civilization as we know it today might not exist without domesticated bovines.

And in no other country are cattle more important than in the United States. The milk of the cow is the most popular single food item in this nation, with the average American consuming 291 pounds per year. Americans also produce and consume about 35 percent of the world's beef, while comprising only five percent of the world's population.

Cattle herds contribute about 85 billion pounds of meat to the world's larder each year, and American cattle account for about 25 billion pounds of that total. But the United States ranks second in overall cattle ownership, with about 115 million head, while the U.S.S.R. and Brazil can both claim close to 100 million. Then which country ranks number one? Of the estimated 1.1 billion head of cattle presently on earth, the largest number—about 176 million—are to be found in India, a nation which does not eat beef!

Beef is now the third most popular food item in the United States—the average American consumes 89 pounds per year. Among the top dozen most popular home-cooked dishes in the United States, five are beef dishes: roast beef, beef stew, meat loaf, pot roast, and swiss steak. The ground beef patty known as the hamburger is far and away the most popular eating-out dish—the McDonald's Corporation alone sells over four billion hamburgers a year!

Still, the American is not the greatest meat-eater in the world. New Zealand leads all countries with a per capita annual consumption of 224 pounds, followed by Uruguay, Australia, Argentina, and the United States.

And let's not forget the cows. Each year, the females of the *Bos* genus donate some 200 billion quarts of their milk to the world's food supply. We should be thankful indeed that, in the words of Ogden Nash:

The cow is of the bovine ilk;
One end is moo, the other milk.

The word "cattle" is often used for all members of the ox family, as well as the particular species we in America call cattle. The ox family includes, in addition to our cattle, the buffalo, bison, yak, and zebu of Africa, and the gaur, gayal, and bantin of India. All but the bison, gaur, and bantin have been domesticated, and all members of the genus can interbreed with one another.

The buffalo was thought to be an exception until recently, when breeders succeeded in crossing cattle with buffalo. In 1974, one of the hybrid creatures, called "beefalo," sold for $2.5 million, the largest sum ever paid for a single bull!

Bovines were without doubt one of the first animals to be domesticated. Early man found that the cow produces milk far in excess of that needed for its offspring, and that the male can be made docile enough for work as a draught animal. Also, the digestive system of these creatures enables them to subsist on roughage and other plant parts that might otherwise be useless to man. For thousands of years, cattle were employed as work animals and raised for their milk; raising cattle for meat is a relatively recent development. There are still parts of the world, like India, in which beef is never eaten, despite an abundance of cattle.

Cattle were probably first domesticated in India and Central Asia, perhaps as early as over 11,000 years ago, and brought by Neolithic migrators to Europe and Africa. There they interbred with native cattle, which are thought to have evolved from an extinct wild ox. The earliest known domestication dates from 6000 B.C., in Greece and Crete. The ancient Egyptians raised cattle for their milk and for use as draught animals, and hunted wild

57

cattle for sport. Domesticated cattle were also used to trample grain on the threshing floor. By Roman times, cattle markets were common sights in many cities—and so were Imperial meat inspectors.

From ancient times through much of the Middle Ages, cattle and wealth were virtually synonymous. Our words "capital" and "chattel" are both derived from the word for cattle—or rather, from the Latin *caput*, "head," from "head of cattle." In the language of the Aryans who invaded India centuries before the Christian era, the word for war literally meant "desire for more cattle." In Europe, cattle were used as the standards of exchange as late as the eighth century.

Cattle came to the New World almost as soon as the Europeans themselves, for Christopher Co-lumbus brought a few head to the Americas on his second voyage. As early as 1611, English settlers at Jamestown were raising cattle; by 1624, the colony could claim 20,000 head. By the mid-18th century, America was already beginning to export its cattle.

The cattle-raising land of the United States has been moving westward ever since then. Around 1800, the cattle industry in the United States was centered around Ohio and Kentucky. By 1850, it had moved to Illinois and Missouri, and by 1870, to the states of the Great Plains and the Southwest. Most American breeds are descendants of the British breeds brought from Europe and the longhorn breeds brought to Mexico by Spanish colonists.

To a great extent, cattle settled the American West. Much of our Wild Western lore centers around the cattle ranch, the cattle trail, and the cowboy. Initially, cowboys not only tended cattle herds, but drove them long distances over cattle trails to cities for slaughter. Beginning around 1850, Western cattle took to the railroad for the ride to the slaughterhouse, and cowboys thereafter drove their herds only to the nearest rail depot. Thus Dodge City, Abilene, and other famous Western "cow towns" were born.

Today, American cattle are raised for beef in the sparsely populated rangeland states of the West, while dairy farming predominates in Midwestern and Eastern states close to urban centers. Texas leads all states in the

---

Names of the several joints of beef, as depicted in Household Management *by Mrs. Beeton, published in London in 1899.*

HIND QUARTER.

1. Sirloin.
2. Rump.
3. Aitchbone.
4. Buttock.
5. Mouse-round.
6. Veiny piece.
7. Thick flank.
8. Thin flank.
9. Leg.

FORE QUARTER.

10. Fore rib (5 ribs).
11. Middle rib (4 ribs).
12. Chuck rib (3 ribs).
13. Leg of mutton piece.
14. Brisket.
15. Clod.
16. Neck.
17. Shin.
18. Cheek.

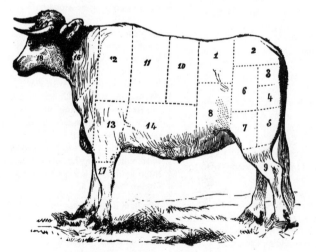

OX, SHOWING THE MODE OF CUTTING UP THE VARIOUS JOINTS.

number of cattle, and most of these are beef cattle. The American "dairy belt" stretches from New England through New York and Pennsylvania to Michigan, Minnesota, and Wisconsin. Southern Wisconsin can claim the heaviest concentration of cows per square mile in the United States.

There are now some 280 recognized breeds of cattle, of which 33 are beef breeds. Generally, cattle breeds were developed to produce animals good for either their meat or their milk, but rarely for both. In the United States, there are about 10 times as many beef cattle as there are milk-producing cows, and about 30 per-

cent of all dairy cows eventually find their way into the meat freezer as low-grade beef.

The most popular beef breeds in the world are the *Shorthorn* and the *Hereford*. Both were originally developed in the British Isles, and are favored for their hardiness and rapid maturation. Henry Clay is credited with introducing the first Herefords to the United States, in 1817. The Hereford is generally the heaviest of all breeds: a cow may weigh up to 1,700 pounds, and a bull may weigh a ton. The largest bull

on record, in fact, was an American-raised Hereford-Shorthorn that tipped the scales at a prodigious 4,720 pounds!

The *Angus*, another beef breed, was originally developed in Scotland. In the United States, the *Angus* was crossed with the *Brahman*, the humped cattle of India, to produce a new breed, the *Brangus*. In the 1930s, breeders at the King Ranch in Texas crossed the Brahman and the Shorthorn to produce the *Santa Gertrudis* breed, which rivals the Hereford for sheer size.

The King Ranch is popularly regarded as the largest cattle ranch of all time. Actually, the largest cattle range in the world

Indian humped cattle.

today is in Australia, covering some 6,500 square miles. Another Australian ranch, now partitioned into smaller units, once covered 35,000 square miles—about the size of the state of Indiana!

The world's most popular dairy breed is by far the *Holstein*, originally developed in Northern Europe and known as a fine milk-producer for over 2,000 years. A Holstein cow can produce up to 14,000 pounds of milk a year, while the average dairy cow of other breeds produces about 11,000 pounds. One Holstein raised in America claims the all-time milk producing record: 50,000 pounds in one year! And it was a Holstein that set the record for the largest amount of money every shelled out for a single cow: $122,000.

Other popular dairy breeds include the *Ayshire*, the *Jersey*, and the *Guernsey*. The latter two breeds were developed on the English Channel islands that bear those names, while the Ayshire was developed in Scotland. All three are now raised almost around the world. The Guernsey is noted for its yellowish milk, due to a pigment in the cow's skin.

Many American city-dwellers would probably have as much trouble distinguishing a steer from a stag as they would a Guernsey from a Hereford. What do those terms mean? Most male cattle are castrated, and become *steers*. In two or three years, they would grow into an *ox*. If left uncastrated, they become *bulls*. A bull, castrated after mating, is called a *stag*. A female is called a *cow* only when it reaches maturity; an immature female is a *heifer*.

Surely a more familiar cattle terminology is that used to identify beef in the supermarket. All beef sold in the United States is graded for quality, and there are eight basic grades. *Prime* is the best—the meat is flecked with fat, or "marbled," and is very flavorful and juicy. Beef of the *Choice* grade is also top-quality beef, though it's generally less marbled than *Prime*-grade beef. *Choice* beef accounts for about 40 percent of all the beef sold in the United States. *Good* and *Standard* are the other grades of beef from young animals. *Commercial, Utility, Cutter,* and *Canner,* the lowest grades, are generally from mature animals, and are used mostly for processed foods such as salami and sausage.

The terminology used to identify cuts of beef may vary from

A Jersey cow.

A Holstein cow.

supermarket to supermarket, but generally the porterhouse, tenderloin, filet mignon, and T-bone, all cut from the short loin, are the most expensive cuts. Sirloin steak is usually not cut from the short loin, but from the loin end section of the beef carcass. The story that King Charles II of England liked loin end steak so much that he dubbed it "Sir Loin" is, though quaint, a complete fiction. The "sir" in "sirloin" is actually derived from the French word *sur*, "over."

Our supermarkets probably wouldn't be filled with beef products at all if it weren't for the peculiar digestive system of cattle. Bovine creatures have four stomachs; the first two are the *rumen* and the *reticulum*. Food is partially digested in these two stomachs, then coughed up in "cuds" a few times so that the animal can chew over, or "ruminate,"

the partially digested food before swallowing it again. A cow may spend up to nine hours a day ruminating. Later, the food passes to the other two stomachs for further digestion.

This hardy digestive system, and the many kinds of bacteria present there, enable cattle to subsist on roughage that human beings could not digest. Therefore, man has historically been able to keep cattle without surrendering part of his vegetable diet. In most of the world today,

HOW THE BUTCHER CUTS A SIDE OF BEEF

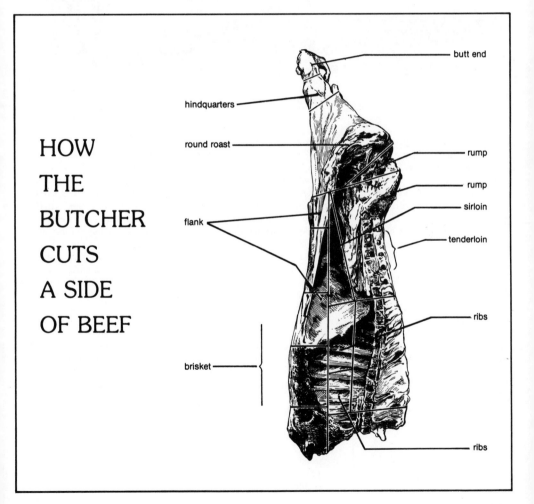

butt end

hindquarters

round roast

rump

rump

sirloin

tenderloin

flank

ribs

brisket

ribs

A Friburg bull.

cattle feed on grass, hay, and other roughage, but in the United States, they're fed grain for fattening. In a single year, American cattle will consume the equivalent food energy of 240 million tons of corn!

In return for this grass and grain, each head of cattle rewards the rancher with about 450 pounds of beef suitable for the retail market, along with 150 pounds of by-products and 150 pounds of low-value salvage. By-products include the hide (for leather), hair (felt, brushes), suet (margarine), and inedible fats (soap), along with the bones used for glue and gelatin, and the blood that in a dried form is used as animal feed.

But it is beef, of course, that is the most prized product of the steer. Beefsteak is regarded by many as the premier meat, especially in England and the United States, and a "thick, juicy steak" is most Americans' idea of gustatorial perfection. The rest of the world by and large does not agree. As late as the 19th century, beefsteak was regarded even by Europeans as primarily an English specialty. French writer Alexander Dumas wrote that beefsteak "must be eaten in an English tavern, with wine or anchovy butter, served on water cress."

The Beefsteak Club was one of the most well-known London social clubs of the 18th and 19th centuries, including among its members such luminaries of the art and theater worlds as William Hogarth, John Wilkes, and David Garrick, plus the Prince of Wales. The club reportedly was so named because its original members met to enjoy a steak dinner. Members were later called "Steaks," and the club the "Sublime Society of Steaks."

Also in England, the ceremonial royal guard—called yeoman of the guard—have long been nicknamed "beefeaters." In 1669, the grand duke of Tuscany noted the size and stature of the guard members during a trip to England, and wrote: "They are great eaters of beef, of which a very large ration is given them daily at the court, and they might be called 'beefeaters.'"

Aside from vegetarians, there are probably few Americans today who don't qualify for that nickname. But if you are a member of that tiny minority, you might take heart in the words of William Shakespeare: "I am a great eater of beef, and I believe that does harm to my wit."

CATS

The oldest domestic cat on record, a tabby owned by a woman in England, died on November 29, 1939, at the ripe old age of 36 years!

Are you an ailurophile or an ailurophobe? In plain English: Do you love or hate cats? Either way, you're in large company.

Ever since the domestication of the feline, the cat has been variously regarded as a representation of the gods or an embodiment of the devil. Even today, there seems to be no middle ground. The dog may be loved, hated, or tolerated, but the cat—well, choose your side.

Dogs and cats are far and away the most popular pets in the world today. But the dog has been a friend of man for much longer, having been domesticated some 50,000 years ago. On the other hand, the cat was not tamed to any extent until just

63

5,000 years ago. Yet the dog, as we know it today, is in evolutionary terms a rather recent development. The cat family, on the other hand, evolved into its present form some seven million years ago, long before most surviving mammals. During the intervening ages, it has undergone little change.

Over the ages, the feline species spread to all parts of the earth, with the exception of Australia and a few islands. The original ancestors of the cat evolved into two general families. One family, called the *Hoplophoneus*, included the Smiladon, or saber-toothed tiger, and other extinct animals. The second group, the *Dinictis*, produced all our modern cats.

There are many ways of classifying the members of the cat family, but the most commonly accepted divides the felines into three genera. The *Panthera* genus includes the great cats, such as the lion, tiger, leopard, and jaguar. The lion is the only gregarious member of the cat family. Its nickname—"king of the jungle"—is something of a misnomer. The tiger is generally larger and stronger than his unstriped cousin. Fortunately, the two creatures rarely meet—there are no tigers in Africa, and few lions anywhere else.

"Ligers and Tigons" may sound like a classic spoonerism, but these animals actually exist. They are the hybrid offspring of the lion and tiger, and there are about a dozen of these creatures in captivity today. When the father is a lion, the cub is called a liger; when the sire is a tiger, the cub is a tigon. And if a liger and tigon mate—well, you figure it out.

The *Acinonyx* genus includes only, since ancient times, the cheetah, a sleek, spotted cat that has been domesticated and used in hunting in Egypt, India, and other Asian lands. The cheetah has been called the fastest animal on earth, and can race along at speeds of 60 miles per hour—though some claim to have clocked this quick-footed cat at close to 75 miles per hour!

The third genus, *Felis*, includes the puma, ocelot, bobcat, serval, lynx, and of course, the common house cat, known rather plausibly in zoological circles as *Felis catus*.

There is no record of domesticated cats before 3,000 B.C., though by that time the kitty was already regarded as sacred in some Near Eastern cultures. The Egyptians tamed a species of wild African cat, *Felis lybica*, an animal about the size of the modern house cat, and put him to work protecting grain supplies from rodents. Egyptian artwork also depicts small cats killing snakes.

Rodent-hunting cats proved so valuable that the Egyptians considered them representations of the gods—a designation that conveniently helped protect the cat from ancient ailurophobes. The Egyptian cat-god *Bast*, was a symbol of the kindly powers of the sun, as opposed to *Sekmet*, the lion-god, who represented the destructive forces of nature. The cat was also worshipped or in some way connected with religious observance in Babylonia, Burma, Siam, Japan, and China, where the domesticated cat first appeared around 500 B.C.

The Egyptians went so far in their ailurophilia as to embalm cats, as they would a member of the royal household. Thousands of cat mummies have been found in Egyptian ruins—along with

even more mouse mummies, presumably entombed to provide food for the resurrected cats. In the 1890s, 180,000 mummified cats found near Cairo were auctioned off in England, where many were used as fuel. The auctioneer used a mummified cat as a gavel to peddle the cats in ton lots.

Legend had it that cats led to the defeat of the Egyptian army in 525 B.C., through a stratagem of the Persian invader Cambyses. The Persian king placed a row of cats in front of his troops, and the Egyptian archers refused to shoot their arrows across the sacred animals, for fear of killing them.

The domesticated African cat spread from Egypt to Europe, where it interbred with a European wild cat known as *Felis silvestris*, literally "forest cat." The Greeks kept few cats which they used as household mousers. Phoenician traders brought the domesticated cat to Italy long before the days of the Roman Empire, and cats were not uncommon as household pets among aristocratic Romans.

The cat would eat fish,
and would not wet her feet.
—John Heywood, *Proverbs*

The first record of domesticated cats in Britain dates from around year 936, when a law was enacted in Wales for their protection. Throughout the Middle Ages, in most countries, cats—especially black cats—were suspected of sorcery, perhaps due to their stealth, independence, and nocturnal habits.

Even today, you find an occasional individual who's convinced the cat has some supernatural powers. As Sir Walter Scott wrote, "Cats are a mysterious kind of folk. There is more passing in their minds than we are aware of."

Today, some ailurophiles entertain the idea that mass cat slaughter during the Middle Ages led directly to the spread of the Black Death, because of the consequent rise in the rat population. Actually, considering the unsanitary conditions of the day, rats, fleas, and the plague would have flourished with or without the intervention of the feline.

Speaking of mousers, you've no doubt heard the one about the traveler who came sadly to the front door of a farmhouse to report an unfortunate accident. "I hate to tell you this, ma'am," he said, "but I just ran over your cat on the road. I'm terribly sorry. Of course, I'll replace him."

"Well, don't just stand there!" the woman snapped. "There's a mouse in the kitchen!"

Domesticated house cats fall into two broad groups: short-haired and long-haired. The long-haired variety developed in Persia and Afghanistan, and the two prevalent types of long-haired cat are now called the Persian and the Angora. As a pet, the Persian has replaced the Angora in most Western countries.

The Abyssinian, a beautiful short-haired feline, developed entirely from the African wild cat.

The tailless Manx cat is common in the Far East, where few long-tailed cats are found. The name comes from the Isle of Man off England, though it is unknown whether the cat was

The Manx cat.

brought there or developed there by mutation.

The Siamese cat, a much favored pet, first reached the United States in 1895 and has flourished ever since. Incidentally, almost all Siamese cats are cross-eyed.

The number of cats extant throughout the world today is anybody's guess. The United States ranks first among ailurophilic nations. There are an estimated 20 to 25 million cats in American households today, but with the inclusion of all alley cats and other strays, the total cat population could well top the 40 million mark, which is the population figure estimated for American dogs. The popularity of cats in this country continues to grow. The cat-care business is now a multimillion-dollar industry, providing cat food and accessories, cat hospitals, kennels, and even kitty cemeteries. Pedigreed cats sell for upwards of $200.

The precise origin of our word "cat" is uncertain, but similar words designate the feline in many unrelated languages. One Latin word for the feline was *catus,* and the Anglo-Saxons dubbed the creature *catt* or *cat.*

In French, we find *chat,* in Italian *gatto,* in Spanish *gato,* and in German *Katze.*

The origin of "puss" is unknown, but "kitty" comes from *chaton,* a diminutive of the French *chat.* Since at least 1450, "Tom" has been used to designate a male. A polecat, by the way, is not a cat at all—in the United States, the term designates a skunk.

According to some accounts, the expression "to fight like Kilkenny cats" dates back to a somewhat ailurophobic custom among Hessian soldiers stationed in Ireland: tying two cats together by the tails and hanging them over a fence or clothesline. One day, the story goes, an officer approached a group of soldiers thus occupied. To hide their deed, one soldier cut off the tails of both tormented animals. The officer was then told that the cats had fought so hard that they'd devoured each other, leaving only the tails.

The notion that a cat can fall from a great height and survive is not an old wives' tale, and may have contributed to the idea that a cat has nine lives. One cat fell from the 20th floor of a Montreal apartment building in 1973 and suffered only a pelvic fracture.

The story of a cat that fell from the Washington Monument and survived has been batted about for years. According to some, the facts are these: during construction of the Monument, workers came across a cat lurking in the framework near the top of the structure. The cat panicked, and leaped from the scaffolding. Incredibly enough, the cat survived the 500-foot-plus fall— but, even more amazingly, the stunned creature was pounced on and killed almost immediately by a wandering dog.

We have no idea how old that unfortunate feline was when it lost its ninth life, but on the average, a house cat can be expected to live from eight to twelve years, with one year in a cat's life equivalent to about seven years in a man's life. However, many cats have survived for considerably longer, and life spans of over 20 years are not at all uncommon. The oldest domestic cat on record, a tabby owned by a woman in England, died on November 29, 1939, at the ripe old age of 36 years!

The average household kitty weighs from eight to twelve pounds, but the largest puss on record, a tom from Connecticut, weighed in at a hefty 43 pounds. And the most valuable cat on record is, depending upon how you look at it, either a tabby inappropriately named "Mickey" who killed more than 22,000 mice during a 23-year career with an English firm, or a pair of house cats which, in 1963, inherited the entire estate of their ailurophilic owner, a California doctor. The estate was valued at $415,000!

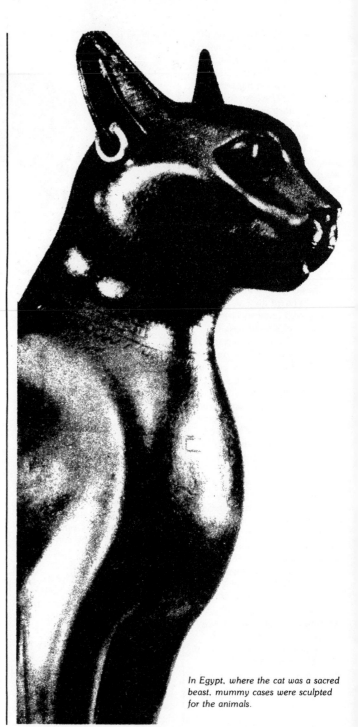

In Egypt, where the cat was a sacred beast, mummy cases were sculpted for the animals.

CAVIAR

Synonymous with opulence is that salty, lumpy marine delicacy known as caviar. The word is rich with princely connotations for almost everyone—including those with no idea what caviar actually is. For it has been said that those who respect caviar's place in the elite of epicurean treats far outnumber those who have actually tasted it. Many who do have a chance to sample the delicacy can only wonder why it is so prized. But as any connoisseur can testify, caviar is an acquired taste that—for reasons of the pocketbook—is best not acquired.

Caviar is the prepared roe, or eggs, of the *acipenser*, a fish found in the Caspian and Black Seas, and the Girond River in France. At one time, the *acipenser* could be found in many European rivers, and even in some North American lakes; but since the onset of the industrial age, that fish's habitat has been reduced to portions of Russia, Iran, and Rumania. Today, virtually all caviar is produced in those three countries.

There are three kinds of *acipenser* that most graciously donate their eggs for the benefit of man's palate, and thus there are three kinds of "true" caviar. The Beluga is the largest fish of the three, growing up to twelve feet in length and weighing up to a ton! One Beluga can produce up to 130 pounds of caviar.

Another species, the Sevruga, is much smaller; four feet long and weighing 60 pounds, the Sevruga can produce only about eight pounds of caviar.

The Ocietrova, or sturgeon, may weigh up to 400 pounds and will produce about 40 pounds of caviar. The term "sturgeon" is often applied to all three kinds of caviar-producing fish, but the Ocietrova is, in fact, the only true sturgeon.

The taste for caviar flourished in the Middle Ages, when sturgeon roe was prepared as a feast for kings. The Cossacks of Russia organized massive caviar- hunting expeditions twice each year, with every member of the community taking part in the two-week campaigns. Among other things, the Cossacks used cannons to stun the fish in the water!

Today, the gathering of roe is somewhat more scientific. The fish live in the salt water of the Caspian and Black Seas but spawn in fresh water, depositing their roe at the bottom of river beds. The fish are caught as they prepare to spawn: the roe, at that time, is barely edible.

Caviar is produced from the roe of the sturgeon fish.
Drawing courtesy of Romanoff Caviar.

The captured fish are placed in submerged floating cages, where due to the lack of food, they are forced to use up the reserve nourishment stored in their roe. When the roe is fit for consumption, the fish are killed and the eggs extracted.

The roe is then pressed through a sieve to remove membranes from the eggs, and then steeped in a brine solution. The production of caviar requires only 15 minutes, but must be carried out with great skill.

The best caviar is sold by weight, is slightly salted, and extremely nourishing. Malossol caviar contains up to 30 percent protein. Due to its salt content, caviar will remain fresh for a long time. But never place it in a freezer or you'll end up with a worthless lumpy broth!

The roe of various fish have been enjoyed as a delicacy by the rich for thousands of years. "Red caviar," however, is a cheap imitation made from salmon roe.

The French have been connoisseurs of caviar from medieval times on. Rabelais speaks of the delicacy in *Pantagruel*, calling it *caviat*. In Shakespeare's day, caviar was recognized as a food for the more discerning, as Hamlet suggested when he said: "The play, I remember, pleas'd not the million; 't was caviare to the general." In other words, the play, like caviar, was pleasant only to a trained palate.

The Czar Alexander I is often credited with introducing caviar to the social elite of Paris. The word "caviar," however, is not Russian in origin (the Russians call it *ikra*), but comes from the Italian *caviola*, derived from the Turkish word *khavyah*.

Today, you can expect to pay anywhere from six to sixteen dollars for an ounce of the prized delicacy—and an ounce is considered scarcely a portion.

Until recently, about 35,000 pounds of fresh caviar were consumed yearly in the United States; a current caviar shortage has reduced American consumption to 20,000 pounds. Sixty-five long tons of caviar were imported into the United States from Iran each year, and the total American retail market for caviar is $6 million annually. But if the treat is beyond your pocketbook, or if you've already tried caviar and have been ashamed to admit that you can't stomach it, take heart. The epicurean chronicler Thomas Mouffet had this to say about the costly treat: "As for caviar, or their eggs being poudred, let Turks, Grecians, Venetians, and Spaniards celebrate them ever so much, yet the Italian proverb will ever be true: *Who eats caviar eats flies, dung, and salt.*"

68

CHAIRS

19th-century English chair, exhibited at the Crystal Palace Exhibition.

The chair is such a simple, necessary, and ubiquitous piece of furniture today, it might seem natural to assume that man has been making chairs for as long as he's been sitting. But there are many material elements of modern life whose present importance belies their relatively late appearance in the household, and the chair is one of them. For this familiar piece of furniture was not common anywhere in the world until just 300 years ago!

That may seem hard to believe, until you remember that there are still parts of the world where the chair remains a rarity. The fact is, your city or town probably contains more chairs than there were in all of ancient Egypt.

If the chair has been popular only for a few centuries, you might wonder what people did sit on for thousands of years. The most common articles of furniture for sitting were the bench, the stool, and the chest.

The bench, a simple plank of wood with two supports, was easy to make and could accommodate a number of people. The stool was also simple to construct, usually being fashioned from untrimmed forest timber. The chest was simply a storage box that could, when closed, double as a seat. You might recall that ancient Romans of means ate their meals at a low table while reclining on couches, so even in the dining room the chair was hardly a necessity.

Ancient peoples did have chairs, but these were almost

69

always reserved for the rich and powerful. As a throne, the chair served for ages as a symbol of authority, an emblem of the state or the seat of religious dignitaries.

In the Middle Ages, even aristocratic households usually owned but one chair, and that chair was reserved for the lord of the house. The historical status of the chair is preserved in our use of the word "chairman" for the head of a group, or in phrases such as "the judgement seat."

Our word "chair" itself was ultimately derived from the Latin *cathedra*. The Romans used that word especially to refer to a teacher's seat, and later it became associated with the seat of a bishop or other religious figure. The word also provided the term "cathedral," which was originally used for the bishop's chair itself and later transferred to the church that contained it, the "seat" of his power.

Few chairs have survived from ancient Egypt, but we know from Egyptian art that the chair was used only by the rich, and especially by political and religious leaders. Egyptian chairs were carved from wood, ebony, or ivory, and many were covered with costly fabrics. The backs were slanted, as they are today, while the legs were often carved to resemble the feet of beasts.

Some of the oldest chairs of which we have a record were depicted on a monument found in the ruins of the Assyrian capital of Nineveh. These were backless chairs with legs carved in the form of lions' claws or bulls' hooves, or supported by caryatides—columns in the shape of human figures.

The art of the ancient Greeks often depicted gods sitting on thronelike chairs. Visitors to the Parthenon, for instance, will find on the frieze of that building a representation of Zeus, seated on a chair ornamented with winged sphinxes. Many chairs depicted in Greek art had legs in the shape of animals' feet, and straight backs that did not conform to the shape of the human spine—but then these chairs may have been designed for gods instead of men.

Ancient Roman households might have included a number of couches and benches, but only the richest had the luxury of a chair. Expensive marble was a favorite building material for these chairs which, like their Greek and Egyptian predecessors, were often elaborately carved and ornamented with costly materials. An early type of Roman chair was the *currule*, a backless folding chair with curved legs that may have originally been reserved for use in a magistrate's chariot. The word itself comes from *currus*, the Latin word for chariot, and is used even today to mean "of the highest rank."

The most famous chair of antiquity is the so-called chair of St. Peter, housed in St. Peter's church at the Vatican. The chair is made of acacia wood with ivory carvings depicting the labors of Hercules, and is actually a Byzantine work of the sixth century A.D. with a few pieces of oak taken from an earlier piece of furniture. This chair is popularly thought to be contained within the bronze chair of Lorenzo Bernini, who designed portions of St. Peter's. But St. Peter's chair is kept under triple lock at the Vatican, and exhibited only once every century.

After the fall of Rome, the Byzantines retained the currule chair, often with a back in the

The chair was not common anywhere in the world until just 300 years ago!

The heraldic chair on the left has sculptured on its surface the arms of the English Saxon kings. Both this chair and its rustic cousin on the right were shown at the Crystal Palace Exhibition during the 19th century.

shape of a lyre, a design common in modern chairs. The rigid, high-backed chairs of the later Middle Ages, or Gothic period, featured pointed arches and carved ornamentation in the form of foliage and geometric designs. In medieval France, chairs were customarily made from stone, while the English preferred wood.

At this time, the chair was still monopolized by aristocrats and religious leaders, and was the seat of authority in both the literal and figurative senses. At the lord's manor, the chair was kept at the head of the dining table, while the rest of the household sat on benches. Some of the thronelike chairs of the period were large enough to seat both the lord and his lady, and might include arms, a high back, a canopy, and a locked storage area underneath the seat. The lord was said to sit "in his chair";

as a result, we still sit "in" an armchair but "on" an ordinary chair.

It was during the renaissance period that the chair came into general use in all households. Since then, the chair has varied more with fashion than has any other item of furniture, and an expert can usually tell from exactly what period an old chair origi-

71

nates simply by examining its stylistic elements.

Until the middle of the 17th century, the majority of chairs in all European countries were made of oak, without upholstery or other cushioning. Gradually, oak was replaced by lighter, more easily carved woods, like walnut. Leather came into use for cushioning, then expensive materials such as silk and velvet. The Louis XIII period saw the introduction of cane backs, decorative gilt ornamentation, inlay, and painting.

In the early 18th century, chairs of the Queen Anne style came into fashion in England. These chairs were smaller, narrower, and lighter than the older oak chairs of that country, and featured less decorative carving. Shell motifs became especially popular. Gradually the high-backed chair faded away, and the chair began to look very much like the modern variety.

But in France, the rococo Louis XV style came into vogue, featuring elaborate detail, sweeping curves, gilded woodwork, and tapestried upholstering. Lacquerwork became fashionable, as did upholstered sides, which previously had been rare. Popular decorative elements included flowing scrolls, cupids, doves, wreaths, and shells.

Toward the middle of the 18th century, chairs began to take the form that was later to be called Chippendale, after the English furniture designer Thomas Chippendale. These chairs stressed practicality over ornamentation, and were solid and sturdy, yet gracefully formed. Mahogany came into wide use for the frames, the backs took on a flowing, interlaced form, and the legs ended in ball and claw feet.

A mahogany Chippendale chair holds the current record as the most expensive chair ever purchased. In 1972, this corner chair dating from the mid-18th century sold at auction for a neat $85,000.

Other English furniture designers, such as George Hepplewhite, Thomas Sheraton, and the Adam brothers, lent their talents to a gradual lightening and refinement of the Chippendale chair, and each gave his name to a distinct style of furniture. The Chippendale with its sturdy, practical construction, and the Hepplewhite with its delicacy, grace, and rounded or oval backs, together determined what might be called the modern chair.

Chair design in America was from the beginning based on the imitation of current European styles, with occasional native adaptations. The first chair factory in the United States actually didn't make its appearance until 1818, in Connecticut. One purely American innovation was the writing-arm chair, typified by the addition of a pear-shaped desk section that could often be raised from the arm. This type of chair, still common in some American schools, is called a "desk" rather than a chair.

But surely the most important and familiar American contribution to chair design was the rocking chair, reputedly invented by Benjamin Franklin. The Boston rocker, with its rounded back and curved seat, has been called the most popular chair ever made.

The largest chair in existence was built in Reykjavik, Iceland in 1977. This chair is indeed fitting for a god of Greek mythology: it stands 24 feet, four inches tall and weighs 12.32 tons!

Since the 18th century, no new style of chair has lasted for any length of time. For the most part, chair design has moved out of the hands of original artists and into the hands of designers who resurrect or recombine older styles to produce the ordinary chair of today—with occasional exceptions such as the sweeping "modernistic" designs of Mies van der Rohe and others.

No matter what kind of chair you prefer, you surely have a few around the house. For in recent centuries, everyone has become a "chairman"—or a "chairperson"—and the ordinary chair is no more a symbol of authority and position than the kitchen table. Even an impoverished recluse like Henry David Thoreau could claim a number of chairs in his forest hut: "One for solitude, two for friendship, three for society."

A Canadian chair exhibited at the Crystal Palace, 19th century.

Chewing Gum

*"Does your chewing gum
    lose its flavor
On the bedpost overnight?"*

The title of this 1960s song may not tickle your funny bone if you don't chew gum, but those who do indulge will certainly get the picture. The sight of a dried up, mouldering piece of chewed gum stuck to the underside of a desk won't strike the non-chewer as very appetizing, but to the gum-chewer—well, a piece of gum is a piece of gum.

And there are gum-chewers galore in this country, male and female, young and old, from every stratum of society. No one knows for sure how many people chew gum, but some 35 *billion* sticks will find their way into American mouths this year. That's about five billion packets, or 25 packets for each man, woman, and child in the United States. At, say, 20 cents a throw, Americans will spend about a

billion dollars on gum this year. And you thought gum-chewing was on the wane?

The urge to masticate seems to be quite strong in the human animal, for gum-chewing has been popular in many cultures over the last 2,000 years. The ancient Greeks chewed a gum obtained from the resin of the mastic tree. Our words "mastic" and "masticate" are both derived from the Greek word for "chew."

Over a thousand years ago, the Mayans and other American Indians chewed chicle-based gums. But the first gums American colonists encountered were spruce gums introduced to the Pilgrims by the Wampanoog Indians in the early 17th century. Made from wads of resin the Indians found stuck to the bark of spruce trees, spruce gums were waxy and tough, more cordial to the teeth than to the taste buds.

Yet spruce gums were to remain the only chews available in the United States for close to 200 years, until the introduction, in the 19th century, of paraffin gums. The first spruce chewing

gum to be commercially manufactured in this country was the "State of Maine Pure Spruce Gum," brought out in 1848 by a Bangor, Maine, entrepreneur named John Curtis. Curtis later sold spruce gums under such names as "American Flag" and "200 Lump Spruce." He also sold paraffin gums dubbed "Licorice Lulu," "Sugar Cream," and "Biggest and Best."

Pioneers settling the American West found the Osage Indians chewing a chicle-based gum made from the hardened sap of the sapodilla tree. The Osage, who'd been chewing chicle for many hundreds of years, had apparently obtained their first chews from Indian tribes living south of the Mexican border, where the sapodilla grows.

The Mexican General Antonio Lopez de Santa Anna—yes, the same Santa Anna of Alamo notoriety—thought that chicle could be used in the manufacture of

73

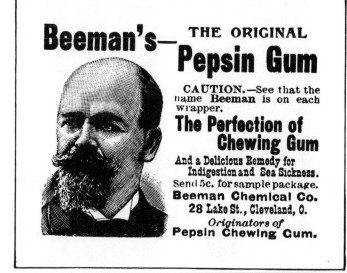

In the days of unregulated advertising, chewing gum manufacturers often made extravagant claims for their product.

rubber. So in 1839, he brought some sapodilla sap to the American inventor Thomas Adams. Attempts to manufacture rubber from the tree sap failed, but by the 1870s, Adams's company was marketing the nation's first commercial chicle- based chewing gums.

Chicle, Adams found, lasted much longer than paraffin or spruce, and carried flavors better than the earlier gums. Adams was soon selling such treats as *Peppermint, Spearmint, Black Jack* (licorice, of course, still popular), *Clove, Pepsin,* and *Cinnamon.* Today, the Adams Company and the William Wrigley, Jr. Company are the nation's largest manufacturers of chewing gums.

Thirty-year-old William Wrigley, Jr. moved to Chicago in 1891 and set up the Wrigley Company with just $32 of his own money and a $5,000 loan. The firm initially sold soap, then branched out into baking powder. In 1892, Wrigley ordered some chewing gum from the Zeno Manufacturing Company to offer jobbers as an inducement to buy

his baking powder. Wrigley's salesmen dispensed two packs of gum with each 10-cent package of baking powder, and the jobbers soon reported that they found it much easier to sell the gum than peddle the powder. It didn't take Wrigley long to see the possibilities.

By the turn of the century, Wrigley's gum was being sold, coast to coast, in stores and vending machines. Chewing gum factories were soon springing up in a number of foreign countries, including Canada, England, Germany, Australia, and New Zealand. By the end of World War II, the taste for Wrigley's product in America, Europe, and Asia was so great that his factories could barely keep pace with the demand.

Today, most chicle comes from Mexico. Sapodilla trees are tapped with grooved cuts and the latex is collected in small receptacles, as in the gathering of

A stick of sugarless gum contains but 6 or 7 calories—while a regular stick contains a whopping 8 calories!

maple syrup. Most productive sapodilla trees are over 70 years old. For best results, each tree is tapped only once every six to eight years. The collected sap is then boiled, coagulated, and molded into blocks.

At the manufacturing plant, the chicle is kneaded into a hot sugar and corn syrup mixture, then flavored and rolled into thin strips. Most modern gums contain 20 percent chicle, 60 percent sugar, 19 percent corn syrup, and one percent flavoring. Of course, after a few hours of chewing, the wad in your mouth isn't likely to contain anything but the gum itself. Some gum manufacturers now use synthetic products to give their gum its chewiness.

Gumdrops are made not from chicle, but from gum arabic, a substance obtained from exudations of certain types of acacia tree. Gum arabic products were used as medicaments for many years, since the slow solution of gum in the mouth allowed a steady release of the active ingredients.

Many gum specialties have come and gone over the 100-year history of chewing gum marketing. For decades, the Adams Company has been selling Chiclets—pellets of gum wrapped in a sugar candy. The 1970s saw the introduction of "squirt" gum, wads of chewing gum with liquid centers that "explode" into the mouth upon the first chew. And the sweet, pink chew known as bubble gum needs little identification.

Bubble gum first appeared in 1933. But it wasn't until 1947, when the Topps Chewing Gum Co. began to offer the familiar Bazooka penny piece, that bubble gum became the ubiquitous source of oral gratification it is today. Later, Topps included baseball cards with slabs of gum.

The earliest baseball cards appeared during the 1880s in packets of cigarettes and tobacco. Candy companies began to issue cards in 1913, and bubble gum manufacturers included cards with their product beginning in 1933. Topps entered the baseball card field in 1951, and has since become the giant of both the bubble gum and baseball card industries, distributing some 250 million cards each year.

The Topps company estimates that there are now more than 100,000 serious baseball card collectors in the United States. Enthusiasts will pay surprisingly high sums for a valuable specimen. The largest collection of baseball cards in the world—200,000 cards—belongs to the Metropolitan Museum of Art in New York, and the most prized Topps card in existence is the 1952 Mickey Mantle, valued as high as $100.

During baseball's spring training period, Topps signs and photographs all rookies and established players whom they believe have a chance to make the major league rosters in the upcoming season. Each player is photographed both wearing a cap and bareheaded. If the player is traded to another club after his picture is taken, the bareheaded photo is used on the player's card. In case you were wondering, a player is paid for the use of his picture—$250 each year a new card appears.

The baseball card trade is not without its lighter side. A number of right-handed practical jokers have posed for the Topps photographer wearing a left-handed glove, or vice versa, and more than one player has appeared on a card bearing another player's name. In 1969, California Angels'

The largest collection of baseball cards in the world—200,000 cards—belongs to the Metropolitan Museum of Art in New York.

In 1975, Kurt Bevacqua of the Milwaukee Brewers won the Topps World Series Bubble-Blowing Contest with this 18" bubble. The prizes were a $1,000 donation to the charity of the winner's choice, a giant-sized baseball card of the player, and a year's supply of Bazooka bubblegum.

third baseman Aurelio Rodriguez duped Topps into photographing the team batboy in his place, and thousands of cards bearing the batboy's image over Rodriguez' name were distributed before Topps caught the error.

Few people buy Topps baseball cards for the slab of bubble gum included in each package. Bubble gum addicts are more likely to get their fix from a piece of Topps Bazooka gum. Bazooka was introduced in 1947, and owes its name to the resemblance between the early five-cent size and the bazookas used in World War II.

Each piece of Bazooka gum comes with a premium of sorts— a Bazooka Joe comic. Topps first

included the comics with their gums in 1953; and in the years since, the firm has developed a repertoire of close to 700 different comics. The company tries not to repeat a title for about seven years so that the comics are fresh for each new generation of bubble gum chewers.

Sugarless gums have been with us since the 1940s, and now account for 10 percent of all chewing gum sales. A stick of sugarless gum contains but six or seven calories—while a regular stick contains a whopping eight calories!

Gum makers have also developed gums that won't stick to dentures, and they are presently working on such earth-shattering innovations as a bubble gum whose bubbles glow in the dark.

In the early days of chewing gum marketing, gum companies tried to sell their products by stressing their value to dental health. Advertisements pointed out that primitive races whose diets demand a great deal of chewing usually have excellent

teeth. When the Wrigley Company began to market its chewing gum in England around 1911, the firm's ads pointed up the values of gum to dental *and* mental health, claiming that gum eased tension and thereby improved concentration.

Wrigley faced an additional challenge in convincing the Englishman to chew gum: to rid gum-chewing of its lower-class connotations. When Wrigley began to advertise heavily in English magazines, he surprisingly chose those publications most read by the social elite. Sure, the ads read, gum may be out of place at the opera or in Buckingham Palace, but gum-chewing can be both proper and highly beneficial at most other times. The results of the ad campaign? Sales of Wrigley's products in England doubled over the next 20 years.

In the Soviet Union, where the manufacture of chewing gum is prohibited by the State, foreign tourists are frequently accosted by young Russian boys clamoring for "tchewing gum! tchewing gum."

Why do people chew gum? Ask the average gum-chewer why he uses gum and you'll most likely receive in response, a shrug of the shoulders. But the answer is simple: gum-chewing uses up excess nervous energy.

Studies have shown that the use of gum rises in periods of social tension, and falls in more tranquil times. For instance, the use of gum in this country soared from a per capita 98 sticks in 1939 to 165 sticks by the early 50s, duplicating a similar rise during World War I. Today's per capita consumption of chewing gum stands at 175 sticks per year. So, as if you needed any further confirmation, the chewing gum barometer suggests that we once again live in troubled times.

Chickens

"A chicken in every pot" is no longer a dream or an idle campaign slogan: it's a reality. The chicken, the most abundant of all domesticated creatures, now numbers over four billion, or one for every person on earth. And the expression "an egg on every plate" might be equally apt, for each year the world's chickens produce some 390 billion eggs—enough to provide every human being with a hundred eggs a year!

That's a lot of chickens and a lot of eggs, considering that the chicken was once no more plentiful than any other jungle bird!

The chicken is such a common creature today that we have more than a half-dozen words for the bird, and the terminology might be confusing to anyone who didn't grow up on a poultry farm. *Chicken* itself usually refers to any member of the *gallus domesticus* species, male or female. The word comes from the Old English *cycen*, which was in turn derived from *kukin*, "little cock."

A *cock* is a male chicken, or a *rooster*. The word *hen*, which designates a female chicken, usually one of egg-laying age, is also derived from an Old English word for rooster, *hana*. A *pullet*, meanwhile, is a hen less than a year old. The term comes from the French word for hen, *poule*, from which our *poultry* is derived. A *capon* is a castrated male chicken, and a *springer* is a female chicken a few months old.

The chicken of today, rooster, hen, pullet, springer, and capon alike, is the product of many centuries of domestication. The wonderful fowl that now graces so many of our dinner plates is believed descended from *gallus gallus*, a jungle bird of India and Southeast Asia. The chicken may not have been domesticated on any large scale until as recently as 1500 B.C., in contrast to the cow and sheep, which were domesticated well before recorded history began.

But the chicken was a common fowl in Europe by the time of the Roman Empire. The Romans may have been the first to raise chickens in batteries, roosts in which large numbers of birds can be raised together cheaply. To improve the flavor of the meat, the Romans sometimes treated their chickens to a diet of barley and milk; to improve their chicken dishes, they often stuffed the bird with sausages, eggs, peas, and other delights. One story has it that the Emperor Didius forbade Romans from stuffing their "hens or roosters" in order to stretch the Empire's food supply. To circumvent the law, Romans castrated roosters and stuffed them, since the castrated birds could not legally be termed either "hens" or "roosters"—and so the capon was born.

The Romans, by the way, ate a great number of birds in addition to the familiar chicken, duck, and goose, and many of these feathered delicacies might seem rather odd dishes to us today. Roman banquets often included such avian treats as the parrot, flamingo, thrush, peacock, pigeon, lark, blackbird, nightingale, partridge, and dove. Hosts sometimes prepared birds'-tongue pie to impress their guests, and we have record of one feast that included a pie made solely from the tongues of songbirds.

During the Middle Ages, European serfs raised chickens for both meat and eggs. Often they turned over a number of chickens each year to their lord as rent for the land they worked. American president Herbert Hoover is frequently credited with the expression "a chicken in every pot," and indeed the phrase was used as a Republican campaign slogan for the 1932 election. But the saying is actually much older: around the year 1600, French King Henry IV used those words in reference to his agriculture plans for France: "I hope to make France so prosperous that every peasant will have a chicken in his pot on Sunday."

Napoleon was an avid chicken fancier. While campaigning, he had his cooks prepare a fresh chicken every half-hour so that one would always be ready when he decided to eat. Napoleon's chef is credited with the invention of one of the most familiar and delicious of all chicken dishes. During the battle of Marengo in Italy, the Little Corporal's chef found himself without butter, so he obtained some native olive oil in which to fry his chicken. To mask the flavor of the oil, he added tomatoes, mushrooms, wine, and herbs. Napoleon loved the dish, and *Chicken Marengo*

77

entered the world of chicken cookery.

In the United States, the chicken didn't become as popular a food item as it is today until the 1930s, when Americans began to raise chickens in batteries, employing scientific feeding systems. Chicken farmers were soon raising birds as plump in seven weeks as they had formerly been in three months, making chicken farming more lucrative.

Today, the chicken population of the United States at any given time is usually around 380 million. About four-fifths are used for meat and the remainder for eggs. The average American consumes 45 pounds of the fowl annually, compared to 88 pounds of beef and about 41 pounds of pork. The U.S.S.R. owns more chickens than any other nation—there are some 565 million chickens in Russian barnyards—while other large chicken producers include China, England, Australia, Ireland, Denmark, Canada, and France.

Pound for pound, chicken is a more economical, nourishing meat than either beef or pork. A hundred grams of chicken meat (about three-and-a-half ounces) contains from 150 to 200 calories, while a like quantity of beef contains 273 calories and pork about 450. Chicken is twice as rich in protein as an equal portion of pork, and contains only a fraction of the fat (from seven to 12 grams per 100) in either beef (22 grams) or pork (45 grams).

To a city slicker, it might seem like a good idea to raise chickens for their eggs and then sell them for meat when their egg-laying days are over. The fact is, most chickens are raised exclusively for either meat or eggs. Generally, egg-layers do not provide good meat, and chickens that are raised as fryers and broilers for the most part do not produce eggs for the commercial market.

Today, there are five classes of chicken: English, Asiatic, Mediterranean, American, and Continental European. Each of these classes includes a number of breeds—there are some 100 breeds and varieties altogether. Only Mediterranean chickens lay white eggs; the others lay mostly brown eggs. But Mediterranean chickens are generally not good for meat.

The most popular breeds of chicken in the United States and Europe include the *Leghorn*, a

A Black-tailed Japanese bantam male.

A Dominique male.

78

A Black Java male.   A single-comb white leghorn male.

Mediterranean breed raised for its eggs; the *New Hampshire,* an American breed noted for its rapid growth that is usually raised for meat; the *Plymouth Rock,* another American chicken raised most often for its meat; the *Rhode Island Red,* an American breed bred for egg-laying and sometimes for its meat; and the *Cornish,* an English breed that makes a fine roaster.

The average chicken weighs from three to six pounds, but some older hens have been known to attain a weight of over 20 pounds. The largest chicken on record, a California native nicknamed "Weirdo," weighed 22 pounds at age four. This fowl, obviously not chicken-hearted, killed a rooster and two cats, and injured a dog as well as its owner.

As long as people continue to enjoy chicken meat and eggs, chicken raising can be a profitable occupation. A single farmer can care for as many as 50,000 chickens at one time, and can bring his flock from egg to market in only three months. In the largest chicken farm in the world, the so-called "Egg City" of Moorpark, California, four-and-a-half million chickens are housed on a mere 600 acres, and turn out over two million eggs each day!

On chicken farms that produce primarily eggs, the male chickens are sold for meat soon after birth, while the females begin laying about 150 days after birth. Normally, a hen would lay about 15 eggs per month during her first year, and about 20 per month in her second year. But chickens are hardy eaters: it takes at least five pounds of chicken feed to produce just a dozen eggs. As a 17th-century Englishman noted, "Children and chickens must be always picking."

A redoubtable egg-laying record was achieved by a Rhode Island Red of recent acclaim that laid 20 eggs in seven days, including seven in one day. At that rate, the prolific hen would have smashed the all-time annual egg-laying record: in 1930, a New Zealand fowl laid 361 eggs in a single year!

While we're on the subject of eggs, the size classifications of the eggs in your supermarkets aren't merely descriptive. U.S. Department of Agriculture regulations specify that to qualify as "Extra Large," a dozen eggs must weigh 27 ounces. A dozen "Large" eggs should weigh 24 ounces; a dozen "Medium" eggs should tip the scales at 21 ounces; and "Small" eggs should weigh 18 ounces per dozen. "Jumbo" eggs are 30 ounces to the dozen.

79

Egg grades refer not to the size, but to the quality of the egg. The best grade is AA; these eggs should have a firm, high yolk and a thick white. Grade A eggs are slightly thinner, but still are fine for baking and other uses where the appearance of the egg is not important.

We have no idea of the grade of an egg laid by a Jersey hen, in 1965, that tipped the scales at close to a pound! The record-setting egg had two yolks and a double shell. And speaking of egg yolks, many eggs contain more than one; the record is nine, set by a hen in New York State.

Crossing the supermarket from the dairy aisle to the meat department, we'll find chickens under such names as *broiler, fryer, roaster, capon,* and *game hen.* All are young birds with tender flesh. Older, mature birds are usually marked *hen, stewing chicken,* or *fowl,* and are certain-ly no spring chickens. A trip to the frozen foods aisle and its host of prepared chicken dinners, pies, and other dishes will show that we've come a long way since the 17th century, when English philosopher Francis Bacon died while trying to freeze a chicken by stuffing it with snow.

Almost every cuisine in the world includes a number of chicken dishes, and America is certainly no exception. Fried chicken is now the most popular single dish in the United States, far surpassing the runners-up—roast beef, and spaghetti. In sheer poundage, chicken ranks number eight among all food items consumed in the United States—and that's not including the 263 eggs consumed yearly by each American!

New dishes for the versatile chicken are probably being invented every day, and will continue to appear as the number of chickens in the world rises steadily. Since there are now about as many chickens in the world as there are people, and the population of the world in the year 2000 is projected to be around eight billion, we might anticipate that there will be some eight billion chickens around by that time!

But then again, that would be counting our chickens before they're hatched.

That expression has been credited to a 17th-century English poet named Samuel Butler, although it was also used by Cervantes, Erasmus, and Aesop, and is surely much older. Coincidentally, it was another Englishman by the name of Samuel Butler, a 19th-century author, who offered the cleverest answer to the age-old question: "Which came first, the chicken or the egg?"

"The hen," Butler wrote, "is only an egg's way of making another egg."

A Bearded Silver Polish male.

A Bearded Silver Polish female.

Chocolate

The fruit of the cacao tree, from which chocolate is produced.

At the market in the Mayan city of Chichen Itza, 10 cacao beans could purchase a rabbit, four beans a pumpkin. A slave was a real steal, at just 100 cacao beans.

It's difficult to imagine a confectionery industry in the West without chocolate. Cocoa and chocolate are virtually unknown as a popular food outside Europe and the United States. Just five nations—the United States, England, West Germany, the Netherlands, and France—now account for four-fifths of all world imports. Ten nations account for over 95 percent. But chocolate is actually a native of Central America, and was totally unknown in Europe less than 500 years ago—and little known outside of Spain until the 17th century!

When Spanish explorer Hernando Cortés arrived in Mexico in the early 16th century, he found the Indians drinking a dark, frothy beverage called *chocolatl*, brewed from the beans of a native plant. The Aztecs regarded the plant as a divine gift brought to earth by the god Quetzalcoatl. Chocolate was so highly prized in the area that both the Aztecs and Mayans used cacao beans as currency. At the market in the Mayan city of Chichen Itza, 10 beans could purchase a rabbit, four beans a pumpkin. A slave was a real steal, at just 100 cacao beans.

The Aztec king Montezuma, who introduced Cortes to the Chocolatl, was said to drink no other beverage than chocolate, consuming some 50 pitchers a day. Over 2,000 pitchers of chocolate were prepared daily for the royal household, usually mixed with honey, vanilla, or peppers, and cooled with ice from nearby mountains. Montezuma consumed a golden goblet of chocolate beverage before he entered his harem, then tossed the cup into the lake beside his palace. Indians were still diving for the golden goblets years after the Spanish began to colonize the area.

An Indian legend maintains that the word *chocolatl* originated when confectioners mixed *atl*, water, with ground cacao beans and stirred the mixture over a flame in huge vats. The bubbling mixture made a sound similar to "choco-choco." But the word more likely comes from the Aztec word *choqui*, "warmth." Today, we use the word *cacao* when referring to the raw bean, *cocoa* for the pulverized bean, and *chocolate* for the solid manufactured product.

Christopher Columbus may have brought cacao beans to Spain. But it was Cortés who first turned the attention of his countrymen to the New World product, writing to Emperor Charles V that he'd discovered a "divine drink . . . which builds up resistance and fights fatigue."

By 1520, cacao had made its first appearance in Spain, where thick, sugared, chilled chocolate beverages became an instant sensation. By 1525, cacao plantations were flourishing on Trinidad. Within a century, large quantities of chocolate were being exported from Venezuela.

The clergy took an immediate distaste to chocolate, as was their wont with any new foodstuff. The churchmen declared chocolate "the beverage of Satan" and "a provocative of immorality," since it was thought that chocolate was an aphrodisiac. The idea did not die easily. As late as 1712, the English magazine *The Spectator* warned that men "be careful how they meddle with romance, chocolate, novels, and the like inflamers."

Chocolate remained popular in Spain for more than a century before it caught on elsewhere in Europe, for the Spanish carefully guarded the methods of manufacturing drinkable chocolate. Late in the 16th century, when the Dutch captured a Spanish ship laden with cacao beans, they considered the unfamiliar cargo so worthless that they tossed the beans into the sea.

In 1606, an Italian named Antonio Carletti introduced chocolate to his country after a trip to Spain. Some historians believe that chocolate then made its way over the Alps to Austria, and was brought to France by Anne of Austria, the queen of Louis XIII. But it's more likely that chocolate was brought to France by the Spanish Infanta, Maria Theresa, when she moved to Paris to become the bride of Louis XIV.

As had been her custom in Spain, the new queen had her maid prepare a cup of chocolate for her each morning. Soon, other women of the court were clamoring for the queen's "naughty beverage." Louis himself enjoyed chocolate as his breakfast drink. And Louis's war minister, the Marquis de Louvois, invented the still popular *Café Louvois*, a mixture of semisweet chocolate, coffee, and whipped cream.

Around the mid-17th century, chocolate houses began to appear in many European capitals. The price of chocolate was still high enough to make the houses fashionable retreats for the wealthy. In 1657, the first London shop opened, selling the exotic beverage Samuel Pepys called "jocolatte." Spurred by doctors' reports claiming chocolate was an effective medicine, with one ounce equal in nutritive value to a pound of meat, chic Londoners began flocking to their chocolate houses, making such establishments as the Cocoa Tree Club and the St. James Club centers of social intercourse and political discussion.

A quaint tale from the early 18th century tells of an Austrian nobleman named Prince Dietrichstein who ordered a chocolate beverage in a Vienna chocolate house and was so enraptured by the waitress who served him that he wooed and eventually married her. The Prince commissioned the noted Swiss portraitist Jean-Etienne Leotard to paint a portrait of his wife, Anna Beltauf, in her waitress garb. Titled *La Belle Chocolatière*, the painting soon found its way to a museum.

In 1872, an American executive of the Walter Baker Chocolate Company saw the painting of Anna Beltauf during a trip to Europe, and purchased it for use as the firm's emblem. Baker chocolate products still bear a reproduction of the Leotard portrait.

The Walter Baker Chocolate Company was manufacturing chocolate in this country as long ago as the 18th century. In 1765, the first chocolate factory in the United States was established in Dorchester, Massachusetts, by one John Hannan. Fifteen years later, Hannan sold the plant to Dr. James Baker, the founder of the Walter Baker firm.

Eating chocolate as we know it today was a fairly recent development. For centuries, chocolate was enjoyed as a beverage, rather than an edible snack. Breakfast cocoa was introduced in 1828, when Dutchman Coenraad Van Houten invented a machine for removing oil from the fermented cacao bean. Milk chocolate was not perfected until 1876, when a Swiss chocolatier named M.D. Peter combined chocolate with milk solids. Today, American chocolate manufacturers use close to 3,500,000 pounds of whole milk daily in the production of milk chocolate candy.

Switzerland and the Netherlands, now the world's foremost producers of quality chocolate, did not begin making chocolate products on a large scale until early in the 18th century.

Assorted filled chocolates of the type now sold by such giants as Fanny Farmer and Barricini's first appeared in 1870, when chocolatiers began covering fresh cream with chocolate liquor as a way of preserving and selling cream. In 1903, the industry received a big lift when a Frenchman invented a machine called the enrober that could mechanically coat candies with chocolate.

The chocolate bar is a 20th century innovation. In 1903, a chocolatier from Lancaster, Pennsylvania, named Milton Snavely Hershey established a chocolate plant on undeveloped property near Harrisburg. The community that grew up around the plant—named, not surprisingly, Hershey—was built entirely by the chocolate company itself, complete with homes and gardens for the workers, streets, sewers, schools, a power plant, a post office, a bank, and a 75-acre park. The plant, the world's largest chocolate factory, now sprawls over two million square feet of floor space, turning out some hundreds of million choco-

late bars each year. In 1973, more than a million tourists visited Hershey's chocolate world.

To Americans, the chocolate bar and the Hershey bar are virtually synonymous. Other chocolate manufacturers began large scale production of the candy bar during World War I. At first, the chocolatiers shipped blocks of solid chocolates to GI's in training camps around the nation. Since the weighing and cutting of smaller blocks became too time-consuming on the bases, manufacturers began wrapping chocolate "bars" individually for shipment to the soldiers, and the candy bar—as we know it—was born.

The Nestlé Company, another major chocolate producer, cornered a large chunk of the American market with the introduction of "morsels" for use in chocolate chip cookies. During

The shape of Hershey's chocolate kisses must be exact for wrapping by automatic equipment.

As late as 1712, the English magazine *The Spectator* warned men to ''be careful how they meddle with romance, chocolate, novels, and the like inflamers.''

An ad for Metcalf's Coca Wine in the latter part of the 19th century.

the 1940s, a Massachusetts restaurant called the Toll House Inn earned a local reputation by serving cookies studded with especially delicious bits of chocolate. When cookie lovers discovered that the "secret" ingredient in the cookies was a certain semisweet chocolate sold in local stores, they quickly wiped out all supplies. So the Nestlé Company introduced their Toll House cookie morsels to satisfy the

demand, and homemade chocolate chip cookie lovers have been grateful ever since.

Today, few Americans are more than a short walk from the nearest chocolate bar. But chocolate itself travels a long road from the tree to the candy store.

Cacao beans come from a tropical plant known as *Theobroma cacao.* The first word literally means "food of the gods." A cacao tree can grow 30 or 40 feet high, but most cultivated trees are pruned to a height of about 20 feet to facilitate harvesting.

Cacao trees begin to bear fruit after three or four years, and reach full production after about eight years. Most trees remain

productive for up to 40 years, and some have been known to bear fruit for almost a century.

A cacao tree bears about 20 pods, each about 10 inches long and four inches in diameter. Each pod in turn contains from 20 to 40 beans. Ripe pods are picked by hand and slit open to remove the beans, which are then fermented in their own pulp and dried in the sun.

At the manufacturing plant, the cacao beans are cleaned, roasted, shelled, and broken into smaller bits known as nibs. The nibs are cleaned and ground into

84

Chocolate for candy comes from a tree that looks like this. This cocoa tree stands in Trinidad.

Today, the annual worldwide production of cacao tops the million ton mark—that's over two *billion* pounds of cacao each year!

a paste, liquifying the fat known as cocoa butter that makes up about 55 percent of the bean. Different processes then produce either cocoa or eating chocolate.

Cocoa is produced by squeezing about half of the cocoa butter from the chocolate paste, then grinding, cooling, and sifting the resultant powder. Eating choco-

late is produced by grinding the paste for days, pouring it into molds, and mixing with additional cocoa butter and flavorings.

On the average, eating chocolate contains about 42 percent chocolate, an equal percentage of sugar, and about 16 percent cocoa butter.

For many years, Central America, Ecuador, and Venezuela were the major producers of raw cacao beans. Today, about 75 percent of the world's supply comes from Africa. The nation of Ghana, which did not begin cacao cultivation on a large scale until 1879, presently accounts for about 30 percent of the African

85

crop. But most African cacao is considered "base" grade, inferior to the "flavor" grades now produced in Central America, Ecuador, and Brazil.

In 1850, the total world production of raw cacao stood at a mere 20,000 tons. By the turn of the century, chocolate lovers were consuming close to 100,000 tons of the bean, and by 1925, the figure had skyrocketed to almost a half-million tons. Today, the annual worldwide production figure tops the million ton mark—that's over two *billion* pounds of cacao each year!

The United States is the largest consumer of chocolate products, accounting for about one-quarter of world imports. About half of the 450-million-pound annual American import of chocolate is used in the production of sugar confectioneries, including ice cream, about a quarter in candy bars, 10 percent in chocolate coverings, seven percent in assorted chocolates, and only seven percent in the production of cocoa. Chocolate byproducts are also used to make cosmetics, and cacao shells provide animal fodder.

About half of all confectionery products in America contain chocolate. All told, America consumes about eight billion pounds of candy each year, making confectionery the eighth largest food processing industry in this country. But per capita, Europeans are far ahead of Americans in chocolate consumption. The average American gobbles up about 16 pounds of candy each year, including about two-and-a-half pounds of chocolate; the average Englishman, about 28 pounds of candy annually.

Western Europe as a whole accounts for up to 60 percent of world chocolate imports, with England, Germany, and the Netherlands the leading consumers.

Without doubt, chocolate must rank as one of the most delectable taste treats ever developed by man. But chocolate is also useful as a source of quick energy, since most chocolate products are high in sugar. Also, cacao beans contain *theobromine*, a mild stimulant, and caffeine. Chocolate's low bulk and high calorific content make it an excellent food for soldiers' ration kits. Queen Victoria sent a half-million pounds of chocolate to English soldiers fighting the Boer War in South Africa, and American GI's helped popularize the candy bar in Europe during World War II. The Hershey Company, the manufacturer of the Ration O bar, reached a peak production of 500,000 bars a day. Wiley Post, the first man to fly solo around the world, ate chocolate bars throughout his journey to keep himself awake.

You may have seen Mole sauce on the menu of a Mexican restaurant. No, the sauce owes nothing to the burrowing animal of that name. Mole sauce is actually a chocolate sauce commonly used with fowl, an invention of nuns in Mexico.

Chocolate is more often consumed in the United States in confectionery items, sold as bars, blocks, morsels, powder, and small candies in an untold number of shapes. Egotistic chocolate lovers might prefer their confections in a more personal form. For $350, Kron Chocolatiers in New York will shape a bust of your head from solid chocolate. Even Montezuma never had it so good!

The average American gobbles up about 16 pounds of candy each year, including about two-and-a-half pounds of chocolate.

CHRISTMAS CARDS

No one could fail to notice that most Christmas cards today have nothing whatsoever to do with Christ or Christianity—but did you know that Yuletide greeting cards were secular from their inception? Sanctimonious individuals may annually decry the deluge of cards and bewail the "loss of religious spirit," but the fact is that few of the customs we now associate with Christmas have anything at all to do with religious commemoration—and some of these customs are a good deal older than Christianity itself!

The date of Christ's birth is purely conjectural—there is no historical evidence that Christ was born on December 25. Mention of a December 25 celebration of Christ's birth first appeared around the year 353, but it wasn't until 440—more than four centuries after his actual birth—that the Church proclaimed that day as the official date for the festival. Conveniently, December 25 already marked a holiday among many Europeans—the celebratory rite of the winter solstice, marking the beginning of lengthening days and the expectation of spring and rebirth. Due to changes in the calendar, Christmas no longer falls exactly on the solstice.

As the celebration of a midwinter Christmas spread with Christianity, people in various cultures retained many of their pagan solstice customs and incorporated them in the

The first Christmas card was designed by John Horsley in 1843.

Christmas rite. At that time of year, the ancient Romans had exchanged gifts to mark the feast of Saturnalia. Celtic and Teutonic tribes kept many customs of their 12-day Yule celebration. Mistletoe, for instance, was prominent in midwinter Druid rites, and holly was similarly used by the Anglo-Saxons. The evergreen tree had long been regarded as a symbol of survival by Scandinavian peoples—though the Christmas tree proper did not find its way to England until 1840, introduced by Queen Victoria's German-born husband, Albert.

By the middle of the 19th century, Christmas was being observed throughout the Christian world very much as it is today—with the notable absence of the Christmas card. The idea, if not the custom, of pictorial representations of seasonal greetings dates back to the Middle Ages. An engraving by one "Master E.S." depicting the infant Christ stepping from a flower has been dated to around 1466, and is thought to be a copy of an even earlier design. Similar works from the 15th century refer to both Christmas and New Year. Calendars in the 17th and 18th centuries often carried Yuletide greetings, with domestic winter scenes, sailing ships, and red-cheeked goddesses among the favored motifs.

As to the first legitimate "Christmas card," there is some controversy. According to many accounts, the idea of a Christmas greeting card sprang from the fertile brain of Sir Henry Cole, the first director of the Victoria and Albert Museum in London. In 1843, Cole commissioned John Collcott Horsley, a fashionable artist of the time, to design his first card. Horsley was well known not only for his artwork, but for leadership of a campaign against the use of nude models by artists—work that earned him the nickname "Clothes-Horsley."

The artist's first card consisted of one unfolded sheet, oblong in shape, with a rustic bower

A Merry Christmas.

A Happy New Year.

This 19th-century Christmas card is one of the 70,000 unusual cards in the Hallmark Historical Collection.

forming a frame for three illustrations. The central scene depicted a typical middle-class Victorian family gathered around a sumptuously laden table, drinking to the health of an absent friend—the card's recipient. The card also showed a moralistic scene depicting a charitable soul feeding the hungry at Christmas. The card also contained a representation of another good Samaritan clothing the naked—though Horsley, true to form, depicted

the naked indigent as fully clothed. Above the tableau, appeared the word "To" followed by a space for an inscription; on the bottom of the card, the word "From" followed by a picture of an artist with a palette and the date "Xmasse 1843." A banner stretching across the bottom of the central scene carried the greeting "A Merry Christmas and a Happy New Year to you." Christmas cards haven't changed much, have they?

Horsley became the world's first Christmas-card sender when he presented Cole with a signed copy of his original design, bearing the brilliantly original inscription:

*"To his good friend Cole
Who's a merry young soul
And a merry young soul is he:
And may he be for many years
to come! Hooray!*

Cole had a thousand copies of the original card printed and issued by Summerby's Home Treasury Office. Only a dozen are known to exist today. Two of these can be found in the

70,000-card Hallmark Historical Collection, the largest and most representative museum of greeting card art in existence.

Initial reaction to the distribution of Christmas cards was hardly favorable. Some critics claimed Horsley's card was too secular, and accused him of encouraging intemperance and alcoholism. Others criticized the idea of cards as a foolish extravagance. In fact, certain Protestant sects refused to condone the Christmas card until the turn of the century.

But Yuletide cards caught on quickly among the general population, and within 20 years were well entrenched in Victorian Christmas celebrations. At first, cards were generally not mailed or signed, but delivered by messenger with a calling card. The penny post, introduced in England in 1840, did much to popularize Yuletide greetings by mail; and by the 1850s, Christmas cards began to appear on the European continent as well.

Victorian Christmas cards were considerably more elaborate than today's, often adorned with layers of lace, silk fringes, tassels, ribbons, dried flowers, satin, or mother-of-pearl. Some were glass frosted. One surviving Victorian card consisted of 750 pieces of material stitched together.

The Christmas card first appeared in the United States in 1874, brought out by Bavarian-born Boston lithographer Louis Prang. Prang's card was designed by Mrs. O.E. Whitney, and based on an English card signed *Charles Dickens* that Prang had brought back from Europe. At first, the cards were produced for export to England, since the custom of sending greeting cards at Christmas had yet to appear in America. But Prang's cards—among the first to depict religious scenes—went on sale in the United States the following year. Christmas-card fever soon became a permanent American ailment.

Through the years, Christmas-card design has often changed to reflect the feeling of the times. During the Depression, many cards spoofed poverty to make light of temporary hard times. Santas carrying flags were popular during World War II, as were inscriptions such as "Missing You" and "Across the Miles." The Cold War years saw an increased demand for humorous cards.

Today, Christmas cards are a multimillion-dollar industry in most English-speaking countries. Hallmark Cards, the largest American greeting card company, boasts annual sales of $400 million. In 1954, Americans sent about two billion Christmas cards; now, the yearly figure stands at close to four billion, for an average of 20 cards per person.

Of course, many Americans send considerably more than 20 cards. One Werner Erhard of San Francisco sent 62,824 cards in a single year. This is believed to be the largest outpouring of Christmas-card generosity in history.

Critics continue to lay the blame for an outlandish waste of time, money, and paper at the feet of overzealous Christmas-card senders. The English magazine *Punch* hit it on the head when, in a 1900 editorial, it declared: "We deprecate the absurd habit of Christmas cards and presents—we refer, of course, to those we have to *give!*"

In 1954, Americans sent about two billion Christmas cards; now the yearly figure stands at close to four billion, for an average of 20 cards per person.

CLOUDS

They look so different at different times—and
the same cloud looks so different to each one
of us.

Today, meteorologists still use a modifica-
tion of Luke Howard's classification of clouds
into four basic types: cirrus, cumulus, stratus,
and nimbus.

Each artist will treat a cloud in his own
manner. There follows a number of unusual
treatments.

*"Califlower clouds" as repre-
sented in a drawing in the* Century Dictionary.

By a Russian painter. Picture appears in Fifty Years of Soviet Art, *published in Moscow.*

By an early German master

*Paul Gustave Dore (1833-1883) was a masterful draftsman, whose book illustrations
are known for their imagination in depicting the weird and the gloomy.*

92

This drawing first appeared in Modern Pen Drawing, *published in London in 1901 by The Studio.*

Cumulus clouds as shown in a drawing from Leslie's, *a famous magazine of the late 1800s*

A drawing from the London Illustrated News *which shows the steam tug Resolute of Liverpool in a storm*

Drawing by Grandville, famous French satirist. This drawing first appeared in Le Magasin Pittoresque

Cocktails

Walk into any American bar today and you'll find dozens of different kinds of spirits lining the shelves. You'll also notice that very few of the patrons are imbibing their favored spirit straight from the bottle. To Americans, the mixed drink may seem quite a time-worn tradition, and the fact is that the cocktail is an American invention—a fairly recent one at that.

The ancient Greeks had a cocktail hour in the late afternoon or evening, complete with hors d'oeuvres. An Athenian gentleman would drop by a neighbor's house during the "happy hour" with a goatskin of wine, and expect to be treated to an outlay of appetizers—the Greeks called them "provocatives to drinking"— that might include caviar, oysters,

nuts, olives, shrimp, and paté. Compare that spread to today's bar-fare of peanuts, cheese, and crackers and you'll agree that in some ways we haven't come very far in the last 2,500 years.

The mixed drink is a recent invention. In the past, not only wine and beer, but hard liquor, too, was usually drunk straight, or at most, diluted with water. As for tomato juice, tonic water, ginger ale, club soda, orange juice, and other mixers, few of these had yet made the trip from the grocery store to the barroom as recently as 200 years ago.

Alcohol itself, of course, has been with us since well before

95

recorded history began. Alcohol still ranks as the oldest and most widely used drug on earth. Primitive man probably discovered the first alcoholic drinks by accident, since any sugar-containing mishmash left exposed to warm air will eventually ferment. Studies of alcohol use among various preliterate societies suggest that alcohol was used by prehistoric man primarily in conjunction with war, religious worship, and various rites of passage—baths, marriages, funerals, and feasts.

The Babylonian Code of Hammurabi, dating around 1750 B.C., set down regulations for drinking houses. Egyptian doctors frequently prescribed alcohol as a medicine. By studying the remains of the Egyptian and Babylonian cultures, we can conclude that alcoholism has been a problem for well over 4,000 years.

The Chinese have been distilling an alcoholic beverage from rice since at least 800 B.C., and the Arabs have swilled alcohol from palm sap for many, many centuries. The earliest alcoholic beverage in the West was wine, brewed either from grapes or honey. Mead, a sweet wine made from honey, was widely enjoyed in Poland as recently as the 19th century.

The Greeks made their wine from grapes, but usually drank it diluted with water. Thus, the wine Athenians quaffed during their cocktail hour was probably less than 8 percent alcohol, a weak beverage by modern standards. In fact, most of the wine the Greeks and Romans enjoyed would probably taste rather crude to the modern palate. After all, we live in an age when an avid oenologist paid over $14,000 for a single bottle of 1806 Chateau Lafite-Rothschild!

Hard liquor is a newer arrival in the West. Around the year 300, the Irish brewed up *usquebaugh* from oat and barley beer. Tenth-century Italians began distilling brandy from wine, and 16th-century Scots first made whiskey from malted barley. The first cognac was distilled by the French around 1750. But it wasn't until Louis Pasteur's research in the 1850s into the action of yeasts and molds that Western man developed the controlled fermentation that makes for a consistently good alcoholic product.

Over the years, there were probably scattered incidents of man mixing hard liquor with a sweet beverage, but the cocktail did not become a popular drink until early in the 19th century. The origin of the word *cocktail* is uncertain. One claim maintains that it comes from a French drink served in New Orleans in the 1800s, called a *coquetier*, named for the tiny egg-cup in which the drink was usually served to women.

There are, however, dozens of other theories. According to some, the first cocktail in America was served in a tavern in Elmsford, New York, where cockfights were often held. The story has it that Betsy Flanagan, a barmaid, decorated the bar with tail feathers of some of the deceased combatants, and inserted one in a mixed drink when an inebriate requested "one of those cocktails." Another story tells us that as a publicity stunt, the proprietor of the tavern regularly inserted the tail feathers of fighting cocks in his mixed drinks, the feathers to be used as swizzle sticks.

In any case, the first mention of the cocktail in print appeared in an 1809 issue of the Hudson, New York, *Balance*, which described the concoction as a "stimulating liquor composed of spirits of any kind, sugar, water, and bitters."

Speaking of bitters, angostura, the most popular modern variety, have been with us since 1824, when a German doctor living in Venezuela prepared them as a tonic for his ailing wife. He reportedly learned the recipe from sailors, who frequently added bitters to rum as a cure for seasickness. When angostura bitters became part of the Manhattan cocktail, their place behind the bar was established forevermore.

The cocktail party is thought to have originated as an outgrowth of the aperitif hour before dinner. As the "hour" gradually lengthened, a buffet of some kind became necessary to allay the appetites of the imbibers. Psychologists attribute the popularity of the cocktail party, and the before-dinner cocktail itself, to their function as a separation between the working day and the evening relaxation. In recent years, many other countries have followed the American example and have adopted both the cocktail hour and the cocktail party.

As a rule, tipplers in most countries prefer a beverage produced from a native product—in effect, the "national drink" of that nation. For instance, vodka, an unaged spirit obtained from potatoes or grain and filtered through vegetable charcoal, is the over-whelming favorite in Poland and the Soviet Union, where the raw materials are plentiful. Vodka, by the way, has recently replaced bourbon as the most popular liquor in America.

Bourbon, America's contribution to the whiskey world, accounted for about one-fourth of all distilled spirits consumed in this country during the 1960s. But that figure has now decreased to about 15 percent, while vodka consumption has doubled over the same period. Vodka drinking now accounts for about 20 percent of the total American alcohol intake. Consumption of scotch whiskey, meanwhile, has held steady at about 12 percent.

Named after the county in Kentucky which may have been its birthplace, bourbon is distilled from a mash that by law must contain at least 51 percent corn. But Jack Daniel's whiskey, which many people consider bourbon, is technically a sour mash whiskey, or a Tennessee whiskey, and not a bourbon at all. Jack Daniel's, produced for over a century in the small Tennessee town of Lynchburg, is filtered through 10 feet of sugar maple charcoal to remove some of the harsh esters. The Federal government decided that this filtering process changed the whiskey's character so much that the drink could not be called bourbon.

Whiskey is usually distilled from the fermented mash of grain—usually oats, barley, rye, or corn. Whiskey is produced primarily in Scotland, Ireland, Canada, and the United States.

Rum is obtained from fermented sugar cane or molasses, and produced primarily in the Caribbean.

Brandy is distilled from wine or the fermented mash of fruit—grapes, cherries, apples, plums, apricots, peaches, blackberries, or whatever.

Tequila is distilled from the sap of an agave plant indigenous to Mexico, not from the mescal cactus, as so many people believe. Flavored spirits like gin, aquavit, and absinthe are produced by redistilling alcohol with a flavoring agent. Juniper is used to flavor gin; caraway seeds to flavor aquavit.

In the Orient, millet and rice are most commonly used for distilling spirits. *Ng ka py* is how you order a shot in Peking. It's made from millet, with various aromatics added. Saké, a beverage made from rice, is the favorite in Japan.

Spirits differ greatly in alcoholic content. Most wines contain from 8 to 12 percent alcohol, with certain aperitif and dessert wines, like vermouth and sherry, as high as 18 percent. The strength of beer ranges from a weak 2 percent brew, produced in Scandinavia, to about 8 percent. Four or 5 percent is the average in the United States. Most hard liquors contain from 40 to 50 percent alcohol, with cognac as high as 70 percent. Cordials and liqueurs contain from 25 to 40 percent alcohol.

The strongest spirits that can be produced are raw rum and certain vodkas which contain up to 97 percent alcohol. Polish White Spirit Vodka is the strongest liquor sold commercially, packing a wallop of 80 percent alcohol.

Most liquor bottlers identify the alcoholic content of their product by "proof." The term dates back to the earliest days of liquor distilling—when dealers would test the strength of an alcoholic product by soaking gunpowder in the beverage, and then igniting it. Spirits with enough alcohol to permit the ignition of gunpowder were considered to be 100 proof—the idea being that the gunpowder test was "proof" that the juice was strong. In England, 100 proof was established as eleven parts of alcohol by volume to 10 parts of water. In the United States, the proof figure was set as double the alcoholic percentage. Thus, 86 proof whiskey is 43 percent alcohol, and pure alcohol is 200 proof.

Just as nations have their favored beverage, most have a favored toast as well. The term originated in the custom of dunking a slice of toast in a glass of wine, for reasons unknown. Englishmen like to toast with *Cheerio, Cheers,* or *Down the hatch.* Scandinavians say *Skoal. Prosit* is a German favorite, though the word is Latin. Italians clink glasses to the tune of *Cincin.* The Spanish favor *Salud,* and the French *Culs secs.* Americans have coined the likes of *Bottoms up, Here's mud in your eye,* and *Here's looking at you*—as well as some more indelicate expressions from the frontier West.

While we're on the subject of word origins: the word *booze* does not, as widely believed, come from a liquor bottler named E.C. Booz. The word is quite old, originating perhaps from the Dutch word *buyzen,* to tipple, or the Middle English *bouse,* to drink deep.

America has nevertheless contributed quite a number of terms to the barfly's dictionary. In the Old West, rotgut whiskey was referred to by such affectionate terms as *old pine top, skull varnish, tarantula juice, Taos lightning, snake water, bug juice,* and *red-eye.*

Today, the names of popular cocktails are somewhat more flattering. The origins of some are obvious; others, lost in history. The *Rickey,* for example, is said to be named after a certain Colonel Rickey. The word *Julep* comes from the Arabic *julab.* The *Black Russian* is named for its primary ingredient, vodka. (It's not black, but it's certainly Russian.) The *Grasshopper,* consisting of green creme de menthe, with creme de cacao, and cream, owes its name to its green color. The *Martini, Tom Collins,* and *Alexander* are named after individuals. The origins of the *Fizz, Sour,* and *Stinger* shouldn't be hard to imagine. As for the *Zombie,* you won't need three guesses—the talk is that three Zombies will turn you into one.

But the names of modern cocktails are certainly not lacking in color. Witness the *Red Devil, Sitz Mark, Bourbon Fog, Hurricane, Barbed Wire Fence, Rhett Butler, Cable Car, Sombrero, Tequila Sunrise, Pink Lady, Pink Elephant, Godfather, Harvey Wallbanger,* and a warm wine-and-brandy concoction billed as the *Instant Cold Cure.*

Among the less exotic—and more popular—cocktails we find the *Old Fashioned,* a mixture of whiskey, sugar, bitters, and club soda. The *Screwdriver* combines vodka and orange juice; the *Bloody Mary,* vodka and tomato juice. A *Daiquiri* includes rum, lime juice, and sugar. A *Mint Julep* usually includes bourbon, mint leaves, sugar, and water. A *Margarita* combines tequila, salt, lime juice, and Triple Sec. A *Manhattan* is made with whiskey, vermouth, and bitters. And the ever popular *Martini* includes gin, a dash of vermouth, and an olive.

Speaking of the Martini, there's the tale about the South

Seas explorer whose friend gave him a bon voyage packet containing bottles of gin and vermouth and a jar of olives. A tag attached to the gift said, *for insurance against loneliness.* When on the high seas, the explorer opened the present. Inside the package, a card contained the following: "I have never yet seen anyone start to make a Martini without someone else coming along and telling him how to do it."

And then there's the one about the man who ordered a Martini in a bar, drank down the cocktail in one gulp, and then began biting the glass. When he'd nibbled the glass down to the top of the stem, he left it on the counter and walked off.

"Did you see that?" a man who had been standing next to the Martini drinker exclaimed aghast to the bartender. "He's nuts!"

"Yeah, he must be," the bartender responded. "He left the best part!"

The production of alcoholic beverages in the United States now stands at over 100 million proof gallons per year, with an estimated half-billion proof gallons in stock. Not bad for a nation in which about one-third of the population are teetotalers.

Today, about 77 percent of adult men and 60 percent of women are regular consumers of alcoholic beverages. Studies have shown that the wealthy and better educated are more likely to be numbered among the drinkers. But in France, where there are few abstainers, those who do swear off the grape are more likely to come from the well-educated, monied classes.

France is the nation with the highest per capita consumption of alcohol: 22.66 liters of pure juice per year, more than twice the American figure. Italians are the highest per capita consumers of wine, downing on the average 153 liters to the American's mere eight. West Germans are the number one swillers of hard spirits—barely beating out the Americans in that category. The Germans are also far and away the leading drinkers of beer and ale, with the average German consuming 182 liters of brew per year. There is a claim, however, that the residents of Australia's Northern Territory far outpace the Germans.

We have no reliable figures for the communist nations, but vodka consumption in the Soviet Union is thought to be extremely high, and Czechoslovakia is said by some to surpass all nations in per capita beer consumption. At the other end of the scale, the citizens of Iceland and Israel rank as the smallest consumers of alcohol.

The above figures may surprise those who think that "light wine" countries such as France and Italy consume less alcohol than "hard liquor" nations like Great Britain and the United States. Great Britain, famous for its whiskies, is often thought to be high on the list of alcohol imbibers, but Britons actually consume less alcohol per capita than the citizens of any country in the West.

That hasn't stopped jokesters from commenting on the soft spot the Scotch have for their famous export. Perhaps you've heard the one about the elderly Scotsman who, while carrying a bottle of whiskey on his hip, slipped and fell on a path of ice. Climbing to his feet and feeling something wet trickling down his leg, he murmured: "I hope it's blood."

Dewar's incidently, is the best-selling non-premium scotch in America; Chivas Regal the best-selling premium. In Scotland, Bell's is the most popular domestic scotch whiskey.

With all that drinking going on, it's no surprise that alcoholism is a major problem in many societies. In the United States, and estimated five million people are alcoholics, and perhaps another four million are problem drinkers. In France, estimates of alcoholism put the figure as high as nine to 15 percent of the total population!

Religious proscription has done little to thin the ranks of the dipsomaniacs. The Koran forbids alcohol use. Devout Buddhists and Hindu Brahmins also spurn the grape. And many Christian sects have forbidden drinking—with mixed results.

As for legal prohibition, the longest on record is a wee 26 years, in Iceland, from 1908 to 1934. Russia tried to illegalize the grape early in this century, but the attempt lasted a mere 10 years. Our own "noble experiment" lasted only 13 years—much too long in the minds of many people.

For a point of view, regarding man's oldest and most popular intoxicant we may turn to the Bible. The Good Book mentions two drinks: ". . . wine, which gladdeneth the heart of man; and water, which quencheth the thirst of the jackasses" (Psalm 104).

Enters the wine, comes out the secret.
—Hebrew Proverb

If all be true that I do think,
There are five reasons
we should drink:
Good wine—a friend—
or being dry—
Or lest we should be
by and by—
Or any other reason why.
—Henry Aldrich,
Five Reasons for Drinking

I drink on every occasion, and betimes on no occasion.
—Cervantes, *Don Quixote*

Spirits, waters, liqueurs, syrups, etc. used in making of cocktails 100 years ago.

100

COFFEE

No one need be told that human beings are lovers of the grape. But did you realize that the brew of the coffee bean is drunk by more people than any other beverage on earth?

Coffee is regularly consumed by about one-third of the world's population, and consumption continues to rise steadily. At the turn of the century, world imports totaled about one million tons. But by 1950, that figure had doubled. Today, the total stands at about three-and-a-half million tons—making coffee the second largest item of international commerce after petroleum!

Americans presently put away about one-and-a-quarter million tons of coffee each year, more than the entire world drank just 50 years ago. Coffee is, to say the least, an institution in this country, with the average American gulping down two-and-a-half cups daily. You won't have to look far to find someone who insists he couldn't live without it. And speaking of institutions, in many states, the coffee break is not only a fixture in almost all offices and factories, it's dictated by law.

Still, Americans are not the world's heaviest coffee consumers—the average Swede consumes close to 30 pounds of coffee each year! In fact, in much of Western Europe, the word for coffee, café, has come to be synonymous with an eating place. Even in this country, we prefer to call our beanery a coffee shop, a coffee house, or a cafeteria—which literally means "coffee store" in American Spanish.

A customer in the cafe called the waiter to his table and asked, "Is this tea or coffee? It tastes like cough medicine."

"Well, if it tastes like cough medicine, it must be tea," the waiter replied. "Our coffee tastes like turpentine."

Americans and Europeans may be avid consumers of the brew, but it's likely that most Western coffee addicts go through their lives without once laying eyes on a coffee bush. The reason: coffee simply won't grow in the climate of Europe or the United States. The coffee plant is a tropical evergreen shrub indigenous to the eastern hemisphere; 25 species grow wild in Africa, Asia, and the Near East. Oh, there is some coffee grown in the United States—but only in Hawaii.

Most coffee shrubs flourish best in year-round temperatures of from 77 to 88 degrees; a temperature dip to around 32 degrees will kill most coffee plants. And many species require more than 60 inches of rain each year.

Two species of the coffee plant are far and away the most common. *Coffea arabica,* the oldest known variety, hails originally from Arabia or Ethiopia, and is now grown extensively in South America. *Coffea robusta* originated in East and Central Africa and is still the major coffee plant of that continent. *Robusta* is not—well, "robuster" than *arabica*. Actually, it's milder in taste and aroma, and is less favored by Westerners; but in recent years, Africa has become increasingly important as a coffee exporter.

The average coffee shrub grows to a height of about 30 feet, with white flowers and red, fleshy fruits. Each fruit contains pulp and two seeds, and it is the seeds—not "beans"—that are used to make the brew. Why? Caffeine, of course.

Caffeine is an alkaloid that mildly stimulates cerebral and cardiac activity—in short, it's a pick-me-up. Try to imagine the difference in American offices and factories if the drug were suddenly to disappear, for caffeine is often the oil that makes the American brain run smoothly. And not without its price: caffeine causes gastric acidity and nervousness as well as heightened cardiac action. But coffee-swillers, take heart. Though theoretically the drug can be fatal in large doses, there is no case on record of a caffeine overdose.

101

The coffee plant produces delicate blossoms and rich berries.

Oddly enough, though coffee is today a fixture from Titicaca to Timbuktu, the beverage was virtually unknown in most of the world just a few centuries ago. For years on end, the tribesmen of Ethiopia and Central Africa crushed coffee berries and mixed them with animal fat to form balls which they devoured before their war parties. The Africans also made a wine from the coffee fruit, though they never brewed a hot coffee beverage.

According to some historians, the *arabica* shrub was taken to Southern Arabia for cultivation sometime before the year 600, though the Arabs didn't learn how to brew the hot beverage until the 10th or 11th century. The word *coffee*, by the way, comes to us either from the Arabic *qahwah*, or from Kaffa, a province in Ethiopia that is reputedly the birthplace of the *arabica* plant.

Arab legend maintains that the coffee bean was actually discovered by goats. According to the tale, a goatherd named Kaldi, living around the year 850, was puzzled one day by the queer antics of his flock. After watching them cavort around the fields on their hind legs, the goatherd discovered that the animals had been nibbling on the berries of a wild shrub, and decided to sample the fruit himself. The snack produced a delightful sense of exhilaration, and Kaldi went on to loudly proclaim his find.

Once the Arabs had learned to brew a hot beverage from the fruit, coffee became very popular on the Arabian peninsula, especially in connection with long Moslem religious services. Orthodox priests soon pronounced the beverage intoxicating and banned its use, but still the dark brew spread throughout the Near East.

Venetian traders were prob-

ably the first to bring coffee to Europe. During the 16th and 17th centuries, the beverage reached one European country after another. In many places, coffee was banned for a while because of religious, political, or medicinal objections. The Italian clergy at first opposed the drink as the beverage of the infidel, but after Pope Clement VIII tasted the brew, he proclaimed it fit for Christians.

Coffee became widely popular in London during the 17th century. The first coffee house opened its doors in 1652. Soon coffee houses became the centers of political, social, literary, and business life in the city. In America, the first popular coffee houses opened as early as the 1680s—and the *Mayflower* listed among its cargo a mortar and pestle to be used for grinding coffee beans.

At that time, almost all European coffee was imported from Yemen and Arabia, since the Arabs had jealously guarded their coffee monopoly by forbidding the export of fertile seeds on pain of death. But around 1700, Dutch traders managed to smuggle some coffee shrubs out of Arabia, sending the embezzled botanica to the island of Java, then a Dutch possession. The growth of coffee plants in Java soon became so prolific that the island's name became synonymous with the brew.

The French, too, managed to get their hands on the coveted shrub, and established coffee plantations in many of their colonies.

The Dutch and French both founded huge coffee plantations in the Guianas of South America; and like the Arabs, tried their best to guard their prize crop. But according to some accounts, a dashing Brazilian officer won the

CHICKEN FAZENDA

2 broiling chickens, quartered
1/2 stick butter
1/2 cup strong coffee
1/2 cup honey
1 1/4 teaspoons dry mustard
1/4 cup vinegar
1/2 cup brown sugar
1 can Mandarin oranges

1. Salt and pepper the quartered chickens to taste.
2. In a shallow baking pan, bake chicken at 350° for 35 minutes.
3. Combine butter, coffee, honey, mustard, and vinegar in a small saucepan. Stir this over low heat until the butter melts.
4. Add the brown sugar, and continue to stir until sugar is completely dissolved. Allow to cool.
5. Brush the cool glaze on the chicken pieces, and continue to bake about 15 to 20 minutes, or until the chicken is brown and crispy on the outside.
6. Garnish each serving with Mandarin orange slices.

Serves 8.

COFFEE OASIS

(As featured at the Oasis Restaurant in Jakarta, Indonesia)

1 clove
1 long, continuous peel of whole orange
1/2 vanilla pod
2 inches cinnamon stick
3 ounces brown sugar
2 1/2 ounces strong black coffee
1 ounce cognac
1/2 ounce Tia Maria coffee liqueur

1. Heat the coffee in a skillet.
2. Add the clove, the vanilla pod, the cinnamon, and the sugar.
3. Put the orange peel on a fork. The orange peel should be long and in one continuous piece. Hold the orange peel high over the coffee.
4. Ignite the cognac, and pour the flaming cognac from the top of the orange peel down the length of the orange peel, so that there is a fire right down to the coffee. Make sure you have a continuous fire.
5. Now drop the peel in the coffee, and heat for a few moments. (Avoid boiling the coffee.)
6. Remove the clove, the cinnamon stick, the vanilla pod, and the orange peel. Add the Tia Maria.
7. Serve in demi-tasse cups.

Note: This exquisite beverage has all the elements of a fine confection.

heart of the wife of the governor of French Guiana. As a token of her affection, she gave him some of the precious beans and cuttings. Brazil began coffee cultivation in 1727, and was to become the largest coffee growing nation on earth.

Coffee is the major export crop of many of the countries between the two tropics. A price drop in coffee can throw the economy of many nations into complete turmoil, as happened in Brazil in the decade between 1925 and 1935.

After Brazil, Colombia is the world's second largest coffee exporter. In 1973, the Ivory Coast ranked third.

Brazil once accounted for 66 percent of all coffee exports, but as African production has continued to rise, that figure has dropped to 40 percent. Today, about 30 percent of all coffee comes from Africa.

The rarest coffee in the world is Jamaica Blue Mountain. That particular coffee is sold in only a few stores in the United States. Only 800 bags, or 100,000 pounds, are produced each year.

Roasted coffee beans can be brewed into a beverage in dozens of ways, but basically, there are two methods: decoction and infusion. In decoction, the brew is produced by boiling the coffee until its flavor is extracted. In infusion, water near the boiling point flows over unheated coffee grounds.

Americans prefer their java brewed by infusion, with either a drip pot or a percolator. The brew is then mixed with milk and sugar. The French prefer *cafe au lait,* an equal mixture of strong coffee and warm milk. Many Europeans prefer *espresso,* a strong infusion drunk without milk.

Cappuccino is a combination of coffee and frothy milk with nutmeg or cinnamon added. Turkish coffee is a heady, usually bitter decoction made from a strong, aromatic bean. Viennese coffee is usually served with a large dollop of whipped cream. And Irish coffee, a mixture of

Coffee beans being ground to powder in the Dutch colony of Surinam.

coffee, whiskey, and whipped cream, can be good to the very last drop—even if you don't like coffee.

Many urban Americans, especially Easterners, are fond of iced coffee, a beverage that is just now being introduced to other areas of the country. And speaking of ice, there's coffee ice cream. Coffee is also used in some chocolates, and caffeine is an important ingredient in another American institution, Coca-Cola.

For those who don't care for caffeine, there's de-caffeinated coffee, a brew made from ground coffee with all but about two percent of its caffeine removed. And for the real caffeine-hater, there are coffee substitutes made from chicory and other herbs. Postum, a popular American drink for more than 75 years, is made from bran, wheat, and molasses.

While we're on the subject of caffeine: the oft-heard idea that caffeine is an effective antidote to inebriation is simply—er, without grounds. Time is the only remedy for excess alcohol in the bloodstream, so coffee is an aid to the intoxicated only insofar as it takes time to drink it.

Instant coffee is actually brewed in the factory and reconstituted in the home. In the spray-drying method of manufacture, a concentrated brew is

Americans are not the world's heaviest coffee consumers—the average Swede consumes close to 30 pounds of coffee each year!

sprayed into a chamber and mixed with hot dry air. The air carries off the moisture, leaving behind the particles you find in your jar of instant.

In the freeze-drying method, a coffee extract is frozen and introduced into a vacuum chamber, where the moisture is sublimed and a solid mass left behind. The mass is then reduced to granules and packaged for those coffee lovers for whom time is more important than taste.

The debate between the instant-coffee connoisseur and the fresh-brewed fancier will probably go on forever. Which makes sense, since among Americans today, there seems to be no middle ground: you either love coffee or you hate it. If you number yourself among the coffee-crazy, drink hearty—and the next time you pour yourself a cup of java, give silent thanks to an Arabian goatherd and his errant flock.

Next time your guest asks for "just half a cup" of coffee, trot out this 3½" ceramic mug, which holds just four liquid ounces.

After-dinner coffee is made quickly with this espresso machine. Water is electrically heated in the chrome center cylinder, then forced through the grounds. Makes up to five demitasse cups of coffee, and puffs the milk for Espresso Cappuccino.

BEEF BRAZILIA

3 lbs. chuck steak cut into cubes
½ stick of butter
1 tablespoon minced garlic, softened in water
3 medium onions, sliced thin
¼ cup flour
1 cup red wine
2 teaspoons salt
½ teaspoon pepper
¼ teaspoon oregano
1 cup strong coffee

1. Melt butter in a deep, heavy skillet.
2. Saute steak until all sides are brown.
3. Now add drained garlic and sliced onions. Cook until onions are soft

and transparent. When done, remove meat and onions from skillet.
4. Using the same skillet, blend flour with remaining butter.
5. Now add wine, coffee, and seasonings, and stir constantly until the sauce is creamy, smooth, and thickened.
6. Then put back the meat and onions in the sauce. Cover the pot. When the mixture is boiling, reduce heat, and simmer for 1½ hours, or until the meat is very tender.

Serves 6.

Comics

ZOWIE! SOCKO! GLUG! WHAP! POW!

Place those words before an American of any age and generally, the reaction will be one of amusement. The comic strip and comic book together form perhaps the largest and the most influential iconographic field in the history of man.

The newspaper comic strip is a relatively new development, but its forerunners are ancient. In the first century B.C., Romans chuckled over tablets with satiric inscriptions sold in the market places of the Eternal City. Chances are, they weren't much different from the editorial cartoons we enjoy today.

Before the invention of the printing press, German artists produced woodcuts arranged in panel form, like the comic strip, dealing chiefly with religious history and current politics. After the printing press came into use, the illustrations took the form of a series of several sheets that could be hung on the wall to form a narrative frieze.

In the 17th century, the Protestant Reformation and the consequent religious wars led to propagandist strips based on political events. A limner by the name of Romeyn de Hooghe was the first artist to devote himself consistently to the narrative strip; he produced pictorial indictments of the persecution of the Huguenots under Louis XIV, and accounts of the accession of William III to power in Holland and England.

German artists began producing crime strips as early as the 16th century. Most strips illustrated, in gory detail, the punishment the perpetrators could expect to receive.

The father of the modern comic strip was Rodolphe Töpffer, a Swiss illustrator and schoolmaster. Töpffer proceeded on the principle that more people can read pictures than can read words. He went on to produce picture-story books and collections of small drawings that were the forerunners of the modern newspaper strip. Töpffer also put out collections of his drawings in oblong albums of about 100 pages. These were the precursors of the comic book.

The dominant comic illustrator in the 19th century was the German Wilhelm Busch, who was the first professional comic-strip artist. His tales of naughty children and pesky animals wouldn't be out of place on today's funny pages. His two infant pranksters named Max and Moritz, his most memorable

It's the comic strip—not film nor television—that reaches one-third of humanity each day.

During the 1930s, Little Orphan Annie achieved heights of popularity. Created by Harold Gray, the character of Annie captured the American imagination, and has been reproduced in everything from dolls to a Broadway hit.

107

characters, were to form the models for the later *Katzenjammer Kids*. Busch's use of oscillations to suggest movement, and his use of conventional signs to suggest emotions, provided a vocabulary for the comic strip artist that is still in use today.

The newspaper comic strip in this country was born out of the rivalry between two giants of the American press. In 1893, the *New York World* published the first full-color comic page in the nation, depicting a set of humorous characters under the title *Hogan's Alley*. Soon afterward, publisher William Randolph Hearst countered with the first weekly full-color comic

Comic strips are popular throughout the world, and China is no exception.

supplement—eight pages—in the *Morning Journal*.

Hearst's supplement featured *Yellow Kid*, a strip by Richard Outcault, whom Hearst had lured away from the *World*. *Yellow Kid* was the first continuous comic character in the United States, and standardized the use of speech balloons for comic strip dialogue. Incidentally, the Italian word for comic strip is *fumetto*, "little puff of smoke," so-named after the speech balloon.

Later, Hearst put out Rudolph Dirks's *Katzenjammer Kids*, the first strip fully developed in form, and the most durable comic strip in history. Dirks's strip used speech balloons and a continuous cast of characters, and was divided into panels—unlike *Yellow Kid*, which employed full panoramic scenes.

With the advent of newspaper syndication, comic strips spread rapidly. In 1904, the first daily black-and-white strip, *A. Piker Clerk*, appeared in the *Chicago American*. Actually, the strip was a horse race tip sheet, as was *M.A. Mutt*—later *Mutt and Jeff*—which eventually dropped its racing connections and developed into a general interest strip.

The period between 1907 and 1920 was the golden age for comics. This era saw the birth of dozens of long-running strips and the development of the genres that predominate today. There was the gag strip, *Bringing Up Father*, brought out in 1913, the first American strip to gain international renown; the family saga strip, *Gasoline Alley*, begun in 1919. The career girl strip, *Winnie Winkle*, was started in 1920; the fantasy and parody strips, *Krazy Kat* came into being in 1911, and *Popeye* was inaugurated in 1919. *Krazy Kat* was the first newspaper strip aimed at the intelligent adult.

In the late 20s and 30s, adventure, detective, and sci-fi strips became popular. *Tarzan* began in 1929, followed by *Dick Tracy* and *Flash Gordon*. Nineteen-thirty saw the birth of *Blondie*, perhaps the most successful strip of all time.

The first true comic *book* was marketed in 1933 as an advertising giveaway. The size, glossy cover, and panel format of that first comic book have remained the same right up to today.

At first, comic books were basically reprints of newspaper strips. In 1938, *Action Comics* appeared. *Superman* and the other super-heroes were not long to follow.

By 1943, comics accounted for one-third of all domestic magazine sales. *Superman* alone had a circulation of 1,500,000 copies per month! By the way, the first issue of *Action Comics* now sells among collectors for close to $5,000!

Early comic books were for the most part brutal, sadistic, blood-and-guts affairs that most parents tried to keep out of the hands of their children. In 1951 and again in 1954, Congress investigated the comic book industry, and—simplistically enough—blamed the rise of juvenile delinquency on sadistic comic books. The industry was forced to adopt a code of self-censorship that still exists.

Comics continued to suffer criticism, especially for their racist, militarist, and fascist values.

Partly as a rebellion against this type of politically Neanderthal comic—*Steve Canyon*, for example—a number of newspaper strips appeared in the late 50s that were heavy with sociological and philosophical overtones. Most took their cue from the earlier *Pogo* (1946) and *Peanuts* (1950). Today, the funnies page is a conglomeration of science fiction, fantasy, adventure, slapstick, and subtle humor—something for every taste.

Without doubt, the comic is the dominant graphic mythology of the 20th century. It's the comic strip—not film nor television—that reaches one-third of humanity each day.

In the last 70 years, an estimated 8 to 12 million comic strip pictures have been produced throughout the world.

Over 100 million Americans—virtually half the population—read one or more comic strips regularly. About 300 strips are presently published in American newspapers. *Blondie* can be found in 1,200 papers across the country, and *Dick Tracy* reaches 50 million readers daily in 500 papers.

109

When Chic Young asked for suggestions for a name for Blondie's second baby, he received 400,000 replies. Al Capp's offer of a prize for the "most gruesome face" for a new *Lil' Abner* character generated over a million replies!

American comics are now read worldwide. *Peanuts*, incidentally, is called *Radishes* in Denmark. In England, a large chain of hamburger stands, the Wimpy Bar, owes its name to a *Popeye* character with a weakness for the burger. Not to be outdone, Texans, in a spinach-growing area in the

eastern part of the state, have erected a statue of Popeye in tribute to his appetite for the vegetable.

Surprisingly enough, studies have shown that the more educated a person is, the more likely he is to follow a comic strip. The peak age for Sunday comic strip readers is—no, you'd never guess—30 to 39 years old!

By the time any American has learned to read, he's likely to have his favorite strips. According to a 1960s survey, the most popular strips countrywide are in order: *Blondie, Dick Tracy, Little Orphan Annie, Peanuts,* and *Rex Morgan, M.D.*

Little Orphan Annie began a run as a successful Broadway

show ("Annie") in 1977. *Bringing Up Father* has been made into a movie 11 times!

Today, most syndicated strips are the work of an entire staff of writers, calligraphers, artists, and editors. In no other art form is the creator so much the prisoner of his creation, for the characters he invents frequently assume lives independent of their creator—and continue to live on, even after the artist's death!

It would be hard to think of a place in which different periods of history are so intermingled as on the funny page. You'll find *Moon Mullins, Dick Tracy, Gasoline Alley,* and other ancient works side by side with new strips like *B.C.* and *Doonesbury.* But they all have a few things in common:

ZOWIE! SOCKO! GLUG! WHAP! POW!

Chester Gould's Dick Tracy *first appeared in 1931. The name has become a synonym for a cagey cop.*

CONFEDERATE STAMPS

Among the rare and valuable American postage stamps in existence today, are those issued by the Confererate States of America during the Civil War.

Shortly after the Southern states seceded from the Union in 1861, the postmasters in various southern cities found it impossible to do business without stamps of some kind. The use of Federal stamps was, of course, taboo. So, the postmasters of many cities and town began issuing their own stamps. Still extant are postage stamps issued by the postmasters in such places as Greenville, Alabama, Ringgold, Georgia, and Petersburg, Virginia.

Lat in 1861, the Confederacy issued its first regular series of postage stamps, with three values: two, five, and 10 cents. The 1861 series was replaced by another in 1863.

The earlier stamps issued by local postmasters are rarer, and therefore more valuable, than the regular Confederate series. As early as the 1890s, some of these stamps were selling for as much as $750.

Postage stamps of the Confederacy used throughout the South during the War of the Secession.

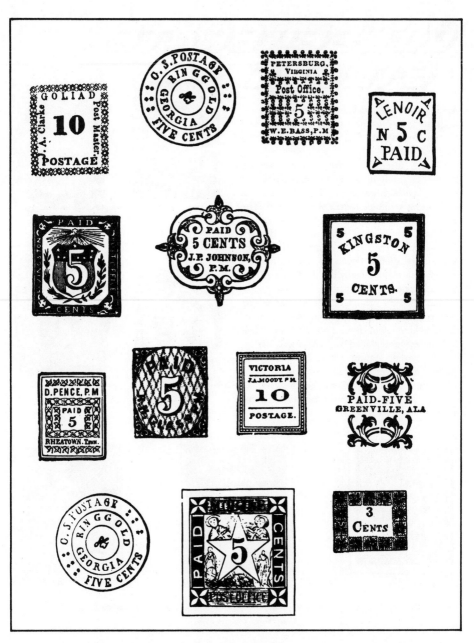

Postage stamps issued by different localities of the Southern States during the War of the Secession.

CROSSWORD PUZZLES

Did you know that an *ani* is a South American bird, but an *ana* is a collection of anecdotes? How about *anil?* It's an indigo dye. *Ara?* That's a genus of birds. And if someone asked you for a "diva's forte," would you respond immediately with *aria?* Well, if you were an addict of that ubiquitous indoor sport known as the crossword puzzle, these words would be as familiar to you as *emu, gnu, ort,* and *ait.*

You'd be in rather large company, too. A 1959 Gallup Poll found that matching wits with crossword compilers is the number one indoor game in this country, surpassing such favorites as checkers, bingo, and poker! An estimated 30 million Americans regularly wrack their brains for the name of "an East Indian shrub" or "an African antelope," and in England, an even larger percentage of the population regularly accepts the crossword challenge. In fact, the crossword puzzle is a familiar sight to speakers of every language that uses the Roman alphabet. And speaking of the Roman alphabet, some stuffy crossword buffs have gone

so far as to construct their puzzles in Latin!

With all of this crossword construction going on, you might think that sooner or later puzzlers would be confronted with the same crosswords that had stumped them in their novice years. No chance of that. A mathematician once computed the number of permutations possible with a standard 11 x 11-square crossword puzzle; that is, given 122 squares and a 26-letter alphabet, how many different puzzles could be constructed? The answer was found to be a number that would blow the lid off any pocket calculator: 24,873 plus 222 zeroes. That's higher than the number of seconds that have elapsed since the beginning of the universe!

Where did crosswords begin? No, the ancient Greeks and Romans did *not* test their wits against the familiar black and white squares. But the crossword does owe a large debt to two

other word games, the acrostic and the word square, both of which date back to classical times.

An *acrostic* is a composition—a verse or a series of words, for instance—in which letters of each line or word, usually the initial letters themselves, form a word or words when arranged in order. For example, the first-letter acrostic of "this heavy elephant" is *the*. The ancient Greeks dabbled with this kind of puzzle, and 12 poems in the Old Testament form acrostics. In Psalm 119, for instance, the first letters of each line form the Hebrew alphabet.

In a crossword puzzle, almost every letter of every word can be thought of as forming an acrostic with letters from neighboring words. Four four-letter words written across, for example, form four words when the letters are read down.

This brings us to the *word square*, a more direct ancestor of the crossword. A word square is comprised of three or more words arranged in a square so that the words read across the

113

same as they read down. For example:

```
P E A T
E A C H
A C H E
T H E Y
```

The ancient Greeks and Romans were both familiar with the word square. A pillar built by the Greeks in Egypt bears a word square with 39 letters on a side, with words reading across, down, and diagonally. A true word square comprised of five-letter words was found among the ruins of Pompeii.

Word squares and acrostics were popular in England during the 19th century, especially in children's books. But both were usually presented as *faits accomplis* rather than as puzzles. Then, during the 1890s, newspapers began to carry word square puzzles in which the boxes of the word square were presented, filled with only a few of the letters or none at all. The clues were most often given in verse form.

The shape was not always square; diamond-shaped word squares such as the one below were not uncommon:

```
      T
   K  E  Y
T  E  N  E  T
   Y  E  T
      T
```

Though word squares most often included just four-letter or five-letter words, word squares with as many as nine letters have been constructed. But if you can con-struct a word square with 10 letters on a side, you will be the first to do so.

It's easy to see the relationship between the word square and the crossword. In effect, each corner of a crossword forms a word square, although in a crossword the across words are not the same as the interlocking down words. Yet, the idea of a crossword puzzle did not enter the heads of any word-square compilers until early this century, when Arthur Wynne, an editor of the New York *World*, produced the granddaddy of all crosswords.

The English-born Wynne was busy preparing puzzles for the 1913 Christmas edition of his paper's Sunday supplement, *Fun*, when the idea struck him: why must the words of a word square read the same down as they do across? Wynne sketched a diamond-shaped grid, reached for a dictionary, and within a few hours compiled a new kind of puzzle he called a *word-cross*.

Wynne's maiden crossword appeared in the December 21, 1913 edition of the *World*, among a group of puzzles that included anagrams and rebuses. The crossword contained 32 words, in a diamond-shaped diagram with a diamond-shaped opening in the center, and no black squares. Clues were keyed to the diagram by the number of the last square filled by each corresponding answer, as well as by the first square, as is the case with today's crosswords.

The response to the initial crossword was immediate and overwhelming. Letters began pouring into the *World* demanding more crosswords. From the very beginning, the newspaper received crosswords compiled by readers at the rate of about six per week. The *World* continued to publish crosswords in its Sun-

A pollster riding the trains in 1924 found that 60 percent of all passengers passed their travel time battling crosswords. The B & O Railroad placed dictionaries on all its main-line trains, and the Pennsylvania Railroad printed crosswords on the back of its diner car menus.

The Nazis recognized the English penchant for the crossword when, during World War II, they showered England with leaflets containing crossword puzzles with propaganda messages.

day supplement until the printers working on the paper—who hated the crossword for the typesetting difficulties it presented—convinced the editors to remove it. But a flood of protests following the puzzle's deletion convinced the editors that their readers' hunger for the crossword was more important than their printers' nerves, and the *World* crossword was permanently reinstated.

For 10 years following Wynne's first crossword, the *World* remained the only paper in the nation to offer the puzzles to its readers. In 1920, the paper hired a young woman named Margaret Petheridge to check the crosswords for printer's errors. Miss Petheridge responded splendidly: she went on to become the most renowned crossword editor in the nation.

Soon after Miss Petheridge's arrival at the *World*, the newspaper began publishing the nation's first daily crossword, edited in part by the noted rhymster Gelett Burgess. In 1924, Burgess penned this paean to his crossword fans:

The fans they chew their pencils,
The fans they beat their
    wives.
They look up words for extinct
    birds—
    They lead such puzzling lives!

By that time, the crossword was already a fixture in many American papers, and a rage throughout the land. A pollster riding the trains in 1924 found that 60 percent of all passengers passed their travel time battling crosswords. The B & O Railroad placed dictionaries on all its mainline trains, and the Pennsylvania Railroad printed crosswords on the back of its diner car menus. Ocean steamers stocked supplies of crosswords for their passengers, along with dictionaries and dozens of copies of *Roget's Thesaurus.*

The crossword craze continued to grow through the mid-1920s, touching almost every aspect of American life. Couples published crosswords in newspapers to announce their engagements. Preachers used crosswords during their sermons to present religious texts. Checked patterns became the rage in the fashion world—one dress manufacturer even included a crossword book with each purchase, offering a discount to any buyer who returned the book correctly filled in.

In 1925, a large crowd filled a hall in New York's Hotel Roosevelt to watch Yale defeat Harvard in the first intercollegiate crossword puzzle tournament.

Some doctors decried the crossword as a cause of eyestrain, while others recommended the crossword to invalid patients as an excellent way to keep mentally alert. The crossword craze reached such heights that many libraries imposed a five-minute limit on dictionary use.

A judge in a New York courtroom had to break up a boisterous gathering of attendants, police, and lawyers battling a stumper crossword in front of his bench. And a Chicago court, faced with a wife's claim that her husband was spending too much time on his crosswords at the expense of providing for his family, decreed that the husband limit himself to just three crosswords a day.

Speaking of crossword court capers: recently, a West German puzzle buff became so frustrated by a particularly difficult crossword, that she woke her husband for assistance three times as she

THE FIRST CROSSWORD PUZZLE

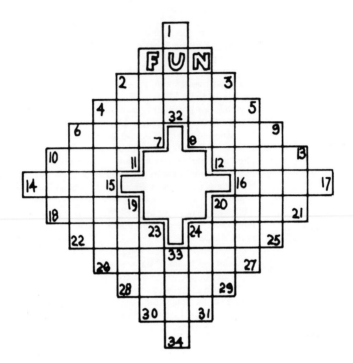

2-3. What bargain hunters enjoy.
4-5. A written acknowledgment.
6-7. Such and nothing more.
10-11. A bird.
14-15. Opposed to less.
18-19. What this puzzle is.
22-23. An animal of prey.
26-27. The close of a day.
28-29. To elude.
30-31. The plural of is.
8-9. To cultivate.
12-13. A bar of wood or iron.
16-17. What artists learn to do.
20-21. Fastened.
24-25. Found on the seashore.
10-18. The fibre of the gomuti palm.

6-22. What we all should be.
4-26. A day dream.
2-11. A talon.
19-28. A pigeon.
F-7. Part of your head.
23-30. A river in Russia.
1-32. To govern.
33-34. An aromatic plant.
N-8. A fist.
24-31. To agree with.
3-12. Part of a ship.
20-29. One.
5-27. Exchanging.
9-25. To sink in mud.
13-21. A boy.

battled the poser through the night. The fourth time the puzzled frau woke her weary consort, he strangled her to death. The court acquitted the husband on the grounds of temporary insanity.

In 1924, two neophyte publishers named Dick Simon and Lincoln Schuster were looking for their newly-formed company's first manuscript when they realized that no book of crossword puzzles had yet appeared in this country. They contacted Margaret Petheridge, who agreed to compile a crossword book along with two of her *World* co-editors. Simon and Schuster presented Ms. Petheridge with a $25 advance, then began searching for a printer who would work for deferred payment. They found one—a crossword addict.

In April of that year, Simon and Schuster brought out *The Crossword Puzzle Book*, an anthology of 50 puzzles from the *World*. On the advice of friends who could see only disaster ahead in the crossword book game, Simon and Schuster omitted their firm's name from the book, opting instead for the Plaza Publishing Company. The book sold for the then rather high price of $1.35, but each copy came complete with a neatly sharpened pencil—provided free by the Venus Pencil Company as an advertising gimmick.

The success of the book was immediate—within three months, 40,000 copies of *The Crossword Puzzle Book* had been sold. A later 25-cent edition was so popular that one distributor placed an order for a quarter-million copies, the largest book order of the time. Volume Two followed later that year, bearing the name of Simon and Schuster, although Plaza Publishing Company was to remain on the firm's crossword

collections until their 50th volume. Within a year, the firm had sold 400,000 crossword books, and they were to follow with two crossword collections per year for decades after. Today, Simon & Schuster is one of the largest publishing houses in the world—and it all began with the crossword!

Across the Atlantic, the English were quick to scoff at the American fascination with crosswords. An article in the London *Times*, entitled "An Enslaved America," estimated that five million hours were being wasted daily in this country by employees who fiddled with crosswords during working hours.

Apparently, the editors of the *Times* were unaware that, five weeks earlier, Arthur Wynne had submitted a crossword to the London *Sunday Express*. Within weeks of the puzzle's publication, the crossword craze in England had reached proportions comparable to the American mania. By 1925, American newspapers were able to announce that Queen Mary was a crossword buff, and that the Prime Minister highly recommended the puzzles for their "educational value."

Crossword addicts in England were no less devoted to their sport than their American counterparts. The London zoo was so deluged with questions that they announced they would no longer answer inquiries pertaining to the names of unusual animals. Libraries began to black out the crosswords in all their newspapers to prevent puzzlers from monopolizing the papers. Advertisers had to pay particularly high prices for the spaces next to crosswords. Some advertisers bought the

spaces and then left them blank—a small notice at the bottom of the otherwise blank space told puzzlers whom to thank for the doodling room. One Liverpool crossword buff went so far as to black out, in the library's dictionary, a key word needed to complete a puzzle contest that the puzzler was intent on winning for himself.

The crossword contest began to appear almost as early as the crossword. In 1924, the New York *Evening Graphic* became the first American paper to offer a crossword contest, or *pruzzle,* so called from a combination of *prize* and *puzzle.* Most contests were lotteries, in which only contestants who correctly completed a crossword were entered. Many were offered as advertising stunts, or as fund-raisers for charitable organizations. Before long, entire pages of newspapers were being filled with crossword contests, and professional puzzle solvers had gone into business, offering to complete contestant's puzzles for a small fee.

The crossword puzzle frenzy has tapered off somewhat in the United States over the decades since its inception, but the English are as fervent as ever in their dedication to the black and white squares. The Nazis recognized the English penchant for the crossword when, during World War II, they showered England with leaflets containing crossword puzzles with propaganda messages. A typical clue might be *warmonger,* with *Churchill* or *Roosevelt* the answer.

But the English put their crossword skills to use in the war as well, occasionally burying coded secret messages in newspaper puzzles. The Hungarian government had recognized the secret-message capabilities of the crossword in 1925, when they ordered that all newspaper crosswords first be submitted to official censors for approval. One crossword not submitted for government approval was the work of a Budapest man who left a suicide note in the form of a crossword puzzle, with the reasons for his act, and the persons to be contacted, cleverly incorporated into the puzzle.

Today, the weekly crosswords appearing in *The Observer*, a London paper, are generally considered to be among the world's most difficult. The first puzzle composer at *The Observer* was Edward P. Mathers, or "Torquemada," who began work during the 1920s and published 670 puzzles before his death in 1939. Torquemada's puzzles, along with those of his successor at the paper, D.S. Macnutt, or "Ximenes," are generally considered to be among the cleverest, most challenging puzzles ever constructed. The few readers who did complete the puzzles required an average of from two to four hours to do the job, although the compilers needed but an hour and a half to construct them.

The crosswords published by the London *Times* are also considered to be among the world's most challenging. The *Times* began publishing daily crosswords in 1930, despite heavy objections from some of the paper's more stodgy readers. Searching for a writer to compile the paper's first puzzle, the editor charged with the task asked the help of a friend, who then recommended his son, 28-year-old Adrian Bell. Previously, Bell had not only never compiled a crossword, he had never even attempted to solve one! Yet, in 10 days, Bell turned out the *Times's* first masterpiece, and over the next 40 years, contributed a large portion of the paper's 10,000-plus stumpers. Today, the *Times* employs an editor and 10 compilers to toil solely on crosswords.

In America, the puzzles of the *New York Sunday Times* are generally recognized as the most consistently challenging, but most American crosswords are child's play compared to their English cousins. Oddly enough, the *Times* was the last major American paper to include a crossword, publishing its first puzzle in 1942 and its first daily crossword eight years later. Margaret Petheridge (later Farrar), of earlier crossword fame, edited the *Times* puzzles until her retirement in 1969.

Petheridge's distinguished tenure at the *Times* was not without its moments of levity. On one occasion, the compiler was searching for a clue for "wooden leg," and opted for "Ahab's distinguishing feature." A reader's letter quickly pointed out that the captain of the *Pequod* in *Moby Dick* had an ivory, not wooden, leg. But the content of the letter was less surprising than the age of its author—an eight-year-old boy!

Errors are far from rare in crossword puzzles. One compiler tells of the time he misread a word in the puzzle diagram and devised the clue "Catholic chief" for what he thought was "pope." The published answer was "dope," prompting a deluge of letters from Catholic readers. A newspaper once published a set of clues with the wrong puzzle diagram, only to find that many readers had successfully reconstructed the correct diagram from the clues!

In 1970, the first annual crossword puzzle championships were held in England, sponsored

A 1959 Gallup Poll found that matching wits with crossword compilers is the number one indoor game in the United States.

118

Measuring six feet long by 18 inches wide, this crossword puzzle is printed on a plastic-coated washable fabric so it can be hung on the wall for posterity. Definitions are printed on a separate sheet, as are the answers.

by the Cutty Sark Distilling Company. Puzzle buffs wishing to participate were asked to complete five puzzles and send them to the contest organizers. Over 20,000 persons successfully completed the puzzles! The finals were held in a BBC studio, with a 43-year-old diplomat named Roy Dean taking first prize—the Cutty Sark trophy, a silver cube mounted on a stand. To the embarrassment of the contest organizers, the crossword diagrams on the cube faces bore a pattern of black squares strikingly reminiscent of the swastika.

En route to his victory, Dean set the all-time record for completing a puzzle from the London *Times* under test conditions—an amazing three minutes, 45 seconds! As a rule, even the best puzzlers require half an hour or so to complete the *Times* crosswords. At the other end of the spectrum, in 1966 a woman wrote to the *Times* to announce that she had just completed a puzzle published in the paper's April 4, 1932 issue!

We wonder how that dilatory puzzler might fare with the largest crossword ever published. Completed in 1975, this giant stumper contained 2,631 clues across and 2,922 clues down, and measured over 16 square feet. A Los Angeles man named Robert Stilgenbauer once compiled—but did not publish—a crossword with 3,149 clues across and 3,185 clues down. Stilgenbauer sent out 125,000 copies of the puzzle—which required 11 years to compile—but none was returned correctly completed. Another ingenious puzzler constructed a three-dimensional crossword, 15 squares on a side, with clues given for words across, down, and depth.

The average crossword is a good deal simpler. Crossword puzzles generally fall into four different categories:

1. Square or rectangular puzzles, usually of symmetrical design.
2. Asymmetrical puzzles, in the shape of a heart, cross, hexagon, or other design.
3. Puzzles without black squares; thick lines indicate where one word ends and another begins.
4. Diagramless puzzles, which simply offer clues, with no hint as to how the diagram is shaped.

But there are dozens of variations, and dozens of ways to disguise a clue. Many puzzles contain unclued words or words with identical clues, revolving around a central theme. Some puzzles ask for answers written in reverse, others for puns or anagrams of the clue. Occasionally, a short word must be deleted from all answers before they are written in the diagram; for instance, if the key word is *cat*, the answer *catatonic* would be written simply *atonic* in the diagram, and the answer *ducat* as *du*.

English puzzle compilers like to use narrative clues, with the answers comprising words left out of a story or poem. Puzzles have been constructed requiring algebraic calculations, with the answers written in the diagram as numbers rather than letters. Some puzzles require a symbol such as the heart or diamond as part of each answer, as *heartless* or *Diamond Lil*. Other puzzles require overlapping answers: for example, an answer such as *teasingleambleedit* might require six clues, one each for *teasing*, *single, gleam, amble, bleed,* and *edit.*

Bilingual crosswords, with clues in English and answers in French, were once common in England, as were English/Yiddish puzzles in New York. One particularly difficult puzzle form provides one set of clues and two accompanying diagrams. Each clue must be used twice, once for each diagram, but no hint is provided as to which answer belongs in which diagram. Sound impossible? Well, English writer Max Beerbohm once constructed what he called the "Impossible Crossword," with nonsensical clues for nonexistent answers. The crossword, published in 1940, came with a warning to readers that the puzzle could not be solved.

You may have seen crosswords that include a number or numbers in parentheses after each clue. These numbers refer to the number of letters in each word of the answer. But at one time, the numbers in parentheses were provided to confirm that a contemplated answer was correct. Each letter was assigned a number (A = 1, B = 2, etc.). The numbers represented by each letter in an answer could be added together, and the sum checked against the number in parentheses.

Crosswords have spawned a number of related games and puzzles. Scrabble, one of the most popular games in America, was invented in 1948, and the present rules formalized in 1953. If you're a Scrabble fan, read this and weep: during the 1970 national championships, the woman who was to become the eventual winner amassed an eye-popping 1,266 points in a single game!

The double crostic, another puzzle similar to the crossword, was invented in 1934 by Elizabeth Kingsley, whose double crostics appeared in every issue of the *Saturday Review* for 18 years. In the double crostic, the puzzler must first answer a number of clues, then transfer each letter of an answer to a corresponding square in the diagram, according to the numbers that appear under the answers. The completed diagram will then contain a quotation, and the first letters of the answers will also form an acrostic providing the author and work from which the quote was taken.

You'd like to try your hand at compiling crosswords? It's not easy, but here are some guidelines. Margaret Petheridge formulated five basic rules for crosswords she might find acceptable. First, all words in the diagram must totally interlock, with no letter of any word dependent on a single across or down clue. No more than one-sixth of the squares in the diagram may be black. No two-letter words are permissible. The word count should be as low as possible— a long word is preferable to several shorter words. Cliches should be avoided whenever possible—and a hackneyed answer must be balanced by a clever, original clue.

To be a successful crossword compiler, you'll need, in the words of one compiler, "practice and a ragbag of a mind that stores away completely unrelated bits of fact."

If you're wondering what kind of individual spends his time toiling over crossword composition, you might be interested to learn that of 100 regular contributors to two New York puzzle magazines, 25 are currently in prison!

Today, the weekly crosswords appearing in *The Observer,* a London paper, are generally considered to be among the world's most difficult.

DIAMONDS

"A diamond is forever" may sound like an advertising slogan devised by the jewelry industry, but it's not far from the truth. Long after the gold band of a wedding or engagement ring—and the finger that wore it—have vanished into dust, the diamond itself will be as hard and brilliant as ever. There is, quite simply, nothing on earth hard enough to crush or chip a diamond—except another diamond. Unless it is cut by man or burned in a furnace, the diamond will, indeed, last forever.

The ancient Greeks had another expression for the treasured gem: "A diamond is invincible." At least, the Greeks called the diamond *adamas,* "the invincible." The word was first applied to all hard metals, then to corundum and certain other hard stones. However, by the first century B.C., the exclusive meaning of *adamas* was diamond. From *adamas* came the later Latin *diamas,* then the Middle English *diamaunt,* and then our words *diamond* and *adamant.*

The diamond owes its extreme hardness to its tightly-knit crystal structure. Atomically, diamond is identical to coal and graphite, two of the softest minerals—all three are composed entirely of carbon. Each carbon atom in a diamond is firmly linked to four equidistant neighbors, while in graphite the atoms are free to "roll" over one another. Its tight crystal structure makes diamond 90 times as hard as the second hardest substance on earth, corundum. Acids can-

not harm a diamond, nor can any but the hottest fires—temperatures over 1,400 degrees, to be exact!

Diamonds may be valuable in industry for their hardness, but it is their brilliance that makes them valuable as gems. The brilliance of the diamond is due to its high refractive powers—much of the light reaching a diamond is reflected back into the stone rather than through it. The best diamonds are transparent and colorless, but diamonds actually range in color from clear to black. The rare pale blue and yellow-tinged diamonds are more highly prized than other "fancy" stones, which may be green, deep blue, pink, or deep yellow in color.

Diamonds are found in four forms, only one of which is used as a gem. *Bort* is a gray or brown crystal, while *ballas* is a powder of minute round crystals. Both are used exclusively in industry, as is *carbonado,* an opaque black or gray mineral. Diamonds are so vital that many industries would come to a complete halt without them. Their many uses include metal-working, stone-cutting, and all kinds of grinding, polishing, and sharpening. Closer to home, diamonds are used for phonograph needles and drill bits—including the one your dentist may use to drill your teeth.

In size alone, the Cullinan diamond is the granddaddy of all famous diamonds. Discovered in 1905 in the Premier Mine in Transvaal, South Africa, the stone in the rough weighed 3,106 carats—1⅓ pounds.

The beautiful gem that might now be sparkling on your finger was formed deep within the earth, where extreme pressures and temperatures forced the crystallization of carbon. Although 4,000 feet is the deepest any diamond has been found, the gems actually originate about 75 miles below the surface of the earth, and are pushed to the surface by volcanic activity. Some are released from the earth by erosion and deposited in river and stream beds. Others remain in the earth, usually in diamond "pipes," funnel-shaped lodes of diamond-rich rock called *kimberlite*. Most diamonds today are mined from pipes, including those found in the world's richest mines, near Kimberley, South Africa.

"'Diamonds in the rough" are usually round and greasy-looking. But diamond miners are in no need of dark glasses to shield them from the dazzling brilliance of the mines, for quite another reason: even in a diamond pipe, there is only one part diamond per 14 million parts of worthless rock. Approximately 46,000 pounds of earth must be mined and sifted to produce the half-carat gem you might be wearing. No wonder diamonds are expensive!

After diamond-bearing ore is brought up from the mine, it is crushed into smaller rocks no larger than one-and-a-quarter inches in diameter, then washed to remove loose dirt. At the recovery plant, the ore is spread on tables covered with grease and sprayed with water. The water moves the rocks off the table, but the diamonds adhere to the grease. Then the grease is

The diamond diggings in South Africa.

boiled off, leaving "rocks" of quite another sort.

Diamonds are weighed by the *carat* rather than by the grain or gram. The word comes from *carob*, a bean once used to weigh gems on a balance scale because of its uniform size. A *karat*, meanwhile, is used in reference to the purity of gold—24-karat gold is pure. An English carat is equivalent to 3.168 grains, or 205.3 milligrams, but in most places the metric carat, equivalent to 200 milligrams, is the standard. The differing values of the carat in various places and during various times has resulted in a good deal of confusion as to the weights of some of the

world's more famous gems. The present metric carat wasn't standardized until early this century.

Diamonds as they are collected at the recovery plant are still a long way from your wedding ring. Skilled craftsmen must transform the shapeless, cloudy stone into a delicate, multifaceted gem. Most diamonds are bought in parcels at diamond "sights" held in London or Johannesburg, then brought to diamond cutters in Antwerp, Amsterdam, and other cities.

Diamond cutting is a slow, painstaking process, involving many steps—and failure at any point could destroy or damage a valuable gem. First, a cutter *marks* the stone, scrutinizing its structure and condition until he decides the best way to cut the stone into smaller gems. Due to its octahedral crystal structure, a diamond will always cut cleanly along a plane parallel to one of the crystal's eight faces. The cutter must decide the best angle at which to cut the stone so that the resultant gem or gems will contain a minimum of flaws.

Next, the cutter *cleaves* the stone along the marked lines, cutting a groove—with another diamond, of course—then inserting a steel wedge in the groove and striking it with a hammer. The rough edges of the gem are then *sawed*, smoothed with a rotating disk charged with diamond dust. Then the gem is rounded, polished, and faceted into the desired shape. The most common diamond shape, called the brilliant cut, consists of 58 facets, 33 above the *girdle* or center line, and 25 below. Other popular cuts include the round, with 18 facets, and such fancy

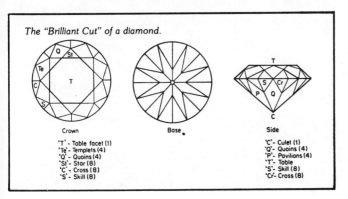

The "Brilliant Cut" of a diamond.

Crown

'T' - Table facet (1)
'Te' - Templets (4)
'Q' - Quoins (4)
'St' - Star (8)
'C' - Cross (8)
'S' - Skill (8)

Base

Side

'C' - Culet (1)
'Q' - Quoins (4)
'P' - Pavilions (4)
'T' - Table
'S' - Skill (8)
'Cr' - Cross (8)

123

cuts as the marquise, emerald, baquette, and pear.

Most of the diamonds of antiquity were found in the gravel of rivers and streams in India, but since the 18th century, most diamonds have come from South America or Africa. In 1740, the discovery of diamonds in Brazil shifted the mining industry from India to South America. But since the discovery of rich kimberlite pipes in South Africa, Africa has become the center of diamond mining. That continent now produces 80 percent of the world's gem diamonds, and 73 percent of all industrial diamonds.

Zaire is the top diamond-producing nation by quantity, but South Africa produces most

of the world's more valuable gem diamonds. Twenty-five percent of all South African diamonds are of gem quality, while only five percent of Zaire's diamonds are of similar value. Diamonds were first discovered in South Africa in 1867, on the banks of the Orange River. Two years later, a second lode was discovered—along with the 85-carat Star of South Africa. By 1870, 10,000 prospectors had joined the diamond rush, panning the gravel of South African river beds much the same way as gold prospectors in California did during the same period.

In 1902, work began at the Premier mine near Pretoria, now the world's richest. Over one-and-a-quarter million carats of diamonds, much of them of gem

quality, are produced by the mine each year. To suggest the importance of the Premier mine, and the scarcity of diamonds: in an average year, diamond production for the *entire world* stands at about 10 million carats—just four-and-a-half tons!

Today, the price of diamonds is set chiefly by DeBeers Consolidated Mines Ltd., the firm that owns most South African mines and controls much of the diamond production of other African nations. The DeBeers concern was formed largely from claims consolidated by Englishman Cecil Rhodes late in the 19th century. Due, in part, to the DeBeers monopoly, the price of diamonds has not kept pace with inflation over the last 30 years. In 1950, a one-carat gem diamond cost from $520 to $1,000. By the mid-1960s, the same diamond could

Washing for diamonds in 1870 at Cape of Good Hope.

124

The diamond fields at Colesberg Kopje.

be bought for from $450 to $1,500. The average gem diamond now purchased in the United States weighs a half-carat, and sells for about $225.

Today, most gem diamonds find their way to wedding and engagement rings, but historically, diamonds have been the playthings of the wealthy. The diamond was first mentioned in 800 B.C., in India. By the first century, the Roman historian Pliny could call it the "most valuable of gems, known only to kings." Even in the East, where diamonds were found, valuable gems were usually the property of sultans and maharajas. Tales abound of a nervous rajah watching over the shoulder of an even edgier diamond cutter, as the craftsman cleaved a precious stone. The craftsman's failure spelled instant execution.

Diamonds have long been the symbols of undying love, their unmatched hardness signifying steadfast devotion, their un-equaled brilliance and beauty a compliment to the beauty of the beloved. The first recorded instance of a suitor presenting his fiancée with a diamond ring occurred in 1477, when Maximilian, Archduke of Austria, sealed his troth with a diamond. Today, 85 percent of all American couples choose diamonds for their wedding rings.

Incidentally, a judge in this country recently ruled in favor of a man who had sued his fiancée for the return of her diamond engagement ring when the planned marriage went on the rocks. In effect, the judge declared that an engagement ring remains the property of the donor until the marriage takes place, but should be returned only if the receiver breaks off the engagement.

A diamond may be a "girl's best friend," but the history of the world's most valuable diamonds suggests that the gem has long known the friendship of thieves as well. As if cursed, many noted diamonds brought only misfortune and death to their often quite transitory owners.

One of the most legendary gems in the annals of diamond lore was the Great Mogul, an Indian gem reputed to weigh 280 carats when cut from a 787-carat rough stone. Its owners included Shah Jehan, the builder of the Taj Mahal. The gem was last seen

125

by a European during the 17th century, but disappeared mysteriously soon after. Some experts believe that either the Orloff or the Koh-i-Noor, two other renowned diamonds, may have been cut from the vanished Great Mogul.

The Orloff diamond once formed the glittering eye of an idol in a Brahman temple in Southern India, until stolen by a French soldier feigning a sudden affection for the Hindu religion. The soldier sold the gem to a ship's captain for $10,000, and was promptly tossed overboard. The gem eventually found its way to Europe. There it was purchased by the Russian Prince Orloff for $450,000. The Prince presented the diamond to Empress Catherine the Great as a peace offering after an earlier fall from favor; Catherine accepted the offering, but never returned the Prince to her good graces. The 199-carat gem now forms part of the Romanov's royal sceptre, on exhibit at the diamond treasury in Moscow.

The renowned Koh-i-Noor diamond had been in the hands of an Indian royal family for generations, when it was seized by an invading Persian sultan during the 14th century. Legend tells that the Indian rajah hid the gem away in his turban, but the sultan managed to exchange turbans with the Indian monarch during a feast. The sultan later unrolled the turban, and when the diamond appeared, exclaimed *koh-i-noor*, "mountain of light," in tribute to the gem's brilliance.

The legend that "he who owns the Koh-i-Noor owns the world" did indeed appear to be true in 1849, when the conquering English brought the gem to London and presented it to Queen Victoria. The gem then weighed 186 carats, but Victoria

had it recut in Amsterdam to 106 carats. The recutting took 38 days. Since 1911, the gem has formed the central stone of the queen's state crown, now on exhibit in the Tower of London along with the other British crown jewels.

The 137-carat Florentine diamond owes nothing to the city of Florence. In 1467, the yellow Indian gem was reputedly worn into battle by the Duke of Burgundy, found by a peasant or soldier after the Duke fell, and sold as presumed glass for a mere florin! The first attempt at recutting the gem in Amsterdam failed; after the successful second attempt, the cutter fainted. For a time, the Florentine formed part of the Austrian crown jewels, but the gem's whereabouts are now unknown.

Three of the world's most famous diamonds disappeared from view when the French crown jewels were stolen shortly after the French Revolution. The 55-carat Sancy, purchased in 1570 in Constantinople by the Seigneur de Sancy, included among its owners Louis XIV, Cardinal Mazarin, and James I of England. Henry IV of France reportedly once sent the gem as security for a loan, only to have his messenger set upon and murdered by thieves. The king ordered the trusted messenger's stomach slit open, and found the diamond where the thieves had not. Stolen in 1792, the gem was recovered in 1828, along with the Regent diamond, and now belongs to an Englishman.

The Regent was found in 1701, by an Indian slave, and eventually found its way into the hands of the Duke of Orleans,

the Regent of France. A favorite of Marie Antoinette, the 140-carat gem was cut from a 410-carat rough stone. The diamond was recovered in a Paris garret after its 1792 theft. Later, the Regent was used by Napoleon as security for a massive loan. For most of this century, the Regent has been on display at the Louvre—except for a short period when it was secreted away to hide it from the Nazi occupational forces.

The third member of the pilfered French trio, the 68-carat Hope diamond, met a considerably worse fate. The sapphire-blue gem, once the property of Louis XIV, was never recovered after the 1792 theft. In 1830, a 44-carat diamond that most experts believe was cut from the original gem appeared in London, where it was purchased by Henry Hope for $90,000. Bought by a New York diamond merchant early this century, the gem is now on exhibit at the Smithsonian Institution in Washington.

In size alone, the Cullinan is the granddaddy of all famous diamonds. Discovered in 1905, in the Premier mine in Transvaal, South Africa, the stone in the rough weighed 3,106 carats—one-and-a-third pounds! Named after Sir Thomas Cullinan, who had opened the Premier mine and was visiting there when the gem was found, the diamond was presented to Edward VII as a gift of the Transvaal government. The king had the diamond cut into nine gems. The largest, called Star of Africa Number One, weighs 530 carats—the largest gem diamond on earth—and now forms part of the British crown jewels.

But even that gem might appear a mere trinket compared with the largest raw gem ever mined, a topaz of 1.36 million

126

The world's largest diamond, the great Cullinan diamond, in its rough state. It weighed better than 3,024 carats.

carats—596 pounds!—that now resides in a glass case in the American Museum of Natural History in New York. The topaz is rather dull-looking, however, and few visitors to the museum pay the huge gem any mind.

The largest stone of true gem quality was a Brazilian aquamarine, discovered in 1910, that tipped the scales at 229 pounds. The hefty stone provided over 200,000 carats of quality aquamarines!

Some diamond owners were more famous than the gems they owned. The Emperor Jahangir of India, who died in 1627, reportedly owned a total of 279,450 carats of diamonds, along with 931,500 carats of emeralds, 376,000 carats of rubies, and two million carats of pearls! The emperor, an avid fisherman, never killed a fish he caught;

instead he slipped a string of pearls through the fish's gills and tossed it back in the water.

The Western madam known as Diamond-tooth Lil owed her nickname to a gold front tooth studded with a large diamond. Immortalized by Mae West's portrayal in a movie called *Diamond Lil*, the Austrian-born madam accumulated husbands as easily as diamonds—she married eight times without bothering to go through the formality of divorce.

Another noted diamond owner, railroad equipment salesman "Diamond Jim" Brady, used a collection of diamond jewelry to dazzle prospective clients. Jim commonly sported a 25-carat diamond ring, a diamond tiepin, cufflinks, and glasses case, and a cane fitted with a diamond handle. When asked if a particular gem were genuine, Jim often proved its worth by using the diamond to scratch his name on a pane of glass. After his death, Jim's diamonds were found to be of generally poor quality.

Most of the world's large, storied diamonds are priceless, and many have been insured for millions of dollars. For the largest amount of cold cash ever laid out

for a piece of diamond jewelry, we must turn to the 69-carat ring bought at a 1969 auction by actor Richard Burton, and presented to his wife, Elizabeth Taylor. The gem set Burton back a neat $1,200,000! His other gifts to Elizabeth include the $350,000 Krupp diamond, a $38,000 diamond, a $93,000 emerald, and a sapphire brooch valued at $65,000.

Burton's record will undoubtedly be broken someday. And the future may hold in store sad tidings for other diamond fanciers as well. Already, the ruby has surpassed the diamond as the world's most valuable gem, carat for carat. Since 1955, when ruby supplies began to dwindle, flawless natural rubies have sold for as high as $5,000 per carat.

Simulated diamonds are certainly no novelty. But the possibility of synthetic diamonds has intrigued scientists since late in the 19th century, when two Frenchmen claimed to have produced a small diamond by a process that, alas, proved unrepeatable. In 1955, the General Electric Company reported that scientists in their laboratories had succeeded in manufacturing a synthetic diamond by subjecting carbonaceous material to pressures of one-and-a-half million pounds per square inch, and temperatures over 5,000 degrees. The synthetic diamonds, the largest of which was a mere one-tenth of a carat, were of industrial quality.

And now jewelers are shuddering at the appearance of cubic zirconia gems, man-made byproducts of laser technology, that can reportedly pass as diamonds to almost any eye—and cost but $12 a carat!

127

DICTIONARIES

"Everything that coruscates with effulgence is not ipso facto aurous" is a rather highfalutin way of saying "All that glitters is not gold," but without a dictionary, you'd never guess it.

"Look it up in the dictionary" is a piece of advice foreign to few ears, but did you realize that until the 18th century speakers of English had no lexicographic authority to consult for the meaning of the thousands of English words now nestled between *aardvark* and *zymurgy?*

The first English work to bear the title "dictionary" (in its Latin form, *dictionarius*, from *dictis*, "saying" or "word" and *dicere*, "to say") appeared around the year 1225. But that first manuscript actually listed Latin words to be learned by rote by students, with only a few English words inserted, here and there, for explanation. Words were not grouped alphabetically, but were arranged according to subject.

English words began to appear regularly in 15th-century dictionaries, but still served only as aids to the study of Latin. One noted dictionary of this era was the charmingly titled *Storehouse for the Little Ones,* or *Promptorium Parvulorum,* brought out around 1440 by a Dominican friar aptly named Galfridus Grammaticus—Geoffrey the Grammarian. The work contained about 12,000 English words and their Latin equivalents. It did not appear in print until 1499 for one rather compelling reason—the printing press hadn't yet been invented.

The *Storehouse* was not the only 15th- and 16th-century dictionary with a colorful title— metaphoric titles were the custom for many years. A work dating from 1500 was dubbed *Ortus Vocabulorum, The Garden of Words,* and a 1573 student's dictionary was somewhat presumptuously named *Alvearie,* or "Beehive."

The first real English dictionary was the *Abcedarium Anglico-Latinum pro Tyrunculis,* a Latin-English work completed by Richard Huloet in 1552. This compendium contained some 26,000 words with their Latin translations. Each word was defined in English. Thus, the *Abcedarium,* though designed as a Latin aid, can be considered a bona fide English dictionary.

The *Abcedarium* was popular in its time, but relatively expensive. So in 1570, a physician named Peter Levins brought out a cheaper version of Huloet's work, entitled *Manipulus Vocabulorum—A Handful of Words.* The entries were arranged—not alphabetically—but according the the spelling of their *final* syllables, making the book, in effect, the first rhyming dictionary in the English language.

Early dictionaries made no attempt to include all English or Latin words, only those that were considered troublesome to students. The title of a 1604 work by Robert Cawdrey explains it best: *A Table Alphabeticall, conteyning and teaching the true writing and understanding of hard usuall English wordes . . . gathered for the benefit and helpe of Ladies, Gentlewomen, or any other unskillful persons.* As for the difference between "Ladies" and "Gentlewomen," you'll have to consult a dictionary.

The more tersely titled *The English Dictionarie* appeared in 1623, compiled by Henry Cockeram, but based to a great extent on Cawdrey's work.

Cockeram's dictionary was hardly the last word in lexicographic precision, as is readily apparent in a definition such as "Hyena: A subtil beast, conterfeiting the voice of a man . . . He is sometimes male and sometimes female."

In 1702, John Kersey—alias "J.K. Philobibl."—issued a wordbook entitled *New English Dictionary* that was the first volume to define words in everyday usage. And in 1721, a schoolteacher named Nathaniel Bailey published the *Universal Etymological English Dictionary*, containing "more words than any English Dictionary before extant."

Another of Bailey's works, *Dictionarium Britannicum*, appeared in 1730, displaying "not only the Words, and their Explications, but their Etymologies." Bailey was also among the first to indicate the pronunciation of words along with their definitions.

In 1791 came the *Critical Pronouncing Dictionary and Expositer of the English Language*, compiled by an elderly actor named John Walker. Walker's book is still considered valuable for its treatment of pronunciation. The phonetician, Isaac Pitman, based his popular shorthand system on Walker's principles.

Perhaps the most remarkable dictionary of the 18th century was the accomplishment of the legendary Samuel Johnson. Johnson's prodigious work—which was completed single-handedly—was brought out in 1755 as *A Dictionary of the English Language*. As Johnson's renowned biographer James Boswell noted: "The world contemplated with wonder so stupendous a work achieved by one man, while other countries had thought such undertakings fit only for whole academies."

Most earlier lexicographers sought to lay down rules for usage and spelling, but Johnson sought more to reflect current usage—to reflect rather than dictate the accepted meaning—explaining in his *Preface* that no scholar "can embalm his language and secure it from corruption."

Said Johnson: "No dictionary of a living tongue can ever be perfect, since while it is hastening to publication some words are budding, and some falling away." Today's dictionaries, likewise, make little attempt to dictate,

In 1755, Dr. Samuel Johnson published a dictionary that was a landmark in lexicography.

From Samuel Johnson's dictionary of the English Language (1755):

Lexicographer: *A writer of dictionaries; a harmless drudge, that busies himself in tracing the original, and detailing the signification of words.*

Oats: *A grain, which in England is generally given to horses, but in Scotland supports the people.*

129

only to reflect the ever-changing meaning of words.

Johnson was the first to use illustrations of word usage gleaned from "the best writers," as do many modern lexicographers. Because of the extensive research involved in gathering the illustrations, Johnson's work—planned to take three years—eventually required eight.

After his long years of toil, Johnson was piqued by an article written by Lord Chesterfield, the statesman and author, in which the Earl claimed undue credit as the patron of Johnson's dictionary. (Chesterfield had actually sent Johnson a 10 pound subscription for the dictionary in 1747.) "I have been pushing on my work through difficulties, of which it is useless to complain," Johnson wrote in his now-famous letter to Chesterfield, "and have brought it, at last, to the verge of publication, without one wit of assistance, one word of encouragement, or one smile of favour . . . Is not a Patron, my Lord, one who looks with unconcern on a man struggling for life in the water, and, when he has reached ground, encumbers him with help?"

Although English dictionaries had been published in America as early as 1788, the first English dictionary compiled by an American was *A School Dictionary*, brought out in 1798 by a Connecticut teacher named—appropriately enough— Samuel Johnson, Jr.

In 1806, another Connecticut resident, Noah Webster of New Haven, issued *A Compendious Dictionary of the English Language* with some 40,000 words. But the most important milestone in American lexicography came in 1828, when Webster published his masterpiece, *An American Dictionary of the English Language*, with about 70,000 entries. Webster's work was the first American dictionary to gain wide acceptance in both the United States and England.

You may be confused by the plethora of dictionaries on the market bearing the name "Webster's." The fact is none of these books—or at least, very few—are directly derived from the work of Noah Webster. The word "Webster's" has become merely an identifying title, like the word "dictionary" itself, and cannot be copyrighted. Anyone at all can publish a book and call it "Webster's Dictionary," although the G.&C. Merriam

Noah Webster compiled An American Dictionary of the English Language *in 1828. Revised versions of this monumental work are still widely used in the United States today.*

The last words of Noah Webster were probably zyme, zymosis, and zymurgy.

Company of Springfield, Massachusetts, claims that their dictionaries are the legitimate successors to Webster's works.

Many stories have been told about the famed American lexicographer—most of them apocryphal. Witness, for example, this droll tale:

One day Mrs. Webster entered the parlor to find her husband locked in an embrace with the maidservant. "Noah!" she sputtered, "I *am* surprised!"

Noah disentangled himself and quickly regained his professional composure. "No, my dear," he told his wife, "It is *I* who am surprised. *You* are merely astonished."

Many other dictionaries have come and gone since the days of Webster and Johnson, but the greatest English dicitionary on either side of the Atlantic remains the *Oxford English Dictionary,* conceived in the mid-19th century, but not completed until 1928. The *Oxford* lists all recorded English words, and their varying usages from the seventh century through the twentieth. Thus, a simple word such as "place," due to its many uses and its long history of change, might occupy 20 or 25 small-print pages. Compiled with the aid of hundreds of research assistants in both England and America, the *Oxford* remains the largest dictionary in the world. Its 12 volumes contain about 415,000 words, almost two million illustrative quotations, and close to 228 million letters and figures!

A glance at a card catalogue in any large library will suggest the tremendous range of dictionaries now available, covering almost every specialized vocabulary imaginable. Witness, for example, *A Dictionary of the Stitches Used in Art Needlework,* or *Dictionary of the Under-*

world: the vocabulary of crooks, criminals, racketeers, beggars and tramps, convicts, the commercial underworld, the drug traffic, and the white slave traffic.

And then there's the *Dictionary of Waste Disposal and Public Cleansing*—published, *naturlich* in Germany.

The number of dictionaries in existence today is difficult to calculate, but in English, there is a dictionary for most of the 5,000 foreign languages spoken throughout the world today.

By the way, the first Bohemian-English dictionary— 626 pages long—was brought out in 1876, and the long-awaited Mongolian-English dictionary was published in 1953.

How many words are there in the dictionary? First of all, no English dictionary but the *Oxford* claims to include anywhere near all the words in the language.

The word "unabridged" in a dictionary title does not mean the work contains all the words in the language, but merely that the book includes all entries appearing in earlier editions of the work.

English, the second most commonly spoken language in the world after Mandarin Chinese, contains the largest vocabulary of any language on earth, an estimated 800,000 words—of which the average person uses only about 60,000. *Webster's Third International Dictionary* contains about 450,000 entries.

You'll find more dictionary entries under the letter *T* than under any other, for *T* is the most common initial letter in our language. The most common letter in English is *E,* and the most common words are *the, of, and,* and *to,* in that order.

Schoolboy wisdom holds that *antidisestablishmentarianism* (28 letters) is the longest word in the language, but the *Oxford English Dictionary* includes the word *floccipaucinihilipilification* (29 letters). The word means "the action of estimating as worthless."

Webster's Third International Dictionary lists *pneumonoultramicroscopicsilicovolcanoconiosis* as a lung disease common to miners.

The longest word in common use is generally thought to be *disproportionableness* (21 letters). And the longest chemical term ever used, the name of an amino acid compound, contains some 3,600 letters.

However, as any lexicographer with a sense of humor will point out, the longest word in our language is actually *smiles*— because there's a mile between the first and the last letters!

Incidentally, excluding proper names, the oldest word in the English language still in use in a comparable form is *land,* derived from the Old Celtic *landa,* "heath." This word is thought to have been in use on the European continent well before the beginning of the Roman Empire.

The dictionary is easily the most useful reference work ever created. Yet there are a number of languages in existence today that are not likely to be recorded in a new dictionary. Why? Well, there are now about 20 languages in which no one can converse, for the simple reason that there are only one or two, or perhaps a few, speakers of the tongue still alive. For example, Eyak, an Alaskan Indian language, is certainly one of the most moribund languages on earth—spoken only by two aged sisters when they chance to meet!

Eggplants

Imagine a dish by the name of "The Priest Has Fainted." Yet possibly the most famous of all eggplant dishes is that *tour de force* known as *Imam Bayeldi*, which owes its name to the Ottoman Turks of the 16th century.

According to legend, a holy man was making a routine call at the home of a particularly beautiful lady. Out of a spirit of hospitality, she insisted that he partake of an eggplant dish she had been preparing. When she bent over to present the dish, her veil slipped off her face and dress, and for a brief moment, the priest caught a glimpse of her two delectable eggplants. Overpowered by the sight and the aroma of the succulent food, the holy man passed out. From that time on, the dish was christened *Imam Bayeldi*, (The Priest Has Fainted).

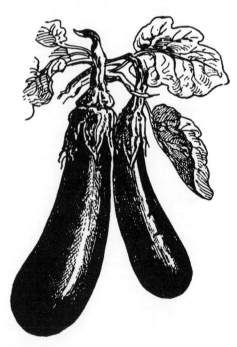

IMAM BAYELDI

3 eggplants
1 12 oz. can tomato puree,
    thinned with 1 tablespoon water
1 lb. ground lamb
½ lb. butter
1 onion, chopped
½ teaspoon celery seed
½ teaspoon garlic salt
½ cup pine nuts
⅛ teaspoon nutmeg
⅛ teaspoon cinnamon
⅛ teaspoon ground cloves
⅛ teaspoon pepper

---

1. Skin eggplants. Cut in quarters lengthwise.
2. Saute eggplants in 3 tablespoons butter, until fairly soft.
3. Slit pieces of eggplant in center, and set aside.
4. Saute ground lamb and finely chopped onion in 2 tablespoons butter, until well browned.
5. Saute pine nuts in 1 tablespoon butter, until slightly browned.
6. Combine all ingredients, and stuff each piece of eggplant.
7. Pour tomato puree over eggplant.
8. Bake for 25 minutes (or so) in 350° oven.

Serves six.

The fact is that there are a number of great culinary expoits that can be performed with the eggplant. This versatile vegetable can be baked, broiled, scalloped, fried, sauteed, stuffed, or marinated. Many countries have their favorite eggplant dishes—Italy, Greece, France, Israel, and Turkey, to name a few. In the Near East and in North African countries, large eggplants are stuffed with meat mixed with onions, tomatoes, garlic, and rice.

The French enjoy a dish which they intriguingly named *Ratatouille*. It is usually baked in a casserole, and consists of eggplant, tomatoes, peppers, onions, and zucchini.

Today, in many Greek restaurants, one of the leading offerings is a dish called *Mousaka*, made from eggplant, lamb, onions, and spices, prepared with an egg sauce. This venerable dish is reputed to have developed in the early Middle Ages.

Most American eggplants come from Florida, Texas, and New Jersey. We produce about a million-and-a-half bushels of the purple fruit each year, and smaller quantities are imported from Mexico. But by and large, the average American isn't very fond of eggplant, and the national consumption comes to about four ounces per year. A pity, because the versatile eggplant has unusual properties, and can be fashioned into a multitude of forms and dishes.

There is a restaurant in Jerusalem whose owner declares he can prepare eggplant in 100 different ways. When the writer questioned him to list his offerings, he only was able to come up with about 16. And yet the statement, "One Hundred Dishes," is really not an exaggeration. There are that many good eggplant recipes around.

Perhaps one of the greatest eggplant dishes ever concocted is a Sicilian specialty called *Caponata*. There are literally dozens of combinations and ways to make this marvelous appetizer. Here is one that never fails to win applause:

CAPONATA

3 eggplants
1 cup olive oil
1 cup shelled walnuts
½ cup pickled melon rind
4 tablespoons garlic salt
½ cup pine nuts
⅛ teaspoon pepper
½ cup drained capers
½ cup finely-chopped sweet mixed pickles
½ cup stuffed green olives, cut in halves
1 cup pitted black ripe olives
1 cup sugar
½ cup cider vinegar
½ tablespoon garlic powder
1 cup finely chopped pimentoes
½ cup small white, sweet pickled onions

1. Cut eggplants in 1" slices; then in 1" cubes. Leave skin on. Discard ends.
2. Fry in 1 cup olive oil for about 30 minutes, until fairly soft and brown.
3. Add all other ingredients, and mix all together in a large pot.
4. Add eggplant and oil, and saute 30 minutes longer.
5. Then fill a very large container and place in refrigerator.

Makes enough for 20 or so good-sized portions of appetizer or 30 smaller portions.
Will keep for at least one month.

ELEVATORS

During the 1977 power blackout in New York City, the business and commercial life of the world's busiest metropolis came to a complete halt for an entire day. Though buses were still running to take people to work and many offices had sufficent natural lighting to make some work possible, the blackout shut off one electrical device without which the modern city is completely helpless: the elevator.

With thousands of offices vacant for the lack of a means of reaching them, and hundreds of thousands of people stranded in high-rise apartment buildings, the importance of the elevator in today's city was drawn sharply into focus.

The idea of vertical transportation, if not the means, has been with us for well over 2,000 years. Ruins from a number of ancient civilizations contain shafts; some archaeologists believe that these shafts were actually hoistways in which goods and perhaps people were lifted. But no mention of an elevator-like device appears in any ancient writings until the first century B.C., when the Roman architect-engineer Vitruvius described lifting platforms that utilized pulleys worked by human, animal, or water power. The Roman Coliseum, built in 80 A.D., used crude lifting platforms to raise gladiators and wild animals to the arena level.

Many medieval monasteries were built atop steep cliffs or surrounded by high walls, and

The elevator in the Convent of St. Catherine on Mount Sinai.

some of the more unsociable cloisters depended upon a device known as the basket elevator for entry and exit. A basket elevator was just that—a basket in which the passenger was lifted or lowered by rope along the outside of the monastery walls. Not the most gracious entry, perhaps, but unwanted guests certainly posed little problem.

In 17th-century France, the "flying chair" occasionally brought passengers to the upper floors of higher buildings. Similar to hoists used by stablemen to lift bales of hay to a loft, the flying chair was operated by a rope running around a wheel at the top of the building exterior. One end of the rope was attached to the chair, the other end to a counterweight. To rise, a passenger threw off a sandbag attached to the chair—the counterweight would then descend and the much lighter

chair and passenger would rise. Not a very pleasant ride, as you might imagine. Even so, at the end of the upward journey, the passenger had to climb in through the window.

In a sense the flying chair was similar in operation to the dumbwaiter, a pulley-and-counterweight device used chiefly to lift food from kitchen to dining room. An apocryphal story credits Thomas Jefferson with the invention of the dumbwaiter; we do know that Jefferson used one of the world's first dumbwaiters in his Virginia home to deliver food from a basement kitchen to the dining room. The dumbwaiter was later used in this country to deliver garbage to the basement of many apartment buildings.

Elisha Graves Otis is often called the inventor of the elevator. Even though he initially contributed only one major safety innovation to elevator design, it was significant enough to make him, in effect, the father of the passenger elevator.

Vermont-born Otis was working in a furniture factory when he was asked to design a machine for lifting lumber and other materials from floor to floor. Otis's invention made its debut at the 1853 Crystal Palace Exposition in New York, where it was billed as "An elevator, or machine for hoisting goods."

Otis's elevator was a simple platform that moved between two guide rails, with a steam-powered windlass at the top of the shaft to raise or lower the cable. The innovation was a safety device that could stop the fall of the elevator in the event the cable broke. The simple device consisted of two metal hooks and a spring, attached to the cable where it met the platform. If tension in the hoist rope was relaxed—in the event of a cable break, for instance—the hooks immediately sprang to a horizontal position, where their ends would catch in teeth cut into the guide rails and stop the

Elisha Otis giving a public demonstration of his safety elevator at the Crystal Palace Exposition, New York City, in 1854.

136

elevator's descent. Sounds a bit shaky? Well, it's basically the safety device modern elevators rely on today—and it's totally reliable.

According to some accounts, Otis demonstrated the safety of his invention by holding regular cable-breaking exhibitions at the exposition. Spectators would watch in amazement as Otis climbed on the platform, rose to the top of the shaft, and then cut the cable! His expected fall would be checked by the safety hooks.

By 1857, Otis had installed the world's first commercial passenger elevator in the Haughwout Department Store in New York. A steam-driven lift, the elevator rose five stories at a speed of 40 feet per minute—barely faster than a stairway. At first, shoppers were reluctant to risk their lives on the newfangled device, but as more and more people took the—er, plunge, it soon became clear that the passenger elevator was here to stay.

Early steam-driven elevators required a large space for the steam engine, and often spewed thick smoke into the shaft. The next step was obvious: an electric elevator. In 1880, a German named Werner Siemens built a crude electric elevator, with a motor under the platform turning cogwheels that fit into notches in the guide rails.

In 1887, William Baxter built an unsuccessful electric machine in Baltimore. The world's first *successful* electric elevator was installed two years later by the Otis Elevator Company in the Demarest Building in New York—and was in continual use until the building was demolished in 1920.

The Demarest Building

elevator's 30-year life span pales next to the endurance record of the world's oldest operating elevators, three hydraulic machines installed in a Gramercy Park, Manhattan apartment building in 1883, and still operating after more than 90 years of service.

By the turn of the century, the problems of speed, safety, and height limitation had been successfully challenged. There remained only improvements in convenience and economy. The push-button elevator, introduced in 1894, was both more reliable and cheaper to operate than the hand-operated manned elevator you can still find in some old city buildings. Automatic leveling, which brings the car to rest precisely at floor level, made its debut in 1915, but the cry of "watch your step" will live on forever. By the middle of this century, automation had rendered the elevator operator nearly extinct.

The Otis Elevator Company, the world's largest manufacturer of elevators, now installs from 20,000 to 25,000 new elevators and escalators each year, and services an estimated 400,000 Otis elevators functioning around the world. As early as the 1890s, Otis was exporting elevator equipment to 31 countries. Nowadays, Otis operates 29 plants worldwide, with over 44,000 employees.

The earliest electric elevators with push-button controls simply carried a passenger from point A to point B without stops—no matter how many people on intermediate floors impatiently watched the car glide by. A modern elevator answers all calls in one direction, then responds to calls waiting in the other direction. Large office buildings

with many elevators use group control systems, which keep the cars correctly spaced and send only the closest elevator to answer a call.

Thanks to Otis, elevators are now almost 100 percent safe—five times safer than a staircase, according to the elevator industry. Cable failure is extremely rare, for each of a modern machine's eight woven steel cables can support a load eight times the capacity of the car. Safety devices similar to Otis's assure that even if the cable does break, the car won't fall very far in the shaft. And a device at the bottom of the shaft, called the buffer, will break the fall of an errant elevator in the unlikely event the car does plummet.

An airplane once crashed into a New York office building and struck directly into the elevator shaft, destroying the cables. The car plunged 17 floors—but the buffer saved the life of the elevator's lone passenger!

Modern elevators travel at many times the speed of the earliest machines, with express elevators in some taller buildings speeding along at 1,200 feet per minute—fast enough to require machinery to adjust changing air pressures in the car. And newer elevators, such as those in the Sears Tower and the John Hancock Building in Chicago, travel at speeds of up to 1,800 feet per minute!

One of the largest elevators in the world—an hydraulic model—raises, lowers, and revolves the stage at New York's Radio City Music Hall. But the largest commercial elevator on record was constructed to raise and lower a full swimming pool on

137

the stage of the Hippodrome Theater in New York. The device had a capacity of 250,000 pounds—that's equal in weight to 35 hippopotami—and moved at a speed of 12 feet per minute, slower than the most sluggish hippopotamus!

A second means of vertical transportation, the escalator, was developed while the electric elevator was still in its infancy. A patent for an escalator was issued in 1859, but the first working escalator was installed by Jesse Reno in 1896 on a pier in Coney Island, New York. About the same time, Charles Seeburger constructed a similar conveyor with horizontal steps. Seeburger coined the word "escalator" for his invention, combining the Latin *scala* ("steps") with the first letter and ending of "elevator." Seeburger's device forced riders to step on and off to one side—at their own risk. The Otis Elevator Company acquired both inventions. By 1921, Otis had developed the kind of horizontal-step escalator in use today.

Escalators eliminated both the need for an elevator operator and, more important, long waits for an elevator car. Escalators were installed extensively in deep subway stations, transporting a steady stream of riders and thereby eliminating bottlenecks at elevator doors. In fact, the longest escalator in the world can be found in the Leningrad subway, with a vertical rise of 195 feet.

The steps of an escalator are moved by an endless chain powered by electricity, usually at speeds of about 100 feet per minute. The underside of each step is triangular in shape, and mounted on four wheels running in tracks under the steps. When the step begins its ascent, the rear wheels rise to keep the top of the step horizontal.

As anyone who's had to climb to the eighth floor of a department store via seven escalators is well aware, the escalator will never replace the elevator for long distances. As buildings rise higher and increase in floor area, engineers have had to keep pace with constant innovation. The major problem faced by the engineers is how to minimize the space taken up by elevator shafts when many elevators are needed for a building. One answer is the dual elevator—two cars running in one shaft. The first dual elevator was place in service in Pittsburgh in 1931, with the upper car running as an express, the lower car as a local. Another development, the double-deck car, was introduced in 1932, with two attached cars that stop one floor above the other.

Round elevator cars serve a Johnson Wax Company building in Racine, Wisconsin, designed by renowned architect Frank Lloyd Wright. Another Wright creation, the Price Tower in Oklahoma, is served by hexagonally shaped elevator cars.

And who says an elevator can go only straight up? The Eiffel Tower boasts elevators that move along dizzily inclined tracks, as does the George Washington Masonic Monument in Virginia. And the outdoor elevator is now coming into vogue, as demonstrated by the new Hyatt Regency Hotel in Atlanta, served by glass-cab elevators running in rails on the outside of the building.

Beats a flying chair, doesn't it?

138

Extinct Animals

Though some of these creatures were extinct 300 million years ago, others did not die out completely until this century—and many other species are in danger of extinction today.

Here are just a few of the creatures that once roamed the earth, but live no more. Let's hope that animals such as the Mexican Grizzly Bear, Giant Otter, Javan Rhinoceros, and Blue Whale—all endangered today—do not soon join this list.

GLYPTODON *The glyptodon was a gigantic mammal, related to the armadillo, that lived in South America more than a million years ago. Later, the glyptodon invaded North America and reached the southern United States.*

DODO *The flightless, swan-sized bird known as the dodo lived on the Indian Ocean islands of Mauritius and Reunion, becoming extinct in 1681. The Dutch called the dodo the "nauseous bird," because cooking would not make it palatable.*

MAMMOTH *This elephantlike creature has given us a word meaning "enormous," but the mammoth was probably no larger than the modern elephant. Remains of the mammoth have been found in many places in the Northern Hemisphere. The creature was hunted by stone-age man, and may have survived in Siberia until relatively recent times.*

STEGOSAURUS *Stegosaurus means "plated lizard." These dinosaurs lived in North America some 150 million years ago. The spiked tail may look fearsome, but the stegosaurus was actually a harmless vegetarian. The largest were 30 feet long.*

139

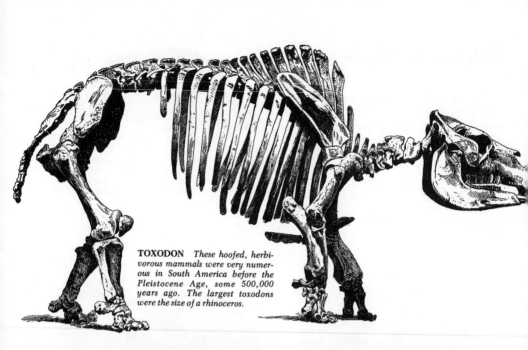

TOXODON *These hoofed, herbivorous mammals were very numerous in South America before the Pleistocene Age, some 500,000 years ago. The largest toxodons were the size of a rhinoceros.*

Riou

ICHTHYOSAURUS *A marine reptile, the ichthyosaurus breathed by lungs but well adapted for life in the water. It flourished throughout the world, but was extinct before the Paleocene Era, 65 million years ago.*

PLESIOSAURUS *This marine reptile was well adapted for life in the open seas. Some measured over 30 feet in length. The plesiosaurus was extinct by the end of the Cretaceous period, 70 million years ago.*

DRACO *This small reptile used the winglike membranes on its sides to glide from tree to tree.*

PTERODACTYL *These winged reptiles lived in many parts of the world some 100 million years ago. The smaller species were the size of a sparrow. But other pterodactyls were the largest creatures ever to fly, with a head four feet long and a wingspan of 18 feet.*

IGUANODON *This amphibious reptile of the dinosaur age was named iguanodon because its teeth resembled those of the iguana lizard. The largest species measured 33 feet in length, and stood 13 feet tall on its hind legs. The thumb formed a spikelike weapon. The iguanodon ranged over Northern Europe and England during the Cretaceous period, more than 100 million years ago.*

MEGATHERIUM *This was the largest of the ancient ground sloths, a group of mammals related to the modern sloth. But the megatherium was much larger, equalling the elephant in bulk. It lived in North and South America during the Pleistocene age, which began 800,000 years ago.*

141

MESOPITHECUS *This ancient primate, an ancestor of the modern ape, lived more than 25 million years ago.*

ARCHAEOPTERYX *This is the most ancient bird of which fossil remains have been discovered. The archaeopteryx had a reptilelike head, teeth, and a lizardlike tail, but also had feathers and wings. About the size of a crow, the archaeopteryx flourished in Europe and other places during the Jurassic period, some 150 million years ago.*

RHAMPHORHYNCHUS *A small pterodactyl, or flying reptile, that lived some 100 million years ago. The body was about four inches long, but the tail grew up to 15 inches in length. The creature lived mainly on fish.*

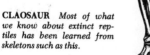

CLAOSAUR *Most of what we know about extinct reptiles has been learned from skeletons such as this.*

HESPERORNIS REGALIS *This aquatic bird lived in North America some 100 million years ago. It measured about four feet in length.*

142

Over 100 million Americans, including two-thirds of all adults, now wear eyeglasses. Another 10 million or so regularly don contact lenses. Eyeglass wearers range from the slightly dim-sighted, who slip on specs for reading or driving, to the virtually blind who would be helpless without their lenses.

aids. A rock crystal lens found in the ruins of the ancient Assyrian city of Nineveh was probably used as a burning glass. In *The Clouds*, Greek playright Aristophanes mentioned the use of lenses to burn parchment and to erase writing from wax tablets. Roman historian Pliny wrote that burning lenses were sometimes

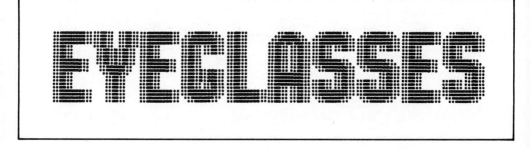

Even those fortunate enough never to need glasses should be grateful for their invention. For corrective lenses rank along with printing, paper, and electric illumination as the major technological milestones along man's road to universal literacy. Today, eyeglasses are considered so vital that it's hard to imagine a world without them. Yet eyeglasses were not commonplace anywhere in the world until about 450 years ago—and precision, individualized lenses date back no further than the 18th century!

What did man do before the invention of eyeglasses? In ancient times, aging scholars often had to give up reading altogether. The more fortunate could afford to pay others to read to them. The Roman dramatist Seneca claimed to have read with the use of a water-filled glass sphere that magnified characters when held just above the page.

Lenses existed even in Seneca's time, but no one seems to have put them to use as vision

used to cauterize wounds—though the "emerald" that he claimed the Emperor Nero used to view the gladiatorial games was probably just a curved mirror.

For many Europeans, the Dark Ages must have been quite literally dark—or, at the least, fuzzy. With no eyeglasses of any kind, medieval man had to rely on medicinal remedies of dubious value. One Anglo-Saxon remedy counseled persons with poor vision to comb their heads, eat little meat, and drink wormwood before meals, and perhaps apply a salve made from pepper, nuts, salt, and wine. Fourth-century Italians believed that a person seeing a falling star should quickly begin counting—the viewer would be free from eye inflammations for as many years as he

143

could count before the star disappeared.

For those too slow to catch a falling star, another medieval antidote to eye inflammation required that the sufferer tie a piece of linen around his neck with as many knots as there were letters in his name. White spots before the eyes? Simply catch a

ber of grains of dust and sand . . . So also we might cause the sun, moon, and stars in appearance to descend here below."

The next step, naturally, was to move the glass closer to the eye. Historians have been unable to determine the inventor of the first eyeglasses, or the exact date

whom the monk conversed with, the man who *invented* eyeglasses?

Some historians believe that man was Alessandro di Spina, a Dominican monk who lived in Pisa. But a document recording Spina's death in 1313 claimed that Spina had seen spectacles on a man who had chosen to remain

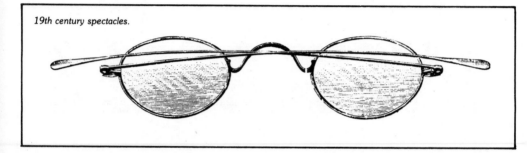

19th century spectacles.

fox, cut out his tongue, tie it in a red rag, and hang it from your neck. As for casting out motes, just touch your eyelid, say "I buss the Gorgon's mouth," and spit three times.

An 11th-century Arab work, *Opticae Thesaurus*, mentioned corrective lenses, but as described, the lenses could not have been suitable for improving vision. It wasn't until the 13th century that some scientists began to deal with vision defects more seriously.

Englishman Roger Bacon was the first to suggest the use of lenses for reading, and the first to describe a practical lens, with a thickness less than its radius. In 1268, Bacon wrote that by holding part of a glass sphere over a page, with the convex side up, a reader could magnify the characters and see them more clearly. He also predicted the use of lenses for microscopes and telescopes, hypothesizing that "from an incredible distance we might read the smallest letters and num-

of their appearance, but we do have a number of clues. In 1289, an Italian named Sandro di Popozo wrote: "I am so debilitated by age, that without the glasses known as spectacles, I would no longer be able to read or write. These have recently been invented for the benefit of poor old people whose sight has become weak." So we can conclude that spectacles first appeared shortly before 1289.

In 1306, a Pisan monk delivered a sermon in Florence that included these comments: "It is not 20 years since there was found the art of making eyeglasses which make for good vision . . . I have seen and conversed with the man who made them first." That would date the invention of eyeglasses to around 1287. But who was the man

unknown. Spina merely copied the invention, and distributed it "with a cheerful and benevolent heart."

A tombstone in Florence credits Armato degli Armati, who died in 1317, as the "inventor of spectacles." But the tombstone has been found to be of relatively recent origin; the claim is a fabrication. All we know for certain is that eyeglasses first appeared in the area of Pisa late in the 1280s.

After Marco Polo visited the Orient during the 1270s, he claimed to have found an old Chinese man reading with the use of spectacles. If this is true, then the Chinese invented eyeglasses before any European. At the time, the Chinese claimed to have learned to make lenses from Arabs two centuries earlier. But this claim is regarded as doubtful.

In any case, the appearance of spectacles in Europe caused little furor among the general populace, since at the time few people could read. For a few centuries, eyeglasses were regard-

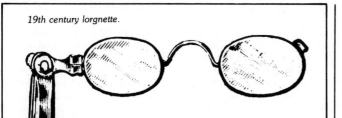
19th century lorgnette.

technical sophistication. Glasses were at first perceived as reading tools only, and no one immediately saw the need to turn a convex lens around for use as a corrective to *myopia*, or nearsightedness. In a myopic person, the eyeball is elongated in such a way that parallel light rays are focused in front of the retina. Concave lenses cause rays to diverge and meet at the retina.

In a person suffering from *hyperopia*, or farsightedness, light rays are focused behind the retina; a convex lens focuses the rays on the retina. *Astigmatism*, caused by an irregularity in the curvature of the cornea, can be corrected with the use of a cylindrical lens—which was not invented until 1827!

The earliest optical lenses were made from beryl or quartz, and set in frames of brass or iron—and later, in bone, horn, gold, or even leather. Single glasses were held in the hand; double glasses were balanced precariously on the nose. Obviously, neither style was suited for continual use, but rather for short periods of reading. Some early spectacles were held on the nose by a hook affixed to the cap. Eyeglass cases, made of decorated wood, metal, or ivory, were usually hung from the belt. One odd eyeglass case from around 1400 was a receptacle built into a book cover, so the reader could leave his specs behind without fear of breakage.

During the 14th and 15th centuries, glass spectacles gradually came into common use. By the 1360s, we can already find references to "spectacles makers." The increased availability of reading matter that followed Gutenberg's printing press gave the industry a major boost. By 1507, a spectacles-makers' guild was firmly established, with Ven-

ed as a sign of respect, suggesting learning and importance. Contemporary paintings often depicted saints wearing spectacles. A portrait of St. Jerome, painted in 1480 by Domenico Ghirlandajo, showed a pair of spectacles dangling from the saint's desk, although Jerome had died a thousand years earlier. Thus it was that St. Jerome later became the patron saint of the spectacles-makers' guild.

The earliest surviving portrait of a man wearing glasses was a fresco of Hugh of Provence, Cardinal Ugone, painted by Tommaso da Modena in 1352—though the Cardinal died around 1250 without ever learning of eyeglasses.

There was another reason why spectacles were not immediately popular in Europe. Early lenses were always convex, and therefore could not be used by nearsighted persons. Concave lenses for myopia were not to appear for several centuries after the invention of convex optical lenses. The earliest surviving painting depicting concave eyeglasses was a 1516 Raphael portrait of Pope Leo X.

The delay in the development of concave lenses was due more to the practical applications of early eyeglasses than to a lack of

ice and Nuremberg the centers of eyeglass manufacture. Spectacles were now cheap enough that everyone could afford them.

Physicians by and large remained skeptical of eyeglasses, clinging to the older medicinal remedies for poor vision. As late as 1583, Dr. Georg Bartisch of Dresden, one of the most famous oculists of the 16th century, advised patients to do without spectacles. "A person sees and recognizes something better when he has nothing in front of his eyes than when he has something there," the doctor reasoned. "It is much better that one should preserve his two eyes than that he should have four."

In the 16th century, when lenses for myopic persons first appeared, eyeglasses were still selected by trial and error. A person seeking eyeglasses stepped into a spectacles maker's shop, and sampled the wares until he found a pair of specs that seemed appropriate. Spectacles makers scratched a number on each lens they made, to indicate the age of the person they thought the lens would suit. It wasn't until the 18th century that lenses were identified by the radius of curvature.

Toward the later part of that century, spectacles makers began to turn their attention to a means of holding the lenses in front of the eye for longer periods of time. First to appear were spectacles held in place by a strap tied behind the head. Next came glasses with two straps, one to loop around each ear, or spectacles with two weighted cords that were tucked behind the ears and hung almost to the wearer's waist. These latter styles were

particularly popular in Spain. The Chinese preferred similar glasses right up to the 20th century, though until recently, Oriental lenses were made from crystal, rather than ordinary glass.

Sunglasses are nothing new in optometry. Tinted lenses were already in common use during the 16th century. By mid-17th century, amber or mica lenses in several colors were available. Samuel Pepys bought a pair of green spectacles in London during the 1660s, and reported their popularity. It wasn't until around 1885, however, that tinted glass spectacles began to appear.

As the use of spectacles became common among all social groups, class distinctions began to arise in eyeglass design. In England, the upper classes preferred

the single-lens eyeglass, or *perspective glass*, which was usually left dangling from the neck by a ribbon. The poor opted for double-lens eyeglasses, most often sold by itinerant peddlers. Some peddlers touted their wares with a claim that viewing the sun or moon through colored spectacles would bring both improved vision and good luck. In Spain, meanwhile, spectacles of any kind were considered so chic that no fashionable man or woman would be seen without them—whether they were needed or not!

The early 18th century saw the first appearance of spectacles with the now familiar rigid sidepieces, or *bows*. The English called the bows *temples*, since they pressed against the temple of the wearer, and dubbed the spectacles *temple glasses*. In France, advertisers promoted "English style" spectacles, by promising that wearers would "breathe more easily" than they

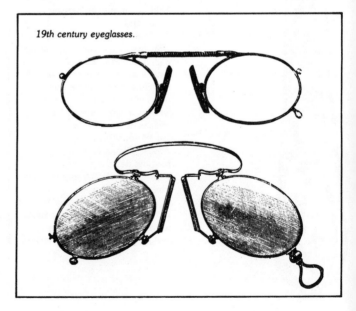

19th century eyeglasses.

146

would with the older, nose-pinching styles.

Scissor glasses were also popular for a time, serving as a compromise for fashion-conscious Europeans who dared not wear double-lens eyeglasses, yet could not see well enough with the more fashionable single eyeglass. Scissor glasses consisted of two lenses joined by a forked handle. When the glasses were held before the eyes, the handle appeared poised to "scissor off" the nose. The spyglass, an earlier invention, also became fashionable—although, for discretion's sake, the spyglass was often hidden in a cane, fan, perfume bottle, or other accessory.

Bifocal lenses were suggested as early as 1716, and may have been first made in London around 1760. However, Benjamin Franklin has generally been credited with their invention. A bifocal lens consists of two semicircular lenses joined together in a frame; the upper portion of the lens corrects for distance viewing, while the bottom half is used for reading. Franklin assembled his first bifocals around 1784, when he tired of carrying around two pairs of spectacles. Bifocal lenses made of fused glass segments did not appear until the 1900s.

Franklin's invention was not without a precedent in nature. The eyes of a tiny tropical fish called the anableps function just like a pair of bifocals. The upper half of each eye is focused for water-surface vision; the lower half for underwater sight.

By the 19th century, European men could wear glasses anywhere, but spectacles remained taboo for fashionable women.

The spyglass was now more diplomatically called an opera glass, due to its nearly universal use at the theater. After the invention of binoculars, in 1823, single and double-lens opera glasses became so popular that a contemporary writer advised: "A bunch of violets, an embroidered handkerchief, a large opera glass, and a bottle of smelling salts—these are the four things a lady of fashion must have at the theater."

The pince-nez—literally, "pinch-nose"—first appeared around 1840, and gradually began to supercede temple glasses. By the end of the century, the pinch-nez was in almost universal use among European and American men, though it was almost never worn by women. The monocle, long associated with aristocratic snobbery, first appeared in England around the beginning of the century, and became all the rage among the European elite— despite warnings from physicians against their use.

By the 1870s, the United States was the world's largest manufacturer of eyeglasses. The trained vision specialist had taken over from the itinerant peddler— though as late as 1960, some Americans still bought their glasses by mail-order. In 1935, the country could boast 10,000 oculists and 22,000 optometrists, with a total annual outlay for glasses topping the $100-million mark. By now, those figures have more than doubled. One of America's largest eyeglass firms, Bausch & Lomb, had its humble beginnings late in the 19th century, when Mr. Bausch sold Mr. Lomb half interest in a supply of miscellaneous optometry equipment for the sum of $66. By 1961, the Bausch & Lomb company alone was selling glasses to the tune of $68 million a year!

147

The terms oculist and optometrist are not interchangeable. An *oculist* is a medical doctor who treats the eyes, while an *optometrist* is an eye-care professional without a medical school degree. An *optician*, meanwhile, is a technician who grinds and sells optical lenses, while an *ophthalmologist* is a medical doctor with several years of specialized training in eye care.

The 20th century marks the first time in history that eyeglasses are fashionably acceptable for any man or woman who needs them. In fact, a 1929 poll found that 53 percent of all spectacles wearers considered their glasses "more or less becoming." Beyond mere social considerations, the most important developments of our century are plastic eyeglasses frames and contact lenses.

Contact lenses—small optical lenses worn directly against the eye—were suggested as early as 1845, by Sir John Herschel, an Englishman. But the first pair of contacts was the work of a German, who constructed a pair of protective lenses for a patient who had lost his eyelids due to cancer. The term *contact lenses* was first used in 1887, by a Swiss doctor named A.E. Fick, but the first pair of contacts did not reach the shores of America for almost 40 years.

In 1938, plastic contact lenses began to replace glass contacts. But until 1950, contact lenses were made to fit over almost the entire eye, with a fluid applied underneath the lens to aid against eye irritation. Today's contact lenses fit over the cornea only, floating on a layer of tears and moving with the eye. Contacts can now be worn by any person who wears eyeglasses, and by some for whom eyeglasses would be useless. The biggest problem contacts wearers now face is finding their lenses, for the average contact is under 10 millimeters in diameter, and usually less than a half-millimeter thick. Incidentally, at present, 65 percent of all contact lens wearers are women.

Sunglasses became all the rage in the United States in 1939, and again after 1947, when *Business Week* called them a "definite style item," reporting that "Hollywood turned them into a fad." The latest word in sunglasses is a lens that darkens or lightens by itself according to the amount of light available.

As anyone who has ever visited a modern optician's shop knows, eyeglasses now come in an almost infinite variety of shapes, utilizing a wide range of materials. Checked or leopard-spotted frames are on the market, as are glasses with one-way lenses—the wearer can see through them, but to anyone else the lenses are mirrors. Glasses have been designed with peekhole-shaped frames, and equipped with roll-down awnings. Fishermen can now purchase goggles that enable them to see through reflections on water, and music lovers can buy glasses fitted with a tiny transistor radio. And grapefruit eaters will be happy to learn that they can purchase a pair of spectacles fitted with miniature, battery-powered windshield wipers!

Many people believe that eyeglasses, exotic or plain, are made for the eyes. This, as we all know, is untrue. As Dr. Pangloss points out in Voltaire's *Candide:* "Noses are made for spectacles; therefore we have spectacles."

Here are a pair of sunglasses with wipers. Powered by a standard battery, these wipers really work. And while this pair will probably turn out to be a hilarious party prank, the water skier and snow skier might find these glasses a boon.

GARLIC

Through most of the 19th century, garlic was so little known to most Americans that a cookbook of the era could recommend that "garlics are better adapted to medicine than cooking."

While there are still many who believe garlic has medicinal, even magical powers, the pungent vegetable has by now found its way into many kitchens in the United States, as Americans discover what their European ancestors have long known: garlic is a useful, flavorful addition to almost any dish.

Garlic is a member of the lily family, and specifically of the *Allium* genus, which also includes the onion, leek, shallot, and chive. We eat only the bulb of this perennial plant. A bulb contains about a dozen cloves, or smaller bulbs, each wrapped in an onionskin-like shell that makes garlic both convenient to use and long-lasting.

Garlic probably first grew in southern Siberia, and it is now found naturally in Central Asia and the Mediterranean. Man has eaten the bulb since earliest times, principally as a flavoring. The Israelites of Biblical times cultivated garlic, and during their exile in Egypt longed for a return to the Promised Land with its bounteous flavorful produce.

The ancient Egyptians also cultivated garlic, though among priests it was considered unclean—no one was permitted to enter an Egyptian temple with garlic on his breath. The workers who toiled on the construction of the Pyramids probably ate garlic and onions in large amounts. The Romans fed garlic to their soldiers in the belief that it promoted strength and courage, but the Senate forbade a Roman to enter the Temple of Sybil after eating the aromatic vegetable. In India, too, garlic was condemned by the priestly class while being enjoyed by the masses.

Our word *garlic* is Anglo-Saxon in origin, a combination of the words *gar* ("spear") and *leac* ("leek"), due to its spearlike leaves. But garlic was by and large spurned in England for centuries, and thus it had little place in the cuisine of early America. The later arrival of large numbers of immigrants from Southern Europe made garlic an American staple—try to find a Mediterranean dish that doesn't include garlic!

Today, about 20 million pounds of garlic are produced in the United States each year, principally in Texas, California, and Louisiana. Argentina is now the world's largest producer, while other nations that cultivate it on a large scale include China, India, Iran, Italy, Spain, and the U.S.S.R. Indeed, garlic is one of the few food items that have long been used in cuisines as diverse as Chinese, Indian, and European.

Garlic is usually employed in small amounts as a flavoring, and therefore it's fortunate that it remains fresh for a long time. Garlic stored in the refrigerator may last as long as 200 days. For those who disdain the chore of

149

slicing garlic or mashing it in a garlic press, there are dehydrated garlic chips, garlic powder, and garlic salt.

A host of legends and superstitions have been attached to garlic in many different cultures. In Europe, garlic has been considered an antidote to witches and vampires, and in some places a clove of garlic was rubbed on an infant's lips at the time of christening. In the Orient, garlic is believed to beautify the complexion and improve the intellect, as well as ward off evil spirits. Peoples from the West and East alike have long regarded it as an aphrodisiac. For a time, garlic was also thought to encourage drinking, as evidenced by a line from the 16th-century English poet Thomas Nashe: "Garlicke maketh a man winke, drinke, and stinke."

Actually, there's some truth to the notion that garlic has medicinal value, for garlic contains an antibiotic and has antiseptic properties. It also promotes elimination and sweating.

But garlic is today far more popular among gastronomists than doctors. Some cooks regard garlic as the most indispensable flavoring item in the kitchen. Among the true garlic lovers we might point to French chef Louis Diat, who wrote that "garlic is the fifth element of living, and as important as earth, air, fire, and water."

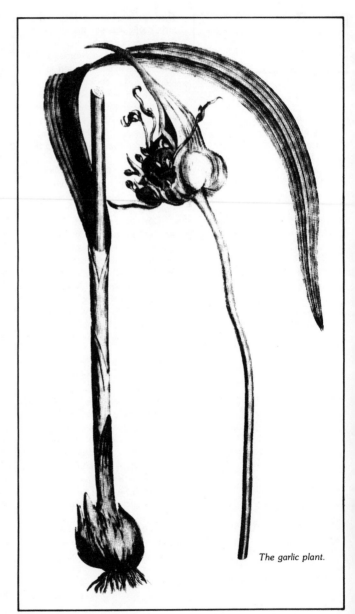

The garlic plant.

150

Hats

Where did you get that hat?
Where did you get that tile?
Where did you get that hat?
Is that the latest style?

It should come as no surprise that the ditty above is the product of another age—the 1890s, in fact. If there is a "latest style" of hat in contemporary America, it's no hat at all. For the first time in centuries, the hat has lost its place in the well-dressed man *and* woman's wardrobe.

That's not to say that Americans don't wear hats to keep themselves warm, or that hats of many styles are not still worn reg-ularly by people around the world. But as a fashion requisite in the Western world, the "tile" has, at least for the time being, fallen into limbo.

Naturally, the hat was worn simply for protection from the rain, sun, and cold long before it became a fashion accessory. But the headdress has also long been a symbol of authority and posi-tion—the warrior's helmet, the bishop's mitre, the king's crown. The significance of the crown is ancient, harkening back to sun worship, for the pointed crown may have originally been a solar emblem.

The first headgear used by primitive man was probably a simple band worn around the head to keep hair from falling in front of the eyes. Ancient peoples in the Mediterranean area wore plaited straw or rushes on their heads to shield them from the sun and rain. In Egypt, ordinary workers wore caps or kerchiefs against the sun, while the wealthy often donned wigs, or curled or braided their hair with beeswax, and wore helmets ornamented with symbols of their rank.

Hats used near the headwaters of the Senegal and Gambia rivers in Africa.

151

Headdress of Chinese woman, Swatow 19th century.

The art of ancient Mesopotamia depicts gods and rulers with tall headdresses, and ordinary men wearing simple caps or no hats at all. By the way, the *beret*, so popular in many countries today, was actually worn in Mesopotamia thousands of years ago. Ninth-century Frankish ruler Charlemagne owned some 500 berets!

European men wore their hair long from the earliest days of recorded history until about the fifth century B.C., then wore their hair short until the end of the Roman Empire, about a thousand years later. Yet neither men nor women in ancient Rome and Greece regularly wore hats. A typical hat of the period was the *petasos*, a flat, circular hat of felt, fur, or leather, similar to the beret. Most of these hats had a band at their edge to keep the hat snuggly on the head; bits of material that protruded from under this band eventually became the hat brim.

In ancient Rome, men's hats were worn mainly by plebians, over short hair. Male slaves were forced to wear their hair long, and a freed slave was often presented with a hat when his hair was shorn. The wealthy wore hats only for hunting and travel, though the Emperor Augustus set a fashion for wearing a lid by always wearing one outdoors.

In military dress, the plumed helmet was common in many parts of the ancient world. Greek helmets often bore horsehair crests, and plumes marked the helmet of the Roman centurion and other officiers. In pre-Columbian Mexico, priests and warriors wore elaborate feather headdresses. North American Indians wore feathered war bonnets, perhaps due to earlier contacts with their southern neighbors. As late as the 18th century, military dress in Europe often featured a tall hat, perhaps ornamented with plumes, to make a soldier appear more formidable to his enemy. A familiar example is the cylindrical *shako*.

Headddress of Papuan.

The expression "a feather in your cap" was first recorded in the 17th century, but feathers in the cap were a sign of nobility more than 500 years earlier. The phrase may be related to the custom of sticking feathers in a soldier's cap to indicate the number of enemy slain.

The Teutonic tribesmen who overran the Roman Empire brought with them round hats edged with fur from the colder regions of Northern Europe. But the hat was still little worn by men and women in the early Middle Ages. Men favored hooded cloaks, while women swaddled their heads in the cloth *wimple* that completely hid their hair. The wimple may owe something to the custom of covering a woman's head in church. (The Christian man bares his head in a place of worship, but the Jewish man covers his.)

The hat remained very much a symbol of rank. Medieval students who had completed a cer-

tain portion of their studies could wear a hat to show that they were no longer subject to their master's rod. In the 13th century, Pope Innocent IV had his cardinals don the scarlet hats they wear today—the color represents the willingness to shed blood for the faith.

Only in the 14th century did the hat truly become part of fashion. Men of the time wore hats shaped like the fez, or brimmed hats remarkably similar to the top hat. The beaver hat first appeared in Flanders, and spread around Europe. Wo-

Fashionable hats of 16th-century Europe.

The most common hat in the world today is the so-called "coolies hat" of China, which is worn by one-third of the people on earth.

153

men's headgear took on fantastic shapes—the tall, conical hat with attached veil, or the "butterfly" headdress with folds of gauze raised above the head on long pins.

In the 16th century, women's hats grew lower, and men's hats regularly took on a brim. But the hat had surely lost some of its association with status; in England, there was a short-lived attempt to force all apprentices to wear wool caps, and in France, an equally abortive effort to force bankrupt merchants to wear a green hat as a warning to prospective customers.

A century later, hats became so chic that they were worn indoors as well as outdoors. Hats with big, floppy brims and feathered plumes came into fashion for men—though Puritans wore hats with stiff, round brims. Styles came and went so quickly that an exasperated King Charles II of England declared no further changes in hat fashion would be permitted at his court.

But of course, that declaration had no effect on fashion. Hats continued to grow and change, reaching the height of their vogue in the 18th century. After that, the gradual shortening of men's hair was eventually to bring in smaller, simpler headgear. One hat of the era was a tiny tricorn worn atop a wig—the smallest we have record of measured just two inches by four inches!

In 1764, a group of dapper English gentlemen formed the Macaroni club, in tribute to the Italian fashions they considered the finest in Europe. The word "macaroni" became associated with English fops in their powdered wigs and fancy hats, and

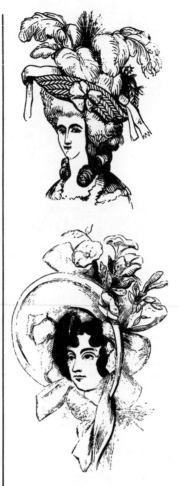

Elaborate hats, 19th century U.S.A.

found its way into that familiar American ditty, *Yankee Doodle*.

Yankee Doodle came to town
Riding on a pony
Stuck a feather in his cap
And called it macaroni.

Italy also gave us the word *millinery*, which now refers to the women's hat industry. The term originally came from *Milaner*, a resident of Milan, since many women's hats were then imported

Ninth-century Frankish ruler Charlemagne owned some 500 berets!

from that city. The term *haberdashery,* which refers to the men's hat industry, probably came from *hapertas,* a kind of cloth used for hats in England and France.

The three-cornered hat, or tricorn, was the universal men's hat in Europe for most of the 18th century. But after the French Revolution, the tricorn was abolished in France in favor of smaller, round hats. These new hats were considered so subversive in the rest of Europe that Russian Czar Paul I gave their wearers a paid vacation in Siberia.

In the 19th century, the shiny black top hat became *de rigueur* for the well-dressed gentleman.

Ladies' bonnets of the 19th century.

A ten-gallon hat, in case you've wondered, can hold about three quarts.

Silk top hat

Straw boater

Derby

Lady's cowboy hat, as shown in a Montgomery Ward Catalog *of the 1890s.*

Gorgeous Easter bonnet of the 1880s, as depicted in Leslie's Magazine.

Various caps and head coverings shown in a Montgomery Ward Catalog *of the 1800s.*

Scene inside a hat factory as pictured in Harper's *in the 1880s.*

Women's hats grew large and showy, with jewels and flowers for occasional ornament. King George III of England helped things along by decreeing that all hats must bear on their linings the name of their maker. By 1850, a writer could confidently declare that the hat had reached its "ultimate degree of excellence."

It may have also reached its ultimate degree of uniformity. Modern hats are made from all kinds of materials, in all kinds of styles, from all around the world—but no single style predominates. Most of the hat styles

of today are from another land or another age.

For instance, you wear a bit of history when you don a fedora, a bowler hat, or a derby. The soft felt, creased *fedora* owes its name to a 1882 production of French playright Sardou's *Fedora*, in which a Russian princess wore such a hat. The *bowler* owes nothing to the kegler. It was named after William Bowler, the English hatter who, around 1850, introduced it as a hard-shelled headgear for horsemen. In the United States, the hat came to be known as the *derby*, after a

famous horse race held in Derby, England.

The *shapka*, the Russian fur hat, originated in the Cossacks' sheepskin hat. Early in the 16th century, it was introduced in England by a Russian ambassador. The felt *Homburg* owes its name not to Hamburg, but to a German town called Homburg where it was first made. The *Panama* hat, made from the leaves of the jijippa plant, has never been made in Panama. Most are manufactured in Ecuador, Colombia, or Peru, but the hat originally reached America through distributors in Panama.

Another South American hat, the *chola derby*—popular among the Indians—may have originated

157

when a bankrupt hat dealer dumped his derbies on the Indians, after other South Americans had spurned them. The Mexican *sombrero,* usually made of felt or straw, owes its name to the Spanish word *sombra,* "shade," for reasons obvious to anyone who's been south of the border. The Spanish *mantilla,* or woman's scarf, probably evolved from the Moorish headscarf.

The colorful *tam-o'-shanter* with its center tassel became popular in Scotland during the 19th century, and was named after a character in a poem by Robert Burns. It's actually a form of an old Celtic hat. The Scottish *glengarry,* creased lengthwise and ornamented with ribbons in the back, was named after a valley in Scotland. The expression "hold on to your hat" may also have originated in Scotland. In the 18th century, Scottish soldiers were exhorted to keep their hats on in battle so that they would recognize one another.

In the East, the *turban* has been the customary headgear for many centuries. The color and shape of a turban has historically indicated rank or occupation. The

French ladies' hats around 1900.

Headdress of South America near Lake Titicaca.

Indian turbans, 19th century.

longest turbans may contain more than 20 feet of material. Some Hindu turbans also contained a circular metal blade that could be hurled at an enemy.

Among Arabs, the common headdress is the *kaffiyeh,* a piece of cloth folded in a triangular shape and secured to the head with a round cord. Another hat from the Near East, the *fez,* was popular as long ago as the 11th century. Most fezes are made from red felt. In a 1920s attempt to Westernize Turkey, the fez was abolished as part of that country's national dress; tradition-conscious Turks who insisted on wearing the hat changed their minds after a few fez wearer's were led to the gallows.

The most common hat in the world today is the so-called "coolies hat" of China, which is worn by one-third of the people on earth. The wide-brimmed hat is made from bamboo, with leaves as padding. The oldest hat in the world may well be the familiar "chef's" hat, which was worn in ancient Assyria as a badge of office in the kitchen. And the most expensive headdress in the world is a hat worn by Napoleon, which recently sold at auction for a handsome $30,000.

Hats of the Malay Archipelago.

The straw hat was first produced in America in 1798, by a 12-year-old girl in Rhode Island. The first hat factory in the United States, opened in Connecticut late in the 18th century, produced crude fur caps. One kind of hat that is distinctly American is the broad-brimmed ten-gallon hat still popular in the Southwest. A ten-gallon hat, in case you've wondered, can hold about three quarts.

If you're thinking of buying a ten-gallon hat in Kentucky, you might be advised that a law still on the books in that state forbids a man to buy a hat without his wife along to assist in the selection.

Who can tell if the hat will make a comeback on the American fashion scene? For hat styles, like all others, rarely remain popular for long—even if that style is no hat at all. As Shakespeare noted, "as the fashion of his hat, it ever changes."

Besides, as an old ballad points out:

*Any cap, whate'er it may be
Is still the sign of some degree.*

The *Panama* hat, made from the leaves of the jijippa plant, has never been made in Panama.

Ice Cream

True or false: (1) Ice cream will cool you off on a hot summer day; (2) Americans invented the dessert; (3) Since mechanical refrigeration techniques were not developed until late in the 19th century, ice cream is obviously a recent arrival to man's dessert table.

Americans presently consume over a billion gallons of ice cream, ices, and sherbet each year—enough to completely fill the Grand Canyon.

If you answered "false" to all three of the above statements, you've proved you really have the scoop on man's favorite frosty confection. In fact, three answers of TRUE would place you among the majority of Americans, who are ice-cold when it comes to the finer points of ice cream lore.

First, ice cream is not a cooler. Oh, it may cool your taste buds momentarily, and its psychological effect may convince you that you're cooling off. But ice cream is chock-full of calories, the unit of measurement of heat. So the ultimate effect of a bowlful of ice cream is to make you warmer, not cooler!

Modern American refrigeration techniques and ice cream infatuation notwithstanding, the frozen dessert is neither a recent concoction nor a product of Yankee ingenuity. Most historians would trace the first bowl of ice cream to 15th- or 16th-century Italy, or perhaps England, but the story of ice cream's rise to gustatory prominence is a good deal more interesting than a simple date.

In ancient Rome, the Emperor Nero had snow transported from nearby mountains to cool his wine cellar, and reportedly concocted some of the first water-ice desserts by mixing the snow with honey, juices, and fruit. But the first frozen dessert made from milk didn't reach Europe until the 13th century, when Marco Polo returned from the Orient with a recipe for a milk-ice, presumably similar to sherbet.

Improvements in ice- and sherbet-making probably led to the invention of ice cream some time in the 16th century. We know that early in that century Italian noblemen were enjoying a frozen milk product called "flower of milk." Yet Anglophiles may proudly point to a 15th-century manuscript reporting on the coronation of Henry V that mentions a dessert called *creme frez*. If creme frez was indeed ice cream, then the manuscript proves that the reputedly Italian invention was actually being made in England before the 16th century.

Italian ice cream arrived in France in 1533, along with Catherine de Medici and her retinue of chefs, when the 14- year-old Florentine moved to Paris to marry King Henry II. For many years, the chefs of various French noblemen tried to keep their recipes for ice cream a secret from other chefs—and from their masters, who were frequently astounded by their cooks' talent for serving a cold dessert even in the warmest weather.

Ice cream remained a treat for the rich and regal until 1670, when Paris's first café, the *Procope,* opened its doors and made the frigid dessert available to the masses for the first time. Other cafés quickly followed— including the *Café Napolitain,* whose proprietor, a Monsieur Tortoni, concocted the creamy delight that still bears his name.

The first mention of ice cream in America occurs in 1700, but the dessert was not made here in any quantity until much later in the century. Both George Washington and Thomas Jefferson were known to be ice cream fanciers. Jefferson, who had learned how to make French ice cream during a visit to France, was one of the first officials to serve the confection at a state dinner. Jefferson once served a dessert of crisp, hot pastry with ice cream in the middle, perhaps the first ice cream sandwich in America.

Ice cream remained an expensive dish until the early 19th century, which saw the invention of the insulated icehouse and the hand-crank ice cream freezer. By the 1820s, the dessert was being sold by street vendors in New York City, who beckoned passersby with shouts of "I scream ice cream."

By the middle of the century, ice cream was so popular that a magazine editor was moved to write: "A party without ice cream would be like a breakfast without bread or a dinner without a roast."

The father of the American ice cream industry was Jacob Fussell. Beginning in 1851 with a small ice cream store in Baltimore, Fussell was soon selling his wares in shops from Boston to Washington. During the Civil War, Fussell sold huge quantities of ice cream to the Union army. By the end of the century, ice cream could be bought almost anywhere in the nation. New inventions such as steam power, mechanical refrigeration, electricity, and the homogenizer made the ice cream plant virtually as modern as it is today.

In the early decades of this century, the popularity of the soda fountain made ice cream an American institution. Temperance preachers urged listeners to give up the grape in favor of the cool confection. Baseball star Walter Johnson—no relation to Howard —boasted that all he ever ate on the day he was to pitch was a quart of ice cream.

Beginning in 1921, officials at the Ellis Island immigration station in New York, intent on serving the newcomers a "truly American dish," included ice cream in all meals served at the station.

By that time, the three mainstays of the ice cream parlor—the soda, the sundae, and the cone—were already popular from coast to coast. The first to appear was the ice cream soda. In 1874, a soda-fountain manufacturer by the name of Robert M. Green was busily vending a cool drink made of sweet cream, syrup, and carbonated water (now known as the egg cream) at the semicentennial celebration of Philadelphia's Franklin Institute. One day, Green ran out of cream and substituted vanilla ice cream. The new treat quickly became a sensation. Green went on to make a fortune selling ice cream sodas. His will dictated that "Originator

Ice cream freezer, circa 1870.

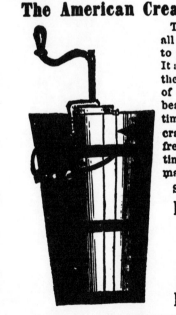
161

of the Ice Cream Soda" be engraved on his tombstone.

The ice cream sundae emerged during the 1890s, and there are many claims for its invention. Contemporary laws forbade the sale of soda on Sunday, and this, undoubtedly, had a hand in popularizing the dessert. The first sundaes were sold in ice cream parlors only on Sunday, and thus were called "Sundays" or "soda-less sodas." The spelling change to "sundae" was made later by ice cream parlor proprietors eager to see the dish shed its Sunday-only connotation.

The best-known explanation for the invention of the ice cream

cone traces its origin to the 1904 Louisiana Purchase Exposition in St. Louis. According to the tale, an ice cream salesman by the name of Charles E. Menches gave an ice cream sandwich and a bouquet of flowers to the young lady he was escorting. She rolled one of the sandwich wafers into a cone to hold the flowers, then rolled the other wafer into a cone for the ice cream.

Ice cream parlors were an integral part of American life early in the 20th century. In these emporia, busy soda jerks developed a lingo all their own. *Adam's ale*, for instance, was water, while *belch water* meant seltzer. *A pair of drawers* could mean only two cups of coffee.

Fortunes were made in the ice cream trade during the heyday of

the soda fountain. Louis Sherry, a Frenchman from Vermont, began his career as a famed restauranteur when he was granted the ice cream concession at the Metropolitan Opera House in New York.

In 1925, Howard Johnson—the father of American franchisers—opened his first ice cream store in Wollaston, Massachusetts. Johnson, incidentally, once sold 14,000 ice cream cones in a single day at his Wollaston Beach stand.

In 1921, the *Eskimo pie* was introduced in Des Moines, Iowa, by the same Russell Stover who was to go on to fame and fortune in the candy trade. The *Good Humor*, meanwhile, was the handiwork of one Harry Burt, and ice cream parlor owner from Youngstown, Ohio. Before starting out in the ice cream business, Burt had sold a lollypop he called the *Good Humor Sucker*. The

bright idea to mount a chocolate-
covered Eskimo pie on a lollypop
stick led to ice-cream-on-a-stick,
and the familiar white wagons
that still ply our streets with their
tinkling bells. Good Humor bars
are now sold in most supermarkets as well.

Today, the manufacture of ice
cream is, of course, mechanized.
Factories first produce a liquid
product made of 80 percent
cream or butterfat, milk, and
nonfat milk solids, and about
15 percent sweeteners. Next they
pasteurize, homogenize, whip,
and partially freeze the mixture.
Then flavoring is added, and they
freeze the product in its
containers at temperatures of
about 240 degrees below zero.
The finished product is frequently

as rich in vitamins as an
equivalent amount of milk.

Frozen mousse is a cold
dessert made from sweetened
whipped cream, flavoring, and
gelatin. *Sherbet* consists of milk,
sweeteners, and fruit flavoring,
while *Italian Ices* is made from
fruit juices, water, and sweeteners. *French ice cream* is definitely
different from other varieties: in
this country, only ice cream made
with eggs can legally be sold as
"French."

The quality of ice cream products differs greatly from brand to
brand, due to such factors as the
amount of fresh milk, cream, or
eggs used, the naturalness of the
flavoring ingredients, and the presence of preservatives and synthetic flavor and texture
enhancers.

Americans presently consume
over a billion gallons of ice
cream, ices, and sherbet each
year—enough to completely fill
the Grand Canyon. Americans
are by far the world's largest consumers of ice cream. The average
person in the United States puts
away about 23 quarts each
year—that's roughly equivalent to
a cone per person every other
day. Only Australians, Cana-
dians, and New Zealanders eat
even half that much. Compare
that figure with the average yearly consumption of 100 years
ago—about one teaspoon per
person!

Only in America, then, could
you expect to find the largest ice
cream sundae of all time. The
3,956-pound monster, concocted
in McLean, Virginia in 1975,
contained 777 gallons of ice
cream, six gallons of chocolate
syrup, over a gallon of whipped
cream, and a case of chocolate

163

"The Soda Fountain" by William Glackens.
Courtesy of the Pennsylvania Academy of Fine Arts.

164

sprinkles. The world's largest popsicle, meanwhile, was a paltry 2,800 pounds.

The largest banana split ever thrown together—measured one mile in length and contained 33,000 scoops of ice cream and over 10,000 bananas! This whopper was the pride and joy of a St. Paul, Minnesota ice cream parlor.

Most ice cream stores today point with pride, not to the size of their wares, but to the sheer length of their flavor list. The Baskin Robbins company lists over 300 flavors in its repertoire, and the number is still climbing—though you'll have a tough time finding half that many in any one store. The winner of the Baskin Robbins America's Favorite Flavor Contest, by the way, was Chocolate Mint ice cream.

The modern ice cream maker will go to any length to outdo the competition with bizarre new taste treats, and novelty flavors such as *iced tea, bubblegum, root beer,* and *mango* ice cream. The newcomers occasionally outsell the old standbys—*vanilla* and *chocolate.*

But don't think that exotic flavors belong solely to the modern ice cream maker. A recipe book dating from 1700 shows that even at that date, French confectioners were turning out such tempting ice cream flavors as *apricot, violet,* and *rose!*

These are just a few of the ice cream concoctions offered by The Flick Ice Cream Parlor *in New York City in 1978.*

SUNDAES

Large Sundae / $2.25

Your choice of 2 flavors ice cream, topping, nuts,
whipped cream and cherry

Extra-Large Sundae / $3.95

4 scoops ice cream, topping, nuts,
whipped cream and cherry

Gibson Girl / $3.95

4 scoops mixed ice cream,
butterscotch sauce, wet walnuts,
whipped cream and burgundy cherry

A Sherbet Delight / $3.95

Fresh fruit topped with
Flick orange and lemon sherbet

Fresh Fruit Flick Delight / $3.95

Giant bowl of fresh fruit,
your choice of 2 flavors of ice cream,
whipped cream and cherry

Flaming Desire / $3.95

4 scoops of ice cream of your choice, topping,
whipped cream and burgundy cherry.
Set aflame and served to delight you

Mission Impossible / $4.25

Egg nog, rum raisin and
burgundy cherry ice cream
topped with hot fudge, marshmallow,
butterscotch, crushed pineapple,
whipped cream and cherry

Virgin's Delight / $3.95

Vanilla, cherry-vanilla,
and cocoanut ice cream
with a blanket of marshmallow sauce,
whipped cream and red cherry

Initials!

It took mankind a long, long time to convert spoken language into written form. Even today, there are more languages which exist only in spoken form than there are languages with a written form.

The first writings of man consisted of pictures, which gradually became conventionalized. This kind of ideographic writing still exists in our numerals, and in Chinese and Japanese writing.

The alphabet was the last stage in the development of writing. The term *alphabet* comes from the first two letters of Greek—*alpha* and *beta*.

The Roman alphabet, which is used for most European languages, and also for the newly-written languages of Africa, consists of 26 letters.

Other alphabets are the Greek alphabet (on which the Roman alphabet was originally based) which contains 24 letters; the Cyrillic alphabet used for the Russian, Serbian, and Bulgarian languages, which contains 32 letters; the Hebrew alphabet which contains 27 letters; the Arabic alphabet which contains 28 letters.

Indian languages, such as Sanskrit, use the Bevanjari alphabet, while other Oriental languages use a system of characters devised from the Chinese characters.

For centuries, fancy letters have been devised to lend interest to stories and titles. Some of the more remarkable effusions of the 19th century follow. These pieces of art are now in the public domain, and may be used freely by anyone.

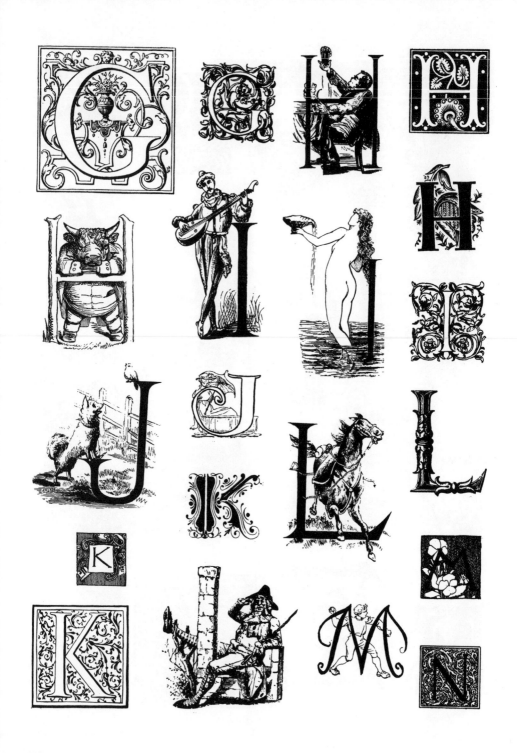

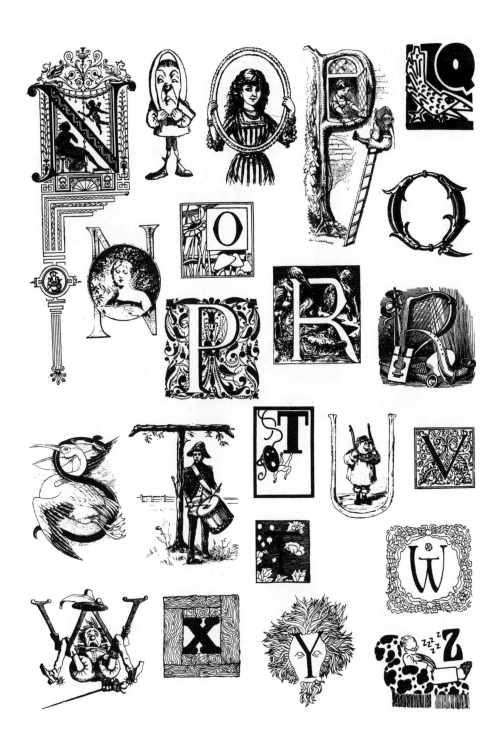

LEVIATHANS

"This is the sea, broad and wide," said the Psalmist. "There go the ships, and this leviathon which Thou has created to disport himself therein."

Since then, and long before, the whale has been a subject of enormous curiosity to man, and myriads of legends and fantasies have grown about this huge beast. There are many species of whales extant, and they differ in interesting ways. Here are a number of these behemoths of the seas:

COMMON WHALE *Like all members of the whale family, this sea creature is warm-blooded and breathes with lungs. The flippers are actually mammalian hands, not fins.*

BLUNT-HEADED CACHALOT *Cachalot is another name for the sperm whale, the largest of all toothed whales. All sperm whales are in fact "blunt-headed."*

WHITE WHALE *The adult of this species is pure white all over, while the young are brown or gray. Most adults measure about 18 feet in length.*

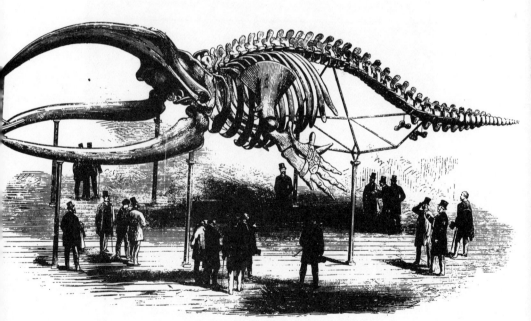

Skeleton of a whale, as depicted in the Illustrated London News.

BOTTLE-NOSED WHALE *This toothed in-habitant of the North Atlantic prefers cut-tlefish as its food. The largest males may mea-sure over 30 feet in length.*

SPERM WHALE *The male sperm whale may measure over 60 feet in length, but the female rarely exceeds 35 feet. The sperm whale lives primarily in tropical waters, unlike most whales, and may descend up to 10,000 feet in search of food.*

172

ATLANTIC RIGHT WHALE *Also called the Biscay whale, this toothless creature averages about 60 feet in length. It lives in the Atlantic near northern Europe, and visits the eastern United States.*

HUMPBACK WHALE *This mammal is found in all the world's seas. The average length is 50 to 60 feet. Humpback whales can communicate with each other from hundreds of miles apart by means of a low-pitched cry.*

LOCKS

Along with the many other advances that have paralleled the evolution of civilization, the progress of man's history has seen a continual improvement of the resourcefulness of two professionals: the locksmith and the burglar. Almost every advance in the locksmith's craft has been matched by a corresponding refinement in the trade of those who covet their neighbor's goods—or vice versa, depending on your point of view.

And the battle of wits between the locksmith and the burglar is far from over: though the former might maintain that many a modern lock is foolproof, and many a haven totally safe, every year burglaries abound.

The use of a lock of some sort probably dates from the time man first acquired goods he wanted to safeguard. But the use of locks among ancient peoples was limited, for a number of reasons.

First of all, most families had few valuables to guard, and had little reason to leave their home untended for any length of time. Most ancient peoples lived in small communities of friends and relatives, where theft was easily detectable and swiftly punished. Since most homes were one-story, and windows lacked glass, a locked door would accomplish little in deterring a determined

thief. Even if a strong lock could be attached to a door, the door itself was often so flimsy that it could be battered down easily, whether locked or not.

Early locks were used mainly by the rich, or by officials to prevent unauthorized entry of a temple or government building. From earliest times right up until today, the essential element of most locks is the *bolt*, the metal or wooden bar that fixes the door to the doorpost and prevents the door from opening. All advances in the locksmith's craft have been primarily in strengthening that bolt, and improving the mechanism that opens and closes it.

The oldest surviving locks were found in the ruined palace of Khorsabad, built by the Assyrians in the eighth century B.C. But locks of similar design were used by the Egyptians more than 4,000 years ago, and may be much older, for their counterparts have been found in places far from the Middle East, among them Norway and Japan. This Egyptian lock was simple in design, and made entirely of wood, but was in principle remarkably similar to the pin tumbler locks we rely on today.

The Egyptian lock consisted of a vertical wooden bar, or *staple*, affixed to the doorpost, and a wooden crossbar, or bolt. The bolt fit into a groove in the staple to lock the door. Pins pro-

The simplest of all true locks.

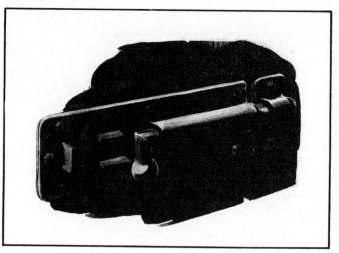

The key to an ancient Egyptian lock and an X-ray picture of an Egyptian lock with the key inside it.

jecting downward from the staple fit into holes in the bolt, and held it firmly in place.

To open the lock, the Egyptians used a huge wooden key, shaped like a toothbrush with a set of wooden pegs in place of bristles. These pegs corresponded to the pegs of the staple. The key was inserted through a hole in the bolt; when the key was levered upward, its pins passed through the matching holes in the bolt and pushed the staple's pins upward and out of the holes, thereby freeing the bolt.

In the homes of the anicent Greeks, as in those of the earlier Mesopotamian peoples, doors and windows usually faced inward on an open courtyard, with only one outer door providing access from the street. To protect this door from would-be thieves, the Greeks designed locks that were intended more for the detection of thievery than for its prevention. One lock of this type consisted of a bolt that was tied to the doorpost with a rope in an intricate knot. A thief could never hope to untie the knot and retie it in exactly the same way, so the owner would always know when the lock had been tampered with.

175

And in those days, discovery meant certain death to the culprit.

Another type of Greek lock utilized a key the size and shape of a sickle, and featured the first known use of the keyhole. The hooked key was inserted through a hole in the door so that the end of the hook fit into a groove in the bolt. A simple twist of the key's handle would turn the hooked end and slide open the bolt. The heavy key, which was up to three feet long, had the added advantage of doubling as weapon.

The Romans were the first to use a metal lock, fabricating the key from bronze and the locking mechanism from iron. The iron has long since disintegrated, leaving us only the keys. Roman keys were sometimes cut with *wards,* notches that align with corresponding ridges inside the lock. In the days before the pocket, the Romans also invented ring keys that could be carried on the finger. Many Romans used the older Egyptian-style wooden locks; these ancient devices are still in use today in some parts of the Middle East. Duplicate Roman keys, by the way, were called "adulterous," probably for more than one reason.

The Romans, along with the Hindus, Chinese, and others, developed the earliest portable lock, or *padlock.* Many padlocks were adorned with elaborate designs of animals and geometric figures, and inlaid with precious metals. The word "padlock" has been linked to the footpad, or highwayman, whose sticky fingers might delve into an untended saddlebag. But the word probably comes directly from *pad,* a Dutch word for a path or road, since the padlock was most often used to safeguard goods while traveling.

In medieval Europe, the doors of most peasant huts were secured by a simple latch that could be opened by sliding a finger or lever through a hole in the door. These latches might secure a door against the wind, but were no proof against thievery. Medieval castles relied more on the brute strength of their locks than on their complexity. The main gates of most castles were secured by a huge wooden latch that required several men to set in place and remove. In many castles, it was easier to scale the walls than to batter down the doors.

Inside the castle, the door to almost every room was fitted with a lock, as were many chests and strongboxes. So, a special attendant was required to guard all the keys—including those to the dun-

The latch on these great doors is a huge hand-hewn plank, weighing hundreds of pounds.

geon. This attendant was called the "keeper of the castle" or *chatelain.* The feminine form of the word, *chatelaine,* is still used for a woman's ornamental chain, especially one worn around the waist.

Locks of the Middle Ages and Renaissance often offered more in the way of decorative beauty than security. Most locks employed intricately designed keyways and obstructions around the keyhole to prevent opening with a pick or false key. Since these locks were often undependable, some featured other discouragements to unauthorized opening: sharp blades inside the keyhole, bullet-firing mechanisms activated by the opening bolts, or knives that sprang toward an intruder. From the East came the puzzle lock, with hidden keyholes and buttons to foil the thief. Other locks were fitted with counters that recorded the number of times the lock had been opened. Such a lock couldn't prevent a burglary, but would indicate readily enough if one had been attempted or committed.

English King Henry VIII included a massive gold-plated lock among his traveling baggage. Whenever the wary monarch stopped for the night, he had a carpenter screw the lock to his bedroom door. In the morning, the lock was removed. The king's precautions evidently paid off: his bedroom remained inviolate and he died at the age of 56 from "a surfeit of quinces."

The history of the modern lock began in the 18th century with the invention of the lever tumbler, which made the lock-picker's work much more difficult. With a lever tumbler lock, the key disengages one or more spring-actuated safety devices that fit into notches in the bolt. Still, burglars kept pace with their gimlets, hacksaws, drills, pass-keys, and picks. And too often, they succeeded.

In 1817, British authorities were so fed up with thievery at the Portsmouth Dockyard that they offered a sizeable cash prize to anyone who could invent a cheap unpickable lock. The winning design was the work of one Jeremiah Chubb. To test Chubb's lock, the government presented it to an imprisoned locksmith and lock-picker, and offered him a pardon if he succeeded in opening the lock. After 10 weeks of effort, the convict had to admit defeat.

Chubb's lock employed six control levers that had to be raised to an exact height by the key. The lock was considered

pickproof because if one of the
levers was raised too far by a
thief's tampering—which was inevitable no matter how skillful the
thief—a set of springs would immediately lock all the levers in
place. The key would then be
needed to reset the lock before it
could be opened. In more than
150 years since Chubb's lock was
invented, it has never been successfully picked!

Evidently, not all locks of the
era were fitted with Chubb's device. A skilled lock-picker jailed in
London's Newgate Prison managed to open not only his cell
door, but four additional doors
and gates that led to freedom.
Once outside the prison, however, the convict lost his nerve
and decided to return to his
cell—picking all five locks a second time on his return trip!

The first lock and key that
we would recognize as modern
was the work of the American
Linus Yale—whose name is still
to be found on keys. Invented in
1861, the device was called the
pin tumbler cylinder lock, or
more simply, the cylinder lock.
It consisted of a cylinder with an
attached bar that passed through
a hole in the door and activated
a bolt on the inside. The cylinder
itself consisted of two cylinders,
one inside the other. Pins of various lengths in the outer cylinder
fit into holes in the inner cylinder,
preventing it from turning.

The key for a cylinder lock
was cut with ridges that lifted
the pins out of their holes, and
allowed the inner cylinder to turn
and thereby open the bolt. By
varying the lengths of the pins,
and the corresponding heights of
the key ridges, over 36,000 variations could be obtained. In other

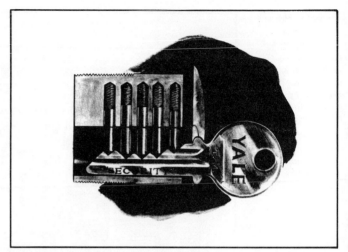

Compare this modern tumbler lock with the large lock used in ancient Egypt.

To open up this padlock, you must line up the four code letters properly.

words, only one key in every
36,000 was identical!

Linus Yale was also credited
with reintroducing the combination lock, which had been used in
China for many centuries. The
older combination lock consisted
of a series of numbered or let-
tered rings revolving around a
bolt. Openings within the rings
had to be aligned perfectly by the
"combination" before the bolt

could be withdrawn. But burglars
developed a skill for opening
these locks with a delicate touch
and a sensitive ear. In 1947,
Harry C. Miller invented a combination lock that was considered
manipulation-proof. In the modern combination lock, revolving

wheels are hidden inside the lock, and turned by a single outer wheel marked with numbers or letters.

Modern locks are basically of six kinds. The *rim* lock fits directly on the surface of the door, with the bolt on the inside and the keyhole on the outside. The modern drop-bolt lock is one example.

The *mortise* lock fits into a cavity within the door, and its bolt slides into an opening in the door frame.

The *key-in-doorknob* lock features, not surprisingly, a keyhole set in the doorknob.

A *cabinet* lock is the kind of simple lock often fitted on cabinet doors or jewelry boxes.

An *electric switch* lock completes an electric circuit when the key is turned; an automobile ignition cylinder is one example. And a *padlock* is familiar to almost anyone who's owned a bicycle or utilized a locker room. The largest padlock in existence, by the way, is manufactured by an English firm, and weighs 100 pounds!

Burglars have shown an equal disregard for all six types of lock, forcing locksmiths to design a number of other kinds for places where security is paramount. Safe-deposit boxes in banks are protected by a lock that requires two keys, one provided to the box holder and the other kept by a security guard. Similar in principle is the master key lock, which employs a separate set of pin tumblers that can be opened by a master key. This kind of lock is often used in hotels, where a chambermaid needs access to a room when the occupant is out.

Banks, naturally, employ the most sophisticated locking mechanisms. The doors of some bank vaults are actually huge locks, equipped with a number of combination dials that must each be

This streamlined padlock and bar offer no starting place for a burglar's tools.

opened by a different person. The odds against guessing the correct combination of just one dial are about 100 million to one. And if you're thinking about lifting one of these vault doors off its hinges, you might keep in mind that such a door may weigh 20 tons!

In 1874, the first *time* lock was installed on the vault of a bank in Morrison, Illinois, and time locks have been widely used in banks ever since. A time lock is fitted with a series of watch movements, and will open only at a predetermined time—no matter how dire the threats of a would-be bank robber and how shaky the knees of the bank employees.

Still, the burglar has not admitted defeat. If the lock of a vault or safe is foolproof, there's always the option of blowing the door away with explosives, or using an acetylene torch to remove the entire locking mechanism. Locksmiths and safe manufacturers have responded by

building safes encased in a metal alloy that can resist even the flame of an acetylene torch!

But few of us can afford the kind of locks used by banks, jewelry stops, and other storehouses of valuables. So most people have decided, like their Greek forefathers, that detection is as good as prevention: more money is now being spent on burglar alarms than on locks.

Fortunately, the best lockpicker in history was not a burglar, but a magician. Harry Houdini, the renowned escape artist, sometimes had himself bound in chains and manacles, placed inside a locked chest, and dropped into water. But he always managed to unfasten the chains and manacles, open the box, and emerge smiling. No locksmith who examined Houdini's equipment ever claimed that the magician used trick locks. To this day, no one knows how Houdini opened his locks, and no one likely ever will.

If nothing else, Houdini proved that, no matter the circumstances, no matter the lock, anything that can be locked with a key can be opened without one.

179

Love

As one wag has put it, love is a ticklish sensation around the heart that can't be scratched. Artists all over the world have got into the act, and here are some of their effusions.

"Hearts Aflutter," by an artist who drew for Harper's Magazine in the 1890s.

From the American magazine of humor, Life, published in the early 1900s.

From Bab Ballads by the famous W.S. Gilbert, the one who cooperated with Sullivan.

From Life, American humorous magazine of the early 1900s.

Drawing by Honore Daumier, noted French satirical artist.

"The Attack Direct," drawn by Ronald Searle, well-known British artist, in 1950 for a book called The Female Approach.

These drawings are from the world famous
English magazine of humor, Punch.

From Art of the Book, *a Russian publication.*

"A Modern Approach" *by a Russian artist, contained in* Fifty Years of Soviet Art.

Love among the bourgeoisie of the 19th century, according to this artist who drew for *Leslie's Magazine.*

Marsupials

Of course, you know what a marsupial is—a mammal that carries its young in a natural pouch on its stomach. The kangaroo comes immediately into mind, and so does Australia.

But there are many other marsupials in addition to the kangaroo, and not all are indigenous to Australia or to the adjacent islands. The opossum, for example, lives right here in North America.

All marsupials do have one thing in common: the extraordinary way in which they bear their young. Baby marsupials are incompletely developed, and very small—a newborn kangaroo may be only an inch long! The young nurse for several months within their mother's pouch, or marsupium, to complete their development.

The Australian marsupials were virtually unknown until Captain James Cook visited Australia in 1770. When Cook saw his first kangaroo, he thought he'd found a gigantic leaping rodent. We now know that the marsupials form their own order within the mammal family, an order that includes some of the most unusual looking creatures on earth.

BANDICOOT *This rabbitlike marsupial spends most of the day inside his burrow, emerging at night to feed on worms and insects. Bandicoots are fairly pugnacious, and fight by leaping into the air and striking at each other with their hind feet. There are about a dozen species, all native to Austrailia and adjacent islands.*

OPOSSUM *The most familiar American marsupial, the opossum, has given his name to the defensive ploy of playing dead when threatened by a predator—though a number of other animals similarly "play possum." This cowardly creature, one of the most prolific of mammals, bears two or three litters each year, with as many as 18 bee-sized babies in each litter.*

KOALA *This small Australian native looks just like a toy teddy bear. But he gets his name from an aboriginal term meaning "no water," for this cute creature never drinks water in his entire life. He's a fussy eater, though: A koala will eat only the leaves of the eucalyptus tree, and spends almost all his time in one of these trees, munching on the leaves.*

WALLABY *The wallaby is more closely related to the kangaroo than any of the other marsupials. In fact, many of the larger wallabies are commonly called kangaroos or bush kangaroos in their homeland, Australia. The smaller wallabies are about the size of a rabbit. They spend their days in rock crevices, and feed on grass at night.*

TASMANIAN DEVIL *This strong, carnivorous marsupial has proved a devil to many Australian sheep and poultry farmers. About the size of a badger, with large, powerful jaws, the Tasmanian devil spends his days in his burrow, and comes out at night to hunt.*

MARMOSET *A close relative of the opossum found in South and Central America.*

WOMBAT *Often called "native badgers" because of their strength and burrowing abilities, wombats are closely related to another Australian marsupial, the koala. This shy, gentle herbivore can grow up to three feet in length.*

185

Music & Musical Instruments

The world is full of music. Everybody loves music and many people play instruments. Here are two pages of musicians as depicted in the world's great humor magazines and publications.

Art Nouveau, U.S.A.

Harper's, U.S.A.

Grandville in *Un Autre Monde, France*

Gebrauchgraphik, Germany

Wilhelm Butch Album, Germany

Comic Almanac, England

Harper's, U.S.A.

Quaint Cuts, U.S.A.

Grandfather's Moneybox, U.S.S.R.

Throughout the centuries, man has attempted to make better and newer and weirder musical instruments, the better to celebrate his joy.

The *Appolonicon* was a gigantic instrument which could be made to sound like a symphony orchestra. First played publicly in London in 1817, the Appolonicon was played automatically or manually. The brilliant arrangement of its five keyboards enabled five persons to play a composition together.

The largest stringed instrument ever constructed for a single player was a *pantaleon* played by George Noel in England in 1767. Played with wooden mallets like a xylophone, the instrument consisted of 276 gut and metal strings stretched over a horizontal soundboard which was 11 feet long by five feet wide.

Since the violin was introduced in the 1600s, several devices have been invented for playing the instrument automatically. But the only one to vibrate the strings with a bow was the *violonista*, which could be found in penny arcades in the early 1920s. The machine was about three feet long, two feet high, and two feet wide, It was electrically operated and controlled by air flowing through the perforations of a music roll.

A certain Austrian by the name of Karl Waetzel, who lived during the last century, had a particularly inventive turn of mind. He built a fabulous conglomeration of musical instruments which he called the *panomonico*, an instrument which could be played by a single person. The panomonico included 150 flageolets, 150 flutes, 50 oboes, 18 trumpets, five fanfares, three drums, and two kettledrums. The whole thing totaled 378 instruments. Waetzel's fantastic invention was purchased by Archduke Charles of Austria. The irony was that the Duke used the panomonico not to produce beautiful music, but for the purpose of annoying noisy courtiers of his royal household.

Playing the Sang, *a Chinese musical instrument.*

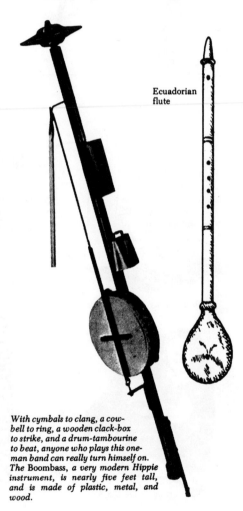

Ecuadorian flute

With cymbals to clang, a cowbell to ring, a wooden clack-box to strike, and a drum-tambourine to beat, anyone who plays this one-man band can really turn himself on. The Boombass, a very modern Hippie instrument, is nearly five feet tall, and is made of plastic, metal, and wood.

188

The nyatiti is made of wood, string, beeswax, and pieces of reed. This eight-string Luo harp is a traditional musical instrument of a major tribe in Kenya.

Around 1850, Don Jose Gallegos, of Malaga, invented a musical instrument which he called the Guitarpa. It combined a harp, a guitar, and a violin-cello, and had 35 strings. Twenty-six strings and 21 pegs acted upon the harp. Six strings belonged to the Spanish guitar, while three silver strings and 18 pegs managed the violin-cello. The pedestal by which the instrument was supported was so constructed that the Guitarpa could be either elevated or lowered at the musician's pleasure

A Chinese Gong, or—as one might say today—a super gong.

Neckties

The clothing of other periods often looks amusing to us, and current fashions always appear stylish and dignified. Yet future periods may judge the clothes we wear today as foolish-looking as we find a 16th-century man's doublet, leotards, and ruff. If our clothes are supposedly designed for comfort and practicality, how can you explain high-heeled women's shoes? Or skin-tight slacks? Or that completely useless and often uncomfortable piece of apparel without which no man can be considered well-dressed: the necktie?

How did the custom of wearing a necktie arise? Did the tie once have a function? Not really. The scarf and neckerchief have long been used to keep the neck warm. Even the ancient Romans wore a chin cloth, called a *focalium,* to protect their necks and throats. Orators especially favored the *focalium* to keep their vocal cords warm. But the necktie of today really evolved from a series of neckwear items whose function was almost always purely decorative.

Before the first appearance of what we might call the necktie, tie, or cravat, fashionable European men wore various kinds of collars, ruffs, ribbons, bows, and other finery around their necks. In the 16th century, the frilly material at the neck developed into a pleated ruff that completely encircled the neck. Later in the century, the full ruff was opened in front to form more of a recognizable collar, and by the end of the century, the ruff was being replaced by the falling collar.

The falling collar was still the fashion when the cravat was born out of an incident in French history. In 1660, a regiment of soldiers from Croatia (part of modern-day Yugoslavia) visited Paris, and paraded before their French allies wearing brightly-colored handkerchiefs around their necks. The fashion caught on immediately in France, then spread to England after Charles II had returned from France to assume the throne.

At the time, the coat and vest—usually very long—were emerging as distinct garments in men's dress, and colorful neckwear quickly found a place in the wardrobe of fashionable men. But in place of the ordinary handkerchief of the Croatians, European nobles opted for neckwear of rich lace and other expensive materials—English King James II bought three neckerchiefs for $600! These early neckties came to be known as *cravats,* from *cravate,* a French corruption of "Croatian." A regiment of French soldiers was even renamed the Royal Cravates!

Another neckwear item that was named after a military incident was the *steinkirk.* In 1692, according to one story, French soldiers encamped near Steinkirk, Belgium, were surprised by an English attack. In their haste to dress, the soldiers tied their cravats very loosely around their necks, and dashed off into battle. The French won the battle of Steinkirk, and a new neckwear fashion became the rage in Paris the following year. Men began to tie their cravats loosely, leaving long, flowing ends, sometimes threading the two ends through a ring. The official uniform of the Boy Scouts of America still includes a ring-secured steinkirk.

Various neckwear fashions came and went during the 18th century, when cravats with ruffles, pleats, layers, or tasseled

190

strings had their heyday. Jeweled stickpins came into vogue, and so did cravats stiffened with wire or stuffed with cushions. Some cravats were tied so high on the neck that the wearer could barely turn his head, or were thick enough to stop a sword thrust!

French monarch and stylesetter Louis XIV favored brightly-colored satin cravats, while his successor Louis XV brought in lace cravats whose ends often reached as far as the waist. Later in the century, cravats of starched linen or cambric came into fashion. Louis XVI, who was to suffer the guillotine during the French Revolution, wore starched muslin cravats around the neck.

The Revolution brought in simpler garments of all kinds—including men's pants. The *stock*, a wide, stiff cravat that encircled the neck, replaced the neckwear finery of earlier periods, and was presented to French soldiers as part of their military dress. According to a tale, Frenchmen of the time believed that a red-faced soldier was a healthy soldier. Men tied their stocks so tightly around their necks during military parades that their faces turned red and their eyes bulged—and so was born the epithet "froggie" for a Frenchman.

By 1840, the stock was still the universal cravat in Europe and America. Extensions to the stock led to a cravat with a slip-knot and hanging ends, called the "four-in-hand" because the wearer described a figure 4 when tying it. A stock with bows on each side evolved into the modern bowtie, while the four-in-hand became the ordinary necktie of today. Both were in fashion by the beginning of this century.

In the United States, almost all cravats were imported from Europe until around 1865, when the cravat was already a must for the well-dressed man. Many books and pamphlets were published advising men how to tie their cravats, including one from 1829 that warned: "In all cases of apoplexy, fainting, or illness in general, it is requisite to loosen or even remove the cravat immedi-ately." The book also advised that "those who are accustomed to sleep in the cravat, should be careful in examining whether it be loose." And regarding the affront of grabbing a man by his cravat, which had long been considered a great insult, the writer declared that "only blood can wash out the stain upon the honor."

The necktie of today was really born in the 1920s, when manufacturers began to turn out stronger ties that would not rip easily and would spring back to shape after untying. Silk knits were the fashion during the 20s, and ties with all-over patterns came into vogue during the 30s, when Americans were already spending $70 million a year for neckties. Average price: 60¢.

During the 1940s, wartime shortages of silk and other expensive materials helped introduce ties of wool and rayon. Wool, silk, and various cotton blends are presently the favored materials for neckties, though manufacturers have produced ties made from such unlikely materials as alpaca, cashmere, fur, glass, and leather!

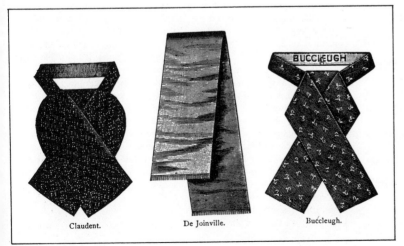

Stylish neckwear from a Jordan Marsh catalog in the early 1900s.

Claudent.   De Joinville.   Buccleugh.

After World War II, the vest faded as part of the well-dressed man's wardrobe, and the necktie consequently became more visible and important. Colorful, decorative neckties became the rule, and so did wider, longer ties. Today, necktie fashions seem to change every few years, with necktie width often following the widening or narrowing of the jacket lapel.

In 1946, the Men's Tie Foundation was formed to propagate the wearing of ties in America, with the slogan: "Wear a tie to look your best." By the end of that decade, the Foundation could report that Americans were spending $191 million a year on neckwear, with the average tie selling for from $1.50 to $2.50, and the average man owned four ties. Any necktie up to five dollars, the Foundation declared, was simply a "tie;" if it cost more than five dollars, it deserved the name "cravat." And if it cost more than $15, well, then it was a "creation."

In 1949, the Tie Foundation reported that the American necktie industry used some 34 million yards of material, not including linings and labels—enough to encircle the globe three times! The bowtie accounted for five percent of necktie sales, while about 85 percent of all ties purchased in the United States were bought by women for men! How did American men respond to the selection of their ties by their wives, daughters, and girlfriends? Less than one percent of all ties purchased that year were exchanged!

The Foundation even provided a breakdown of the nation in terms of the favored colors and designs of particular areas. Chicagoans favored green ties. Bostonians purchased far more red ties, while men and women in Dallas seemed to have a liking for blue ties. We don't known what color fashion plates from Omaha favored, but we do know that one Omaha man owned a collection of neckties that would warm the heart of any tie manufacturer: 7,000 ties, cravats, and creations.

The cornhusker's necktie collection surely must have included some of the so-called novelty ties that make their appearance regularly to commemorate an event. Most of the presidential campaigns of this century have produced a collection of commemorative neckties, all of which presumably had a short wearing life. There was even a necktie commemorating the dropping of the atomic bomb on Hiroshima, in production less than 24 hours after the explosion! This necktie attracted far less attention, though, than a tie bearing the reproduction of a painting of a nude woman—authorities raided the tie manufacturer and confiscated the offending neckties!

The future of the necktie is anyone's guess. It's possible that the necktie might be obsolete by the end of the century, so you might as well begin your collection of these fashion curiosities right now. But no matter how proud you might be of your necktie collection, don't ever accept an invitation to a necktie party—the term is American slang for a lynching!

Chicagoans favor green ties. Bostonians purchase far more red ties, while men and women in Dallas seemed to have a liking for blue ties.

Octopi and Squids

The octopus and squid belong to a class of sea creatures, called Cephalopods, that are found in almost all the world's waters. The octopus alone comprises some 140 species, ranging in size from just an inch to 28 feet in diameter.

The word "octopus" means "eight legs," but the tentacles of this creature might just as easily be called "arms." Each of the octopus' arms contains rows of suckers with which the octopus can grip its prey. But before killing a victim, the octopus paralyzes it with a secretion from its salivary glands. Octopi have been known to capture men with their tight-gripping tentacles, and are among the more ferocious creatures to be found in the deep.

The octopus also uses its tentacles to crawl along the ocean floor. Most live in shallow coastal waters, while others have been found in the deep sea. They prefer crabs or other crustaceans as their meal, but an octopus in captivity may devour its own arms—even if other food is available!

The squid has ten legs—or arms—equipped with suckers. Two of these tentacles are longer than the other eight. The squid uses the shorter arms to capture its prey, then transfers the catch to its mouth with the longer, more mobile arms. Squids range in size from just an inch or so to 52 feet in length, and the larger squids are the biggest invertebrate creaturs on earth.

Some squids are equipped with light organs in various regions of their body that make the creature phosphorescent. Others "fly" by leaping across the surface of the water, and can occasionally leap right onto the deck of a ship.

The most distinguishing feature of the squid, however, is its ability to squirt an inky substance into the water when set upon by a predator. The ink, or sepia, forms a screen to hide the squid, and also a dark "dummy" shape that the predator often attacks in place of the squid. After squirting its sepia, the squid becomes transparent and slips away in the darkness of the deep.

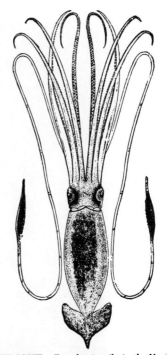

GIANT SQUID *Found primarily in the North Atlantic, this is the largest invertebrate creature on earth, growing up to 52 feet in length. Most are only seven feet long.*

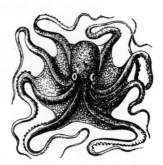

OCTOPUS VULGARIS *This is the common octopus, found in all the seas of the world. It may span over six feet with its tentacles.*

193

MUSK OCTOPUS *Like all octopi, this creature uses its tentacles as both arms and legs.*

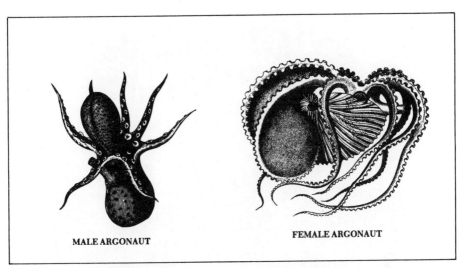

MALE ARGONAUT   FEMALE ARGONAUT

ARGONAUT *Also called the paper nautilus, this Mediterranean denizen usually measures just an inch in length. The young develop in the female's spiral shell.*

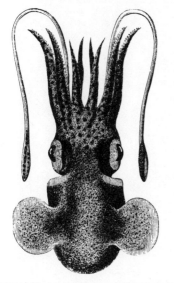

SEPIOLA *Some members of this genus bear phosphorescent light organs. The creature takes its name from sepia, the inky protective fluid it secretes when attacked.*

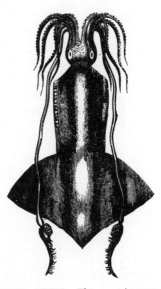

HOOKED SQUID *This carnivorous marine cephalopod has a long, tapered body, with tapered fins on either side. A horny plate is buried under the mantle of the squid. In the United States, this creature is used for fish bait, while in Mediterranean and Oriental countries, the squid is eaten as a delicacy.*

195

GIGANTIC CUTTLE-FISH   *This cuttle-fish was caught by the French Corvette Alectaon near Tenerife.*

ONIONS

If you were asked to guess the most widely used vegetable in the world, you might think first of corn or potatoes, or perhaps lettuce or tomatoes. Because it is most often used in the United States as a flavoring to other foods, the plant that rightly deserves the award for culinary prevalence might not even come to mind as a vegetable at all. We're talking, of course, about the odorous, oft-derided vegetable that is so essential to any chef, and so unessential to any chef's eye—the onion.

In total production, both the potato and tomato surpass the onion, but neither is used in such a wide variety of cuisines as the onion. The list of recipes, Western and Oriental, that require the services of the onion or its cousins would probably fill a small library. And since it appears both as a flavoring in much *haute cuisine*, and as a staple in much peasant cookery, the onion has traditionally been one of the few vegetables popular with both commoners and kings.

The onion is not only the most widely-used vegetable on earth, it is also one of the oldest. In the book of Numbers in the Bible, chapter II, verse 5, the Israelites bewailed "We remember the fish,

which we did eat in Egypt freely, the cucumbers, and the melons, and the leeks, and the onions, and the garlic," to a harassed Moses. A native of Western Asia, probably Pakistan or Afghanistan, the onion has been grown and eaten for so long it no longer exists in a wild state. By the time the ancient Egyptian civilization began to flourish some 5,000 years ago, the onion was already a staple food throughout the Mideast.

It's been said that the Pyramids owe their existence to the onion, since the workers who constructed them subsisted largely on the vegetable. The Roman historian Herodotus claimed to have seen an inscription on the Great Pyramid at Giza that listed the amounts of onions, garlic, and radishes eaten by the workers who built the monument. For some reason, Herodotus also maintained that the onion was good for sight, but bad for the body. Many a tearful cook might disagree.

The upper classes in Egypt also ate onions, though more often as a complement to other foods than as a staple in itself. The historian Pliny wrote that the Egyptians invoked the onion when taking an oath, and one variety was considered divine. The vegetable was depicted on a number of Egyptian monuments as a symbol of eternity, due to its layer-upon-layer formation within the shape of a sphere. Similarly, our word *onion* comes from the Latin

term *unio,* which has also given us *union* and *united.*

The ancient Greeks and Romans cultivated onions extensively, as do the people of Greece and Italy today. The Romans fed onions to their soldiers, believing the vegetable would make them brave. The Emperor Nero favored the leek, a member of the onion family eaten in the Mediterranean area since Biblical times, because he thought it would improve his singing voice.

Phoenician traders had brought leeks to the British Isles before the arrival of the Romans. The leek has been the national emblem of Wales since the year 640, when victorious Welsh soldiers pinned leeks to their caps so that they would not inadvertently bludgeon one another instead of the enemy. But some historians discount the tale, pointing instead to a confusion by English writers between the Welsh words for the daffodil, *cenine,* and the leek, *cenin,* for the daffodil was another Welsh national symbol. In any case, the Welsh still pin leeks to their hats on the feast day of St. David, their patron saint.

Medieval Europeans who did not fancy onions had a difficult time putting vegetables on their table. Meat, fish, game, and baked goods comprised most meals of the time, and among the vegetables, only onions and leeks were widely used. Onions mixed with chopped flowers were the staple food at many medieval monasteries.

The Spanish first brought the onion to the New World, planting the vegetable in their West Indian colonies. Onions had become a staple in America before the Revolution.

Today, New York and Texas are the primary suppliers of the American onion crop, which usually stands somewhere around the three-billion-pound mark annually. Europe produces about twice that amount each year. Even without taking into account the mammoth onion production of the Soviet Union, the worldwide figure is usually over 20 billion pounds a year!

The onion is a species of lily known as *Allum cepa. Cepa* and the Italian word for onion, *cipolla,* come from *caepa,* one of a number of Latin words for the vegetable. Onions contain volatile oils heavy with sulphur compounds that account for the pungent fumes so familiar to onion peelers. These oils disturb the eyes, which tear in order to wash away the offending fumes.

If you've been finding your onions a bit too lachrymal for comfort, try chilling them before you begin

198

cutting. You can remove onion odors from your hands by rubbing them with lemon juice before washing. If onion aroma clings to your knife, just run the blade through a raw potato.

Onions are sensitive to the length of day in the area in which they're grown. Varieties that thrive in northern latitudes are usually grown in the summer, when the days are long, and will not produce large bulbs if transplanted in southern regions. Conversely, onions grown in southern areas are usually grown through the winter. If transplanted in the north during the summer months, the onion will stop growing and ripen before it can produce a large bulb. Onions grown in the north, such as the familiar globe, are usually harder and more sugary and the white onion and others grown in southern regions.

The onion family consists of two main branches, the *dried onion* and the *green onion*. We eat the bulb of the former, and the green top and unformed bulb of the latter. But there are hundreds of individual varieties, for onions grow in the widest range of types among all vegetables.

The globe onion, round, yellow-skinned, and pungent, is the most commonly used dried onion in America. The Grano-Granex onion, better known as the "new" onion, is milder and sweeter than the globe. The new onion is best used raw, while the globe is best suited for cooking. The red onion is another sweet variety often served raw in salads, but it disintegrates when cooked.

White onions, which contain a high percentage of water, often taste best when creamed, pickled, or boiled. The pearl onion is not a separate variety, but a white onion harvested when small. The Gibson, a martini with a pearl onion instead of an olive, is named after New York artist Charles Dana Gibson, though the drink was invented not by Gibson, but by his bartender.

The Bermuda and Spanish onions are the largest members of their family. Both are mild, with a yellow to red skin, and are best eaten raw in salads or atop hamburgers. The Spanish onion, often used for fried onion rings, hails from Central Spain, while the Bermuda onion originated in the Canary Islands.

Green onions are harvested before their bulbs have had time to enlarge, though some green onions are harvested from non-bulbing varieties. Green onions include the scallion, leek, shallot, and chive. All are most often used as flavorings in the United States, although in some parts of Europe the leek is eaten as a vegetable. In France, the leek is known as "the poor man's asparagus."

If you've been finding your onions a bit too lachrymal for comfort, try chilling them before you begin cutting. You can remove onion odors from your hands by rubbing them with lemon juice before washing. If onion aroma clings to your knife, just run the blade through a raw potato.

199

ONION SOUP

Slice three large onions and brown in three tablespoons of butter or oil. Sprinkle in a tablespoon of flour, and heat for another 10 minutes, stirring occasionally.

Meanwhile, heat a quart of rich beef stock or bouillon. Add the onion mixture and simmer until tender.

Spread grated Parmesan cheese thickly over slices of toasted bread and melt the cheese under a grill.

Pour the soup in tureens and add a slice of toast to each bowl.

Or you can cover each bowl with Swiss, Gruyere, or Mozzarella cheese and bake for 15 minutes.

Onions can be stored for longer periods of time than any other fresh vegetable. But cooks looking for shortcuts—or protecting their tear ducts—can resort to an array of even longer-lasting onion products, including dehydrated minced or flaked onions, onion powder, and onion salt.

The proportions of sugar and water in onions determine the taste of particular varieties. But the way in which an onion is cut or cooked will also influence its taste. A finely-cut onion will more easily lose its oils in cooking, resulting in a milder flavor. Onions cooked in liquid quickly lose water, increasing the proportion of sugar and resulting in a sweeter-tasting, less odorous onion. As Jonathan Swift noted:

But lest your kissing should be spoil'd
Your onions must be thoroughly boil'd.

All types of onion are relatively low in nutritional value, and thus are seldom eaten alone like most green leafy vegetables. As a tribute to its flavoring power, the onion has been called "the vegetable whose absence spoils the stew." But too many onions can spoil the stew just as easily. English writer Sydney Smith advised moderation:

Let onion atoms lurk within the bowl,
And, scarce suspected, animate the whole.

The versatile onion may be boiled and combined with other vegetables, sauteed and piled atop steak or liver, stewed, or made into soup. And speaking of onion ingenuity, one recipe calls for large Spanish onions stuffed with—yes, pearl onions.

French onion soup is considered a gourmet treat in this country, but during the Middle Ages, onion soup was the poor man's staple. If you'd like to try your hand at onion soup, there's a recipe above.

If you'll believe a number of old wives' tales, your homemade onion soup might provide more than a pleased palate and a full belly. The onion has been used medicinally since the days of ancient Egypt. It was thought to ward off evil spirits, and because it induces perspiration, to cure colds. It's also been called into action against such maladies as earaches, insect stings, and warts. A medieval superstition holds that to remove a wart, simply cut an onion in half, rub the exposed inner flesh against the wart, tie the onion back together and bury it. When the onion has decomposed, the wart will have disappeared.

Most likely it's the onion's pungent aroma that has contributed to its place in legend and superstition. Many writers have advised judicious use of the vegetable, especially by lovers. A character in Shakespeare's *A Midsummer Night's Dream* warned: "Eat no onions nor garlic, for we are to utter sweet breath."

Indeed, for pungent aroma the onion's reputation towers above that of all its vegetable relatives—with the possible exception of garlic, which can be considered another member of the onion clan. An old poem correctly ranked the offending vegetables in the order of their olfactory powers:

If Leekes you like, but do their smelle disleeke,
Eate Onyons, and you shalle not smelle the Leeke;
If you of Onyons would the scente expelle,
Eate Garlicke, that shall drowne the Onyon's smelle.

The author obviously "knew his onions."

Oysters and Clams

"He was a bold man that first ate an oyster," wrote Jonathan Swift, in homage to the first human being who deigned to swallow the pulpy meat of that slippery mollusk. No, we don't know the name of the fearless individual, but we can conclude that he lived thousands of years before the written word, and—judging from the popularity of oysters forever after—that he probably found the morsel quite delicious!

Oysters, and their bivalve relatives, clams, have always been popular food items in the West. The clam retains its popularity, but oysters were much more widely enjoyed in the past than today, when the hard-shelled critter is considered an expensive delicacy by most people. There's no evidence that the Egyptians ate oysters, and no mention of the food in the Bible, but archaeologists excavating in Denmark have found oyster and mussel shells among pottery shards dating from 8000 B.C.

Oysters and clams are members of the family of mollusks known as bivalves, so named because they consist of two valves, or shells, enclosing a soft body. The word *oyster* is used to designate a particular genus of bivalves. But the word *clam* is a generic term used to designate some 12,000 species of bivalves. In Scotland, the word refers to the scallop. In the United States, *clam* usually refers to the *quahog*, or hard-shelled clam, and the *steamer*, or soft-shelled clam, though the two sea creatures belong to two entirely different genera of bivalves.

The Royal
Thorny oyster.

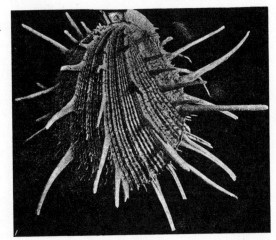

201

Hard-shelled clams, found along the Atlantic coast of North America, are the clams you're likely to enjoy on the half-shell. Also called the *quahog*, the hard-shelled clam belongs to a genus of mollusks named *Venus* because of the beauty and symmetry of its shells. The most popular eating clam is that northern quahog, or *cherrystone*. Young quahogs are sold as *Little Necks*.

The ancient Greeks—who gave us the word *oyster* from their *ostreon*—feasted regularly on mollusks. They also used oyster shells for casting votes, scratching the name of the chosen candidate on the inner shell—making Greek politics a real shell game. Greek juries also used the shells in recording their verdicts. Thus a person condemned to exile was "ostracized."

The Romans, too, were voracious oyster eaters. The Romans went so far as to establish a colony at Camulodunum (present-day Colchester, England), where oysters could be gathered and sent back to the Roman dinner table. The first known oyster bed in Italy itself was established by Sergius Aurata in 102 B.C. The famed Roman epicurean and cookbook author Apicius hosted orgiastic banquets featuring oysters. Apicius invented a system to keep his oysters fresh— he stored the mollusks in pewter vessels treated with pitch and vinegar. Eventually, Apicius committed suicide rather than face the poverty that resulted from his largesse.

For a time, the French considered oysters a brain food. King Louis XI feted the Sorbonne professors on oysters once each year "lest their scholarship become deficient." The girthsome gourmet Brillat-Savarin customarily consumed two dozen oysters before breakfast—tuning up, most likely, for the 45-course dinners he regularly attended—and one of Napoleon's marshals devoured over 100 oysters each morning.

Oysters were considerably cheaper in Napoleon's day, but modern oyster-eaters need not hang their head in shame. In 1975, a 48-year-old Florida man gulped down 588 in just 17½ minutes, and in 1977, a man devoured 212 in five minutes. And clam-eaters, take heart: in 1975, in Washington, a man slid 424 of the slimy critters down his gullet in just eight minutes.

In medieval England, an entire bushel of oysters could be bought for about four pence. As late as the mid-19th century,

Filling oysters with liquor in the kitchen of a gourmet restaurant of the Old South. (1872)

oystermen peddled their wares from wheelbarrows on the streets of London for about four pence a dozen. Dr. Samuel Johnson bought oysters regularly for his pet cat, Hodge. Presumably, he shelled them, too. In fact, oysters were so cheap that the saying arose: "Poverty and oysters always seem to go together." How times do change!

Clams and oysters were long popular among American Indians, who used the shells of a certain hard-shelled clam for *wampum*, or money. The Indians were the first to enjoy a clambake, burying clams along with lobsters and corn in sand pits lined with seaweed and hot coals.

New England colonists quickly made the clambake a culinary custom in that part of the United States. And settlers moving from New England to Ohio were not inclined to surrender the custom simply because there were no clams in Ohio. They buried chickens along with corn instead, but continued to call the feast a clambake. "Chickenbake" just doesn't have the same ring.

Oysters baked in the shell were served at the first American Thanksgiving feast, and oyster roasts were common in Thomas Jefferson's day, with hundreds of the savory sea critters roasted in hot ash until their shells popped open. As early as 1779, the state of Rhode Island set aside part of the public domain for oyster beds. Oyster fishing soon became a big industry on the Atlantic coast, particularly around Long Island—the inlet and town called Oyster Bay attest to this.

German immigrants settling around Cincinnati further popularized oyster eating in the United States. For a time, "oyster parlors" were common meeting places in the city. A rail and river network known as the "oyster express" transported fresh shellfish from Baltimore to Cincinnati. By the 1870s, oysters were a status symbol at dinner parties throughout the nation, and their price had begun to rise.

Oysters planted in tributary of Maryland bay.

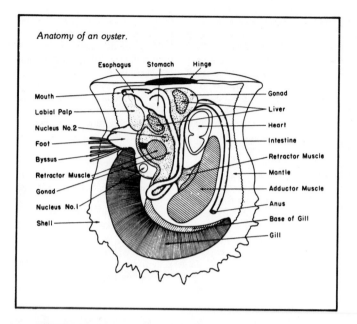

Anatomy of an oyster.

Esophagus   Stomach   Hinge

Mouth
Labial Palp
Nucleus No.2
Foot
Byssus
Retractor Muscle
Gonad
Nucleus No.1
Shell

Gonad
Liver
Heart
Intestine
Retractor Muscle
Mantle
Adductor Muscle
Anus
Base of Gill
Gill

Oysters are cultivated in farms at sea, then transported to beds near the mouth of a river. Many kinds of oyster actually change sex four times each year, alternating between male and female, and each full or part-time female will release two million eggs in the summer—of which only about 50 will survive.

Bivalve larvae are parasites, hooking onto the fins and gills of fish and feeding on the fish's tissues. After a few months of freeloading, the larvae let go of the fish and settle into the mud wherever they land. A newborn oyster will grow from one to four years before it's ready for the dinner table.

A clam can live as long as 10 years if not disturbed by a human or other predator. But clams and oysters see little of the briny deep during their life span, spending their adult lives buried in the mud at the bottom of the water.

Bivalves are equipped with two tubes, called *siphons*, that reach into the water from the creature's half-buried shell. Water flowing through one siphon provides the bivalve with oxygen and food before it flows out the other siphon. An average-sized clam can filter more than 6,000 gallons of water each year through its siphons.

Clams and oysters *can* move, however, pushing along with a small hatchet-shaped foot protruding between the two shells. When danger threatens, the bivalve simply withdraws its foot and siphons and "clams up," closing its shell so snugly only a chisel can pry it open.

Clams are considerably safer from their human enemies at high tide than at low tide, when clam beds are more easily accessible to clammers. The expression "happy as a clam" is actually a shortening of "happy as a clam at high water."

The record for oyster devouring was set in 1975, when a 48-year-old Florida man gulped down 588 in just 17½ minutes. And clam-eaters, take heart: the same year, a Washington man slid 424 of the slimy critters down his gullet in just eight minutes.

204

Oyster beds in Brittany, France.

The clamshell's gripping power is merely a nuisance to the clam opener, but it could be quite treacherous if you happen to be a pearl diver in the area of the Great Barrier Reef. That's the domain of the *Tridacna gigas*, the world's largest bivalve, which grows to an average of four feet in diameter and weighs about 200 pounds. The largest known specimen, now preserved in the Museum of Natural History in New York, had a body weighing 20 pounds encased in a shell that weighed a quarter of a ton!

Speaking of superlatives, the largest oyster farm in the world is—as any gastronomist might expect—in France, in the Arcachon Basin off the Bay of Biscay. The development of the Arcachon beds came about by complete accident. A Portuguese cargo ship carrying oysters was shipwrecked off the coast of France, and the surviving mollusks founded a colony in the nearby Basin.

The French soon began devouring *huitres* at such a pace that, in 1750, a law was passed that forbade the gathering of mollusks in the Basin for four years. Afterward, oyster gathering was declared illegal from May to October—a law which, coupled with the false rumor that a breeding oyster is inedible, may have led to the belief that oysters are taboo in any month without an "r" (May, June, July, August). Actually, oysters may be eaten at any time of the year.

Another mistaken belief holds that a lucky oyster-eater will occasionally find a small pearl lodged inside his dinner. The fact is the edible oyster does not produce pearls. Pearl oysters are found only in tropical waters, and are not considered fit for consumption. The beautiful iridescent jewel is composed of carbonate of lime, or mother-of-pearl, secreted by the shell lining.

Today, oysters are served raw, grilled, fried, deviled, and in oyster soup. Smoked oysters are imported from Japan and sold as a canned delicacy. Then there's *Oysters Rockefeller*, a gustatory treat created by New Orleans chef Jules Alciatore, which combines oysters with chopped bacon, scallions, spinach, parsley, and bread crumbs. The dish has nothing at all to do with the Rockefellers—the name was

205

selected to suggest the opulence of the dish.

The invention of the oyster cocktail is credited to a California miner of the 1860s, who ordered a glass of whiskey and a plate of oysters and then used the emptied whiskey glass to mix the oysters with Worcestershire sauce, catsup, and pepper sauce. The enterprising bartender thereafter began selling glasses of "oyster cocktail" at 50 cents a throw.

Clam chowder was invented by a group of Breton sailors shipwrecked off the coast of Maine. The venturesome seamen gathered clams and mixed them with salvaged pork, crackers, and potatoes in a large cauldron, or *chaudière*. Milk was added to the recipe later to produce New England clam chowder, and tomatoes to produce Manhattan clam chowder.

The famed Marennes oyster owes its origin to a peculiar incident that took place during the 17th-century religious wars. At the siege of La Rochelle—described in Dumas' *The Three Musketeers*—the Huguenot

An oyster dredger of the 19th century.

defenders began tossing oysters from the parapets of the city when they ran out of more potent ammunition. Some of the missiles landed in the nearby salt marshes. Peasants who later found the oysters discovered the meat had turned an odd green color. The characteristic Marennes green proved to be the result of diatoms (algae) living in the marsh water.

But the most curious oyster anecdote of all comes to us from 19th-century London. A tavern owner was frightened one evening by a peculiar whistling sound emanating from his storage cellar. Fearing a thief, he tiptoed into the cellar and began gingerly trying to locate the source of the plaintive wailing. What he found was so remarkable that he invited a number of his usual patrons to a special dinner the following night—when Charles Dickens, William Thackeray, and other London notables were delighted by the performance of a singing oyster!

Oyster culture in France.

PAPER

Egyptian papyrus was so vital to the Roman Empire that a papyrus crop failure during the reign of Tiberius nearly brought all official and commercial business in Rome to a complete halt.

A Chinese man by the name of Ts'ai Lun is considered by some to be among the 10 most influential persons in all history.

You ask: "Who on earth is Ts'ai Lun? Though his name is unfamiliar to most Westerners, Ts'ai Lun has been credited with the invention of a most important item, without which many other products—including this book—would be impossible—Tsai Lun invented paper.

Before the appearance of paper in the second century, Chinese culture was generally inferior to that of other contemporary civilizations in the West, at least in literacy and technology. But with paper as a tool, Chinese civilization leapt forward to a prosperity unmatched in the West. Then, around the 15th century, Western technology once again gained the ascendancy. The new Western hegemony was due in large part to two new tools: Gutenberg's

printing press and, equally important, cheap and plentiful paper to replace expensive papyrus and parchment.

The papyrus reed, or *biblos*, was cultivated in the Nile delta at least as early as 3500 B.C. The Egyptians used the reed for food and fuel, utensils, boats, and ceremonial garlands, but the membranous tissue of the plant's stem was reserved for use as a writing material. Papyrus sheets were made by laying strips of stem tissue together in a cross-hatch pattern, and sealing them together with a paste most likely made from bread crumbs soaked in boiling water. The Roman historian Pliny claimed that the Egyptians made their paste solely from the water of the Nile.

Egypt supplied papyrus for the entire ancient world, for the *biblos* has never been grown in any quantity outside that country. Egyptian papyrus was so vital to the Roman Empire that a papyrus crop failure during the reign of Tiberius nearly brought all offi-

cial and commercial business in Rome to a complete halt. Most papyrus documents in Europe vanished long ago due to fire, vandalism, war, or dampness, but the arid climate of Egypt has preserved a number of ancient papyrus scrolls. Arabs continued to use papyrus as a writing material until the eighth or ninth century, but by the 12th century, papyrus had been completely superseded by parchment.

Parchment, made from the skins of calves, goats, sheep, rabbits, and other animals, was competing with papyrus in Europe as early as the second century. A king named Eumenes, who ruled the city of Pergamum in Asia Minor during the second century B.C., is sometimes credited with developing the technology of parchment production. Our word *parchment* is derived from the name of his city. From the very beginning, the finest parchment

was made from the more delicate calves' skins, and the word *vellum*, designating the finest parchment of medieval times, is derived from the French word *veau*, "calf."

While the papyrus supply was limited by the size of the crop in the Nile Delta, the supply of parchment was limited by the expense of animal skins. Consequently, both papyrus and parchment remained quite costly through much of their history. In ancient times, wax tablets were used for everyday writing. Characters were pressed into the wax with a sharp stylus, and the wax was melted and was reused afterwards. Medieval monks frequently erased writing from older scraps of parchment and reused them. Fortunately, many of the older writings are visible today under ultraviolet light.

During the Middle Ages, the royalty and clergy were among the few to afford parchment in any quantity. Medieval monarchs published their proclamations on

In the year 105, a privy counselor named Ts'ai Lun presented Emperor Ho Ti with samples of a new writing substance made from some combination of bamboo, mulberry, and other vegetable fibers, along with fish nets and rags —the substance we now call paper.

MAKING PAPER

FROM LEFT TO RIGHT:

(1) Cut bamboo is washed and steeped in a water pit to prepare material for making paper.

(2) Digesting the bamboo pulp.

(3) Making a sheet of paper.

(4) Pressing the sheets of paper.

(5) Drying the sheets of paper.

parchment dyed royal purple, as had been the custom in Rome and Constantinople. The finest Bibles were written in gold or silver on precious stained vellum.

The use of parchment ultimately made possible the replacement of the written scroll by the book, as we know it. A papyrus scroll was constructed of overlapping squares of papyrus pasted together, with the text written in columns across the eight to 15-inch breadth of the scroll. Standard length was from 15 to 20 feet, but a single scroll containing *The Odyssey* or *The Iliad* could stretch up to 150 feet. The Greeks called the scroll a *biblion*, the source of *Bible, bibliography*, and other common words. The Latin word was *volumen*.

To examine a scroll, a reader had to unwind it from the left roller to the right, then rewind it completely when he'd finished. Quick references were, of course, impossible. The difficulty of un-winding and rewinding scrolls has been cited as a reason for the frequent inaccuracy of ancient writers when quoting other authors. Many writers chose simple to rely on their memory rather than take the trouble of dealing with a cumbersome scroll.

Parchment had two advantages over papyrus. First of all, it could be folded without cracking, and therefore could be organized into folded leaves instead of merely being rolled up. Parchment could also be prepared for writing on both sides, an essential quality for any writing material arranged in leaves. The introduction of parchment led to the use of the *codex*, or parchment-leaf book, that was already replacing the scroll by the time of Jesus.

Neither papyrus nor parchment was used at any time in China for a very simple reason: from the second century on, the Chinese had a far better writing material at their disposal. Prior to that, the Chinese had relied on books made of bamboo, which were extremely heavy, and silk, which were very expensive. In the year 105, a privy counselor named Ts'ai Lun presented Emperor Ho Ti with samples of a new writing substance made from some combination of bamboo, mulberry, and other vegetable fibers, along with fish nets and rags—the substance we now call paper.

Alas, Ts'ai Lun's paper profited the rest of humanity far more than it profited its inventor. The eunuch Ts'ai Lun enjoyed a brief period of wealth before becoming involved in a palace intrigue that resulted in a summons to the imperial judges. Instead of appearing in court, Ts'ai Lun retired to his home, took a bath, wrapped himself in his best robes, and and drank poison.

Some historians doubt that Chinese paper manufacture was the achievement of one man alone. But those who extol the accomplishments of Ts'ai Lun point out that, unlike many other inventions, the discovery of paper

209

was not inevitable even if its inventor had never lived, but rather the work of one gifted individual. Indeed, Europe, which could not boast a Ts'ai Lun of its own, was not to begin manufacturing the paper until 1,000 years after the Chinese inventor had been at it, and then only because Europeans learned the secrets of its production from others.

The use of paper had spread to Korea and Japan by the year 600, but the Chinese continued to guard the secrets of its manufacture from foreign traders and visitors. Then, in 751, Arabs who had occupied the city of Samarkand in Central Asia were attacked by a Chinese army. The Arabs repelled the attack, and captured a number of Chinese skilled in the art of papermaking.

The use of paper made from linen, cotton, and other substances spread quickly throughout the Arab world. We find mention of a paper document in 11th-century Greece, but paper did not reach Europe on any scale until the following century, when the Moors introduced its manufacture to occupied Spain. The Arabs also brought paper to Sicily, and it is on that island that we find the oldest European document written on paper, a deed of King Roger of Sicily that dates from the year 1102.

During the 13th century, the first great paper mills of Europe appeared in the area of Fabriano, Italy, and it is there that we also find the first known watermark. By the 15th century, paper was the most common writing substance in Europe, ousting papyrus completely and relegating the use of parchment to official documents. And just in time: the invention of a practical mechanical printing press by Gutenberg around the middle of the century resulted in a sharp rise in the demand for writing materials. By 1500, close to 40,000 volumes had been printed in 14 different European nations, the majority in Italy and Germany.

The use of the watermark to identify the manufacturer of a piece of paper was unknown in China. Watermarks were used in Fabriano during the 1290s, but the oldest surviving watermark, a circle surmounted by a cross, dates from the year 1302. Watermarks are formed by pieces of wire or wax set in the frame in which the pulp dries. Since less pulp can settle along the outlines of the watermark figure, the paper will be thinner along those lines, rendering the figure visible.

The first watermark in the United States, the word *company*, appeared on paper produced by a mill near Germantown, Pennsylvania, the first paper mill in America. Erected in 1690 by William Rittenhouse and William Bradford, the mill turned out handmade linen paper on the order of 250 pounds per day. Less than a century later, disruptions caused by the American Revolution resulted in a paper famine that spurred the construction of many new mills. F ; 1810, there were over 200 paper mills in the United States.

210

Until the 19th century, most paper was made from substances derived from old linen and cotton rags, and later, from straw. In 1799, a Frenchman named Louis Robert obtained a patent for the manufacture of paper by mechanical means. The resultant increase in paper production, along with a steadily rising literacy rate, created the need for a cheaper, more plentiful raw material for paper manufacture.

Inventors experimented with a number of substances, including hemp, from which the familiar Manila paper has been made here since 1843. By the middle of the 19th century, several processes had been patented for the production of paper from wood pulp. Paper makers at last had an inexpensive, seemingly inexhaustible supply of raw materials for their product, and the forest fire became the single most dangerous threat to world literacy.

World production of paper and paperboard now stands at an astounding 140 million tons per year. How much paper is that? Well, if the entire supply were used to produce standard 20-pound bond typing paper, the yearly world production figure would exceed 40 trillion sheets—10,000 sheets for every person on earth!

And how many trees must be felled to produce that prodigious figure? The answer is difficult to calculate, but 1,000 pounds of pure pulpwood paper require about one cord of wood, or 128 cubic feet.

The United States now leads all other nations in the manufacture of paper and paperboard, producing over 47 million tons a year. (Paperboard is the term applied to any wood pulp product more than .012 inches thick.) Japan ranks a distant second, at about 13 million tons, with Canada and the U.S.S.R. rounding out the top four. The United States is also the home of the world's largest paper mill, the Union Camp Corporation's plant in Savannah, Georgia, which turns out over a million tons of paper annually—an amount equal to 10 percent of the total Canadian production!

As forest land dwindles and paper production soars, wastepaper and other non-pulp materials are becoming increasingly important in paper manufacture. Wastepaper now accounts for about 19 percent of all the paper produced in this country. In West Germany, where the supply of pulpwood is more limited, 45 percent of all paper is made from waste; in forest-rich Finland, only three percent of the paper is made from waste.

Paper is now produced in a nearly infinite variety of kinds and sizes. Bond paper, with or without rag content, is most commonly used for typing paper and stationery. Kraft paper is the coarse, brown substance you see most familiarly in brown paper bags. Blotting paper dates back to at least 1465, and was in common use in Europe by the 16th century. On a more exotic note, handmade Finnish writing paper with a watermark in the form of the buyer's portrait sells for as much as $80 per sheet. More exotic, no doubt, are writing materials from pre-Columbian Peru and Mexico, now in the Vatican Library, which were made from human skin!

Sheet paper is customarily sold by the *ream*. Originally, a ream consisted of 480 sheets, or 20 *quires*, but today, a ream usually contains 500 sheets. The

About one-third of the 18 million volumes in the Library of Congress, the world's largest book and manuscript repository, are too brittle to be handled!

thickness of the paper is indicated by a figure designating the weight of a ream of that paper cut in two-by-three-foot sheets. For example, with "20-pound bond," 500 sheets measuring two-by-three feet will weigh 20 pounds.

If you've ever read the publishing history of an old work of literature, or examined a library card catalog, you may have come across terms such as *folio*, *octavo*, and *foolscap*, and dismissed them as the esoterica of the bookbinder's craft. These terms refer to the dimensions of the leaves of a book, and the manner in which the pages were folded for binding.

A folio (f) is a book assembled from sheets of paper each folded once, producing two leaves and four pages from each sheet.

A quarto (4to) is a book made from sheets of paper folded twice, producing four leaves and eight pages from each sheet.

An octavo (8vo) is comprised of sheets of paper folded three times, each sheet producing eight leaves and 16 pages.

Foolscap, crown, and *demy* refer to the dimensions of the original sheet of paper. A *foolscap*, for example, is a sheet of paper measuring about 13½ by 17 inches. A *foolscap quarto* is an edition made from foolscap sheets, each folded twice. Each foolscap quarto page will therefore measure about 8½ by 6¾ inches.

The term *foolscap* may be derived from the Italian *foglia*,

"leaves." But a more interesting derivation traces the term to the period of the English Civil War. Charles I declared that all paper manufactured in England should bear the royal arms as a watermark. When Oliver Cromwell toppled the monarch in 1649, he ordered that a fool's cap and bells be substituted for the royal arms on all English paper. Most of the other terms referring to paper size, such as *demy*, *crown*, and *royal*, were also derived from a customary watermark.

There is no term for the size of a sheet of paper produced in 1830 by the Whitehall Mills in Derbyshire, England, that measured four feet in width and three miles in length!

The introduction of pulpwood paper has made writing material affordable to all persons, but modern paper does have one major drawback. Pulpwood paper is less durable than paper made from linen or cotton, and the alum-rosin compounds used to coat pulpwood paper produce acids that eat away at the paper. While many parchment manuscripts from the Middle Ages remain in good condition, books printed today are not likely to survive more than 40 to 50 years without turning yellow and brittle.

It would cost an estimated 50 cents per book to use paper durable enough to survive more than a century, compared to over $300 to restore a book once it has suffered the effects of old age. The additional expense might be well worth considering. Already, about one-third of the 18 million volumes in the Library of Congress, the world's largest book and manuscript repository, are too brittle to be handled!

World production of paper and paperboard now stands at an astounding 140 million tons per year. How much paper is that? Well, if the entire supply were used to produce standard 20-pound bond typing paper, the yearly world production figure would exceed 40 trillion sheets— 10,000 sheets for every person on earth!

The peanut might seem to be a plant that can't quite make up its mind where it belongs in the world of botanical classification. What's your guess? A nut, you say? Nope—the goober is actually more a pea than a nut. The tasty morsel we call the peanut is the pod or legume—not the nut—of the *arachis hypogea* plant.

But the peanut is an unusual member of the pea family, since its pods have the peculiar habit of ripening underground.

food for Africans being carried across the ocean on slave ships. Eventually, some African peanuts were brought to Virginia and planted for livestock fodder. Thus, the peanut made two transatlantic journeys before becoming a North American crop.

Peanuts were used in Virginia as fodder for pigs, and the soft, juicy ham made from peanut-fattened hogs has ever since been known as *Virginia Ham.*

for the crop after it had become over-abundant in the United States as a foodstuff. Carver discovered some 300 derivatives of the goober, including cheese, milk, flour, coffee, ink, dye, plastics, soap, wood stains, linoleum, cosmetics, and medicinal oils.

Peanut butter is one peanut derivative we can't thank Carver for. That great favorite of the schoolboy was introduced by a St. Louis doctor in 1890 for patients who needed an easily

After the plant's flower is pollinated, a stalklike structure called a *peg* begins growing from the base of the flower toward the soil. Only when the tip of the peg is below the surface do the fertilized ovules begin to develop their characteristic pods.

The one to three "nuts" found inside the shell are the seeds of the plant, and the tiny morsel found inside the nut when it's split open is the only part of the seed with reproductive powers.

The peanut is a native of tropical South America. Spanish conquistadores exploring the New World found South American Indians eating what many called *cacohuate,* or "earth cocoa."

The goober was gradually transplanted in West Africa as a food and fodder crop. Slave traders found that the peanut could provide cheap, nutritious

The peanut has also been called *groundnut* and *earthnut,* both aptly suggestive of the plant's peculiar subterranean habits. The word *goober* is reputedly of African origin, from the Bantu *naguba.*

George Washington Carver is the man most responsible for wide-spread cultivation of peanuts in the United States. Carver's work in the early part of this century showed that the peanut could help free the South from its dependence upon cotton, and restore needed nitrogen to soil depleted by cotton cultivation. When Carver began his research in the 1890s, the goober was not even recognized as a crop; by 1940, the peanut ranked as one of the six leading crops in America, and the largest crop in the southern United States after cotton.

Carver, the son of a slave, not only demonstrated the ecological advantages ' peanut cultivation, but found new uses

digestible form of protein. Today, about half of the United States' annual peanut harvest of some four billion pounds is used for peanut butter, with the remainder going to salted nuts, candies, oil, and livestock fodder. Only about 10 percent of our crop is used to manufacture peanut oil.

Planters Peanuts, the world's largest dealer in peanut products, was founded in 1906 by Amadeo Obici, an Italian immigrant who had journeyed alone to America as a 12-year-old boy. Starting as ı peanut vendor in Wilkes-Barre, Pennsylvania, Obici built Planters into a 10 million dollar a year business within a quarter-century.

"The Nickel Lunch"

IT'S not a real beach unless equipped with sand, sea, sunshine and Planters Pennant Salted Peanuts. When once you've tasted these flavory, golden peanuts you'll see how necessary they are. You just can't resist them. The biggest, plumpest peanuts in the whole crop—fresh and crisp as a sea breeze—roasted to a healthy tan and with the salty tang that adds to appetite. You can eat all you want of them. They're as wholesome as all out doors. "The Nickel Lunch".

Even though taken from the Planters can, and sold in the Planters jar, they are not Planters Salted Peanuts unless they are in the glassine bag with the "Planters" name and "Mr. Peanut" on it.

Planters Nut & Chocolate Co., Wilkes-Barre, Pa., Suffolk, Va., San Francisco, New York, Chicago, Boston, Philadelphia

MR. PEANUT
REG. U.S. PAT. OFF.

Planters
PENNANT SALTED
PEANUTS

Remember the days of the "nickel lunch?" Today this small bag of peanuts costs a quarter.

"Mr. Peanut," the company's trademark, began his association with Planters in 1916, when the firm offered a prize for the best trademark suggestion. A 14-year-old Virginia boy submitted a drawing for an animated peanut, another artist added the familiar cane, hat, and monocle, and "Mr. Peanut" was soon appearing promoting Planters peanuts everywhere.

The peanut requires at least five months of strong sunshine and 24 inches of rain annually, and thus is restricted to the warmer regions of earth. India is the largest peanut-producing nation, followed by China and West Africa, with the United States fourth in total production.

As a food, the goober is one of the most concentrated sources of nourishment known to man. Pound for pound, the peanut provides more protein, minerals, and vitamins than beef liver, more fat than heavy cream, and—dieters beware—more calories than sugar. Recent experiments in Africa have shown that the discarded shells of the peanut can also be used as animal fodder!

Peanuts may be basically a snack food in the United States, but in many parts of Africa and Asia the goober is an indispensable part of the diet. To demonstrate the importance of the peanut in other nations, we might note that the first American to be honored with a monument in India was none other than George Washington Carver. In 1947, the peanut growers of India unveiled a monument in Bombay to commemorate the American's outstanding work.

214

PEANUT SOUP

¼ cup margarine or butter
¼ cup minced onion
½ cup peanut butter
¼ cup chopped celery
1 tablespoon flour
4 cups beef bouillon
2 teaspoons lemon juice
½ cup chopped roasted peanuts
1 tablespoon chopped parsley

1. Melt the butter or margarine.

2. Sauté the onion and celery in the shortening until tender.

3. Put these ingredients into a double boiler. Add peanut butter, flour, beef bouillon, and lemon juice, and blend well.

4. Bring the water in the bottom of the double boiler to a boil, and cook for 20 minutes. Stir the mixture occasionally.

5. Before serving, sprinkle the soup with chopped peanuts, and a dash of very finely chopped parsley.

Serves eight.

PEANUT PIE

1 cup sugar
¼ cup light corn syrup
½ cup margarine
3 eggs
½ teaspoon vanilla extract
1½ cups roasted peanuts
1 nine-inch pastry shell

1. Combine sugar, corn syrup, melted margarine, eggs, and vanilla in a large mixing bowl. Blend thoroughly.

2. Stir in the roasted peanuts.

3. Turn the mixture into the unbaked pastry shell.

4. Bake in 375° oven for 45 minutes.

Serve warm as is. If you serve the pie cold, garnish with large dollops of whipped cream.

Pianos

Ornate piano of the 19th century.

> *Most pianos are harmless things, if people would only let them alone.*

Twenty-one million Americans— about one of every 10—now play the piano, more than the number who play all other musical instruments combined.

About 180,000 new pianos are sold in the United States each year, close to double the annual total for the 1930s. We have no idea how many of those pianos are played regularly, and how many merely occupy space in a living room. But there's no question that the piano, though less than 300 years old, is the most popular musical instrument throughout the Western world. If the present trend continues, the piano may someday be No. 1 in the Orient as well!

About 750,000 pianos are produced worldwide each year. What manufacturer would you guess to be the world's largest piano producer? Steinway? Baldwin? Another old, distinguished European firm? Well, only about 60,000 pianos are currently produced in Europe each year—in addition to the 170,000 manufactured in the Soviet Union. In fact, since 1960, the largest piano manufacturer in the world has been Yamaha, a Japanese firm that turns out close to 190,000 pianos a year! Japan is presently the largest piano producing country, manufacturing over 280,000 pianos annually. Even more surprising, most of those pianos are sold in Japan, which by and large was not introduced to the instrument until this century!

The Japanese did not invent the piano, of course. Traditional Oriental music cannot be played on any of the popular Western keyboard instruments. The piano and its precursors—the clavichord and harpsichord—directly embody the structure of Western music, and their design was altered as that music evolved from medieval plainsong to the tonal music familiar to our ears today.

There are two basic ways to produce musical tones: with wind or with vibrating strings. Wind was first employed by a keyboard instrument as early as the third century B.C., Ctesibius of Alexandria built a hydraulic pipe organ activated by a keyboard. A keyboard may have been applied to a stringed instrument as early as the 10th century, but the keyboard instruments that led to the invention of the piano did not appear in Europe until four centuries later.

The immediate precursor of the first stringed instrument with a keyboard was the monochord. This instrument consisted of a wooden sounding box with a single string and a movable bridge. The bridge could be shifted at fixed intervals to determine the length of the string, and hence, its tone. The ancient Greek philosopher Pythagoras used the monochord to investigate the nature of musical sound. In later centuries, monochords were constructed with more than one string. Then, during the 14th century, an unknown inventor devised a stringed instrument in which the length of the strings was fixed by hammers activated by a keyboard. This was the clavichord.

The word clavichord—formed from the combination of the Latin clavis, "key," and chorda, "string"—was first mentioned in 1404, but the instrument probably appeared during the preceding century in England, France, or Spain. By the 15th century, the clavichord was well known by musicians throughout Europe. In some ways, the clavichord was closer in function to the piano than the harpsichord and other later keyboard instruments.

The rear end of each clavichord key was fitted with an upright metal tangent. When the key was depressed, the tangent rose to strike one or more metal strings. In early clavichords, the strings were of equal length; the tangent itself formed a second bridge when it struck the string, thus determining the length of the string and its tone. The harder the key was struck, the harder the tangent's impact, and hence, the louder the sound. But the clavichord's sound was generally small, making the instrument unsuitable for play with an ensemble.

The harpsichord, which marks the next stage of keyboard evolution, provided a louder, more resonant sound, and therefore was commonly used along with other instruments. While the clavichord sounded a string by striking it with a hammer, the harpsichord plucked the string with a short quill called a plectrum. The rear end of each harpsichord key was fitted with an upright jack bearing a plectrum made from crow quill or leather. When the key was depressed, a felt damper was lifted from the string to be sounded, the jack rose, and the plectrum plucked the string. When the key was released, the jack fell back into place, while the plectrum swung away on a pivoted tongue so that it could not again pluck the string.

Like the organ, the harpsichord offered no dynamics—no matter how hard the key was struck, the plectrum plucked the string with the same force. Composers writing for the instrument had to provide their own dynamics, adding or subtracting tones to thicken or thin the texture.

The harpsichord—so called because its strings were thought to resemble a prostrate harp—appeared in Europe before 1425, and for a time developed, side by side, with the clavichord. While the organ was retained in church, the harpsichord became the predominant keyboard instrument in the theater or concert hall. At home, cheaper harpsichordlike instruments called the spinet and the virginal were most common. The rectangular virginal, a favorite of Queen Elizabeth, was often small enough to be placed on a table or in the lap. The term is derived from the Latin word for girl, since a small keyboard instrument was largely conceived of as feminine, in contrast to the manly lute.

Early in the 18th century, when the piano first appeared, Western music was undergoing fundamental changes that made most earlier keyboard configurations obsolete. The predominant form of music from the days of ancient Greece up through the Middle Ages was modal, built on seven scales called modes. Thus, the earliest keyboards contained only seven tones in various octaves: A through G, with no chromatics (black keys). Since there was no way of otherwise distinguishing the keys, the letters A through G were often marked directly on the keys.

Then, through the Renaissance period, music gradually evolved from modality to *tonality,* with only two modes or keys, major and minor. Tonality created the need for *chromatics,* or intervals between the A through G notes— the black keys. First to appear on a keyboard was the B-flat key— the flat symbol was originally just a small *B.* Most 15th-century keyboards contained nine tones per octave: seven white keys plus a B-flat and an F-sharp. Full chromatic keyboards had appeared on organs by the 14th century, but the earliest full chromatic keyboards to appear on stringed instruments contained a separate black key for each sharp and flat—the B-flat was not equivalent in tone to the A-sharp.

Then, beginning around 1690, the *tempered scale* was gradually adopted. It's difficult to explain the tempered scale without delving into mathematics and acoustical physics, but basically the tempered scale equalized the intervals between a black key and its neighboring white keys—B-flat and A-sharp became identical tones. Frequent key changes were possible, and keyboards now matched the modern piano—seven white keys and five black keys within each octave. Early in the 1770s, Bach demonstrated the versatility of the tempered scale by composing his *Well-Tempered Clavier,* which consisted of two pieces of music in each of the 12 major and 12 minor keys.

Through the 18th century, *polyphonic* music, consisting of two or more independent melodies, gave way to *homophonic* music, in which a predominant melody was played over a chordal accompaniment. Hand in hand with the development of homophonic music came the need for keyboard instruments with dynamics—the capability of playing a note loudly or softly. As the composer Couperin wrote in 1713: "The harpsichord is perfect in its compass and brilliant in itself; but as one cannot increase or diminish its sounds, I will be forever grateful to those who . . . will succeed in rendering this instrument capable of expression." Couperin probably did not know that such an instrument had already been invented—the piano.

Italian letters dating from 1598 mention a keyboard instrument called the *piano e forte,* but the instrument they describe was merely an improved harpsichord with a mechanism to provide dynamics. The invention of the first true piano was undoubtedly the work of an Italian genius named Bartolomeo

Cristofori, harpsichord maker and tender of musical instruments for Florentine Prince Ferdinand dei Medici.

Sometime between 1693 and 1700, Cristofori removed the plectra from the harpsichord's upright jacks and instead attached the jacks to leather-tipped hammers. When a key was depressed, the jack rose and threw the hammer against the string. The key also lifted a damper from the string to be sounded, allowing the string to resonate until the key was released.

In *piano e forte* models built in 1720 and 1726, Cristofori added a device that prevented the hammer from falling back to its original place immediately after striking the string, allowing for quick repetition of a note. But what was more significant about Cristofori's invention, the touch on the key determined the force with was that the hammer struck the string—the harder the touch, the louder the sound. In fact, Cristofori called his invention a *gravicembalo col piano e forte*—"harpsichord with soft and loud." Cristofori's 1720 piano is now on exhibit at the Metropolitan Museum of Art in New York.

Word of Cristofori's work soon reached Germany, inspiring organ builder Gottfried Silbermann to construct a piano of his own. In 1736, five years after Cristofori's death, Silbermann showed two of his pianos to Johann Bach, but the master did not find them to his liking, complaining that the touch was too heavy and the upper registers too weak. Ten years later, Silbermann demonstrated an improved piano to King Frederick the Great of Prussia, and the monarch ordered a number of them—three of which survive.

The harpsichord remained in common use through most of the 18th century, but the higher cost of maintaining the harpsichord's plectra made the piano a more attractive home instrument for most people. Although Voltaire called the piano "a boiler-maker's instrument," the piano gradually gained in popularity until it was recognized as a distinct new instrument rather than an improved harpsichord.

During the 1770s, Muzio Clementi became one of Europe's first pianists of renown, composing keyboard music in a new style suited to the piano. After 1790, Haydn abandoned the harpsichord in favor of the piano, and Mozart wrote almost all of his later keyboard music for the piano. But Mozart's piano pieces—as well as Beethoven's first piano sonatas— were composed for the then contemporary pianos which had only five octaves.

During the 1760s, a student of Silbermann named Johann Zumpe began making pianos in Lon-

218

don, introducing the first English *square piano*—a piano in an oblong horizontal case, similar in shape to the earlier virginal. By 1800, the square piano had become the most popular keyboard instrument in middle-class parlors throughout Europe, and had even found its way to Mideastern harems, where its legs were shortened so that a player could reach the keys while sitting on a pillow.

By that time, harpsichord making had virtually ended. But most 19th-century pianos were far from perfectly dependable. Composer/pianist Franz Liszt often attacked his piano so violently that hammers would fly from the carriage, and strings would snap from the force of his blows. Audiences came to expect such accidents, and felt cheated if Liszt did not break at least one string during a concert performance.

Upright pianos and harpsichords had appeared during the 18th century, but the cases of these early instruments were extremely tall. Then, in 1800, John Hawkins, an Englishman who had emigrated to Philadelphia, patented the first upright "portable grand" similar to the shorter upright piano of today, with the vertical strings reaching to the floor. By 1900, the upright was by far the most popular home piano in the United States. In 1904, when the piano manufacturers' convention met in Atlantic City, New Jersey, the conferees symbolically ushered in the reign of the upright by burning a collection of old square pianos.

The upright piano may be smaller, cheaper, and more convenient to transport than the concert grand, but it cannot match the latter instrument in tone quality. With a concert grand, the floor underneath the horizontal strings acts as an additional sounding board, and the raised lid helps project the sound. Also, the concert grand employs gravity in part to return a hammer to place after it strikes the strings, while the hammer of an upright is returned by a spring mechanism. Thus the grand has slightly better action.

By 1900, the Pleyel firm of France, Bechstein of Germany, and Broadwood of England were virtually synonymous with the piano in those countries. The earliest pianos in America were imported from Europe; but by 1775, Americans had piano manufacturers of their own. The first U.S. piano was produced that year by a German immigrant in Philadelphia. Within a decade, piano factories were common in New York. By the end of the 19th century, the best American pianos were recognized as equal to any produced in Europe. American piano sales were climbing toward their peak year of 1909, when 364,500 new pianos were purchased there.

The firm that did the most to establish the quality of American pianos was founded in 1853, when a German immigrant named Heinrich Steinweg and four of his sons began manufacturing pianos in New York. By 1859, a huge factory was turning out pianos bearing the family name—changed by now to Steinway—that were to become the premier concert pianos in America. In 1867, Steinway pianos earned the plaudits of Europeans when displayed at a Paris exposition, with composer G.A. Rossini proclaiming the Steinway "as great as thunder and the storm, and sweet as the piping of the nightingale."

In 1903, the Steinway Company presented its 100,000th piano to the White House, where it resided until 1938, when it was replaced by the firm's 300,000th model. Today, the Steinway remains for most pianists the last word in fine American pianos, but in sheer numbers the largest piano producers in this country are Aeolian, Baldwin, Kimball, and Wurlitzer.

The standard concert grand piano is now almost nine feet long, with a compass of seven octaves plus a minor third, although some European pianos have a compass of eight full octaves. Ebony has long been used for the black keys—according to some, it

19th-century piano that could be turned into a table.

was originally adopted to better show off feminine white hands—but many pianos now use black plastic instead. Concert grands still employ ivory as a covering for their white keys, but most upright pianos substitute a white plastic substance. The modern piano, incredibly intricate in construction, contains close to 12,000 individual parts.

Even more intricate is the *player piano,* probably the only musical instrument in history that replaced the musician altogether. Patented in the United States in 1897, after an earlier English model, the player piano employs a spinning roll of perforated paper; the pattern of perforations governs the passage of air acting on a valve, which in turn sets the keys in motion. All the proud owner of a player piano has to do is preset the tempo for a particular piece of music. Some player pianos were self-contained units, while others were attached to a regular piano for automated playing. Though player pianos enjoyed a brief resurgence during the 1960s, they have, by and large, disappeared in the wake of radio and phonographic records.

Other piano novelties include a 1780 model with a circular keyboard, so constructed as to bring all keys perpendicular to the player. Pianos have been designed with all keys level and of the same color, or with a keyboard of alternating black and white keys.

In 1882, a Hungarian patented a piano that employed six keyboards, three tuned a half-tone higher than the other three. Designed to facilitate the fingering of certain chords and arpeggios, this piano enjoyed a brief vogue during the 1890s, when schools teaching the instrument's playing style were established in New York and Berlin.

Another piano constructed during the late 19th century contained a number of special-effects keyboards, including a "bassoon" pedal that brought a piece of parchment into contact with the lower strings to produce a buzzing sound reminiscent of the reed instrument; a pedal that activated a triangle and cymbal; and another that beat a drumstick against the underside of the soundboard.

Still another piano that enjoyed passing success during the 19th century was the pedal piano, which was equipped with a full pedal keyboard similar to that of the organ.

Most modern pianos are equipped with only two pedals— the *soft* pedal produces a softer sound by bringing the hammers closer to the strings, or by shifting the hammers so each strikes two instead of three strings; the *sustaining* pedal lifts the dampers from all the strings to sustain harmonies and allow each string to vibrate along with the sounded strings.

American pianos sometimes contain a third pedal, the *Sostenuto,* which allows all sounded strings to continue resonating until the pedal is released.

The most recent arrival on the keyboard scene is the *electronic piano,* which first came into widespread use during the 1960s. These instruments electronically amplify tones most often produced by hammers striking metal bars. Though its sound lacks the overtones of a true stringed instrument, an electronic piano can be amplified to high volume for use in large jazz or rock bands, or attached to special-effects devices that alter the piano's timbre. Just as keyboard players gradually came to recognize the piano as an instrument distinct from the harpsichord, many pianists now regard an electronic piano as a distinct instrument rather than an amplified piano, with a playing style all its own.

If nothing else, the much lighter electronic piano could someday put the piano mover out of business. Another piano that might have driven even the brawniest piano mover to seek other employment was manufactured in 1935 by Challen of London, measuring 11 feet, eight inches in length, and weighing over one-and-a-third tons. The longest string of this piano, the grandest grand of all times, was nearly 10 feet long!

But the most astounding superlatives associated with the piano are related not to size, but to endurance. In 1894, an Englishman set the first recorded mark for long-term piano playing by tickling the ivories for 48 consecutive hours—without repeating a single song!

An even more impressive endurance record was established in 1967, when 67-year-old Heinz Arntz played continually—except for two hours of sleep daily—for 1,056 hours. Beginning his stint in Germany, Arntz was carried in a van to a seaport, traveled by steamship to the United States, and finished his performance at Roosevelt, Long Island, 44 tuneful days later!

Alas, Arntz's transatlantic marathon remained a world's record for only three years. In 1970, James Crowley of Scranton, Pennsylvania, played consecutively for almost 45½ days—except for the allowed two hours of sleep daily. We're not sure if Crowley was paid for his feat, but if so, his fee probably did not approach the $138,000 that American pianist Liberace once earned for a single New York performance. Adjusting for inflation, however, the highest paid classical pianist of all time was probably I.J. Paderewski, Prime Minister of Poland around 1920, who amassed a fortune of some five million dollars for displaying his keyboard wizardry in concert.

220

Pinball Machines

In an age when amusement arcades offer their patrons electronic tennis, basketball, baseball, hockey, auto racing, tank, airplane, or rocket warfare, and an unlimited array of other video-screen games, an older, simpler pastime still holds center stage in most modern arcades: the venerable pinball machine.

Despite the allure of competing video games, pinball buffs in unprecedented numbers are now feeding coins into their favorite machine for a chance to test their reflexes against a flashing, ringing device that offers neither a cash reward, prize, nor congratulatory acknowledgment. Pinball is, quite simply, man versus machine. And though the machine is almost always the winner, man has been undauntedly accepting the challenge for close to 50 years—with no sign of surrender.

Games in which round objects are propelled into holes or against pegs probably predate written history. But the most immediate precursor of pinball may be the game of *bagatelle*. Popular during the 19th century, bagatelle was played on an oblong slate or cloth-covered board, with players using a cue stick to shoot balls into nine numbered scoring cups. Obviously, bagatelle was much more like billiards than modern pinball.

In 1871, a Cincinnati man named Montague Redgrave patented a game that might be considered the "missing link" between bagatelle and pinball. Called *Improvements in Bagatelle*, Redgrave's game employed a spring plunger rather than a cue stick to propel the balls onto the playfield, pins to alter a ball's direction, and bells to indicate a high score—all familiar elements of modern pinball. Redgrave's invention spawned many imitators, including the *Log Cabin* of the 1880s, a table-top game with pins that many people mistakenly call the first pinball game. Gradually, bagatelle-type games began to resemble pinball, but it wasn't until the 1920s that games similar to modern pinball really caught on in the United States.

Amusement arcades had been popular here since the turn of the century. But games of skill or chance usually took a back seat in the arcades to fortune-telling machines, mechanical peep shows, and strength-testing devices. As coin-operated amusement machines found their way into drugstores, bars, candy stores, tobacco shops, and other establishments, the demand for new types of mechanical games increased.

In 1928, one manufacturer produced *Billiard Skill*, the first

A political cartoon from 1863 showing American President Abraham Lincoln playing a game of bagatelle, an early forerunner of present-day pinball.

221

game in which steel balls were propelled by a plunger onto a horizontal playfield. Two years later, a Chicago firm turned out *Whoopee*, a game similar to *Improvements in Bagatelle* played on a 24-by-48-inch board. In arcades, a nickel bought a play of 10 balls. Neither of these games bore a strong resemblance to pinball. But 1930 also saw the appearance of *Little Whirl-Wind*, the game most often credited for the surge in pinball popularity that occurred during the next few years.

Though *Little Whirl-Wind* was to provide an impetus for the subsequent growth of the pinball industry, the game actually resembled modern pinball a good deal less than some of its predecessors. Invented by one Howard Peo of Rochester, New York, *Little Whirl-Wind* was an upright game small enough for a countertop. For one penny, a player could propel five balls around a spiral maze and into scoring holes; the farther through the maze the ball traveled, the higher in value the scoring holes. The game was easy to maintain, inexpensive to purchase, and challenging enough to attract players by the droves. Advertisers billed it as the "Greatest Legal Penny Amusement Machine Ever Put on the Market." The pinball boom had begun.

One of the first entrepreneurs to move into the pinball industry was David Gottlieb, a Chicago-based film distributor and arcade machine manufacturer. In 1931, Gottlieb produced a counter top game called *Baffle Ball*, the first widely successful horizontal pinball game. *Baffle Ball* was a simple game by modern standards: for one penny, players attempted to shoot seven balls into four circular scoring areas, or into lower-scoring slots at the bottom of the playfield. A ball shot into a cup called the "Baffle Point" doubled the score of the entire table, provided it was not knocked off by a subsequent ball. The added challenge of the Baffle Point struck the fancy of pinball players from coast to coast. Within a year, Gottlieb was producing 400 *Baffle Ball* machines a day.

One of Gottlieb's West Coast jobbers was Harry Williams, considered by many the true father of the modern pinball industry. At a 1929 convention, Williams was intrigued by a coin-operated game called *Jai Alai*, in which players attempted to flip balls into scoring hoops mounted on an upright playfield. Williams immediately took out a franchise for *Jai Alai;* then founded a manufacturing company in Los Angeles and began turning out his own coin-operated games.

At first, Williams bought and modernized old bagatelle-type machines, designing new playfields and installing them in the old bagatelle cabinets. Later, he began to invent entirely new games, devising many of the features still common to pinball machines around the world. His first invention was called *Advance*, a 10-ball game whose intricate design demanded more skill of players than any previous game. More importantly, *Advance* was the game that spawned the familiar "tilt" mechanism so detested by avid pinballers.

Early pinball machines were vulnerable to sharp blows by players that could jar a ball into a desired hole, making pinball a game of brute force rather than finesse. When Williams observed a player smacking the bottom of an *Advance* machine to jar open mechanical gates that were supposed to be opened only by a well-aimed ball, he decided to devise a mechanism to prevent such rough treatment. His first attempt was crude: nails were hammered into the underside of the machine to provide a painful surprise to players attempting to slap the board from underneath.

Soon after this, Williams devised a more gentle deterrent. Called a "stool pigeon," the device consisted of a small ball set atop a pedestal, with a metal ring underneath. When the machine was lifted or pounded too heavily, the ball fell from the pedestal to the metal ring, stopping play. A player trying out the newly-equipped *Advance* game, surprised when his strong-arm tactics ended the game, exclaimed: "Look! It tilted!" And "stool pigeon" became "tilt" forevermore.

Williams was also the inventor of the electric "pendulum tilt" built into many modern machines. The device consists of a plumb bob hung by a wire, with a thin metal rod protruding from the bottom of the bob. If the machine is pushed too far in any direction, the rod makes contact with a metal ring, completing an electric circuit that stops the machine and illuminates the "tilt" light. Needless to say, this device is not overly popular among pinball fans, but it does increase the challenge of the game and limits wear and tear on the machines.

In 1933, Harry Williams broke new ground with the invention of the first electric pinball machine feature. Included in a game called *Contact*, the battery-powered device was the forerunner of the modern kick-out hole. A ball landing in a certain hole completed a circuit that triggered an electrically powered peg and ejected a ball placed in another hole. Shortly after, Williams added an electric doorbell to one of his games. Other electrical innovations followed, completely revolutionizing an industry that had heretofore been entirely mechanical.

Williams included his first electric tilt mechanism in *Multiple*, a game produced in association with the Bally Company, founded by Chicago manufacturer Ray Moloney. Moloney had been a coin machine distributor for Gottlieb and other firms until 1931, when he built his first pinball machine, *Ballyhoo*. The game included a "Bally Hole," similar in principle to the Baffle Point. At 10 balls for a penny, *Ballyhoo* was an immediate sensation, launching Moloney on a pinball-machine making career, and laying the groundwork for the Bally Manufacturing Company, today the world's largest producer of slot machines and other electric coin game equipment.

The back glass—the upright portion of the modern pinball machine—made its first appearance during the late 1930s. Originally intended to hold various electric features such as the point totalizers, the back glass was soon sporting the comic artwork so much a part of the modern pinball machine. Artwork quickly began to appear on the playfield itself. Attracted by the colorful illustrations, the electric buzzers and bells, and the continuing innovations of Williams, Gottlieb, Moloney, and others, gamesters began swarming around pinball machines in unprecedented numbers.

But at the same time that pinball manufacturers were turning out new electric games to challenge the growing number of players, pinball came under increased opposition from political and church groups opposed to gambling. During the early 1930s, slot machines and other pay-out games were still legal in many parts of the country. Since pinball was a novelty game played for fun only, many players began to turn their attention to games that offered cash as well as self-satisfaction for a skillfully played, or lucky, game. In 1933, Bally introduced *Rocket,* the first automatic pay-out pinball machine. Now a player reaching a certain score, or hitting a special target, received an immediate cash pay-out from the machine—a highly attractive feature to Americans of the Depression era.

Until then, pinball had suffered little from legal restraints. But once Bally, Williams, and other manufacturers began to produce pay-out games, opponents of gambling cast a suspicious eye toward pinball. Newspapers carried stories incorrectly linking pinball operators with organized crime. Politicians accused pinball makers of teaching and encouraging gambling among teenagers. In 1939, the city of Atlanta passed a bill stipulating a fine of $20 and imprisonment of up to 30 days for operating a pinball machine in the city. Other cities and states rushed onto the anti-pinball bandwagon, banning not only the pay-out games, but all novelty pinball games as well.

In 1941, the police commissioner of New York City took a stand against pinball, declaring that "children and minors who play these machines and frequent the establishments where they are located sometimes commit petty larceny in order to obtain funds, form bad associations, and are often led into juvenile delinquency and, eventually, into serious crime." In 1941, Mayor Fiorello La Guardia went on the campaign trail with a sledgehammer in hand, personally smashing pinball machines for the benefit of newspaper photographers. In December of 1941, pinball was declared illegal in New York.

As pinball machine factories were converted to other uses for the war effort, it appeared for a time that pinball was dead in the United States. But, after the war, those pinball manufacturers who survived began campaigning for a relaxation of the laws against machines without pay-outs, claiming that pinball was a game of skill rather than chance. In 1947, the Gottlieb Company brought out *Humpty Dumpty*, the first machine equipped with flippers. Flippers are the short arms near the bottom of the board activated by control buttons on the side of the game. By manipulating the flippers, a player can return a ball to play when it is about to drop through the outhole. Pinball makers could now claim that flipper pinball was completely a game of skill, and as such should not be outlawed along with gambling games of chance.

In 1956, a Federal court decision made a distinction between gambling devices and flipper games without a pay-out. Soon all pinball machines were fitted with flippers, and the pay-out pinball machine disappeared almost completely. To make the game more rewarding, manufacturers substituted free games or "add-a-ball" bonuses in place of cash pay-outs. Even today, pinball machines intended for use in different parts of the nation are manufactured differently to comply with local standards, since add-a-ball, free games, and automatic plungers are still illegal in some places.

Most anti-pinball legislation was erased from the books during the late 1960s. In 1972, pinball addicts could again exercise their reflexes legally in Los Angeles. In 1976, pinball again became legal in Chicago, the city of its birth. And the same year, the New York City Council voted to allow pinball machines in the Big Apple—though thousands of illegal machines were already in use there at the time. Pinball was once again respectable.

Today, few people think of pinball as anything but a harmless, fun game for players of all ages. Pinball machines are turning up in shopping malls, department stores, airports, college dormitories, and restaurants, as well as in the video game center, the modern version of the penny arcade. The success of the movie Tommy, which featured a "pinball wizard," did much to spur a new interest in the game. In 1975, after the release of the movie, Bally's Wizard became the fastest-selling pinball machine in the United States.

Along with Bally, D. Gottlieb and Company, Williams Electronics, and Chicago Coin are the major pinball manufacturers in the nation. To suggest the size of the pinball industry: the Gottlieb Company was recently sold to Columbia Pictures for the sum of $47 million!

Each of the four major manufacturers now brings out from six to 12 new games every year. It's a long road that takes a new machine from the designer's head to the arcade floor. After a new design is presented by one of the company's staff, a mock-up of the new playfield is constructed and tested. Care must be taken that the game is neither too easy nor too difficult—and most important, that an average game will be completed in about two-and-a-half minutes, considered the ideal time for a pinball game. Designers aim for a game that demands about 75 percent skill, but allows for 25 percent luck, so that unskilled players can enjoy playing, too.

After all features are in place in the final mock-up, from 50 to 200 complete test samples are constructed and shipped around the world for on-the-floor testing. If the game meets with the approval of its most demanding critics—pinball players—the game is placed in full production. The success of the test models in various countries will determine where most new models will be shipped.

A new pinball machine will cost over $1,000. But if a machine were kept in continual operation for, say, six hours a day, one machine could return close to $15,000 a year to its owner. If you'd like a pinball machine in your home, you might look at a used model. Machines from two to five years old, removed from an arcade to make room for new models, can be purchased for $500 to $800. Older, rebuilt machines cost under $500.

Surprisingly, over 60 percent of all pinball machines manufactured in the United States are exported, the majority to Western Europe. Americans first traveling to Europe are often stunned by the ubiquity of the "American" pinball game there. But Europe has enjoyed decades of uninterrupted pinball growth, while development of the game in the United States was hampered for 25 years by anti-pinball legislation.

In England, "pin tables" are a fixture in most pubs. Since payout devices are legal in that country, many pinball machines in Britain offer an immediate cash reward for the skillful pinballer.

The competitive Germans most often enjoy Kampf Flipper as a four-player game. In France, les flippers machines are everywhere—in cafés, restaurants, stores, and in palaises des jeux, or game arcades. In quieter cafés, the bells are sometimes removed from pinball machines so that players won't disturb other patrons. Spain, the only European nation that does not permit the importation of American machines, has nine pinball manufacturing companies of its own. The Spanish maquinas del millon are usually built with more of an incline than their American counterparts, providing a faster, more challenging game.

The popularity of pinball in Europe may be due, in part, to its price. In France or England, a player can enjoy two games for about 20 cents, while most American games cost 25 cents per play. Dutch and Spanish pinballers can battle their machines for just about seven cents a game. It's no wonder that many Americans who never play pinball in their own country become avid gamesters the moment they reach Europe.

Each European country has developed a pinball lingo all its own, but we don't have to delve into any foreign languages to find a colorful array of terms pertaining to America's most popular coin game. *Gunching,* for instance, is body English applied to the machine. *Kickers* are targets made with stretched rubber that send a ball rebounding quickly in the opposite direction, while *kickout holes* are holes in the playfield that electrically propel a captured ball back onto the playfield. *Drop-targets* may be struck only once by each ball, falling below the playfield after contact.

Thumper-bumpers are the large circular targets, usually equipped with a bell and a light, that send a ball careening off rapidly after each score. Motion is imparted to the ball by a spring system that spins the thumper-bumper when a ball makes contact with it. Most thumper-bumpers bear the words "100 Points When Lit," or some such legend to explain the scoring provided by the target. A *free game* mechanism is just that—a player attaining a certain score, or hitting a certain target, moves a numbered drum inside the machine that allows him to push a button for a replay without inserting another coin.

The names of modern pinball machines are no less imaginative than their earlier counterparts. Old machines bore names such as *Wang Poo, Who's Goofy, Stop and Sock, Jiggilo,* and *Hell's Bells.* Newer games include *Cue Tease, Op-Pop-Pop, Rawhide, Hula-Hula,* and *Love Bug.* A list of all machine names, old and new, would include well over 1,500 entries, so only the most dedicated pinballer can claim to have played even half the games now in existence.

Now that most anti-pinball legislation has been removed from the books, the future of pinball looks bright, indeed. A small home pinball machine recently sold 50,000 models in its first week on the market. Manufacturers are now experimenting with games that can be played by two persons at once, games with multi-level playfields, and machines with video back screens.

Speaking of video screens, the first all-electronic video pinball machine was *Spirit of '76,* constructed in 1976 by Mirco Games. A pinballer can now battle wits with video pinball machines whose playfields change design every half-minute or so, or after a certain score has been attained. Video pinball games use blips instead of balls, and an entirely different range of sound effects. It's too early to tell whether pinball buffs will take kindly to these games. But the keenest players will likely remain loyal to the older electric games, for body English (twisting one's body to exert slight pressure against the machine in a particular direction), one of the most important elements in a good game of pinball, is completely useless against a video machine.

There is one trend in the pinball industry that is indeed disheartening to players of any ilk. Pinball machines must now compete in many arcades with a complete range of video games, most of which have a shorter playing time than their pinball neighbors. To discourage arcade managers from removing pinball machines in favor of the shorter-playing and therefore more lucrative video games, pinball manufacturers are now turning increasingly to games that offer just three balls per play, rather than the customary five.

Experienced players will undoubtedly cry "tilt!"

To suggest the size of the pinball industry: the Gottlieb Company was recently sold to Columbia Pictures for the sum of $47 million!

Playing Cards

Ask even a hard core cardsharp about the origin of playing cards and, pointing to the king and queen in their Renaissance raiment, he may well answer smugly that, of course, cards originated in Europe during the 15th and 16th centuries. Well, the reply would be half correct; yes, the design of modern playing cards can be traced back to 15th- and 16th-century Europe. But the cards themselves are a good deal older than the paper money often used to wager on them.

The exact origin of playing cards remains uncertain, but most historians agree that China is their most probable birthplace. But no matter where they originated, cards—like their gaming counterparts, dice—were probably used, at first, exclusively for fortune telling.

In early times, cards were connected with various religious rites. Some ancient Hindu cards, for instance, were divided into 10 suits representing the 10 incantations of the god Vishnu. The four-suit deck may be symbolic of the four hands of the god, as represented in Hindu statuary.

No one seems quite certain how cards found their way to Europe. Marco Polo may have brought them back from China in the 13th century. Other theories credit—or blame—the gypsies with bringing cards from Arabia to Europe, or claim that the Arabs themselves introduced cards in Europe during their occupation of Sicily and Spain. Probably, all of these sources were, in some part, responsible.

The first reference to playing cards in Europe appears in an Italian manuscript of 1299, although cards did not become well known on the continent until the 14th century. A receipt,

Card parties are no novelty—this scene depicts a card party of the 15th century.

dating from 1392, shows that Charles VI of France purchased three decks of cards in "gold and diverse colors." By 1495, playing cards were so well established in Europe that card manufacturers in various nations petitioned their kings for protection against imports.

Many believe that Tarot cards are the forerunners of the modern deck. The fact is the two decks developed independently—Tarot cards were unknown in China, and playing cards were virtually unheard of in Europe before the 13th century.

The Tarot deck consists of 21 pictorial representations of material forces, elements, virtues, and vices, plus the Fool—the precursor of the joker that found its way into the playing card deck. For centuries gypsies have claimed the ability to foretell the future based on their interpretations of the Tarot cards, which show characters and dress strikingly similar to those of the Romany tribe.

Renaissance Venetians were probably the first to combine the 22-card Tarot deck with the then current 56-card playing deck. The playing deck of the time consisted of a king, a queen, a knight, a page, plus number cards from one through 10 in each of four suits—*cups, coins, swords,* and *wands.* Several games derived from the combined 78-card deck—22 Tarot plus 56 playing cards—are still played in some countries.

Further combinations of number and picture cards resulted in decks of 32 or 36 cards in Germany, 40 cards in Spain, and 52 cards in France. The English

adopted the French deck, with its designs which originated in 15th-century Normandy. The picture cards were in royal dress from the period of Henry VII.

The English retained the French symbols for the four suits, but changed their names. If you want to call a spade a spade in France, you would say *pique,* literally "pike." The French *carreau* ("tile" or "square") became in England the diamond; the *trèfle* ("cloverleaf") became the club; and the *coeur* ("heart") remained the heart.

In Germany, the spade, diamond, club, and heart are known respectively as the *Grun* ("leaf"), *Schelle* ("bell"), *Eichel* ("acorn"), and *Herz* ("heart"). In Italy, it's *spada* ("sword"), *denaro* ("coin"), *bastone* ("rod"), and *coppa* ("cup").

In Soviet Russia, government officials once tried to replace the "corrupt" monarchy face cards with proletarian revolutionary figures, but the tradition of Russian card design was so well entrenched that the attempt had to be abandoned. The famous 19th-century poet Pushkin wrote a novel, *Queen of Spades,* in which card playing leads to the death of the three main characters, and then Tchaikovsky based a celebrated opera on Pushkin's novel.

The earliest European playing cards were laboriously hand painted. Later, they were printed with wood-block techniques. German card makers were perhaps the first wood-block engravers in Europe.

In 1832, Thomas de la Rue invented a typographic process for card manufacture, and institutionalized the design of "double-headed" cards, readable from either end.

Early mass-produced playing cards were printed on paste-

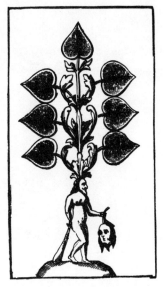

These old German tarot cards were used to tell fortunes. The top card is the seven of clubs; the bottom card is the seven of spades.

227

This engraving shows a Fench card factory in the era of Louis XIV.

board, with two sheets gummed together and lacquered.

At various times, card makers have tried to introduce different types of decks. One such effort was a deck with five suits.

Metal cards, intended for play on magnetized boards, have been manufactured, and these come into view occasionally on a windy day at the beach. But basically, card design has remained unchanged for centuries.

European governments have always found playing cards an ideal subject for heavy taxation. England began taxing card imports in 1615. By 1628, the tax on each deck had risen to a then exorbitant half-crown. Taxes on playing cards once became so high in Austria that card makers began selling oversized decks that

since Las Vegas casino operators probably account for a large chunk of the total—owing to their practice of throwing away a deck after just a few rounds of blackjack.

The number of games that can be played with cards is virtually limitless. New games are invented continually. Yet, almost all games can be divided into one of two categories: rank games and combination games.

The earliest Chinese games were rank games, in which the player turning over the highest card won the round. Many modern games are based on that simple ideas with variations, such as the trump suit—designating which beats any card of the other three suits. Among the popular games in this category would be *loo, euchre, whist,* and *bridge.*

Combination games are those in which the winner of a round is determined by the entire hand held and the combinations formed by the cards—for example, *poker* and *gin rummy.* Games which are a combination of the two are: *pinochle* and *klobiash.*

Poker became popular in the United States in the 19th-century, especially among gold-digging forty-niners. The game was actually based on an older Spanish game called *primero* that included elements of betting and bluffing just like the modern game. According to Shakespeare, Henry VIII played *primero* the night Queen Elizabeth was born. The term *poker* comes to us from the German *pochen,* "to brag" or "to knock," or from a similar German game called *pochspiel.*

Reportedly, there are over 350 different versions of that great boon for a rainy day— *solitaire.*

The popularity of a card game varies greatly from country to

could be gradually trimmed as their edges became worn, thus lasting two or three times as long as a regular deck.

Did you ever wonder why the ace of spades in every pack is so distinctive, with the central spade by far the largest symbol in the deck? Well, the ace of spades was the card designated to bear the tax stamp. Even today, card makers use the ace of spades to carry their trademark or brand name.

More than 70 million editions of what the Puritans termed "The Devil's Picture Book" are now sold in this country each year— one deck for every three persons. The figure is misleading, though,

229

ODDS AT POKER

Hand	Number Possible	Odds Against
Royal Flush	4	649,739 to 1
Other Straight Flushes	36	72,192 to 1
Four of a Kind	624	4,164 to 1
Full House	3,744	693 to 1
Flush	5,108	508 to 1
Straight	10,200	254 to 1
Three of a Kind	54,912	46 to 1
Two Pairs	123,552	20 to 1
One Pair	1,098,240	4 to 3 (1.37 to 1)
Nothing	1,302,540	1 to 1
	2,598,960	

country, and from one era to the next. In the United States today, most people have at least heard of canasta—a Latin American invention—and also are familiar with poker, rummy, bridge, gin, blackjack, war, go, cassino, keno, pinochle, and old maid. In the past, such games as faro, whist, and euchre were more popular.

Blackjack is easily the most popular casino game in the United States today. Actually, all popular casino games—baccarat, banque, chemin-de-fer, and blackjack—date from the 15th and 16th centuries. All were extremely simple to play. In each of these games, the object is to reach a number close to—but not above—a predetermined limit. In blackjack, it's 21; in baccarat, it's nine.

You may have been confused in the casino, or in your reading, by the games of baccarat and chemin-de-fer. The rules of play are actually the same in both games, but the betting procedure is different in each. Baccarat is the big-money game in most American casinos, while chemin-de-fer remains more popular in Europe. In both games, six 52-

card decks are used, shuffled together and placed in a wooden box known as the sabot.

Speaking of rules, Edmund Hoyle has been credited with formulating the rules of many popular card games. Actually, Hoyle wrote only two books on cards, and never heard of most of the games for which he is supposed to have formulated the rules. Among them is poker, which was not invented until almost 100 years after Hoyle's death.

If you're a real card freak, you may want to take a gander at some of the world's great playing card collections. The most notable are in the British Museum in London, the Morgan Library in New York, and the Cincinnati Art Museum, which includes a display donated by the U.S. Playing Card Corporation.

Morrisey's Gambling House at Saratoga, New York was a popular 19th-century casino.

230

KING OF CLUBS
(Spanish, c. 1500)
The Spanish and Italian decks were the only early decks containing the clubs suit. Our modern deck has retained the word "clubs," but not the clubs symbol.

KING OF MONEY
(Spanish, c. 1500)
The circular figure in the right-hand corner represents a gold coin. The Spanish called the suit *oros*, or "gold pieces."

TWO OF SWORDS
(Spanish, c. 1500)
The swords suit of the Spanish deck became the French *pique* (pike), and eventually, the English spades.

JACK OF CUPS
(Spanish, 18th century)
In this deck, the court figures of each suit wore the garb of a different period. The cups suit figures wore costumes of the Carlos I period, around 1550.

KNIGHT OF SWORDS
(Spanish, 18th century)
Spanish decks of the period included a King, Knight, and Jack, but no Queen. The swords suit figures in this deck wore clothing from the Roman Empire.

232

And talking about card freaks: Carter Cummins holds the record for building the greatest number of stories in a house of cards— 51 stories in a tower of 2,206 cards, 9½ feet high. Joe E. Whitlam of England built a house of 73 stories—a stupendous 13 feet, 10¼ inches—but Joe cheated a bit by bending some cards into angle supports.

We might also mention what must be the single largest loss in a game determined by the turn of one card. William Northmore of Okehampton, England, an inveterate gambler of the early 18th century, lost his entire fortune of $850,000 on the turn of an ace of diamonds!

Northmore's tale does have a happy ending, though. After the game, Northmore vowed never to gamble another penny. The townspeople of Okehampton, in sympathy for his plight, elected Northmore to Parliament, where he served for 19 years until his death.

Without doubt, the card game most widely played over the world today is *Contract Birdge*, a partnership game played by four persons. Bridge is derived from *Whist*, which can be traced back to 1529. The earliest treatise on Whist written by Edmund Hoyle in 1742, was a best-seller.

Duplicate Whist was played in London as early as 1857. The idea of Duplicate Whist was to eliminate luck and transform the game into a contest of skill.

In 1891, the American Whist League was established. My, how the game has grown! Today, bridge is played by over 30 million people in the United States, of whom 200,000 are dues-paying members of the American Contract Bridge League.

William Northmore gambled $850,000 on the ace of diamonds— and lost!

It is estimated that over 60 million people play bridge throughout the world. In Sweden, Holland, and Belgium, the game is even more of a rage than it is in the United States. Today, champions compete on television, and there are bridge columns in newspapers throughout the world.

During the 1930s, the big name in bridge was Ely Culbertson, who developed a system of bidding which took the bridge world by storm. With a host of bridge teachers under his tutelage, Culbertson turned the game into a multi-million dollar business. He wrote a number of books on the Culbertson System, which sold in the hundreds of thousands. Included in his hoopla were matches played by himself and his wife as partners against such topnotch bridge stars as Sidney Lenz and P. Hal Sims. These Culbertson matches became parlor chitchat throughout the country and turned the name of Culbertson into a household word.

During the 1940s, the ascendant star was Charles H. Goren, who ruled the world of bridge for some 20 years.

Apart from being played in tournaments, bridge is, of course, also played for money; sometimes, it is rumored, for fairly high stakes. In the early days of the game, Charles F. Schwab, the steel magnate, is reputed to have run a game where the stakes were a dollar a point. In today's clubs, the stakes run as high as 10 cents a point, which on a bad evening when Lady Luck frowns, might cost a player around $500.

SUIT DISTRIBUTION AT BRIDGE

The odds against finding the following distributions are:

4-4-3-2	4 to 1		7-4-1-1	about 249 to 1
5-4-3-1	9 to 1		8-4-1-0	about 2,499 to 1
6-4-2-1	about 20 to 1		13-0-0-0	158,755,357,992 to 1

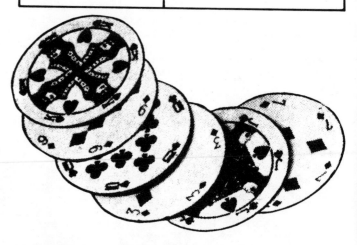

The well-rounded card player might like these round cards, which can be read no matter how you hold them.

Ely Culbertson was a critical figure in the history of bridge playing. Culbertson turned bridge into a multi-million dollar industry.

This 80-blade English pocketknife, inlaid with gold and mother of pearl, was exhibited at the Great Exhibition of 1851 in the Crystal Palace, in Hyde Park, London.

POCKETKNIVES

The pocketknife is obviously a recent invention, right? After all, the technological skill required to craft a workable fold-up knife must be a product of the industrial age. Besides, what need would men have had for a pocketknife in the days before pockets? Well, don't be surprised if you come across a rusty, time-worn pocketknife in the display cases of a museum—a tool, say, 2,000 years old!

Knives themselves, of course, have been with us since the Stone Age. Primitive man used cutting tools and weapons made from stone and flint, and later, from bronze and iron. The ancient Romans were skilled metalworkers, spreading their craft throughout their Empire—and the Romans left us the world's first known fold-up pocketknives.

The Roman implements were about three inches long when shut, fashioned without a spring or "nail nick"—the groove used to open the blade. The handles were often elaborately carved. One pocketknife surviving from the first century features an

235

ivory handle skillfully carved into the shape of an armored gladiator. Another Roman knife, now in the British Museum, had the carver's name scratched into the handle.

Table knives did not exist in the Middle Ages— each diner was expected to bring his own knife which, between meals, doubled as a dagger. Nor did innkeepers provide table cutlery. Affluent travelers often carried sets of elegant tableware in their baggage. Obviously, the pocketknife would have been an ideal all-purpose tool for the medieval European, but few pocketknives were in existence at the time. Most men preferred an nonfolding knife in a scabbard to a pocketknife—owing either to lack of good spring knives or to the shortage of pockets.

Until the 18th century, the only kind of pocketknife generally available was the jackknife, a heavy tool with one blade that closed into a groove in the handle. Then cutlers began using springs to secure the blade in both the open and closed positions, providing a safer, firmer tool. From that time on, pocketknife manufacture became known as spring knife cutlery.

As the craft improved, multibladed tools began to appear—the penknife by far the most important. No, *penknife*, is not, strictly speaking, interchangeable with *pocketknife*. A penknife was a specialized pocketknife with one blade at each end of the handle. The smaller of the two blades was used to trim and sharpen quill pens.

Throughout the 18th and 19th centuries, anyone who wrote had to own a penknife, and spring knife cutlery became a major industry in Europe and the United States. The penknife was the premiere product of the cutler's craft, for the fitting of a spring knife demands highly skilled work. The blades were made from high-grade steel, tempered slightly harder than table knives. The more expensive models were finished by jewelers, with handles fashioned from silver, ivory, pearl, horn, ebony, and tortoise shell. An American cutlery catalogue from 1893 lists some 1,500 pocketknife models, which might suggest both the size of the industry and the variety of product available at the time.

Since at least the 14th century, English cutlery had been centered around the city of Sheffield, while German knife makers from Solingen have long excelled at their craft. It was 19th-century Sheffield cutlers who began fitting pocketknives with various other tools, among them buttonhooks, files, leather borers, tweezers, gimlets, saws, and implements curiously known as "castrating blades." One interesting Sheffield creation sported both a pistol and a dagger.

The jack-of-all-trades knife—often known as the sporting knife—is today the most popular kind of pocketknife, fitted with nail files, clippers, scissors, corkscrews, forks, spoons—you name it. Special sporting models have been designed for fishermen, engineers, and campers, some combining a toolchest of implements into one handy pocketknife.

The Norfolk Sportsman's Knife, manufactured in 1851, was fitted with 75 blades, and took two full years to manufacture. But the award for pocketknife-blade proliferation surely goes to the Year Knife, made—like the Norfolk—by the world's oldest cutlery firm, Joseph Rodgers and Sons Ltd. of Sheffield. This knife, introduced in 1822, contained 1,822 blades, and the firm has added one blade to the knife each year since. By now, of course, it's far from a "pocket" knife. In 1977, this one-of-a-kind tool was fitted with its 1,977th blade, and the number will continue to match the year until 2000 A.D., when there will be no further room for blades in this gargantuan tool.

Though we have little need for the penknife today, pocketknives are still widely manufactured. In the recent past, young boys often carried pocketknives for whittling, or for games like mumblypeg; but after the teenagers of the 50s took to carrying switchblade and push-button knives for less savory purposes, we no longer look kindly upon knife-wielding youths. Laws have been passed in some states stipulating the maximum length for a pocketknife blade—a longer blade is considered a deadly weapon.

If you number yourself among the ranks of pocketknife owners, take note: pocketknife manufacturers warn that their products demand constant attention. The spring joints of each blade should always be kept well oiled. And most important, a pocketknife blade should never be used as a screwdriver or lever. The blades are made from special steels tempered to maintain an edge, but not to withstand the strains of bending. If you need a screwdriver, you'll have no trouble finding a pocketknife fitted with one.

236

Potatoes

"Meat and potatoes" are the foundation of most American cooking, and of many European cuisines as well. The spud is so rooted in Western cooking that it's hard to believe the vegetable was totally unknown in Europe just a few hundred years ago.

In the mid-16th century, Spanish conquistadores in South America discovered that the Incas ate a white tuber they called "papa." (Perhaps it was the "father" of their diet.) The Incas used the plum-sized vegetables in hundreds of ways, baking them in hot ash, eating them raw or dried, and even pounding them into a flour.

The Spaniards thought the tuber was a form of truffle, since the Incas found them underground. Pedro Cieca, an officer of Juan Pizarro, shipped a load of the spuds back to Spain. From there, they were sent to the Pope for inspection, and eventually to a Belgian botanist for classification.

The botanist called the vegetable *taratoufli*, "little truffle," a word recognizable in the present German word for potato, *kartoffel*. But the Spaniards found the spud similar to the sweet potato, called *patata* after the African *batata*, and christened the new vegetable by the same name.

Within 20 years of their arrival, white potatoes were being grown, sold, and eaten in Spain, though far less than the sweet potato. After Sir Walter Raleigh planted potatoes on his Irish estate, spud farms began to sprout up all around the Emerald Isle. But in England and Scotland, the potato remained unpopular for 200 years—defamed as "Ireland's lazy root."

In the late 17th century, the German monarch Frederick William decided that the potato could solve his nation's food shortage, and he decreed that all peasants should plant spuds. Those who refused, would have their noses and ears cut off. It's unknown how many farmers lost their features because of the bog apple, but Frederick's decree may help explain why potatoes have become so popular in Germany.

The English did not become large-scale potato eaters until the latter half of the 18th century. The Scots, meanwhile, continued to resist the spud, with some Presbyterian clergymen declaring that since the vegetable was not mentioned in the Bible, it could not be fit for human consumption.

France was the last European nation to accept the potato. A soldier who had spent considerable time in Germany returned to his homeland to convince fellow Frenchmen that the potato was both edible and delicious, despite medical advice that the vegetable was "toxic and the cause of many illnesses."

The first potato to reach the shores of North America arrived around 1622, imported by Virginia colonists as a food. The first potato cultivation didn't begin in America until 1719, when Irish immigrants planted spud fields in New Hampshire. Thomas Jefferson, by the way, was the first American to serve french fries with beefsteak, a combination now as institutionalized in America as the Declaration of Independence. And it was the German immigrants you can either thank or blame for potato salad.

Of all the foodstuffs indigenous to the Americas, none is as useful as the potato. Potatoes are easy to cultivate and can be stored for long periods of time. To give you an idea of the fecundity of the potato, in 1968, an English farmer reported that just six seed potatoes had yielded a whopping 1,190 pounds of spuds.

The potato is also one of the most versatile vegetables. You can do almost anything to the spud and still it insists on remaining edible. Potatoes can be *home-fried, French-fried, deep-fried, mashed, hash-browned, baked, boiled, oven-roasted,* or made into *chips, sticks, salad,* or *pancakes.* They can be coal-roasted as *mickies,* or powdered into *instant potatoes*—well, you get the idea.

The well-known *Saratoga chips* were invented, not surprisingly, in Saratoga, New York, when a guest-house chef, appropriately named George Crumb, lost his patience with a guest who insisted on thin French fries.

237

Crumb cut a potato into paper-thin slices, dropped them in oil, and—presto!—another American institution was founded.

In 1969, Australian Paul Tully set a record for potato chip devouring by consuming 30 two-ounce bags in 24½ minutes—without a drink. And while we're on the subject, the record for potato gobbling is three pounds in one minute and 45 seconds, set in Worcestershire, England in 1976. We have no idea if the spuds were peeled or unpeeled—or served with or without Worcestershire sauce.

To settle an oft-heard dispute: no, the sweet potato and the yam are *not* the same vegetable. The yam is in fact almost never seen in this country—no matter what food packagers claim to the contrary!

More than one American tourist has been known to ask his confused French waiter for *French fries*. The French actually call them *pommes frites*—and the French word for potato is *pomme de terre*, literally "earth apple."

The French have also contributed *pommes soufflées*, or souffled potatoes, to our gastronomic repertoire. The delicacy was reportedly created by the personal chef of Louis XIV. In this case, necessity was definitely the mother of invention. One afternoon, the king left the palace to inspect his army, then engaged in warfare with the Dutch. On the return voyage to the palace, the Sun King's coach was delayed by a downpour that made the roads impassable. When his master did not appear at the expected hour, the Royal Chef began to panic. The Great Monarch was a most fastidious diner, who insisted that his repasts be served the instant he arrived at the royal dinner table. The cook had prepared a huge batch of the king's beloved *pommes frites*, but as the hours passed and still Louis failed to appear, the fries began to frazzle and turn cold and soggy.

Suddenly, a herald announced the entrance of the king. The agitated chef, in dismay, grabbed the deep-fat fryer and submerged the wilted French fries in sizzling oil, shaking the fryer madly from side to side. Et violà!—a dish fit for a king was born. The potatoes emerged from this second bath in deep hot oil all puffed up—golden brown and heavenly delicious.

To make *pommes soufflées* is a culinary feat. The heat of the oils must be perfect. Consult a good cookbook and try it. You, too, might achieve gastronomic immortality.

According to another tale, however, the origin of the souffled potatoes is considerably less regal. A 19th-century French chef was charged with preparing a banquet to celebrate the opening of a new railroad line. While preparing the repast at one of the new stations, the chef was notified that the train carrying a coachload of dignitaries to the banquet would be delayed. So he took his half-cooked French fries out of the oil and began preparing a fresh batch. Then he was notified that the train was pulling into the station, on time after all. Frantic, the chef plunged the half-cooked potatoes back into the fat, and the soggy fries puffed into crisp ovals—*pommes soufflées!*

Today, Americans consume literally billions of spuds each year—production usually hovers around 34 billion pounds—with the most well-known varieties hailing from Idaho, Maine, and Long Island.

Potatoes remain, pound for pound, one of the cheapest foodstuffs available, perhaps because they can be grown so easily. If you believe some mothers, they'll even grow behind the dirty ears of little boys.

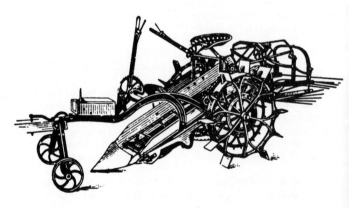

This potato digger is a handy contraption for unearthing spuds from the soil.

RAIN

As if there were any choice. This universal phenomenon carries with it beneficence or disaster. Many large populations pray for the blessing of rain, without which their food supply would parch and put their very existence in grave peril.

Rain, too, can bring floods and other unpleasantnesses.

The theme is so universal that mary artists have tried their hand at limning rain. Here follows some unusually drawings on the subject.

Woodblock print by noted Japanese artist Hiroshige.

Drawing by Crawford Young which first appeared in Caricature, *a magazine published in New York in the 1890s*

This magnificent drawing appeared in a most unexpected place, a humor magazine named Judge, which was published in the United States during the early part of the 20th century.

Drawing which originally appeared in Judge, a humor magazine which flourished in the United States in the 1920s

A painting by Anatoly L-vovich Kaplan, a great Soviet artist

From Punch, *the great English magazine of humor*

241

Drawing by the great French artist, Honore Daumier (1808-1879), noted for his political caricatures, satirizing social inequity.

A refrigerator is a place where you store leftovers until they are ready to be thrown out.

REFRIGERATION

A prominent encyclopedia has suggested that the invention with the greatest impact on worldwide economic life since the railroad is—no, you'd never guess—the refrigerator! Isn't the refrigerator more of a convenience item? Hardly. Refrigeration technology has completely revolutionized farming and has led to the rapid development of a world-wide food trade. It would be difficult, indeed, to find a person in the world today who has not benefited in some way from the

This ice-house was used by George Washington at Mount Vernon to preserve food.

introduction of refrigerated food preservation.

The growth of cities and suburbs in the last century has steadily moved most of us further and further away from our food source, the farm. Without food-preservation techniques, especially refrigeration, it's doubtful that this urban growth could have moved ahead so rapidly. And since the advent of refrigeration, a nation no longer has to feed itself—the abundant supply of one nation can balance the scarcity in another, allowing many nations to industrialize

more quickly. Improved food preservation has also helped increase the world's food supply by eliminating much waste. Foods that would otherwise perish can remain in storage until needed.

Refrigeration may be a recent advance, but food preservation itself has engaged man's attention since the beginning of time. Cheese and butter may, in a sense, be regarded as preserved milk; wine, as preserved grapes. For thousands of years, meat and fish have been preserved by salting or drying, or more recently, by curing with sugar or nitrate compounds. Most of these early stratagems were discovered by chance—they worked, but no

243

one knew why. Only when the existence of bacteria and their influence on foodstuffs became known, could man begin to deal adequately with food preservation.

Without bacteria, edibles would last almost indefinitely. All food-preservation techniques, then, are designed to kill or limit the growth of bacterial life. For instance, the process of drying works because bacteria cannot grow in the absence of moisture. Sterilization by heat—cooking— will completely destroy bacterial life, but the effects are temporary. Cooked food will spoil as rapidly as uncooked food if left untreated.

Cooling does not kill bacteria, but it does stop their growth. Once scientists learned that most bacteria cannot grow at temperatures below the freezing point of water, and also that long-term freezing or cooling of foods does not influence their nutritional content, they knew what was needed for the perfect food-preservation system—a refrigerator. It remained only to invent one.

It had long been known that low temperatures would, for some then unknown reason, preserve food. People in Arctic lands often stored their meat in snow and ice. But to preserve

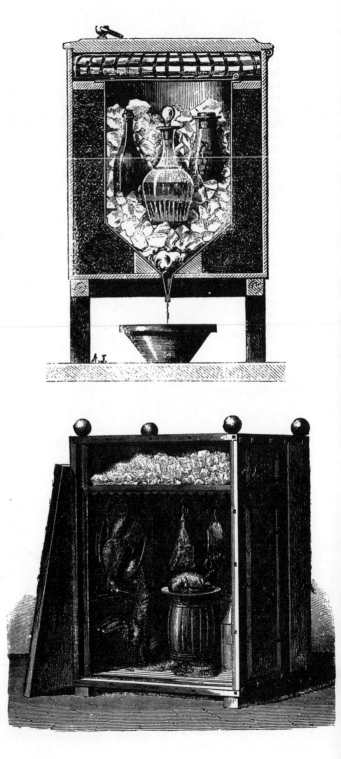

TOP RIGHT:

A primitive icebox used in India in the 1870s.

BOTTOM RIGHT:

This Victorian precursor of the refrigerator had detachable parts that were easy to assemble and disassemble.

244

food, people in warmer climes needed man-made ice.

Ancient Indians made ice the simplest and least dependable way possible—leaving water in special outdoor receptacles overnight. The ancient Romans cooled their wine cellars with snow brought from nearby mountains. They also discovered, as did the Indians, that water could be cooled with the addition of saltpeter. The Romans sometimes chilled liquids by immersing bottles in vessels filled with water and saltpeter, and rotating the bottles rapidly.

Primitive cooling techniques could chill food and drink, but not freeze them; the beneficial effects were temporary. During the 18th century, many scientists developed an interest in mechanical refrigeration, but with neither electricity nor the means to manufacture large quantities of ice, the scientist's road to the new "ice age" was a long and difficult one.

The first "refrigerator" in the United States was invented in 1803 by Thomas Moore of Baltimore, but Moore's machine was

This advertisement appeared in Century Magazine in 1888.

really a "thermos" device—two boxes, one inside the other, with insulating material in-between. Food stored with ice in the inner box would remain cool for a long time, but not cool enough to inhibit bacterial growth for very long.

The next giant step toward successful refrigeration came in 1834, when Jacob Perkins, an American living in England, developed an ice-making machine functioning on the compression principle. Gases subjected to high pressures will remain in the liquid state at temperatures beyond their normal boiling point. Perkins showed that when these compressed liquids were used as refrigerants, they would absorb a great deal of heat before changing to the gaseous state.

The 1870s saw vast improvements in refrigeration techniques. A refrigerator car— really a rolling icebox—had made its earliest appearance in 1851, when several tons of butter made the journey by rail from Ogdensburg, New York to

Boston. But the first application of refrigeration technology to marine food transportation came in 1880, when the steamer *Strathleven* carried a meat cargo from Australia to England. Oddly enough, the meat was meant to be cooled, not frozen—but freezing did take place, and the excellent results led to the subsequent freezing of all meat cargoes.

The domestic refrigerator was not to be used on any scale until this century. In the past, urban Europeans had often hung dairy products out the window to keep them cool for a time. The larder was also used throughout the West for temporary preservation. Earlier in this century, most American homes relied on the icebox for their victuals. The icebox, however, left much to be desired, especially when the iceman did not cometh.

The modern domestic refrigerator is based to a great extent on the work of the Frenchman Edmond Carre. In the 1830s, Carre perfected the first refrigerating machine to be widely adopted for individual use. Carre's machines were used in many Paris restaurants for the production of ice and ice cream products. The first household

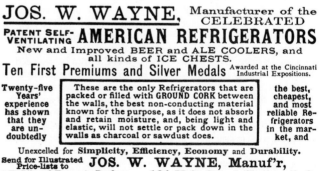

refrigerator patent in the United States was granted in 1899 to one Albert T. Marshall of Brockton, Massachusetts.

Modern refrigerators and freezers use a circulating refrigerant that continually changes from the gaseous to the liquid state. Most machines use dichlordifluoromethane and other refrigerants mercifully known under the trade name of Freon. The liquid refrigerant changes to a gas in the evaporator, then absorbs heat from the food chamber and carries it to the condensing coils, where the refrigerant is cooled by air passing over the coils, and is reconverted into liquid. The cycle is then repeated, spurred on periodically by a small electric motor. Incidentally, your refrigerator is probably your greatest electricity consumer—after your air conditioner.

Wartime restrictions limited the growth of the domestic refrigerator in this country, but after World War II the 'fridge found its way into almost every American home—and so did frozen foods. The American, Clarence Birdseye, is responsible for the development of methods for freezing foods in small packages for the retail trade. The General Foods Corporation introduced the now familiar Birds Eye commercial pack in 1929. Since then, the use of frozen foods has grown with the refrigerator. As early as 1944, Americans were consuming some three billion pounds of frozen meats, vegetables, fruits, fish, and dairy products each year.

During and after World War II, military and industrial research led to the development of the science of cryogenics, the study of matter at extremely low temperatures. Basically, cryogenics—from the Greek word *kryos*, "icy cold"—deals with the production of temperatures below that of liquid oxygen (-297 degrees F.). You hardly need such frigid temperatures to keep your eggs fresh, but cryogenic engineering has had an impact on many elements of modern life, from medicine to space travel.

Scientists are now freely discussing the ultimate cryogenic marvel, suspended animation. Living organisms, including man, can theoretically be kept in a deep freeze almost indefinitely, and resume normal life functions upon thawing. Persons with presently incurable diseases could be frozen before death in the hope of reviving them when cures are found. Intergalactic space travelers could be frozen and revived upon reaching their destination thousands of years later. And think of the possibility of a living time capsule, a human being frozen for thousands of years, to be resurrected by some future civilization to see how we lived in the 20th century!

Restaurants

The restaurant is such a seemingly natural and necessary institution that you'd suspect it's · been with us for as long as man has lived in cities. But the restaurant, as we know it today, is a surprisingly recent development. That's not to say there weren't any commercial eating places before our time. But the menu, with its choice of dishes, is only about 200 years old. The fact is that the diner or the coffee shop in which you may have lunch today offers more of a menu selection than the best of restaurants of the world did just a few centuries back.

The earliest forerunners of the restaurant were the medieval tavern and cookshop. The tavern customarily provided a daily meal, or "ordinary," at a fixed hour and price, usually serving just one dish, much like a household cook providing dinner for a large family. Cookshops primarily sold cooked meat for carry-out, but some did, on occasion, serve food on the premises.

By the 16th century, Englishmen of all classes were in the habit of dining out often. Local taverns offered fixed price meals, wine, ale, and tobacco, and served as a meeting place and informal clubhouse to boot. Entry was generally restricted to men. Among the more famous Elizabethan taverns in London were *The Falcon,* a popular haunt of actors, and *The Mermaid,* oft frequented by William Shakespeare.

Beginning in England around 1650, the coffee house began taking over many of the tavern's social functions. At first, the coffee house served only coffee, tea, and chocolate—all new arrivals to Europe. Then, the coffee houses began providing wine, ale, and occasional hot meals. Another attraction was its supply of gazettes and newsletters regularly kept on hand for coffee swillers on their way to and from work. The clientele evidently was quite varied. An early 18th-century writer noted: "Some shops are a resort for learned scholars and wits; others are the resort of dandies, or of politicians, or again of professional newsmongers, and many are temples of Venus."

For the first real restaurant, we must naturally turn to France.. In 1765, a soup vender named Boulanger opened a shop offering diners a choice of dishes rather than the then standard "ordinary" or "table d'hôte" dinner. The sign above Boulanger's door read *"Restaurants,"* meaning "restoratives," referring to the hot soups and broths available inside. The term restaurant or a derivative, was eventually adopted by many other nations and languages, although the word was not generally used in England until the late 19th century.

Hungry Parisians so enjoyed the new eating place that hundreds of similar establishments began springing up around the city, one offering close to 200 different meat dishes daily.

The first "luxury" restaurant to open its doors in Paris was *La Grande Taverne de Londres,* founded in 1782 by Antoine Beauvilliers. He was later to write a cookbook that became a standard work on French culinary art. According to the rotund gastronomist Brillat-Savarin, Beauvilliers' establishment was the first to offer the four essentials of a fine restaurant: "an elegant room, smart waiters, a choice cellar, and superb cooking."

Prior to the French Revolu-

The Old White Hart Tavern on Bishopsgate Street, London, a popular Renaissance establishment, was one of the precursors of the modern restaurant.

tion, aristocrats maintained elaborate culinary staffs. When the aristocracy was driven from power, their cooks were likewise driven from the kitchen. Many sought work in restaurants or opened their own eating places. By 1804, there were well over 500 restaurants in Paris.

The great culinary establishments of 19th-century Paris included the *Very*, whose menu listed 12 soups. 24 fish dishes, 15 beef dishes, 20 mutton specialties, and scores of side dishes. In 1869, the *Very* was merged with a neighboring restaurant to form the *Le Grand Vefour*, which still ranks near the top among French restaurants. Another great restaurant of the era, the *Cafe Anglais*, had a chef, Adolphe Duglère, who created the famed "Three Emperors Dinner" in 1867 for

Waitresses with bloomers are used in a San Francisco restaurant to attract customers. The drawing is from a Police Gazette of the 1890s.

three well-heeled diners: Tsar Alexander II of Russia, his son, the future Alexander III, and William I, the future emperor of Germany.

Across the English Channel, by the end of the 19th century, the tavern had given way to the restaurant and the tea shop. The first teahouse opened in 1884, initially serving only teas. Later, it offered full meals. Teahouses became immediately popular among women, who, for the first time, had a place where they could eat in public without a male escort. Meanwhile, the lower classes turned to cheap eateries nicknamed "dives" due to their customary underground location.

In the United States, the earliest restaurants on record appeared in Philadelphia around 1680. The *Blue Anchor Tavern* was among the first. New York's *Fraunces Tavern*—the site of George Washington's farewell to his troops—was a popular watering hole in Revolutionary times, and still operates today.

The major American innovations in the field of eateries were the self-service restaurant and the automatic restaurant. The first self-service eatery in New York opened in 1885, but self-service establishments called *cafeterias* first became popular in San Francisco of the gold rush era.

The first automatic restaurant was opened by the Horn & Hardart Baking Company in Philadelphia in 1902, using mechanisms imported from Germany. Other American innovations were the specialty restaurant—the steak house and seafood restaurant, for example—the Pullman diner car, and the riverboat dining room.

By 1955, there were close to 200,000 eating places in the United States—one for every 800 persons—serving over 60 million meals a day with a staff of 1.3 million workers.

The dollar lunch was still a possibility at the posh restaurant, Rector's, in 1894.

Rector's Specialties

Onion Soup   *Lobster, Thermidor*
Chicken casserole, Catalane   *Sweetbread, Prince of Wales*
Boneless Squab en cocotte, Nerac   *Venice Peaches, Mephisto*

Luncheon

OYSTERS 25   CLAMS 25

Soups

Julienne, Pea or Tomato 25 .40   Chicken Gumbo 35 60
Mongole 25 40   Consommé Brunoise 25 40   Oyster Stew 50

Fish

Filets of Sole, Marguery 40 75 *9 minutes*
Aiguillette of Kingfish, Rector 50 90 *9 minutes*
Oysters and Oyster Crabs, Opera 75 *6 minutes*
Brook Trout, maître d'hôtel 45 80, *10 min.*   Bluefish au gratin 40 70, *12 min.*
Frogs' Legs, Poulette 60 1 10, *5 minutes*   Filet of Bass, Mornay 40 70, *7 minutes*

Hot

Roast Beef 40 60   **Spring Lamb**
Braised Beef with noodles 35 60, *ready*   **Irish Lamb Stew 35 60,** *ready*
Shirred Eggs, chicken livers 50, *5 minutes*   Omelette à l'Espagnole 50, *5 minutes*
Emincé of Lamb, green peppers 40 70, *4 min.*   Lamb Fries, Béarnaise 40 70, *8 min.*
Pig's Feet, sauce moutarde 35 60, *6 min.*   Calf's Brains, brown butter 35 60, *4 min.*
Corned Beef Hash browned, poached eggs 40 70, *7 minutes*
Brochette of Chicken Livers, Madeira sauce 40 70, *9 minutes*
Tripe en casserole, nouvelle mode 40 70, *4 minutes*
Deerfoot Sausage, purée of peas 35 60, *6 minutes*
Ham and Spinach, demi-glace 40 70, *5 minutes*
Fresh Mushrooms on toast 60 1 00 *9 minutes.*

Vegetables

New Peas or Beans 50   **New Asparagus 1 00**
Potatoes Sarah 20 30   Oyster Plant 30   Egg Plant 40   Spinach with egg 25 40
Bouldin Island Asparagus 35 60   Asparagus Tips au gratin 35 60
Céleri braisé au jus 30 50   Macaroni, Spaghetti or Noodles 25 40

Game, Etc.

Ruddy Duck 2 00   Squab Chicken 1 25   Teal Duck 1 00
Squab, Plover, Snipe or Railbird 80   Spring Chicken 1 50 75
Broiled Half Capon 1 25   Half Spring Turkey 1 50

Salads

Hot House Tomato or Cucumber 35 60   Chiffonade 40 70   Rector 45 75
Lettuce, Chicory, Celery or Escarole 30 50   Romaine 35 60
Fetticus with beets or dandelion 30 50   Mayonnaise 10

Dessert

Fresh Strawberries with cream 75   French Pastry [assorted] 25
Brandied : Figs, Peaches, Cherries or Plums 25 40

Ices

Fancy Ice : Plombière au kirsch 40   Souveniers : Pin Cushion 50
All Plain Cream or Ices 25   mixed 30
Cheese   Fruits
COFFEE : French 15   Turkish 20   Special 25

HALF PORTIONS FOR ONE PERSON ONLY

Rector's

THE FOOD STALLS OF SINGAPORE: *A series of restaurants open to the public under the aegis of the city-state. The interior may consist of 30 or so individual food emporiums. Stalls specialize in dishes. There is a stall that sells roast duck, another that sells roast pork, still another that sells fruit juice, another cake, etc.*

You walk around in these restaurant complexes, and you select the food you want. Each table is numbered. When ordering, you give the stall keeper the number of your table. A few minutes later, your order is delivered to you. The food is good, clean, and exceptionally well priced. These pictures show the food stalls on Tanglin Road.

251

Annual sales totaled about nine billion dollars, making the restaurant the third largest retail business in this country. About 20 percent of all restaurant sales are now rung up on the cash registers of large American chains. These include *Howard Johnson's*, *McDonald's*, and other various hamburger drive-ins.

> *Two men sat down in a restaurant and ordered their main dishes. Then they closed their menus. The waiter said, "Thank you, gentlemen, and would any of you wish a beverage with your meal?"*
>
> *One man said, "Well, I usually have coffee, but today, I think I'll have a glass of milk."*
>
> *The other man said, "That sounds good. I'll have milk, too. But make sure the glass is clean!"*
>
> *"Very good," said the waiter, and he left.*
>
> *Soon he came back with a tray and two glasses of milk, and said, "Here you are, gentlemen. Now which one of you asked for the clean glass?"*

Today, the last word in gastronomic excellence is the guide published by the Michelin Corporation, a French tire firm. Michelin annually rates restaurants in thousands of towns and cities, awarding each from zero to three stars according to culinary quality. One star indicates good quality in its class; two stars suggests the restaurant is well worth a detour; and three ranks the establishment among the best in the world.

In a recent typical year, Michelin rated a total of 3,036 restaurants in France: 2,382 were rated as unstarred; 581 received one star; 62 received two stars; and only 11 restaurants earned the highest Michelin compliment of three stars. Five of these gastronomic palaces were in Paris, among them *Grand Véfour* and *La Tour D'Argent*, the oldest surviving restaurant in Paris.

Many culinary connoisseurs, however, maintain that for the best in *haute cuisine* you'll have to travel to Vienne, near Lyons, where you'll find the renowned *Pyramide*. Other gourmets would name Paul Bocuse's *Auberge Pont de Collonges*, near Lyons, as the world's premier restaurant, or perhaps the *Auberge de l'Ill* in Illhausen, Alsace, or the *Hotel Côte D'Or* in Saulieu, near Dijon.

France, of course, has no monopoly on fine food. (Modern French cuisine, by the way, is Italian in origin.) Many gourmets avow that Chinese cuisine is actually the world's finest, and excellent Oriental restaurants can be found in most cities of the world.

It's been estimated that a New Yorker can dine out every night of his life until age 65 without visiting any establishment twice!

Among New York's restaurants, *Lutèce* and *La Grenouille* have been given high marks by Michelin, and certainly rank among the finest restaurants on this side of the Atlantic. *Windows on the World*, located atop one the 110-story World Trade Center towers, has been lauded for its view more than its food. Reservations for dinner at the sky-high restaurant must sometimes be made weeks in advance. And any list of Gotham's posh restaurants must include *The Palace* where dinner prices are, at this writing, $75 per person— without drinks!

It's been estimated that a New Yorker can dine out every night of his life until age 65 without visiting any establishment twice!

ROSES

The Madame de Watteville Rose

The red rose whispers of passion
And the white rose breathes of love;
O, the red rose is a falcon,
And the white rose is a dove.

—John Boyle O'Reilly, *A White Rose*

Quick, name a flower. Well, you may not have said *rose*, but if you were to experiment with the question you'd probably find that, of the estimated 300,000 species of plants on earth, the rose is the first flower to pop into most minds.

Why? It's difficult to say. Many other flowers are larger, more colorful, more fragrant, or more valued. But no single flower is so universally known, so closely connected with the culture of many civilizations, so rich in poetic and mythologic significance as the rose. Symbol of beauty, romance, love, secrecy, perfection, elegance, and life itself, the rose has figured in legend, heraldry, and religion, and has served as the favorite of poets and artists from time immemorial.

Immortalized in songs, such as *The Last Rose of Summer, Sweet Rosie O'Grady,* and *My*

The Papa Gontier Rose

Wild Irish Rose, the rose has been, and will likely forever remain, the queen of flowers.

The botanical family Rosaceae, which includes close to 200 species and thousands of hybrids, has flourished for millions of years. Indeed, roses have been cultivated for so long that it's impossible to determine where or when the flower was first domesticated. The Egyptians were familiar with cultivated roses by 3000 B.C., building rose gardens in their palaces and often burying roses in their tombs. By the time of Cleopatra's reign, the rose had replaced the lotus as Egypt's ceremonial flower.

The mythologies of various ancient cultures touched on the rose. Most agreed that the flower was created when the gods were still on earth. The Greeks called the rose, "the king of flowers" until the poet Sappho, in her *Ode to the Rose,* dubbed it as the "queen of flowers" forevermore. According to the Greeks, the rose first appeared with the birth of Aphrodite, the goddess of love and beauty. When Aphrodite (in Roman mythology, Venus) first emerged from the sea, the earth produced the rose to show that it could match the gods in the creation of perfect beauty. The well-known painting by Botticelli, *Birth of Venus,* depicts dozens of roses in a scene of the goddess emerging from the sea.

Another myth tells of a beautiful maiden named Rhodanthe (*rhodon* in Greek means "rose") who was tirelessly pursued by three suitors. To escape her pursuers, Rhodanthe fled to the temple of Artemis, where her attendants, convinced that Rhodanthe was even more beautiful than Artemis, flung a statue of the goddess from its pedestal and demanded that Rhodanthe

be represented there instead. The god Apollo, angered by the insult to his twin sister, Artemis, turned Rhodanthe into a rose and her attendants into thorns. The three suitors were changed into the three courtiers of the rose: the bee, the worm, and the butterfly.

Yet another myth blames the god Eros, or Cupid, for the rose's thorny stem. According to the tale, the god of love was enjoying the aroma of the thornless rose

when he was stung by a bee lurking in the petals. To punish the flower, Cupid shot the stem full of his arrows, and the rose forever after was cursed with arrowhead-shaped thorns. Yet, according to a Chinese proverb, "The rose has thorns only for those who gather it."

The word *rosary* comes to us from the Latin *rosarium,* meaning a "rose garden," and later the word came to mean "a garland of

roses." Christian legend tells of a monk who made a garland of 150 roses each day as an offering to the Virgin Mary. Later, the monk substituted 150 prayers for the flowers.

Though various mythologies have explained the origin of the rose differently, almost all ancient cultures valued the rose for its beauty and fragrance. Roman aristocrats strewed roses around their banquet halls and served a wine made from roses. Moslem monarchs in India bathed in pools with rose petals floating on top of the water. According to the *Thousand and One Arabian Nights*, the Caliph of Baghdad served a jam made from roses that held captive anyone who ate it.

The use of the rose as a symbol of beauty, frailty, and love is quite understandable, but the flower has also symbolized crea-tion, secrecy, the Church, and the risen Christ. The rose windows featured in most Gothic cathedrals are thought by some to represent life and creation, or hope radiating from faith and the Church.

A root in the right soil,
Sun, rain, and a man's toil;
That, as a wise man knows,
Is all there is to a rose.

—Orgill Mackenzie,
Whitegates

As a symbol of love and romance, the rose needs little introduction. As some are fond of noting, *rose* is an anagram of "Eros."

Robert Burns compared his "love" to a "red, red rose, that's newly sprung in June." And a German custom dictated that a groom send a silver rose to his bride before the marriage ceremony—a custom that forms the basis of the plot of Richard Strauss's opera *Der Rosenkavalier*.

Since classical times, the rose has been a symbol of secrecy. In 16th-century England, a rose was sometimes worn behind the ear by servants, tavern workers, and others to indicate that the wearer heard all and told nothing. In Germany, roses in a dining room suggested that diners could speak freely without fear that their secrets would travel beyond the room. The expression *sub rosa*, which literally means "under the rose," actually means "secretly," and is thought to originate in the custom of carving a rose over the door of the confessional in a Catholic church.

Roses are distilled to make perfume.

Exactly why the rose came to be a symbol of secrecy is open to speculation. Perhaps the un-opened rosebud suggests beauty or truth hidden by the closed petals. In any case, medieval alchemists used the rose as a symbol of the need for secrecy in their art, and as a representation of certain highly guarded scientific principles important in their work. The secret society of the Rosicrucians—from "red cross"—used a cross with a red rose as their symbol.

In medieval England, many families employed a represen-tation of the rose in their coat of arms: the red rose of Lancaster and the white rose of York are two well-known examples. During the 15th century, these two houses fought for control of the English crown in a struggle that came to be known as the War of the Roses.

The rose has, of course, proved useful in more ways than the symbolic. Rose water was first distilled around the time of the Crusades. When the Moslem leader Saladin retook Jerusalem from the Crusaders, he refused to enter a mosque until all the walls and the objects had been purified with rose water. Over 50 camels were required to transport the aromatic cargo from Baghdad to Jerusalem.

Rose oil, used in perfumes and lotions, likewise originated in the Near East, and did not appear in Europe until 1612. A 17th-century German book lists 33 diseases that supposedly can be cured by rose water or oil.

During the 18th century, rose petals occasionally were included in English salads, and essence of roses was used to flavor ice cream.

Today, roses are grown ex-tensively in many parts of the world, especially in France, India, and the Balkans, and attar of roses is used in perfumes, cos-metics, and flavoring syrups. Rose hips, the fruits of the rose plant, are used to make tea, or as a source of Vitamin C.

The Empress Josephine of France, the wife of Napoleon, put the rose to a more singular use. Josephine built a huge rose gar-den at her estate at Malmaison, with over 250 varieties of the flower flourishing—every variety known at the time. The Empress often carried in hand a Malmaison rose that she could raise to her lips when smiling, since she was particularly sen-sitive about her imperfect teeth.

The rose has been cultivated and hybridized for so long that there are, strictly speaking, no species of purely wild rose left on earth. The flowers extant today range in size from just half an inch in diameter to varieties that spread to more than seven inches. Colors range from white through yellow, pink, red, and maroon.

Some roses smell like—well, roses, while others suggest green tea, hay, or various spices. Biologically, the rose's fragrance is quite important, since roses normally do not secrete nectar and depend mostly on aroma and color to attract pollinating in-sects.

There are about 35 species of rose thought to be native hybrids of North America. Various roses are the state flowers of Iowa, North Dakota, and New York. While the Greeks and Romans named their roses after gods, and the English after court figures, in America the preference is for de-scriptive or geographical names, such as the *pasture*, the *prairie*, the *smooth*, the *prickly*, or the *California rose*. The Chinese, meanwhile, have long used metaphoric names for the flower. The names of some Chinese rose varieties translate as *After Rain*, *Clear Shining*, *Tiny Jade Shoulders*, and *Three Rays of Dawn*.

Speaking of poetic descrip-tions, the prominent metaphoric use of the rose through the ages has left us with a considerable body of "rosy" verse. Robert Her-rick wrote *Gather ye rosebuds while ye may*, William Blake gave us *The Sick Rose*, and W.B. Yates, *The Rose of the World*. But surely the simplest observa-tion concerning the queen of flowers came from the pen of Gertrude Stein, whose poem, *Sacred Emily* includes the line, "A rose is a rose is a rose is a rose."

Rulers

Here's something to think about: a dry goods dealer has a five-yard piece of 32-inch wide material, and wishes to sell a customer one-and-a-half yards. But neither a yardstick, nor a tape measure, nor any other measuring device is available. Can the dealer complete the sale?

Yes, it can be done, as you'll discover later; but for now, take our word for it. Using a ruler or a tape measure would be a lot easier than figuring out this problem in your head. In fact, much of our commercial life would be next to impossible without implements for estimating length and distance. Why "estimate?" Well, if the American mission that landed a man on the moon had depended upon measuring devices only as accurate as the ruler in a schoolboy's briefcase, our astronauts would most likely have missed the moon altogether!

No ruler or measuring device is completely accurate; in fact, no measurement of any kind is ever *absolutely* correct. A measuring device is, in effect, only a reproduction of an arbitrary standard. While the standard itself is perfectly accurate, the reproduction *never* is. For instance, the standard of length measure in the United States is the yard. Theoretically, a yard is a yard is a yard, but no yardstick ever measures *exactly* 36 inches.

The first common unit of length was the *cubit,* used by the Egyptians and Babylonians thousands of years ago. Originally, the cubit was defined as the length of a man's arm from the elbow to the end of the middle finger (the word comes from the Latin word for "elbow"), but the actual length of the cubit varied from place to place and from

257

time to time. Through most of Egyptian history, the cubit was equivalent to about 20.6 inches. One advantage of the cubit was that in the absence of a measuring device the unit could be easily—handily, you might say—approximated. Presumably, long-armed merchants were quite popular in Egypt.

In Egyptian, the cubit was called the *meh,* and divided into units called *sheps,* or "palms." There were seven *sheps* in a cubit, and the *shep* in turn was divided into four parts, called *zebos,* or "digits." "Let's see—I'll have two *mehs,* six *sheps,* three *zebos* of that linen..."

The ancient Greek cubit was about 20.7 inches, but another unit of measurement, the *foot,* was more widely used. The Greek foot was about 12.5 inches, divided into 25 digits. The Romans adopted a *pes,* or foot, of about 11.6 inches, divided into 16 digits.

Prior to the 19th century, each country in Europe had its own system of weights and measures. In medieval England, for instance, the foot was equivalent to 13.2 inches, with six feet to a *fathom,* 10 fathoms to a *chain,* 10 chains to a *furlong,* and 10 furlongs to an *old mile,* equivalent to about 6,600 feet. The English units of measure evolved from many origins, some as old as the Roman conquest.

By 1800, length measure standards were fixed in England at their present values. The unit of length measurement was the *yard* (from the Anglo-Saxon *gyrd,* "measure"), divided into feet and inches. English kings kept a bar known as *the standard yard* in London as the ultimate arbiter of the yard's exact length.

The idea of a physical standard is an old one. Physical standards are kept, not to settle every measurement dispute by direct reference to the standard, but to have a permanent—or so it was thought—record of each measuring standard. But even a physical standard can be inaccurate. It's been estimated that the new British standard yard has decreased by .0002 inches since it was cast a little over a hundred years ago.

The original standard yard was lost when the Houses of Parliament burned in 1834. Scientific studies followed to determine a new standard and to produce a unified system of weights and measures. In 1878, the British imperial yard was defined as the distance at a specified temperature between two lines engraved on gold studs sunk in a certain bronze bar.

Measurement systems from England, France, Spain, and Portugal were all brought to America by colonists, and all were used here briefly in various places. By the time of the American Revolution, standards of measurement here were identical to those current in England. In 1832, an American physical standard was adopted, defining the yard as the distance between the 27th and 63rd inch of a certain 82-inch brass bar kept in Washington, D.C. Since 1893, the U.S. standard yard has been defined in terms of the meter.

The yard is still the standard of length measurement in this country, of course; but most other nations, including England, have gone over to the metric system. Although a decimal system for measurement was first proposed as long ago as 1670, the essentials of today's metric system were embodied in a

report made by the Paris Academy of Science in 1791.

The original plan for a metric system defined the meter as one ten-millionth part of a meridional quadrant of the earth Larger units were formed by the addition of Greek prefixes (deca-, hecto-, kilo-), and smaller units with Latin prefixes (deci-, centi-, milli-). A platinum bar was cast according to this definition for use as the physical standard, although few scientists at the time were satisfied with its accuracy.

The new measuring system did not catch on immediately. Many years passed before it was widely adopted in France and other countries. In 1875, a treaty was signed assuring international unification and improvement of the system. Four years later, the standard meter was newly defined with reference to a bar of platinum-iridium alloy. In 1927, a supplementary definition described the meter in terms of light waves, for while a platinum bar can be destroyed or altered, light wave measurement will always be available. With such a standard, a unit of measurement can be verified anywhere in the world without risking damage in transit to the physical standard.

Along with the United States, only Liberia, Southern Yemen, and a handful of other small nations still employ the so-called British system, and the metric system will soon be introduced in most of these countries as well. The exact date for total metric conversion here has not yet been fixed, but Canada began the switchover in 1977.

A number of other terms are sometimes used for length measurement. For instance, have you ever wondered what a *furlong* was? The term originated with the word "furrow," and at one time was thought to be the length most suitable for a plow furrow. The furlong is now defined as 220 yards.

The word *league* has varied in meaning in different times and countries. In England, the league was equivalent to about three miles. For centuries now, the word league has been used chiefly in a figurative sense.

The *knot* is not a measurement of length, so if you ever hear a sailor say "knots per hour" you'll know he's a landlubber in disguise. The knot is actually a measurement of speed, equivalent to one nautical mile per hour.

The *nautical mile* is defined three different ways, since navigators once regarded the nautical mile as the length of one minute of the meridian at the place where they were taking the reading. The U.S. nautical mile has been identical to the international unit since 1959, measuring 6,076 feet.

The *fathom* was originally thought to be the length to which a man can extend his arms—if you can fathom that. Today, the fathom is equivalent to six feet, and is used most often in reference to water depth and cable length.

The smallest unit of length measurement in the world is the *atto-meter*, equivalent to a mere quintillionth of a centimeter. Your pinky is probably about 7,000,000,000,000,000,000 atto-meters long!

For a measuring device, early man probably first used his arms or his foot—but even during the Egyptian era, when the cubit was the unit of length measurement, a ruler of some kind was more often used. There are two basic kinds of length-measuring devices: the end standard, and the line standard. With an end standard, the unit is defined as the length from one end of the device to the other; with a line standard, from one calibration on the device to another. Most modern rulers are end standards; that is, a foot ruler is one foot long from end to end, and a yardstick is one yard long.

How accurate is a modern ruler? Suppose you want to draw a two-inch line on a piece of paper. First of all, the calibrations on the ruler are a fraction of an inch thick. Thus, a dot that looks correctly placed to you, may appear off-center to another eye. The calibrations themselves are never absolutely precise, and the edges of most rulers are slightly warped. The chance of your line measuring precisely two inches, then, is slim, indeed.

Rulers come in many shapes and sizes, among them the three-edged or triangular ruler so often used by students—both for measuring and for launching rubber bands across the classroom.

A tape measure is used for very long measurement, or for the measurement of a bent surface. Calipers consist of two prongs joined by a pin; they are best for measuring thickness or the distance between two surfaces.

As any draftsman can tell you, there's a world of difference between a ruler and a straight edge. No draftsman worth his T-square would use a ruler for drawing an accurate straight line, since rulers are designed chiefly for measuring, not line drawing.

With this map-measure, you can calculate anything from centimeters to miles.

259

For a crisp, straight line, it's best to use a triangle or other device specifically designed for line drawing.

Measure for measure, these modern devices pictured below achieve maximum accuracy.

Left: The Disc Ranger measures distances from 6 feet to almost as far as the eye can see, in yards, nautical miles, and statute miles.

Right: The Tapeless Tape Measure is a skid-proof, mar-proof wheel that glides along surfaces and measures distances on a digital counter.

Bottom: The Manpo Measure Meter tells you at a glance how far you've walked.

You remember our dry goods dealer and his measuring dilemma? Well, here's what you would have to go through to cut the material without a measuring device.

The customer wants one-and-a-half yards, or 54 inches. Without a ruler, this will have to be measured out along a strip of paper. First, fold the five-yard piece of fabric in half. It now measures 90 inches long. Overlap the material so that you divide it into three equal parts. Each part will be 30 inches. Lay this on the piece of paper and mark off the 30 inches. Now, unfold the material. This time fold the width in half; this will give you 16 inches. Mark off 16 inches next to your 30-inch mark on the paper. Now fold the width in half again, giving you eight inches. Mark off an additional eight inches along your piece of paper. You now have marked off a total of 54 inches. Lay your length of material along the marked paper and cut your customer the desired one-and-a-half yards.

And next time, get yourself a ruler or a tape measure!

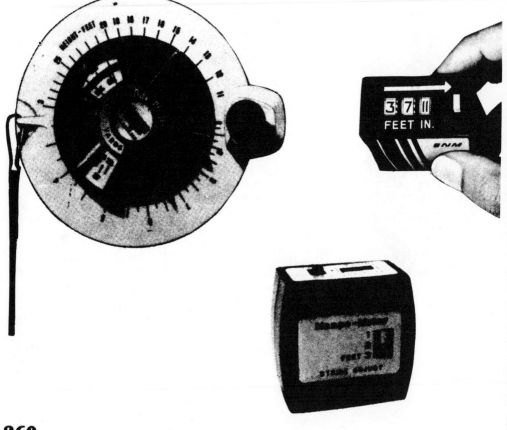

Safety Pins

On April 10, 1849, a New Yorker by the name of Walter Hunt was granted patent Number 6,281 for a device he called the safety pin. Never heard of Walter Hunt, you say? Well, Hunt was not destined to be pinned with the tag "inventor of the safety pin" for one simple reason: the safety pin, or devices virtually identical to it, had been in use for more than 2,500 years—since the days of ancient Greece!

The earliest fasteners used by man were straight pins, usually simple thorns. Relics of prehistoric man 20,000 years old include bone needles with eyes, and pins with decorated heads. The art of pin making actually predates agriculture, pottery, and metalworking.

The Egyptians didn't use the safety pin or button, but they did fashion straight pins and needles from metal. Bronze pins eight inches long have been found in Egyptian tombs, many with decorated gold heads.

Every period of classical Greece and Rome had its own forms of safety pin and clasp. In fact, the forms of each period were so distinctive that a safety pin can frequently be used to accurately date an entire archaeological find. During some periods, safety pin heads commonly took the form of serpents, horses, and lutes; other periods produced heads with abstract designs.

Homer tells us that a dozen safety pins were presented to Penelope, the wife of Odysseus by her suitors, suggesting that the Greeks considered pins fitting gifts, even for royalty. Presumably, almost all early Greeks used safety pins to fasten their tunics, since the button wasn't to arrive from Asia Minor until considerably later.

Athenian women used long, daggerlike pins to fasten their chitons over their shoulders. According to Herodotus, when a group of angry women used the pins to stab to death an Athenian soldier, the city forbade the wearing of all but the Ionion tunic, which did not require pins. The law was later revoked; but by then, women were using buttons as well as safety pins.

This elaborate Etruscan safety pin dates from the third century B.C.

The Romans called the safety pin *fibula*, a term still used for a clasp, and also for a certain leg bone. A bust from the late Empire shows a consul wearing a tunic fastened by two safety pins as long as his head, suggesting that in Rome the size of a *fibula* may have indicated rank.

In Medieval Europe, the wealthy used elaborately fashioned safety pins of ivory, brass, silver, and gold, while the poor had to make do with simple wood skewers. By the 15th century, pins were being manufactured from drawn iron wire, and a pin-making industry was well established in France.

But for centuries, metal pins remained rare and costly items reserved for the rich. You've heard the expression *pin money*, meaning a small sum allotted by a husband for his wife's use, or money for incidental items. Well, when the term originated in the 14th century, "pin money" was just that, for at that time, pins were expensive enough to be real items on the budget. By custom, a husband would present his wife on the first or second of January with enough money to buy her pins for the year. "Pin money" went by the boards in the 19th century, when mass-production made pins the inexpensive purchase they are today.

The father of the American pin industry was Samuel Slocum, who in 1838, founded a pin factory in Poughkeepsie, New York, capable of turning out 100,000 pins a day. Though Slocum was not the first to design a machine for manufacturing pins, his pins were the first to be mass-produced in America. Slocum's pins had solid heads, and came to be known as *Poughkeepsie pins*. Slocum was also the first to devise a machine for packaging pins in grooved paper boards.

There's another reason why Walter Hunt is forgotten as the "inventor" of the safety pin. The would-be pin magnate rather hastily conceived his idea, made a model, and sold his patent rights for the sum of $100—all within three hours! In any case, diaper-wearing babies have expressed their gratitude ever since, with hours of sob-free slumber.

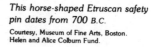

This horse-shaped Etruscan safety pin dates from 700 B.C.

Courtesy, Museum of Fine Arts, Boston. Helen and Alice Colburn Fund.

"Diamond Dee" "Skirt Grip."
COMBINATION BELT AND SKIRT SUPPORTER
"Patent 1 Dec. 29, 1896."

UTILITY,
SECURITY,
SIMPLICITY.

Holds the Skirt Up. Holds the Belt in Position. Holds the Waist Down.

For Sale at all the Leading Retailers
At Wholesale only No. 7 E. 17th St. N.Y.

The safety pin made a critical contribution to the wasp-waist look of the gay 90s.

The 19th century was the big era for fasteners of all kinds. Buttons are thousands of years old, but it wasn't until 1863 that Louis Hannart invented the *snap.*

And 1896 saw the first patent for a "slide fastener," a device invented five years earlier by Witcomb Judson as a "clasp locker and unlocker for shoes." The term we use today, *zipper,* originally referred only to a boot equipped with a slide fastener.

Judson, a Chicago inventor, became so tired of lacing and unlacing his high boots that he set out to devise a quicker, easier way of fastening them. At first, he peddled his invention door-to-

door as the *C-Curity Placket Fastener,* using the slogan "Pull and It's Done." But Judson's zipper, a series of hooks and eyes, was crude by modern standards, and tended to open or stick.

Judson eventually sold his patent rights to Lewis Walker, who, with the aid of a Swede named Gideon Sundback, developed the first modern zipper in 1906. Zippers began to appear on tobacco pouches, mailbags, and galoshes around 1920; but by and large, the garment industry regarded the zipper as a passing fad. At the time, the only garments fitted with zippers were theatrical costumes for quick-change artists.

The 1930s saw the development of an improved zipper, with the metal teeth die cast directly onto the zipper tape fabric. Die cast teeth with rounded edges made the zipper completely dependable for the first time. Soon, everyone was using zippers.

Those of you who are presently struggling with torn, toothless, or unlockable zippers might be interested to know that modern zipper manufacturers claim their products can withstand 200,000 openings and closings without showing signs of wear. Tell it to the marines!

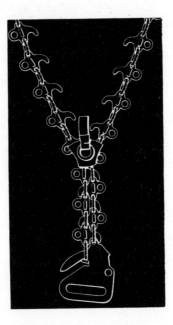

The first zipper was invented in 1891 by an engineer named Witcomb L. Judson.

263

SALT

Interior of a salt mine.

When we eat and drink, we consume hundreds of chemicals combined in an appetizing form, and our bodies do the work of separating and distributing them. But there are two chemicals that we consume largely in their pure form, and these are two of the most important: H_2O and $NaCl$—water and salt.

Fortunately, these are also two of the most abundant chemicals on our planet. Two-thirds of the earth is covered with water, and the oceans are about three percent sodium chloride—that's the chemical term for ordinary table salt. Considering its abundance, it might seem odd that salt has been so highly valued by man throughout the ages—salt not only *costs* money, in some places it has been used *as* money!

Salt occurs in crystals of various sizes, made up of any number of individual molecules, each of which contains one atom of the element sodium, and one atom of the element chlorine. In the body,

salt bathes all living tissues and helps flush out wastes. Unfortunately, it will also flush out water from our cells. For if a man could drink salt water, there would be no need for many of the extensive water-carrying systems we've constructed through history to bring water to our cities. And there would be little need for a salt trade.

But salt water, instead of replenishing living cells with water, has the opposite effect: Salt water, denser than pure water, draws water out of the cells through osmosis. Thus, even a man dying of thirst dares not drink salt water, as Coleridge's Ancient Mariner bemoaned in the oft-misquoted lines:

> *Water, water, everywhere,*
> *Nor any drop to drink.*

As you might expect, the use of salt dates back to the oldest of man's civilizations, though there are still peoples today who do not use it. Before the beginnings of agriculture, nomadic man subsisted on milk and roasted meats, which retain their natural salt, and therefore he did not need additional salt in his diet. But the rise of agricultural societies, with their vegetable and cereal diets, created the need for salt supplements.

We know that the ancient Sumerians ate salted meat and used salt to preserve food as long ago as 3500 B.C. According to a Mesopotamian legend, the benefits of salt were discovered when a wounded pig ran into the ocean and drowned. The pork thus soaked in brine was found to taste better than unsalted meat. The value of salt as a preservative and purifier was well known by Biblical times, for Job said: "Can nothing which is unsavory be eaten without salt?" Salt trade routes connected Mesopotamia, Egypt, and India at a very early date.

Because the habitual use of salt accompanied man's transition from nomadic to agricultural society, salt has long been esteemed as an object of religious significance and a gift of the gods. According to a Finnish myth, the god of the sky struck fire in the heavens, and the sparks fell to the ocean and turned into salt. Another ancient myth held that our salt water oceans are made up of all the tears ever cried. Early man often included salt in his sacrificial offerings to the gods, and used salt-filled pendants to ward off evil.

Salt was also used to seal covenants among ancient men, for its preservative qualities made it a fitting symbol for an enduring agreement. The Arab expression "there is salt between us" means a binding agreement has been reached, while the Persian "untrue to salt" refers to a broken covenant. The Biblical phrase "salt of the earth" still implies "elite."

Homer called salt divine, and mentioned its use at feasts. The ancient Greeks ate salted fish, and sometimes used salt in bartering for slaves and other items. The expression "worth his salt" may have first been uttered by a satisfied slave buyer who'd made his purchase with a quantity of salt.

Salt was a major commodity in ancient Rome. The *Via Salaria*, or salt route, was one of the oldest roads in Italy, the route by which salt was transported from salt pans near Ostia to other parts of the peninsula. By Imperial times, the salt oases of Northern Africa were linked by caravan routes, and other trade routes brought salt to Italy from salt pans around the Black Sea. Roman soldiers were given a ration of salt, called a *salarium,* which later became an allowance of money with which to buy salt—thus the origin of our word "salary."

The phrase "with a grain of salt" also dates back to Roman times. The Triumvir Pompey was known to add a grain of salt to his drinks as a supposed antidote to poison. Therefore to take something *cum grano salis* is to regard it with suspicion, or accept it with reservations.

Salt was used as currency in Tibet, Ethiopia, and other parts of Africa, in some cases until relatively recent times. During an invasion of Ethiopia in the late 19th century, Italian soldiers found blocks of salt stored in bank vaults along with more familiar forms of currency. Tribal Africans have been known to prefer salt to cash as payment for their wares, explaining "you can't eat dollars." And when salt has not been used by governments as official currency, it's often been used to *raise* money. European monarchs at various times taxed salt so heavily that it became affordable only on the black market.

The first American colonists had their salt shipped across the ocean from England. But a salt factory was established in Virginia as early as 1630, just a few years after the arrival of the colonists at Jamestown, and was probably one of the first factories of any kind on this side of the Atlantic. Americans continued to rely largely on imported salt until the War of 1812 cut off English shipments, at which time an American salt industry began to flourish in the area around Syracuse, New York.

In 1848, the company that was to become Morton Salt, the largest salt producer in the United States, was founded in Chicago. Morton now maintains salt processing plants in a number of states, and works almost every large salt field in the nation, with major deposits in New York, Pennsylvania, Ohio, West Virginia, Michigan, and the Great Salt Lake area of Utah. The Morton girl, with her umbrella and salt cannister, has graced packages of the firm's salt since 1914, though she's been redesigned a number of times since then.

Salt is found on earth in three basic forms: salt water, brine deposits, and rock salt crystal. The oceans hold by far the largest supply. Each gallon of sea water contains about four ounces of salt. It's been estimated that all the seas of the world contain some 4.5 billion cubic miles of salt, an amount equal to over 14 times the bulk of Europe!

Sea water close to the polar regions contains slightly less salt than water near the equator. The salt content of enclosed seas such as the Red Sea and the Mediterranean is also higher than ocean water. The most saline of all water, the Dead Sea, covers only about 350 square miles, yet contains some 11.6 billion tons of salt. The highly saline River Jordan pours six million tons of water into the Dead Sea daily, which after evaporation leaves behind about 850,000 tons of salt each year, much of it sodium chloride. The peculiar taste and smell of the salty Dead Sea water moved ancient Arab writers to call it "the stinking sea."

Rock salt deposits are almost entirely the result of sea water evaporation in areas once covered by the oceans. In Utah, salt can literally be scooped up off the ground, but in other places salt domes may be found more than 1,000 feet below ground. The Wieliczka mine near Cracow, Poland, is one of the world's most famous, with almost 70 miles of multi-leveled tunnels, a restaurant and two chapels with rock-salt walls and statues hewn from salt, and an underground salt lake that tourists can row across.

About 45 percent of the salt mined today comes directly from sea water. But in the United States, the largest supply comes from the evaporation of natural and artificial brines. In an artificial brine, water is pumped into a salt dome and then brought back to the surface, where the water can be evaporated and the salt collected.

The brine is first placed in settling tanks to remove impurities, then fed to a vacuum pan evaporator to eliminate the water. Invented in 1886 by the American Joseph Duncan, the vacuum pan evaporator allows salt producers to turn out the uniformly-sized cubic grains of salt we're likely to see in our salt shakers. Before the vacuum pan, salt was packaged in crystals of varying shapes and sizes.

After the salt is removed from the pans, it's filtered again, dried by heat, and passed through screens to produce grains of the desired size. Chem-

265

Russian convicts at work in the salt quarry at Iletsk, in Siberia, in the 1880s.

icals such as magnesium silicate and tricalcium phosphate are then added to table salt to make it free flowing. Since 1924, potassium iodide has also been added to some table salt to assure that Americans living inland receive an adequate supply of iodine, normally supplied by fresh seafood.

The United States is presently the world's largest producer of salt, turning out about 45 million tons each year. Other large salt-producing nations include the U.S.S.R., China, India, France, West Germany, and the United Kingdom. Annual worldwide production stands at around 160 million tons.

That may seem like a lot of salt for the salt shakers of the world. But the fact is, less than 10 percent of the salt produced in the United States is used in food industries, and only about three percent as table salt. Salt is now produced predominantly for use in the manufacture of major chemicals and household products such as bleaches, glass, soap, cement, paints and dyes, plastics, and water softeners. On the farm, salt is fed to livestock in large

blocks. And since salt lowers the melting point of snow, it's often strewn over icy roads to speed up melting.

Once one of the most highly prized materials on earth, salt is now one of the cheapest products available in the supermarket—it costs only about 15¢ per pound. In fact, salt is so cheap and plentiful that the overuse of salt has become a bigger health problem than salt deficiency. The sodium in salt can contribute to high blood pressure and other ailments. Nutritionists have begun to petition the food industry to remove some of the salt now added to almost all prepared foods.

But convincing Americans to forsake salt may be a difficult task. After all, salt cellars will be found on the tables of every restaurant, diner, and coffee shop in the nation. Salt is still one of the very few things that you can get for free!

Scissors

Scissors are one of those ubiquitous everyday objects so common and useful today that it's hard to imagine a time when they weren't around. You don't have to—scissors of one kind or another have existed for almost as long as man has had something to cut!

Scissors are probably as old as the loom, but the oldest pair still in existence is a bronze tool from Egypt, dating from the third century B.C. These scissors were richly decorated with figures of metal inlay, and the blades could be detached for separate sharpening. But they probably belonged to a wealthy family, and were not typical of the kinds customarily used by ancient people.

Most early Egyptian and Greek scissors resembled the Roman *forfex*, which consisted of two blades connected by a curved bowspring handle. There was no pivot screw, and the tool was forged usually from one piece of iron. The scissors were worked by finger pressure against the handle or the blades themselves. A pair of *forfices* from Pompeii with crude iron blades and a bronze spring, along with comments by contemporary authors, suggest that a trip to the Roman *tonsor* for a haircut or shave could indeed be an uncomfortable experience.

Used for clipping wool, trimming plants, and a host of other tasks, as well as for cutting hair and thread, scissors of the Roman type remained in widespread use into the Middle Ages. These primitive shears were still being made as late as the 16th century—and in the Far East, the 19th century.

But pivoted shears, with a pivot pin of some kind connecting the blades, were in occasional use as early as the first century, and perhaps earlier. Most of these ancient shears looked more like a pair of modern pliers than the scissors we're familiar with today. By the fifth century, shears with pivot pins were in common use by the tailors of Seville—and yes, by the barbers too. Steel blades were already replacing iron blades before the end of the Roman Empire, due in part to the metalsmiths of Damascus and their work with hard "Damascus" steel.

Scissors managed to find their way into the mythology of the ancient world, too. The Three Fates of Greek myth were Lachesis, who determined the length of the thread of life; Clotho, who spun the thread;

These three ornate scissors were exhibited at the Crystal Palace in London during the 19th century.

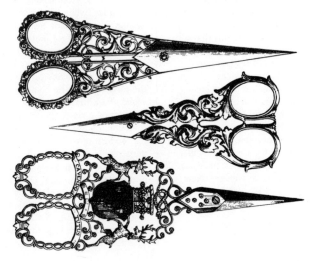

and Atropos, who used shears to snip the thread. And while we're on the subject of legend and superstition, an old belief of Northern Europeans held that the giving of cutlery as a gift would lead to the severing of a friendship—unless the receiver of the gift gave a penny to the donor.

The Roman word for scissors, *forfex*, has given us "forficate," an adjective meaning "forked." But our word "scissors" actually came from two other Latin words. One was *cisoria*, the plural of the word for a cutting instrument. The other was *scissus*, a form of *scindere*, a verb meaning "to cut," which spawned the Latin *scissor*, "one who cuts." *Cisoria* led to the Old French *cisoires* (the modern French is *ciseaux)*, and in turn to the Middle English *cysowres*, while the Latin *scissor* produced *sisours*. The latter word and *cysowres* together became the modern "scissors."

The production of scissors and cutlery of all sorts has long been centered in the European cities of Thiers, France, and Solingen, Germany. In England, Sheffield was already noted for its cutlery by the time of Chaucer. All three cities are situated near mountain streams that turn waterwheels to produce the power needed for grinding and sharpening blades.

From earliest times, New England was the center of the cutlery industry in the United States. But the man who was largely responsible for the development of the American cutlery industry, Jacob Wiss, plied his trade instead in Newark, New Jersey. In 1847, Wiss immigrated to the United States from Switzerland and joined the old cutlery firm of Rochus Heinisch. A year later, Wiss founded his own company—with his power initially provided by a dog running on a treadmill!

Wiss and his descendants found a way of utilizing two metal alloys together to produce the sturdiest, longest-lasting scissors. By 1914, Jacob Wiss & Sons was the largest producer of fine shears in the world. Wiss's firm was also responsible for introducing pinking shears on a national scale—pinking shears have notched blades that produce a saw-toothed cut—and for popularizing scissors whose handle can double as a bottle opener.

The manufacture of a pair of scissors or shears from raw metal may require as many as 175 individual steps. Formerly, the blades were sharpened by grinding on a natural stone, and polished with a wooden wheel. Today, the blades are die cast, then forged, trimmed, ground, heat-treated, polished, and finished. That leaves only about 165 other steps.

Modern scissors usually have steel blades, while the handle section may be made from aluminum or other light metals. The pivot screw is made of hard steel, and firmly riveted to one blade; the other blade turns on the pivot screw. The blades are slightly bent toward each other to produce a close contact along the cutting edge.

Modern scissors are plain, utilitarian tools, but in past centuries shears sporting fanciful shapes and designs abounded. During the 18th century, scissors with shanks in the shape of women's legs—called *Jambes des Princesses*— were the rage in France. The 19th century saw scissors in the shape of castles, butterflies, and birds, with the blades forming a bird's bill. Today, there are scores of specialized shears, scissors, nippers, and snips, from barbers' to bankers', surgical to cuticle, ranging in size from tiny scissors fitted to pocketknives to huge tailors' shears up to 16 inches in length.

Have you ever wondered what the precise difference is between "scissors" and "shears"? The use of the two words is fairly arbitrary. Generally, the former is used for a pair of blades less than six inches in length, with usually two small matching finger holes in the handle. "Shears" is generally applied to a tool longer than six inches, with one small hole in the handle for the thumb and one larger hole for a finger.

And haven't you ever wondered if the word "scissors" is singular or plural? The dictionary tells us that "scissor" is much less preferred than "scissors," but that the latter word may take either a plural or singular verb. To avoid the question completely, you might opt for "pair of scissors"—for what's one "scissor" without the other? As Charles Dickens wrote in *Martin Chuzzlewit:* "We are but the two halves of a pair of scissors, when apart . . . but together we are something."

Shoes

An Egyptian silver sandal.

Roman sandals.

Step into a modern shoe store and take a look around. High-heeled and platform shoes, boots, sandals, moccasins, wooden-heeled clogs—quite a variety for today's shopper. Recent fashions? Well, not one of the footwear styles you see today is less than 400 years old!

The loftiest high-heeled and platform shoes you can find today are flat pumps compared with some of the shoes in fashion during earlier European eras. No, our ancestors didn't don stiltlike monsters to raise themselves above muddy streets, or for any other utilitarian reason. In former times, as today, shoe style was dictated by fashion—among the upper classes, at least. Class distinction via footwear? Yes—differentiation of shoe styles to indicate social rank is as old as Western civilization.

In ancient Egypt, the sandal demonstrated a person's rank in society. Slaves either went barefoot or wore crude sandals made from palm leaves. Common citizens wore sandals of woven papyrus, consisting of a flat sole tied to the foot by a thong between the toes. But sandals with pointed toes were reserved

only for the higher stations of society, and the colors red and yellow were taboo for anyone below the aristocratic rank.

Shoes have been regarded as a sign of dignity since well before the Christian era. Going barefoot has often demonstrated humility and piety in the presence of God. Hindu documents, thousands of years old, warn worshippers to remove their footwear before entering a shrine; and Moslem tradition demands that shoes be removed before entering a place of worship. In the book of Exodus, 3:5, when God appears to Moses in the burning bush, His first command was "Put off thy shoes from off thy feet, for the ground whereon thou standest is holy ground."

In the days of ancient Greece, aristocratic women owned as many as 20 pairs of shoes, with a style to match every occasion. Slaves were employed solely to carry a supply of their lady's shoes when she left home, assuring that she would be appropriately shod throughout her travels.

The Chinese custom of binding women's feet to keep them small is many centuries old. Originally, the practice owed little to pedal aesthetics—bound feet were thought to insure faithfulness, since with such deformed feet the wife would supposedly find it difficult to travel very far on her own.

In the West, shoes have had a place in marriage ceremonies for many centuries. In some cultures, the bride's father threw his shoes at the newlyweds to signify the transfer of authority from father to husband. In Anglo-Saxon ceremonies, shoes were as indispensable as the wedding ring is today. Instead of exchanging rings with her betrothed, the bride customarily passed her shoes to her husband, who then tapped her on the head with a shoe.

During the Middle Ages, in the colder climes, the sandal gave way to more protective footwear. Often, a single piece of untanned hide was wrapped around the foot and tied with a leather thong. Beginning in the 12th century, the sabot, a shoe cut roughly from a single piece of wood, was the predominant

269

LEFT:
Chinese women bandaged their feet and wore dainty, embroidered shoes.

RIGHT:
Poulaines, or crakows, were long, pointed-toe shoes popular in Europe in the 14th and 15th centuries. The shoes were named for Crakow, Poland, where the fashion originated.

footwear of the European peasant. In those times, the Dutch were not unusual in their use of the wooden shoe. In England, the sabot took the form of the clog, a fabric mounted on a wooden platform. In Japan, wooden shoes mounted on thin blocks three or four inches high have been worn for centuries. The Japanese traditionally selected their wooden shoes with an ear for the sound made by the wooden blocks, for a discordant pair of clod-hoppers were considered the epitome of poor taste.

The long journeys undertaken by European crusaders made stronger, longer-lasting shoes a necessity, but medieval aristocrats still took their cue from fancy. The wearing of elaborate, unwieldy footwear was an indication of lordly rank, demonstrating that the wearer did not—and could not—perform manual labor. Such shoes were genuine "loafers."

Pointed shoes became the vogue in France, reportedly because of a Count of Anjou who wished to hide his deformed hooves. To assure that the peasantry did not ape the aristocrats, the 12th-century French king Philip Augustus decreed that the points of his subjects' *souliers* should be between six and 12 inches long, depending upon one's station.

But the rush toward outlandishly long shoes went on unabated. Fashionable shoes were soon so long that their toes had to be stuffed to prevent the wearer from constantly tripping over the ends. In the 14th century, the points of shoes grew to such monstrous lengths that some had to be fastened to the wearer's leg just below the knee. The clergy objected vehemently to the fashion, claiming that the long-pointed shoes prevented the faithful from kneeling in church. In many communities, shoe-point length was eventually limited by law to about two inches.

In the 16th century, aristocratic French women began wearing high-heeled shoes so steep that the—er, well-heeled wearer was literally standing on her toes when she wore them. Later, stiltlike wooden platform shoes became the rage in Venice. The heels eventually became so high that women could not walk

Among 16th-century Venetian prostitutes, the vogue for stiltlike shoes was carried to absurd lengths. Eventually, high heels were prohibited by law, because of the high death rate resulting from ladies of the night tripping and falling to their deaths.

It wasn't until the invention, in 1818, of the left-shoe last and the right-shoe last that the left shoe was constructed differently from the right shoe. Prior to that, either shoe could be worn on either foot with equal discomfort!

in them, and servants were hired to help the ladies in and out of their gondolas. The fashion reportedly owed much to the Venetian husband's desire to make sure his wife didn't travel far while he was away—the same concern that motivated the Chinese to bind their women's feet.

Among 16th-century Venetian prostitutes, the vogue for the stilt-like shoes was carried to absurd lengths. Eventually, high heels were proscribed by law, because of the high death rate resulting from ladies of the night tripping and falling to their deaths.

During the 16th century "elevator shoes" were worn by Venetian prostitutes.

Henry VIII initiated the vogue for wide-toed shoes in England, presumably to hide his gout-swollen feet. Shoes soon grew to such widths that Parliament passed a law limiting the width of a shoe to six inches.

That European lawmakers have historically taken such an oppressive interest in their subjects' footwear can be partly explained by the way in which fashion was dictated in earlier centuries. To a great extent, the king himself was often the trend-setter, the aristocracy was expected to follow suit, and the peasantry was forbidden to emulate their betters.

Many monarchs opted for shoes that would best veil their physical shortcomings. If the fashion didn't catch on naturally, well, laws could guarantee its implementation. For instance, the custom among men of wearing high-heeled shoes at the court of Louis XIV grew out of the Sun King's desire to mask his diminutive stature.

Compared to modern footgear, the shoes of earlier centuries were, for the most part, highly uncomfortable. It wasn't until the development of woven stockings in the 17th century that footwear could be made snug-fitting and shaped to the foot.

To give you an idea of the crudity of earlier shoes, it wasn't until the invention in 1818 of the left-shoe last and the right-shoe last that the left shoe was constructed differently from the right shoe. Prior to that, either shoe could be worn on either foot with equal discomfort!

Until the introduction of mass-produced footwear in the 19th century, shoes were usually handmade in the cobbler's shop, with nails or pegs used to bind the sole to the upper. As mechanization set in, machines were

In 1851, a shoe exhibition was held by one J. Sparkes Hall of London.

TOP LEFT AND RIGHT:
14th century English slippers.

BOTTOM LEFT:
Blue satin slipper decorated with honiton lace for Queen Victoria.

BOTTOM RIGHT:
This shoe, worn by the Duchess of York in the early 19th century, was notable for its small size.

devised for sewing shoes together. By 1900, most footwear was being made, at least in part, by machine.

The first shoe manufactured in the United States was the handiwork of one Thomas Beard, a *Mayflower* pilgrim, who nailed together the first pair of American shoes in 1628. At that time, the colonists also learned how to make animal-hide moccasins from the Indians, and the moccasins became so popular in the mother country that the colonies began exporting moccasins to England as early as 1650. America's first factory for mechanized shoe production was established in Lynn, Massachusetts in 1760.

Tanned leather has been a favored material for footwear since the Arabs introduced fine leatherwork in Spain in the eighth century. The leather-making trade of the Spanish Arabs was centered around the city of Cordova—to which we owe the origin of the cordovan, a soft, fine-grained leather shoe.

By the way, the average American woman now buys about five pairs of shoes each year, and the average man, about two pairs—as a rule men's shoes last longer and remain in fashion longer than women's footwear.

Each model of a modern shoe is manufactured in some 150 sizes, with length designated by a number and width by a letter. But a size 10 shoe is not 10 inches long—so where does the number come from? Believe it or not, it stands for 10 barleycorns!

The English king Edward II decreed in 1324 that an inch was equal to three average-sized barleycorns laid end to end. The normal shoe was declared to measure 39 barleycorns, and this size, for some reason or other, was designated with the number 13. Other sizes were graded from this standard, with one barleycorn difference between each successive size.

Today, the foot-measuring system used in England is one size different from the American system in both length and width. In metric countries, one size indicates a difference of about two-thirds of a centimeter.

Speaking of shoe size, the largest pair of shoes ever sold—apart from those specially built for elephantiasis sufferers—were a colossal size 42, built for a Florida giant named Harley Davidson. (Yes, it's the name of a British motorcycle manufacturer.) Let's see—a size 42 equals 39 barleycorns plus 29 for a total length of some 22½ inches!

The average person has literally thousands of styles to choose from today, from the modern machine-stitched leather shoe, or the rubber-soled sneaker, to such ancient favorites as the sandal, the clog, the platform shoe, and the pump. The pump is thought to owe its name to the early use of the shoe for ceremonies of "pomp." Footwear ranges in price from rubber *thongs* selling for less than a dollar to mink-lined golf shoes—with 18-carat gold ornamentation and ruby-tipped gold spikes—selling in England for some $7,000 a pair.

The U.S. Patent Office has on file a design for boots with pockets—for use by nudists. A bit outlandish? Well, if the shoe fits, wear it!

Silhouettes and Shadows

The form of pictorial art known as the silhouette dates back to stone-age man, who traced the outline of a person's shadow on the wall of his cave, then filled it in with colored pigments. The ancient Greeks also traced shadows to draw profile portraits.

Profile portraiture became popular in Europe in the 17th century, when artists used a candle or lamp to cast their subject's shadow against a wall or screen. When paper came into abundant supply, artists began to cut out their profile portraits from black paper and mount them on light-colored backing. This kind of silhouette construction was all the rage in Europe around the middle of the 18th century.

The term we use to refer to these outline drawings comes from Etienne de Silhoette, the French finance minister in 1759. Silhoette instituted a series of new taxes that were particularly odious to the wealthy, and attempted to cut back the expenditures of the royal household. He was forced to resign after only a few months in office, but his name was applied to a new kind of men's pocketless trousers, and *a la Silhoette* came to mean "on the cheap" in reference to his parsimonious fiscal policy.

Partly because cut-out paper portraits were considered art "on the cheap," and partly because Silhoette himself produced paper profiles as a hobby, these black outline drawings soon came to be known as "silhouettes."

As an art form, silhouettes go back to ancient times—to the black figures that adorn Etruscan and other Greek pottery. But the great era of silhouette art dates from the final decades of the 18th century. During that period, the new interest in the science of physiognomy developed by Lavater and the general revival of interest in classical art combined to make silhouettes a dominant art form, supplanting miniature painting in France and Germany. Silhouettes also became popular in England and America, and their popularity continues.

275

SNOW

You may occasionally curse snow for the inconvenience it causes, but no one could find fault with an individual snowflake. Each snowflake that falls to earth has its own unique crystal design, and many of these designs are among the most beautiful symmetrical forms to be found anywhere in nature.

Snowflakes generally assume a hexagonal form, but they're found in a wide range of patterns. The smallest flakes, called "diamond dust," may be just .005 inches in diameter, while others may be several inches across. An average-sized snowflake takes eight to ten minutes to fall to earth from a height of 1,000 feet. Approximately ten inches of snow contain water equal to an inch of rain.

Since 1940, scientists have had a means to produce replicas of snowflakes so that their structure may be studied. A chemical compound is spread over a glass plate on which the flakes settle. As part of the compound evaporates, the snow crystal is left encased in a plastic shell. When the flake melts, the shell remains, forming a perfect replica of the original flake. In all studies of snowflakes, no two flakes with the same crystal design have ever been discovered.

A painting entitled "Late afternoon in winter" which originally appeared in Harper's Magazine

A winter scene in the woods as depicted in a 1800s drawing in Leslie's Magazine

"Travelers in a snowstorm" is the title of this Japanese drawing which first appeared in Harper's Magazine *around 1890*

A drawing by the great French satirist, Grandville, which appeared in Un Autre Monde, published in Paris in 1844

A painting by Malcolm C. Salaman in a publication New Woodcuts, published in London in 1930

278

A drawing of jolly old England during a snowstorm, as seen in the columns of Punch

This winter scene appears in a book entitled "The Book of the Revolution" by Benson J. Lossing, published by Harper's in 1860.

A winter scene in Czarist Russia, as depicted by a Soviet artist of the 1970s.

A winter scene of woods covered with snow.
The drawing appeared in the London Illustrated News *of 1886.*

280

SOCCER

To an American sports fan, soccer and football appear so dissimilar that it's hard to believe the games were once virtually identical. And even today, outside the United States, the names for the two sports are identical. The word *football* is used around the world to refer to the game Americans call "soccer." Only in America is the terminology confusing, because only in America is there a difference between the two games.

When it comes to football, America stands alone. Football is the only spectator sport that's played exclusively in the United States. Baseball has spread to Latin America and the Far East; basketball and hockey are played in many countries. The Irish play Gaelic football, but that game is a variation of soccer; Australian football is actually a good deal like rugby; and even Canadian football has some major differences from its American counterpart. Football remains strictly an American sport.

Soccer, relatively unknown in the United States until a decade or so ago, is now the most popular sport in the world. It's played in over 140 nations under uniform rules, and in most countries is either the only or the major professional sport. Soccer matches regularly draw the world's largest sports crowds, and soccer players are among the highest paid of all athletes.

Why is soccer so universally popular? Think of the amount of equipment and organization necessary for a simple high school football game—and think of the complex rules. A soccer game, on the other hand, requires little more than a ball, and can be played on a field of almost any size. The play is swift and continuous, involving both individual effort and teamwork—and the rules are simple enough to learn in a minute!

You'd probably guess that soccer is a good deal older than its American cousin, football. In a sense that's true; but surprisingly, organized soccer competitions played under uniform rules are less than a decade older than football.

The first soccer organization was formed in 1863, and the first intercollegiate football game took place just six years later. (Coincidentally, both football and baseball had beginnings of sorts in the year 1869, when the Cincinnati Red Stockings became the first professional baseball team.) But the origins of football undoubtedly go back to a much older game whose evolution has produced not only soccer and American football, but rugby as well.

Some historians believe that the true forerunner of football was a Greek game adopted by the Romans some time before the beginning of the Christian era. We don't know much about how the game was played, but its object was probably to drive a ball beyond a line drawn behind the opposing team. Most likely, the game was not played with the foot alone, since the name of the game, *harpastum*, was derived from a Greek word meaning "handball."

It's quite possible that Roman soldiers played *harpastum* during their occupation of Britain, the nation most often credited with the origin of football and its related sports. But according to a British tradition, football had its beginnings sometime during the 11th century, when workmen excavating the site of an earlier battle came upon the bones of a Danish soldier and began kicking around the skull of the hated invader. A group of young boys noticed the workmen's diversion, and dug up a skull of their own to kick around. Shortly after, an inflated cow bladder was substituted for the skull, and thus was born the game of "kicking the Dane's head" or "kicking the bladder."

The story may be fiction, for it was also reported that the first "football" was not the skull but the actual head of a slain Danish brigand. But in any case, the new sport gained popularity in Britain over the next century as football games were staged annually in various towns. For many years, the drapers of the town of Chester held a football match on Shrove Tuesday (the day before Ash Wednesday),

281

using a leather ball. Derby claims that the first football matches were held there on Shrove Tuesday, in
celebration of a victory over the Romans in 217. In
one Scottish parish, an annual football match pitted
the married women against the spinsters. It was
reported that the married women almost always
won handily.

Most of these early football games were really
free-for-alls, violent melées between teams whose
players could number in the hundreds. Matches
were often held between adjacent towns, with the
ball put in play midway between the towns and each
team seeking to attain victory by driving the ball
into the middle of the rival town. There were few
rules, and many casualties, both to players and by-
standers.

To limit the damage to town and player alike,
English authorities began to restrict the matches to
vacant areas that could be marked off to form a sort
of playing field. But around the middle of the 12th
century, when the game was already being called
"futballe," English kings began to take a sterner view
of the sport.

Henry II banned football for fear that Englishmen were spending too much time playing it, to the
neglect of the more militarily useful sport of archery.
King Edward II banned the game due to "great
noise in the city caused by hustling over large balls
from which many evils might arise which God for-
bid." Other monarchs, including Richard II, Henry
VIII, and Elizabeth I, also tried to eradicate the
sport, with little success.

During an Anglo-Scottish war late in the 12th
century, English soldiers reportedly sought to settle
the dispute on the football field instead of the battle-
field—which suggests not only the popularity of the
sport, but its violence. At the end of the 16th
century, the game remained so violent that an English writer claimed it seemed more like "a bloody
and murdering practise than a felowly sporte or pastime . . ." often involving "fighting, brawling, con-
tention, quarrel picking, murther, homicide, and
great effusion of blood."

In the 17th century, when archery was no longer
important in warfare, James I lifted the official ban
on football and the game quickly found its way into
almost every town in the British Isles. Matches were
still held between adjacent towns, with the "goal
lines" as far as three or four miles apart. And the
sport was still quite violent, with tripping, shin-kick-
ing, and rough tackling an integral part of the game.

The game as played from the 11th century to
the middle of the 19th century was basically a kicking game, much closer to modern soccer than to

**The word *football* is used
around the world to refer to
the game Americans call
"soccer." Only in America is
the terminology confusing,
because only in America is
there a difference between
the two games.**

football or rugby. Rules varied from place to place and from school to school, but there was one universally observed rule: the ball could not be picked up with the hands. It was the flagrant violation of that rule that was to spawn the game of rugby, and in turn, American football.

In 1823, a student at the Rugby school by the name of William Webb Ellis, frustrated after failing to kick a bouncing ball, picked it up and dashed downfield. Ellis was severely criticized for his infraction, but word of his deed spread throughout England, and other players began to experiment with new rules. In 1838, players at Cambridge decided to try "the game at Rugby," and within 10 years the new game was being played at almost all English schools.

Gradually, the games of football and rugby began to diverge, with some clubs and schools adopting the new game and others staying with the older "feet-only" sport. In 1863, a group of football enthusiasts met in London and adopted a set of rules that forbade using the hands, publishing them under the title of *Rules of the London Football Association*. From the term *association football* came the modern word *soccer*. But many other players continued to enjoy "rugger."

During the 19th century, both rugby and soccer were played in the United States, especially at Eastern colleges. Football of any kind was banned for a time at Harvard and Yale, but in 1867, a set of rules was drawn up at Princeton. Two years later, a team from that school took on a squad from Rutgers University at New Brunswick, New Jersey, in a match often called the first intercollegiate football game in America. But the fact is, the game that day was soccer and not football: each team consisted of 25 men; a round ball was used; and running with the ball was not permitted.

A young student by the name of Irving Lane was a member of the Rutgers squad that won the match, 6-4. In 1938, Lane—the last survivor of the game—was in attendance when Rutgers again defeated Princeton, 20-18. That marked the first time in 69 years that Rutgers had beaten their old foes. Lane died a few days later.

Two years after the first Princeton-Rutgers meeting, students at Harvard adopted a sport, known as "the Boston Game," that like rugby permitted a player to run with the ball. So in 1873, when Princeton, Rutgers, Columbia, and Yale met in New York to draft a code of rules for football, Harvard refused to attend. The decision was momentous in the history of soccer and football. If Harvard had gone along with the four other colleges and adopted a set of rules forbidding players to run with the ball,

the game of soccer would most likely have developed as the major academic sport in the United States, and American football may never have been born. Hereafter, the paths of what became soccer and American football would continue to diverge.

Other American colleges soon began to follow Harvard's lead, and abandoned the kicking game. In 1875, the first game of true "football," between American universities pitted Harvard against Yale. The Crimson won 4-0. The following year, a new set of rules based loosely on those of rugby was adopted by the newly formed Intercollegiate Football Association. Yet the administrations of many colleges remained less enthusiastic than their student players. When students at Cornell requested permission to travel to Cleveland to meet a squad from the University of Michigan, the Cornell president replied: "I will not permit 30 men to travel 400 miles to agitate a bag of wind."

Despite such protests, American football continued to evolve from a rugby-like game to the unique sport it is today. By 1888, football was being played in the United States on a field 110 yards long, with 11 players on a side and the familiar egg-shaped ball. By 1906, when the forward pass was legalized, football was the national academic game of America, played in a way recognizable to any modern fan.

Also easily recognizable by that time were the differences between the game and its earlier cousin, "association football," or soccer. While American football had evolved into a running and passing game incorporating elements of both soccer and rugby, football enthusiasts in England had stuck by the kicking game. The rules of English football had become codified at the 1863 meeting of the London Football Association (F.A.); by 1870, soccer was played in the British Isles with 11 men on a side, as it is today.

During the 1871-72 season, the F.A. organized a competition among member football clubs for a trophy, the F.A. Cup, which was soon to become the most highly regarded soccer prize in the world. The following year, a similar tournament was organized for a Scottish F.A. cup. As the level of competition rose, professional players quickly began to outnumber amateurs. So in 1894, another competition for amateurs only was established. The two trophies, the Association or Challenge Cup and the

League or Amateur Cup have been awarded almost every year since then—though in 1895, the original Association Cup was stolen from a Birmingham shop and never recovered.

If baseball is the American pastime, and the major leagues the premier baseball organization in the United States, then the British Football League is the "major league" of England. In 1889, this professional soccer league was formed with 12 teams, and a second division was added three years later. A rule was soon put into effect establishing that the two best teams from Division II would replace the two poorest teams from Division I each year, a rule that is still in effect. A Division III was established in 1921, and another section of Division III soon after, with a similar provision for dropping two Division II teams to Division III at the end of each season— surely an attractive idea to American supporters of perennial also-rans.

By the mid-1950s, the British Football League included 22 teams each in Divisions I and II, and 24 teams in each of the two sections of Division III—for a total of 92 teams! The teams that have won the Division I title the most times are Arsenal, Liverpool, and Manchester United. The Challenge Cup has been in the hands of the Aston Villa squad more than any other team.

As soccer grew in the British Isles, the game was continually spread around the Commonwealth by British soldiers, administrators, and travelers, until a football association of some kind existed in many countries. In 1904, these associations joined together to form an international governing body called, in a curious combination of languages, the Federation Internationale de Football Association, or F.I.C.A.

In 1930, the F.I.C.A. instituted the first world competition for the Jules Rimet Cup, or the World Cup, which is probably the most prized sports trophy in the world today. Uruguay won the first competition. Since then, the World Cup competition has been held every four years, except in 1942 and 1946, with Brazil the only team to win the Cup three times. Other winners include—in addition to Uruguay (twice)—West Germany (twice), Italy (twice), and Argentina. In 1928, the British Football Association left the F.I.C.A., but it rejoined the body in time for the 1950 competition. In 1966, England finally won the Cup.

Both professionals and amateurs are allowed to compete in the World Cup series. Amateurs may also exhibit their skills at the Olympic Games, which have included soccer matches since the turn of the century. Over the last 20 years, teams from Eastern

At the soccer stadium in Rio de Janeiro, the playing field is surrounded by a moat seven feet wide and five feet deep to keep overenthusiastic fans from the players—and the referees.

284

Europe have dominated the Olympic soccer competition.

But it's the professional soccer leagues in many countries that have made soccer the most popular sport in the world. The total attendance at all the games played each year is almost inestimable; it certainly outshadows the total attendance of hockey, basketball, and other worldwide sports. In 1937, an incredible 149,000 people packed into a stadium in Hampden, England, to watch a match between teams from Scotland and England, setting the all-time attendance record for that country. Today, crowds of 80,000 or more are not uncommon.

In 1950, the world record for soccer attendance was established at the World Cup finals in Rio de Janeiro, when 205,000 people tried to cheer their Brazilian team to victory—but Brazil lost to Uruguay. At the stadium in Rio, the playing field is surrounded by a moat seven feet wide and five feet deep to keep overenthusiastic fans from the players—and the referees.

Soccer in the United States is only now starting to catch on as a popular sport. Toward the end of the 19th century, when soccer was mushrooming in Britain, the game was played here chiefly by small groups of English, Scottish, and Irish immigrants. In 1913, a governing body for American soccer was formed, called the U.S.F.A., and an affiliation was established with the F.I.C.A. But there was still little interest here in the sport, due to most Americans' conception of soccer as a "foreign" sport, and the then growing popularity of baseball and American football. Even the shocking victory of the U.S. team over England in the 1950 World Cup series gained little notice in the United States; in 1953, the return match at Yankee Stadium drew only 7,271 people.

Today, professional soccer matches in the United States often attract five or more times that number—though attendance is far below the 58,000-per-game average of professional football and the 35 million annual total of college football. The soccer boom in America began slowly after World War II, when soldiers stationed overseas first learned the game, and has been spurred by the influx of European and South American immigrants. The biggest spur to American soccer development, however, was the formation of the professional North American Soccer League.

In 1968, the NASL began with 17 teams, but partially collapsed during the next two years. Then the steady upswing in soccer's fortunes began. Between 1970 and 1975, the league grew from five to 20 teams; by 1974, the game was attracting more than a million fans annually. The year 1975 was the key year for the league, due to a big rise in attendance and, most importantly, the signing by the New York Cosmos of a Brazilian player named Edson Arantes do Nascimento—better known as Pelé. During his 18-year career in Brazil, Pelé had scored 1,216 goals in 1,254 games—almost a goal a game—and had become the most famous athlete in the world.

The rules of soccer are fairly simple, and the game can be learned quickly by any novice—that's one of the major reasons for its widespread popularity. Soccer is played on a field from 100 to 120 yards long and from 55 to 75 yards wide. Goal posts at each end of the field are eight feet high and 24 feet apart, connected by a crossbar, with a net in the rear. Each team has 11 players, including a goalkeeper. Players advance the ball by kicking it or playing it with any part of the body except the arms and hands; the goalkeeper can use his hands. A team scores one point for each ball they play into their opponent's net. A game consists of two 45-minute halves, and the play is continuous, with a time-out called only for a serious injury.

Unlike football or basketball, the clock continues to run in a soccer match even if the ball is played out of bounds. Whenever a player drives the ball off the playing field, the ball goes over to the opposing team. If the ball goes beyond the side line, or "touch line," the opposing team throws it in with a two-handed toss. If the ball is driven beyond the end line, or "goal line," by the attacking team, the defenders are awarded a free kick, similar to the kick-off in football; if the defending team drives the ball beyond its own goal line, the attacking team is awarded a corner kick, playing the ball in from one corner of the field.

A penalty kick is awarded an attacking team for certain infractions committed by a defender within his own penalty area, which is 44 yards wide and extends 18 yards from the goal line; a penalty kick is taken from a spot 12 yards in front of the goal. Aside from a few other basic rules, that's about all there is to the game of soccer!

As soccer grows in the United States, there's sure to be a controversy about the relative merits of the game and its historical cousin, American football. There's already a debate as to which game is the more violent.

Football is surely more of a hard-hitting contact sport. As long ago as 1906, President Theodore

A picture of the Brazilian soccer star, Pelé, working his magic on the field. He is seen bouncing the ball on his knee.

Roosevelt threatened to abolish the game unless it was made less brutal, and the injury rate among football players has certainly not tailed off since then. In a recent season, professional football teams suffered an injury rate close to 50 percent—one reported injury for every two players. Among nonprofessionals, an estimated 35,000 college students and 375,000 high school players suffer football-related injuries each year!

But football players are protected by pounds of equipment to soften the blows. The soccer player, engaged in a rough and tumble contact sport, wears only knee guards and a pair of shorts. The action can get quite rough, at times approaching the free-for-all of the medieval game. To quote the remarks made by a Frenchman after witnessing an 18th-century game of football in England, "If this is what the English call playing, it's impossible to tell what they might call fighting."

SPICES

Some spices were even worth as much as gold and silver. One pound of ginger could buy a sheep; a pound of cloves, seven sheep. Spices were often included in wills, or given as part of a marriage dowry.

As any schoolboy can tell you, it was the desire of Europeans to find a faster, cheaper route to the spice supplies of the Far East that spurred the great explorations of the 15th and 16th centuries. Have you ever wondered why men were eager to undertake those long, dangerous journeys in pursuit of such lightly-regarded items as pepper, ginger, and cinnamon?

The answer is simple: spices were as valuable to contemporary Europeans as the gold so avidly sought by California prospectors a century ago. A shipload of spices could make a man rich for life, and the nation that controlled the spice trade to a great extent controlled the commerce of Europe.

Spices were highly prized at the time not only because of their rarity, but because of their extreme importance in daily life, and the wide variety of uses they served. In the days before refrigeration, spices were needed to preserve food, to disguise poor-tasting, often tainted dishes, and to salvage sour wine. Herbs and spices were also used for embalming, and to make incense, perfume oils, and medicines. In fact, the earliest known treatise on medicine was a 2700 B.C. Chinese work entitled *The Classic Herbal*.

As early as the seventh century B.C., the Assyrians of Mesopotamia were importing dozens of spices from India and Persia, including cinnamon. The ancient Egyptians used spices for embalming as well as food flavoring and preservation. Spices were valued so highly in Egypt that many monarchs, including Cleopatra, had supplies placed in their tombs along with jewels and precious metals.

Since Biblical times, caravans laden with spices had traveled from India and points east to the Mediterranean. There are four references to cinnamon in the Bible. The ancient route brought caravans through Mesopotamia to the Phoenician port of Tyre. After Alexander the Great captured Tyre in the fourth century B.C., the city of Alexandria in Egypt gradually became the center of the spice trade in the Mediterranean.

The ancient Romans used a wide variety of spices and imported them in large quantities. Spices were so valuable during Imperial times that a single sack of peppers could pay a man's ransom. In the fifth century, the Visigoth chieftain Alaric accepted 3,000 pounds of peppers as part of a tribute to lift the seige of Rome.

The barbarian invasions of the Empire killed much of the spice trade in Western Europe, but some shipments from the East continued to reach Europe via Constantinople. Throughout the Middle Ages, spices were far too costly for the average person.

Spice cabinet, a Jewish religious object, made in Nurnberg.

The nutmeg tree and its fruit.

Besides aristocrats, only monks, who used spices to make medicines, could afford them in any variety. Most commoners had to content themselves with onions. Oddly enough, saffron, one of the few affordable spices in medieval times, is now the most expensive spice in the world.

The long distances spices had to be transported to reach Europe only partly explains their great expense at the time. Until the 13th century, Arab merchants owned a virtual monopoly on the spice trade, and closely guarded the secrets of where they were obtained.

To justify their high prices, the Arabs maintained that they had brought back their wares from "paradise," or from barbarous lands frought with danger. Cinnamon, they claimed, grew only in deep glens infested with poisonous snakes. Since few Europeans had visited the Far East, the

In the days before refrigeration, spices were needed to preserve food, to disguise poor-tasting, often tainted dishes, and to salvage sour wine.

Produced from the dried inner bark of a small, bushy evergreen tree, cinnamon is one of the few spices made from the bark of a plant rather than from the leaf, root, flower, or seed.

general public was ready to believe almost anything.

The "secrets" of the Arab spice trade had been exposed by the time the Crusaders seized the ports used for spice export. The cost of spices fell quickly in Europe, and the demand increased. Gradually, merchants from Genoa, Pisa, and especially Venice, took control of the Mediterranean trade.

At the time, spice supplies were still brought overland by caravan from the East. The main route followed the Euphrates River and ended in Constantinople or the Levant. High custom duties imposed by kingdoms along the route forced many caravans to cross Arabia and the Red Sea and trek through Ethiopia and Egypt to the port of Alexandria. Venetian merchants then transported the cargo across the Mediterranean and sold their wares in French and Italian ports. From there, spices were shipped over the Alps or up the Rhone River to Northern France and Flanders, then on to England.

It was largely the demand for spices—and the great profits that could be made by selling them—that triggered the great discoveries of the era. The Portuguese explorer Vasco da Gama was searching for a cheaper, all-water route to the East when he rounded the Cape of Good Hope and sailed to India. In 1503, he returned to Portugal laden with supplies of cinnamon, nutmeg, ginger, pepper, and other spices from ports on the Malabar Coast. And it was Columbus' attempt to find a faster western route to the Far East that led to his discovery of America.

Without cargo ships suitable for ocean travel, the Venetians quickly lost their spice trade. Portuguese merchants soon owned a monopoly on much of Europe's Eastern imports. Then the Dutch, and later the English, began to roam the Eastern seas, seizing many of the lands where the Portuguese had carried on their trade. By the beginning of the 17th century, Portugal had a monopoly on only one spice: cinnamon.

At the time, cinnamon thrived along the Malabar Coast of India, which was still in the hands of the Portuguese. But in the mid-17th century, the Dutch deviously took control of cinnamon commerce, buying the rights from Malabar kings to destroy all cinnamon plantations in the area to enhance the value of the new Dutch plantations on the island of Ceylon. Thus, when the English seized Ceylon in 1795, they inherited the Dutch monopoly.

The spice trade was still quite lucrative at the time. In the 15th century, a pound of pepper cost an Englishman about six times the average daily wage of a laborer. As late as the 17th century, a load of spices bought in the East for 3,000 pounds could be resold in England for as much as six times that amount.

Black pepper plant.

289

Drying cardamom in Ceylon.

Understandably, many of the herbs and spices shipped to Europe found their way into the hands of the wealthy. One 15th-century German monarch insisted that his women bathe in tubfulls of expensive aromatic oils. French noblemen at the court of Louis XIV often enjoyed perfumed foods, such as meats sprinkled with rose water, eggs flavored with musk, or cream mixed with ambergris.

What's the difference between an herb and a spice? A spice is an aromatic vegetable used to season food. An herb is defined as a seed plant that does not develop woody tissue, but is more or less soft or succulent. An herb may have either a medicinal or culinary use, while a spice is always primarily a flavoring.

Cinnamon has been used in Europe longer than most other spices, since it is native to India rather than the more distant East Indies, where a majority of spices originate.

Biologically, the cinnamon plant is known as *Cinnamonum zeylanicum*. The second word is derived from the Portuguese name for Ceylon. *Cinnamon* itself comes from the Greek *kinnamon*, in turn derived from the Hebrew *qinnamon*. The Germans call the spice *Ceylonzimt*, while *cannelle* is cinnamon in France.

Produced from the dried inner bark of a small, bushy evergreen tree, cinnamon is one of the few spices made from the bark of a plant rather than the leaf, root, flower, or seed. Untended cinnamon trees will grow up to 40 feet high, but to facilitate harvesting they are usually pruned to about eight feet.

At the plantation, the bark is stripped from the trees, fermented, scraped, and dried. The yellow, rolled strips of bark are then inserted one within another for shipping, forming solid rods about three-eighths of an inch in diameter and three feet long. Some of the bark is instead pounded, macerated in sea water, and distilled to produce cinnamon oil.

Ceylon, now known as Sri Lanka, still produces the world's best cinnamon. Other supplies hail from India, Indonesia, Brazil, and the West Indies.

Cinnamon and other spices cost but a fraction of their worth just a few centuries ago, but international spice trade still totals over $200 million a year. Pepper accounts for about a quarter of the total.

Some 150 million pounds of herbs and spices are imported by the United States yearly, with a value of over $70 million. Cinnamon oil alone accounts for about 200,000 pounds of the total import figure.

Spanish saffron is presently the world's most expensive spice, selling in England for as much as $780 per pound. About 32,000 saffron flowers are required to produce just one pound of the powder.

At the other end of the scale, Portuguese rosemary and Canadian mustard are the cheapest spices available today, selling for as little as seven or eight cents a pound in the United States.

If the value of spices has dropped sharply over the last few centuries, so has our need for them. No longer employed on a large scale for food preservation or medicine, most spices are used today as simple flavorings. Cinnamon, with a warm, sweet flavor, is used mostly in confectionery and baked goods. Much European chocolate contains cinnamon, as do many liqueurs. Mincemeat spice, pumpkin pie, baked apples, and the coffee concoction known as *cappucino* all include cinnamon as an essential ingredient. And without cinnamon, could you hope to bake the grandmother of all American desserts, apple pie?

290

SPORTS

Sports have existed since the day that primitive man could take a slight breather from the serious business of self-preservation.

In addition to the use of language, it is play that distinguishes the lower orders of living things from higher ones. The animals that display the least amount of playfulness are those most bound by the instinctual functioning. The higher we go on the evolutionary scale, the more playful the species— witness the dolphin and the human child.

What distinguishes sports from other playful pastimes is that, whether engaged in by an individual or a group, conformity to agreed-upon, prescribed rules is required.

Stone arrowheads uncovered by archaelogists indicate that archery was a hunting skill way back in primordial days. This activity became transformed into an organized sport in the 3rd century, when contests among archers became popular.

Sports are of interest to both men and women—to people of all ages. All over the world, artists have translated the excitement of athletic contests. Here are some of the most fascinating graphic interpretations of the 19th and early 20th centuries.

Bizarre Magazine *was published during the 1960s in Paris. This drawing graced its pages.*

Racing as depicted in the Police Gazette.

In the famous fight between Sullivan and Kilrain, Sullivan lands his right in the 15th round—smack on Kilrain's jaw. This is how the artist of Police Gazette *saw the action.*

291

Tennis played on ice was the subject of this drawing in Punch in 1876.

Un Autre Monde, *published in Paris in 1844, was the work of Grandville.*
This caricature of horse and jockey was one of the drawings that made Grandville famous.

From the noted humorous publication, Life, *which flourished in the early 1920s.*

Scenes of lawn tennis among the upper echelon of American society as depicted in Frank Leslie's Popular Magazine, *published in New York during the 1880s.*

Two scullers, as they appeared in a French magazine of the day.

In 1893, on Thanksgiving Day, Yale defeated Princeton in football. The captains of the teams and some of the action were depicted in the Police Gazette.

Some of the oldsters are trying this monstrous game of football. Here's how the artist of Life Magazine *saw it.*

294

From Voyages and Travels, *a book published by E.W. Walker & Co. of Boston around the turn of the century.*

The Police Gazette *was practically standard equipment in every barber shop during the late 1800s. This magazine featured sports pictures. This drawing of the Kilrain-Sullivan fight of 1889 shows some of the action. Kilrain claimed that Sullivan fouled him in the third round.*

A Lacrosse scene, as depicted in Harper's Magazine.

Lady fencer, from a French magazine of the 1890s.

In the early part of the 20th century, Simplicissimus, *a magazine of humor published in Munich, was the outstanding German publication in the field. This drawing of a man skating appeared in 1913.*

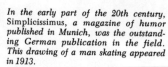

From Punch *of 1879.*

Drawing by the great French satirist Grandville, which first appeared in a book entitled Petites Miseres de la Vie Humaine. *This drawing was published in Paris by Fournier in 1843.*

296

Streetcars

Imagine a vast network of streetcar lines connecting America's cities, with trolley cars whisking passengers between neighboring towns at speeds of seventy or eighty miles an hour. A prospect for the distant future? No, a fairly accurate description of American interurban travel around the turn of this century. Yes, that's right, we said *trolley cars!*

Today, most people would think of the streetcar as a creature of the big city. True, most American cities have operated trolley systems at one time or another. But before the country was laced with freeways and interstate highways, streetcar travel was the best means of transportation to and from the city, as well as within its boundaries. Trolley lines took salesmen to small towns to peddle their wares, and trolleys brought farmers and housewives into town to shop or deliver goods, and trolleys carried city dwellers to nearby beaches and resorts.

Interurban streetcar lines operated with heavy, individually powered cars, quite unlike the lighter, locomotive-drawn railroad cars. Trolleys ran more frequently than mainline trains, and they usually served areas inaccessible by railroad. It was common, too, for a streetcar company to construct an amusement park in an otherwise inaccessible suburban area along its trolley line in order to increase weekend and night travel on the line.

The first interurban streetcar line in this country connected the cities of Granville and Newark, Ohio, beginning in 1889, and the first high-speed interurban trolleys ran between Cleveland and Akron in 1895. Within a few decades, many of America's cities, large and small, were linked by streetcar lines, especially in Ohio, Indiana, Illinois, and Michigan. No burgeoning town was considered major league until it was connected by streetcar line with at least one neighboring city.

Early in this century, it was possible to ride by trolley from New York all the way to Boston for less than four dollars! Of course, there were frequent changes of line.

The longest continuous streetcar route—again with frequent changes of line—ran from Freeport, Illinois to Utica, New York, a distance of over 1,000 miles!

One Colorado line climbed over a 10,000-foot peak to reach the mining boomtown of Cripple Creek.

With even the fastest modern trains rarely exceeding 60 miles per hour, it now seems hard to believe that the normal operating speed of the interurban streetcar line was *80 miles per hour.*

Incredible as it seems, cars of the Crandic Line between Cedar Rapids and Iowa City in Iowa once claimed top speeds of 110 miles per hour!

Within the city, streetcars were the first motor-driven means of public transportation. Streetcars provided the first dependable intra-city travel in the days before the bus, auto, and subway. Dependable, yes; fast, often not. The first streetcar in this country, in fact, was powered by only a few horsepower—provided by, yes, a few horses!

This horse-drawn conveyance was constructed by John Stephenson in Philadephia, and placed in service in New York City in 1832 by the New York and Harlem Railway. Called the *John Mason* after a prominent banker who had organized the railroad company, the car seated 30 passengers in three unconnected compartments. It ran between Prince Street and 14th Street in Manhattan, with a later extension to uptown Manhattan. The fare was a then rather steep 12½ cents. No, we don't know what the conductor did for change of a penny if you didn't want a round- trip ticket.

The earliest electric trolleys were powered by storage batteries, which proved expensive and inefficient. The first electrified streetcar tracks, too, often short-circuited in the rain.

One of the world's first electric lines was constructed in London in 1860 by the American G.F. Train—that's right, Train—with two more tramlines following shortly after in that city. But it was the invention of the electric generator that led to the application of transmitted power to streetcar lines and fostered the proliferation of tramlines throughout Europe and the United States.

There are three kinds of electric streetcars. One is drawn by cable; another is powered by an electrified third rail; and the third is powered by overhead transmission lines, with the car connected to the power lines by a collapsible apparatus called the *trolley*.

Strictly speaking, then, only a streetcar powered by overhead lines can be called a "trolley."

There are two varieties of trolley system, one utilizing two overhead wires—the European preference—and the second using one wire and one electrified track to complete the electric circuit. The later type is the overwhelming favorite of American lines.

Berlin got its first electric tramway in 1881, Budapest in

In the 1870s, steam-powered trams provided public transportation in Paris.

1897, and Paris in 1901. A gas-powered streetcar was placed in operation in Providence, Rhode Island in 1872, while the first commercially owned electric streetcars in this country plied their course in Baltimore in 1885. The first "soundless, shockless" tracks were laid in New Orleans in 1930.

The famed San Francisco cable cars were the world's first cable-drawn cars. The Bay City's cable car was invented by Andrew Hallidie, and introduced in 1873 on Sacramento and Clay Streets.

Cable cars were drawn by an endless cable that runs in a slot between the rails. Cable cars are best suited for steeply inclined streets—thus, their early popularity in San Francisco and Seattle. But a cable car can run only at a constant speed, and a cable jam can stop every car on the line.

By the turn of the century, most cable car lines had been replaced by electric trackage, although Seattle retained its system until the 1930s.

The San Francisco cable car lines still operating today are

The Constantinople trolley was making its rounds in the 1870s.

maintained chiefly as tourist attractions, with most lines long-since replaced by buses or trolley-bus systems.

Streetcar lines in general began to rapidly disappear in the 1930s, in the face of competition from cars and buses. An intermediate step in the trolley-to-bus transition was the trackless trolley, a buslike vehicle that ran without tracks but was powered by electricity from overhead lines, like the trolley. The first trackless trolley began service in 1910 in

Los Angeles. Despite its present automobile mania, LA once boasted one of the nation's finest streetcar systems. Brooklyn, New York, maintained trackless trolleys as late as the 1950s.

London did away with its last trolley in the 50s; Paris had ripped up its streetcar tracks about 20 years earlier. Today, the streetcar is virtually extinct in America, but the trolley is still widely used in Germany, Austria, Switzerland, and Eastern Europe.

But trolley-lovers, take heart. You can still catch a glimpse of the ancient streetcar in various museums throughout the country. The museum in East Hartford, Connecticut, contains 92 trolleys, ranging from some 1880 relics to a New York model from the 1930s. In that museum, trolley buffs can ride an open-sided car—complete with bell—over a two-mile route.

Streetcars were inexpensive to construct and clean. Although dependable, they were not without disadvantages. Among these was the danger posed to idle strollers by a speeding trolley. The Brooklyn Dodgers of baseball fame were not so-named because of their agility on the playing field. Initially, the team was called the "Trolley Dodgers," in tribute to the maze of trolley lines crisscrossing Brooklyn at the height of the streetcar era.

The tram was a fixture of city life in Valparaiso, Chile, in 1890.

SUN

The earth in circumference measures less than 25,000 miles. A single sunspot on the surface of our nearest spectral neighbor can extend more than 185,000 miles. Yet even that is no more than—well, a spot compared to the size of the sun over 864,000 miles in diameter, with a mass 330,000 times that of the earth.

We're hurtling through space at about 66,620 miles per hour as we circle the sun, 93 million miles away in the center of our solar system. Our planet is literally bathing in the sunshine of the sun's energy, which is fueled by 4.5 million tons of gas each second! Temperatures on the surface of the sun approach 11,000 degrees F.; temperatures at the core, an unfathomable 36 million degrees F. Sunspots, which appear dark on the sun, are actually blazing away at about 7,200 degrees F.

But sometimes, neither the size nor power of the sun can be as breathtaking as the kind of perfect sunscopes illustrated here.

Published in Moscow in 1967, The Art of the Book *contained hundreds of premier pieces of Soviet art. Here are two which depict a burst of sun through the clouds.*

A Russian drawing which first appeared in a book entitled Graphic Arts of Lvov, *published in Kiev in 1975.*

This excellent drawing of the sun on hills first appeared in a book entitled Modern Woodcuts and Lithographs by Jeoffrey Holme, which was published in London by The Studio in 1901.

From an album called Fifty Years of Soviet Art, published in the Soviet Union under the editorship of A. Kupetsian of Graphic Arts.

"The Last Furrow," a drawing from Modern Pen Drawings: European and American by Charles Holme, published in London in 1901.

This delightful drawing derives from a publication entitled Grandfather's Moneybox, which was published in Moscow in 1972.

A charming drawing found in a collection called Russian Book Plates, published in the U.S.S.R. in the 1970s.

This drawing comes from Art of the Book, a Moscow publication of 1967.

This drawing derives from a book called Pictures and Stories from Forgotten Children's Books, published in 1969 by Dover Publications, Inc., of New York.

One Thousand Quaint Cuts from Books of Other Days, was published in London by the Leadenhall Press. Here is one of the many fine statements from that book.

This charming headpiece comes from Century Illustrated Monthly Magazine, which was published in the 1880s and 1890s in New York City.

This drawing, by the great French caricaturist known as Grandville, first appeared in Un Autre
Monde, published in Paris around 1860. Grandville was born in 1803, and died in 1847. Grandville's real name was Jean Gerard. His illustrations for classics, such as La Fontaine's Fables are
classic, as are his humorous drawings of human beings with animals' heads.

TOBACCO

"The pipe draws wisdom from the lips of the philosopher, and shuts up the mouth of the foolish," wrote W.M. Thackeray a hundred years ago; and to this day, pipe smoking retains a certain connotation of sophistication. The hoi polloi may take their tobacco by cigarette or cigar, but a true connoisseur of the brown leaf wouldn't think of any means of fumigation aside from the pipe. Perhaps the veneration of pipe smoking stems partly from its long popularity, for centuries in Europe, the pipe was virtually the only means of tobacco smoking.

The common myth about the introduction of tobacco in Europe credits Sir Walter Raleigh with bringing the leaf from Virginia to England in the late 16th-century. True, Raleigh's tobacco created an immediate sensation at the court of Elizabeth I, but tobacco smoking actually first came to Europe by quite another means, involving neither the English nor the North American Indian.

Christopher Columbus observed the Indians of the Caribbean smoking tobacco, writing of "men with half-burnt wood in their hands." According to one story, the first European to smoke was Rodrigo de Jerez, one of Columbus's crew members, who sampled tobacco in the West Indies and brought a pinch home with him to Spain. Jerez's wife, so the tale goes, later denounced him to the Inquisition as a man who "swallows fire, exhales smoke, and is surely possessed by the devil."

Spanish explorers in Mexico found the Aztecs smoking crushed tobacco leaves in corn husks. Tobacco reached the European continent at least as early as 1558, when a Spanish physician named Francisco Fernandes, sent to the New World by King Philip II to report on its products, brought back some plants and seeds. The following year, Jean Nicot, the French ambassador to Portugal, sent tobacco seeds to the French court of Catherine de Medici. The queen reported that tobacco cured her of crippling headaches, and she immortalized Nicot by proclaiming the new plant

Nicotiana, a name recognizable in our word for tobacco's most baleful element, nicotine.

Sir Walter Raleigh may not have been the first to introduce tobacco in England. Some historians claim that one John Hawkins brought back the leaf in 1565 after a voyage to Florida. In any case, we know that Sir Walter had a large hand in popularizing tobacco smoking in Europe.

Raleigh sent Sir Francis Drake on an expedition to colonize Roanoke Island, North Carolina, in 1585. When the expedition failed, Drake returned to Europe. He brought some tobacco and smoking implements to Sir Walter, who soon became the most notorious smoker in Renaissance England. A die-hard smoker indeed, Raleigh even "tooke a pipe of tobacco a little before he went to the scaffolde."

By 1600, the "dry drink" was fashionable in much of Europe. Many pipe smokers of the time carried hand-carved tobacco rammers, used to press the shredded leaf into the pipe bowl.

305

Some of the more ornate rammers doubled as large finger rings. Smokers also had to carry ember tongs to hold the burning embers of juniper wood used to light their pipes.

Cigarettes were little known at the time. It was the beggars of Seville who get credit for creating the first paper-wrapped smokes.

Seventeenth-century doctors prescribed tobacco as a cure-all, fashioning the leaf into pills, plasters, poultices, oils, salts, tinctures, and balms. During the London plague of the 1660s, many people smoked tobacco as a preventive. Even in the later part of the century, doctors continued to prescribe the leaf for such disparate ailments as hiccoughs, imbecility, jaundice, corpulence, syphilis, and "general lousiness,"—for everything except a bad cough.

Some physicians even recommended a tobacco-smoke enema for various ailments. The enema—administered with a device known as the Clyster pipe—was said by one doctor to be "excellent good against colic." And James I of England proclaimed that the Clyster pipe was the only way to take one's tobacco. Well, different smokes for different folks.

It's odd that James would comment favorably on tobacco,

At Myrtle Grove, Sir Walter Raleigh was soothing his mind with the tobacco he had brought from Virginia, when his Irish servant, thinking his master was on fire, dashed water on him.

From the 1850s, tobacco connoisseurs have shopped at the original Philip Morris store on Bond Street, London.

in any form or guise, since the monarch had always been a bitter foe of the leaf. In his *Counterblast to Tobacco*, James described smoking as "a custom loathsome to the eye, hateful to the nose, harmful to the brain, dangerous to the lungs, and the black stinking fume thereof nearest resembling the horrible Stygian smoke of the pit that is bottomless." And you thought the Surgeon General was harsh on tobacco!

Tobacco cultivation was important in the American colonies from their earliest history. In fact, before the Revolution, tobacco was legal tender in several Southern colonies with large plantations. Virginia enacted a law ordaining that taxes be paid in tobacco. George Washington, you'll remember, was reported to have written from Valley Forge: "If you can't send men, send tobacco."

American cigarette manufacture dates from the Civil War, when Greek and Turkish tobacconists in New York City began hand-rolling expensive imported tobaccos. By that time, the cigarette—from the Spanish *cigarito*—was already the favored tobacco product in some parts of Europe. It wasn't until the 1880s, when natural leaf cigarettes made from domestic tobaccos began to dominate the market and machine-rolled butts first replaced the hand-rolled varieties

that cigarettes became affordable by all. Yet cigars and pipes remained more popular until 1920. By the 1950's, cigarettes accounted for over 80 percent of all American tobacco consumption.

In the early days of cigarette manufacture, a factory worker could hand-roll about 18,000 cigarettes per week. Crude machines for cigarette-rolling began to appear in the mid-1870s. In the following decade, the machines replaced hand-rollers almost completely, with one machine doing the job of 50 workers. A modern machine can turn out about 1,500 cigarettes per minute, or 36,000 packs in an eight-hour day.

In 1880, American cigarette production stood at a mere half

307

billion. By 1895, the figure had soared to four billion. A large increase following World War I pushed the figure up to 124 billion. Another big rise after World War II brought the total to 400 billion. In 1975, cancer not withstanding, American cigarette consumption passed the 600-billion mark for the first time.

Has the increased awareness of the dangers of tobacco smoking lowered cigarette use to any great extent? In 1964, the year of the Surgeon General's first warning regarding smoking, 52 percent of all men of presumed smoking age were regular smokers; by 1976, the figure stood at only 32 percent. But smoking among women showed an increase over the same period, and total consumption has risen since 1971. By 1975,

> One day, Dr. Creighton, Bishop of London, was riding on a train with a meek curate. The Bishop who ardently loved his tobacco, took out his cigar case, turned to his companion, and said with a smile, "You don't mind my smoking, do you?"
>
> The curate bowed, and answered humbly, "Not if Your Lordship doesn't mind my being sick."

there were an estimated 30 million former-smokers among the ranks of the non-smokers, with some 50 million persons still clinging to the habit.

Despite the Surgeon General's warning—repeated on every pack of American cigarettes—the United States still leads the world in per capita cigarette smoking. In 1973, the average American 15 years of age or older smoked 3,812 cigarettes—that's about a half pack daily for each person, and well over a pack for each smoker. Japan is close behind with 3,270 cigarettes per capita annually, the United Kingdom third with 3,190, and Italy fourth with 2,774. West Germany, Denmark, and Sweden round out the top seven.

Cigarettes today are sold in three basic sizes—regular non-filter, regular filter, and 100-mm. king size—but in the past, butts have been sold in a wide range of sizes. In the 1930s, when cigarettes were taxed individually in some places, to save tax, one manufacturer brought out "Head Plays," each cigarette 11 inches long.

In 1933, a diminutive bellboy named Johnny immortalized Philip Morris cigarettes with his famous "Call for Phil-lip Mor-ress."

Philip Morris's "Marlboro" remains the most popular cigarette on earth, the 136 billion sold annually making the entire world "Marlboro Country."

In the early days of the tobacco industry, as today, manufacturers vied with each other in creating eye-catching advertisements.

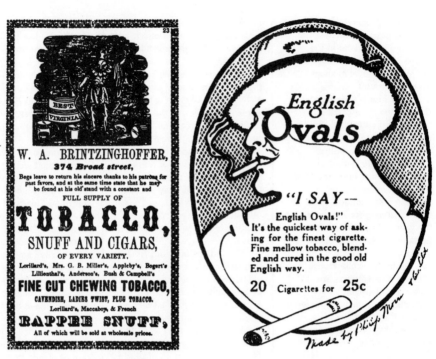

"Lilliput" cigarettes, only one-and-a-quarter inches long, appeared in England in the 1950s. And "English Ovals" are just that—oval in shape instead of round.

Philip Morris's *Marlboro* remains the most popular cigarette on earth, the 136 billion sold annually making the entire world "Marlboro Country."

Long before cigarettes became popular here, the pipe was well entrenched. Pipe smoking was common even among women for a time, and the wives of two American presidents—Andrew Jackson and Zachary Taylor—were wont to light up in the White House. Women pipe smokers are still numerous in China, where cigarettes are rarely encountered outside the major cities.

Speaking of female pipe smokers, perhaps you've heard the one about the young lady who retired to the cafeteria during her coffee break and lit up a pipe. "That's a despicable habit," remarked an elderly woman sitting nearby. "I would rather commit adultery than smoke!"

"So would I," answered the young lady, "but there just isn't enough time during a coffee break."

The first men—or women—to smoke probably managed without any implements at all, simply inhaling smoke billowing from a bonfire of burning leaves. The Greek historian Herodotus reported that certain Scythian tribes "drank smoke" from a fire, inhaling the fumes of what was most likely marijuana.

The first pipe fashioned by man was probably a tube pipe, a simple hollow cylinder of wood or bone. Tube pipes have been found in almost every cranny of civilization, some dating back as

far as 200 B.C. And the use of a curled-up leaf as a makeshift tube pipe later led to the invention of the cigar.

In some cultures, the earliest pipe was the "mound pipe," a small mound of earth with a depression hollowed out on top to hold the tobacco, and hollow reeds protruding through the mound as rudimentary pipe stems. To make use of a mound pipe, the smoker had to lie on the ground on his belly and slip the reed through his lips. These primitive pipes were still being used by Indian soldiers in World War I.

The Indians of South America frequently built communal mound pipes, with as many as 150 people gathering around to share a smoke. When the first reed and clay pipes appeared among the Indian tribes, smoking was still regarded as a communal pastime. Thus arose the custom of passing the pipe around among the group.

Europeans exploring America in the 16th-century found some

Indians smoking a kind of tube pipe shaped like the letter "Y"— the smoker inserted the two upper prongs of the pipe into his nostrils and aimed the lower tube at a mound of burning leaves. Archaeologists in Africa have found tube pipes made of clay or reed measuring up to six feet long.

Indians of the Central United States carved stone pipes with either straight or curved stems. They smoked a blend they called *kinnikinnik*, made of tobacco, sumac leaves, and the bark of the willow tree. The Indians, who considered tobacco a sacred herb and regarded smoking as a sacred art, frequently shaped their pipe bowls in the form of animals and other totems. Historians have been unable to explain why some pipes found in the ruins of ancient Indian settlements were carved in the form of elephants and sea cows, two creatures the Indians had presumably never seen.

The calumet, or peace pipe, was usually a long, slender pipe with a wooden stem and a shorter stone end-piece containing the bowl. The calumet was considered a token of peace and

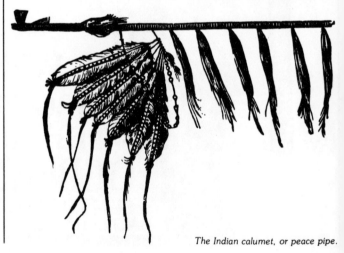

The Indian calumet, or peace pipe.

The hooka, an Oriental water pipe.

friendship, and pioneers exploring the American West often took along calumets in the event they ran into hostile Indians. No instance has ever been recorded of an Indian violating the peace-pipe compact.

Incidentally, the word *tobacco* comes from the Indian word for the tube of the calumet, not from their name for the plant. When East Coast Indians introduced smoking to the Europeans, they presented their pipe and repeated the word *tobacco* to urge the stranger to put the calumet tube in his lips. The Europeans naturally assumed the Indians were referring to the substance they were smoking, and the leaf was forever after known as tobacco.

The water pipe, a popular means of smoking in the Near East for centuries, was probably invented by the Persians for smoking hashish. The earliest water pipes were called *nargeelehs,* from the Arabic word for coconut, since the coconut was used as the base for the first hydro-cooled fumigators. Later, the Arabs fashioned more elaborate pipes from glass crystal.

The *hookah* is a kind of water pipe with a number of flexible stems, called *narbeeshes,* each from six to 30 inches long. British officers in India often employed servants called *burdars,* whose sole duty was to attend to their master's *hookah.*

In a water pipe, smoke is drawn from the bowl into the base, where it is cooled by water vapor and then drawn through the stem. Some Persian men were so partial to the taste of smoke-flavored water that they regularly forced their wives to smoke four or five bowlfuls of tobacco or hashish in succession to produce a well-flavored drink.

The earliest pipes popular in Europe were made from clay. Clay pipes with small bowls were favored in England, the story goes, because in the first days of tobacco smoking the English-man's desire for the leaf far outpaced the supply; to indulge frequently, then, the Englishman had to content himself with a small pinch at each light-up.

The clay pipe had the distinct disadvantage of heating up rapidly, which might also explain why its bowl was so small. The French, true to form, developed clay-pipe making to a fine art, molding their pipe bowls to depict religious, military, and domestic scenes.

There were two basic types of clay pipe popular in 17th-century England, the cutty and the churchwarden. The small cutty, equipped with a stem of about three inches, was the more popular among the general populace, selling for as little as three for a penny. But the cutty stem was often so short that a pipe took on the nickname of "nose warmer."

The churchwarden was fitted with a stem of some eight to ten inches, and a more decorated bowl. As a rule, the wealthy opted for the churchwarden, and frequently bought elegant cases in which to carry their prize pipes. When the lower classes began smoking churchwardens to emulate the rich, the case was still beyond their means, so many an Englishman took to carrying his long pipe in a hole cut through his hat brim.

Washington Irving, in his *History of New York,* presents a tongue-in-cheek account of Dutch settlers in New Amsterdam who were ardent smokers of the long pipe until their leader, William the Testy, proclaimed smoking illegal. The furious populace refused to obey the edict, so William compromised by permitting smoking only from short-stemmed pipes. But the short pipes brought the bowl so close to the smoker's face that the fumes "befogged the cerebellum, dried up all the kindly moisture of the brain and rendered the people . . . as vaporish and testy as the governor himself."

The clay pipe is now but a curiosity piece. Only a handful of claypipe artisans remain to satisfy the smoker with a taste for the unusual.

Today, there are basically five kinds of pipe popular throughout the world. Many Alpine people prefer the porcelain pipe, usually fitted with a long, curving stem and two bowls, one for the tobacco and one for the residue of juices. Other smokers prefer cherrywood pipes. The most popular varieties by far are the meerschaum, briar, and corncob.

Meerschaum is a magnesium silicate compound mined extensively in Asia Minor. The Germans thought the substance in its raw form resembled petrified sea foam, and dubbed it *meerschaum*—literally, "sea foam." Turkish craftsmen today still carve meerschaum pipe bowls by hand, favoring busts of Cleopatra, Bacchus, and other gods and notables.

The briar pipe owes its existence to a French smoker who journeyed to Corsica in the 1820s. Arriving on the island and discovering that his prized meerschaum pipe had been shattered in transit, the Frenchman asked a local artisan to carve a new pipe from the wood of the *bruyere*, or heath tree, which grows extensively on the

island. The smoker was so delighted by the finished product that he sent heath wood and roots to France and began manufacturing the *bruyere*, or briar pipe. Today, the briar pipe is the most popular pipe in the world.

The corncob is an American invention. John Schranke, a Dutch immigrant farmer living in Washington, Missouri, first whittled pipes from corncobs as a hobby. In 1869, Schranke brought one of his creations to the shop of a friend, Henry Tibbe. Tibbe improved the pipe by filling in the uneven surfaces with plaster of paris, and then he began to market the pipes. A hundred years later, corncob pipe production stood at around 10 million per year. The president of the largest corncob pipe manufacturer in the world still uses Tibbe's workshop as his headquarters.

Corncob pipes have the overwhelming advantage of being dirt cheap. At the other end of the scale, the most expensive pipe in the world is the Charatan *Summa Cum Laude,* a straight-grain briar-root pipe that sells in the vicinity of $2,500!

But even such an expensive pipe won't guarantee a perfect smoke. To some tobacco connoisseurs, there's only one kind of pipe you can count on, as Henry Brown noted, in 1896, in a poem that begins:

There's clay pipes an' briar pipes
  an' meerschaum pipes as well;
There's plain pipes an' fancy
  pipes—things just made to sell:
But any pipe that can be bought
  for marbles, chalk, or pelf,
Ain't ekal to the flavor of th' pipe
  you make yourself.

The Churchwarden pipe, made of clay, has an ultra-long stem to cool the smoke.

The odor-free Electra-Pipe reduces tar and nicotine and furnishes a cooler smoke.

312

Toilets

Through all the films set in days gone by, and all the historical novels purporting to show how our ancestors lived during various eras, one particular element of daily life is forever conspicuous by its absence. You may have wondered, as Ramses, Nero, Sir Lancelot, or Marie Antoinette moved across the screen or page: how and where did they go to the toilet?

In a few areas of technology, civilization has regressed rather than progressed through the ages. Indoor plumbing is one such area. It's true that during some past eras the sanitation facilities of even the wealthiest households were far less convenient than the lowliest of modern American bathrooms. But if we go back far enough in time, we can find plumbing facilities superior to anything in the United States just a century or so ago!

The earliest known indoor plumbing facilities in Europe were found in the palace of Knossos, Crete, which dates from about 2000 B.C. Terra cotta pipes were ingeniously constructed of tapered sections and fitted together, narrow end into wide end, to give the water a shooting motion. One latrine at Knossos with a wooden seat over an earthenware pan evidently had a reservoir and piping for flush water. With a few scattered exceptions, no such sanitary device was to appear in England until the 18th century.

Around the time of Knossos's construction, people in the Indus Valley of present-day Pakistan were enjoying the luxury of in-door latrines flushed with stored water and connected by conduits to street drains. Some of the earthenware pipes and sewers installed in ancient Mesopotamian cities are still in workable order today. In Egypt, aristocrats relished the comfort of limestone seats on their latrines. But the vase positioned below the key-hole-shaped seat opening had to be removed for cleaning quite often.

The Romans were the first to construct water-supply and drainage systems on a large scale. Thirteen aqueducts brought water to the Imperial City from nearby mountains, though contrary to general belief, most of these aqueducts were underground. Of the 220-mile total length of Rome's eight main aqueducts, only 30 miles were constructed above ground. At its peak, the water-supply system of ancient Rome provided about 300 gallons of water per person daily. Today, the London water system provides only about 50 gallons per person each day.

By the fourth century, many private homes in Rome were equipped with flush toilets. Stone reservoirs stored flush water, and drains connected the latrines to outdoor sewers. Some homes found in ruined Pompeii were equipped with as many as 30 water taps. But most of the less fortunate Romans had to content themselves with public latrines, of which there were never more

The earliest known indoor plumbing facilities in Europe were found in the palace of Knosses, Crete, which dates from about 2000 B.C.

313

than 144 in the presumably odoriferous capital.

The Romans evidently brought the first flush toilets to England, for fortresses constructed along the Roman-built Hadrian's Wall included bathhouses and latrines with drains. Comfort was still at a premium: one latrine consisted of a 31-foot-long trough covered by wooden seats. Wooden seats were common in England right up to the 18th century, when Dr. Samuel Johnson expressed the view that "the plain board is best."

As the Roman Empire perished, so did plumbing in Europe. Monasteries could boast the best plumbing facilities of the later Middle Ages. Most monasteries included a sanitary wing, known as the *rere-dorter,* that contained all of the monastery's latrines. The schedule of the monk was so tightly regulated that most members of the monastery were required to use the latrine at the same time. Therefore, the reredorter was usually quite large—145 feet long at Canterbury.

A rere-dorter usually consisted of a long line of latrines partitioned from their neighbors, each with a seat set against the wall, and often, a window. Flush water was provided by stored rainwater or the waste water from lavatories or baths. A drain under the latrines carried off the waste, although frequently the reredorter was built over a diverted stream.

In England, Tintern Abbey employed the rising tide of the nearby Severn River to flush out its latrines. At Redburn Abbey, a private latrine for the Abbot was constructed after monks complained that they were "ashamed when they had to go to the necessary in his presence." At the abbey at St. Albans, latrines were

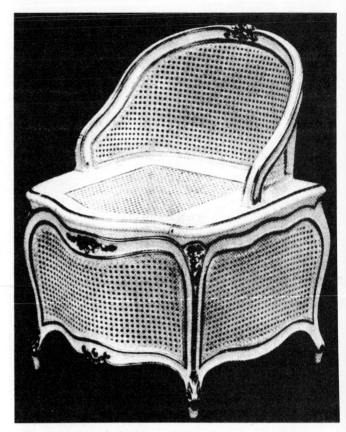

Chaise Percée. Unquestionably the snazziest john extant. Designed to fit over a water closet, this hand-carved, wooden cane seat, with cane back and cane sides, is finished in antique white and gold. This contraption is patterned after the chaise percée used by the French kings.

positioned over a 25-foot ditch that, hundreds of years later, still contained some of the buckthorn seeds the monks used as a laxative. Also found in the ditch were pieces of cloth torn from old gowns that the monks used for toilet paper.

The first toilet paper manufactured in the United States, incidentally, was unbleached pearl-colored manilla hemp paper made in 1857 by a New Yorker named Joseph Gayetty. Gayetty's name was watermarked on each sheet. The paper, which sold for 50¢ per 500 sheets, was called "Gayetty's Medicated Paper," and billed as a "perfectly pure article for the toilet and for the prevention of piles."

Medieval monks usually referred to the latrine with the euphemism *necessarium.* But the most common name for the privy during the Middle Ages was *garderobe,* or "wardrobe," a term euphemistically comparable to the

314

modern *rest room, water closet, comfort station,* or *john.*

The word *john* probably comes from an older term for the latrine, *jakes,* which in turn may be derived from the common French name Jacques. The word *privy,* of course, comes from "private." A score of jokes to the contrary, the latrine has absolutely nothing to do with the English position of Privy Councilor. Even our word *toilet* is a euphemism, adapted from the French *toilette,* a woman's dressing table or room, in turn derived from *toile,* a kind of cloth.

Garderobes were usually set within the thick stone walls of medieval castles, or in niches in turrets or buttresses. Each garderobe contained a wooden or stone seat, with either a shaft underneath to carry away the waste, or a pit that had to be cleaned out from time to time. Frequently, garderobes were mounted one above another on each floor of the castle, as is customary in modern apartment buildings. The drainage shafts usually emptied directly into the moat. Originally defensive, the moats must have quickly become rather offensive. Before you scoff, you might remember that even today most American cities channel their raw sewage directly into the nearest body of water.

A modern visitor to a medieval castle might find the garderobes rather cold, bleak places to spend one's precious time. Actually, many garderobes were quite cozy. Some were positioned beside chimney shafts to provide warmth, with wood paneling, matting, or papered walls, and even bookshelves! St. Gregory highly recommended the latrine

as a place for reading and serious thought.

As the castle gave way to the city, public latrines began to appear over urban streams and watercourses. Like the moats performing similar duty, these watercourses quickly became foul-smelling cesspools. As early as 1307, the River Fleet in London was inaccessible to ships due to the accumulation of filth. During the 14th century, the London street Sherborne Lane became known as Shiteburn Lane in tribute to the pungent watercourse to which it ran parallel. Frequently, latrines were attached to the second or third story of a house, overhanging a street or alley. Streets and watercourses had to be cleaned out periodically by specialists known as *gong-fermors.*

The London Bridge, which at the time carried over a hundred homes, could boast just one privy. Most bridge dwellers, therefore, opted for a more direct route to the River Thames, leading to a popular definition of London Bridge as a structure "wise men go over and fools go under."

Leonardo da Vinci designed a latrine with a flush toilet, ventilation shaft, and even a door that would close automatically in the event that the previous user was negligent. In 1499, a London man built a water closet with a flushing mechanism. But Leonardo's suggestions went unheeded, and the early water closet went unnoticed, resulting in a few more centuries of unnecessary olfactory offense.

During the 16th century, the garderobe was replaced by the *close stool,* a portable, lidded box. The user flipped the lid, sat down on the open seat, and made a contribution to a removable pot inside the box. European

noblemen often had their close stools decorated with ribbons and gilt nails, and more importantly, velvet-padded seats. Some were even fitted with lockable lids to guard against unauthorized usage.

Of course, the close stool did not solve the problem of what to do with the collected waste. As cities continued to grow during the 17th and early 18th centuries, open fields and yards for dumping vanished. For the most part, close stool pots had to be emptied out the window. City residents customarily emptied their pots in the evening, shouting out "gardy-loo," a corruption of the French *gardez l'eau,* "watch the water," to warn passersby below. Since the streets were not cleaned until morning, a walk at night could be treacherous for more than one reason.

One enterprising Scot of the era may have invented the world's first pay toilet when he carried around a bucket and shielding cloth for any fastidious pedestrian who would not condescend to relieve himself in the nearest alleyway. Temporary rental of the bucket and cloth would set you back a mere half-penny.

Members of royal households enjoyed considerably better accommodations. French monarch Louis XIV made use of a comfortable, highly decorated close stool euphemistically known as a *chaise percée* (open chair), *chaise d'affaires,* or *chaise necessaire.* His palace at Versailles at one time included 264 stools, but Louis' favorite was a black lacquered box with inlaid mother-of-pearl borders, a red lacquered interior, and a padded seat of green velour. The monarch's *chaise percée* sometimes served as a throne, and it was considered a high honor to be granted an audience with His Majesty while he was heeding the call of nature that all men, rich and poor, are similarly obliged to answer.

During the early 18th century, Europeans apparently became more self-conscious of their sanitary habits, for close stools began to appear hidden away inside pieces of furniture. A common custom of the time was to cover the lid of a close stool with a pile of dummy books. To correctly identify the apparatus they shielded, the dummy books always bore the title of *Voyage au Pays Bas* or *Mysteres de Paris. Journey to the Low Country* makes some sense—but *Mysteries of Paris?* The period may also have seen the first appearance of the "Men's" and "Ladies'" rooms. The host of a 1739 Parisian ball had the words inscribed on latrine doors to designate the sex for which each was reserved.

The *bidet,* that peculiarly Gallic instrument for feminine hygiene, also made its first appearance during the early 18th century. The device, first mentioned in 1710, must have been unfamiliar to many Frenchmen in 1739, when a dealer offered a bidet as a "porcelain violin-case with four legs." By 1750, portable metal bidets with removable legs were commonly secreted inside pieces of furniture.

Today, bidets are prominently displayed in almost all French hotels, and in many hotels in Italy, Greece, and Spain as well, though the device is rarely seen in any but the finest English or American hotels. The Ritz Carlton Hotel in New York was originally equipped with bidets, but the hotel was forced to remove them after a flood of complaints from outraged puritanical guests.

It was late in the 18th century that the water closet, or W.C., began to appear in Europe. Developed mainly by Englishmen Alexander Cummings and Joseph Bramah, the earliest W.C.'s consisted of a stool with an attached handle. When the handle was pulled, water from a reservoir mounted above the stool was channeled into the bowl, while a plug was opened to drain the latrine. Oddly enough, the English patent office had been opened for 158 years before it received its first application for a water closet patent, that of Cummings in 1775—almost 300 years after an unnamed genius built the first London W.C.

Early water closets were far from perfect, however, and the drains that carried waste to the sewer or cesspit frequently filled with muck that might remain undisturbed for up to 20 years. When the stench became unbearable, it was time to summon the *night men,* the descendants of the earlier gongfermors and the ancestors of the modern plumber.

By 1815, water closets were in general use in fashionable English homes. But the poor still had to content themselves with public privies, which were sorely lacking in both quality and quantity—many blocks had but one privy. At night, most people had to make use of the chamber pot, called *jerry pot* in England. The jerry was descended from the medieval *orignal,* a widemouthed vase usually kept at the foot of the bed so that those in need might relieve themselves without surrendering the warmth of their blankets.

Nineteenth-century jerries often bore humorous drawings or poems, both inside and outside. Popular thunder-mug ditties included this gem:

Use me well and keep me clean,
And I'll not tell what I have seen.

One jerry-maker with a sense of humor devised a pot with a concealed music box that chimed into song when the pot was lifted.

"Carriage pots" were often placed under the seats of carriages for those in too much of a hurry to duck into the bushes. A woman could lift the seat cushion, then sit down on the open board below, and shielded by her wide hoop skirt, relieve herself in broad daylight as her coach rattled through a crowded city street.

In case you were wondering, "jerry-built" most likely has nothing to do with the jerry. The term, which means cheaply, shabbily constructed, is usually traced to either the city of Jericho, jelly, the French word *jour* (day), or a presumably disreputable Liverpool contracting firm known as Jerry Brothers. But it may be related to the gypsy term for excrement.

By the mid-19th century, the waste deposited in privies, water closets, and jerries still found its way to the nearest cesspit or stream, a practice that was both odious to the nose and dangerous to the health of the populace. It wasn't until the 1860s, when a cholera outbreak in England was traced to poor sanitary facilities, that modern drainage systems began to appear in English cities. Around that time, London's most offensive stream, the already bridged-over Fleet Ditch, was finally recognized for what it had become—a sewer—and replaced with a large sewer main.

In 1889, D.T. Bostel of Brighton invented the washdown water closet, the basic prototype of the modern toilet. In the washdown W.C., a tube attached to an overhead reservoir sprayed water over the sides of the bowl after each use. An S-shaped drain allowed clean water from the last flush to remain in the bottom of the bowl between uses.

By the 1890s, water closets for the most part resembled rather elaborate versions of the modern toilet. Some bowls were hidden by sinks that could be swung away when the bowl was needed. Other bowls were placed inside chairs, or fitted with elaborately styled supports in the shape of lions and other animals.

By the way, you can still buy a similar chair to conceal your home's least savory accoutrement. For about $550, a New York firm will send the man or woman who has everything a hand-carved caned seat to fit over a toilet bowl.

People in some Oriental countries prefer to squat over a simple hole in the floor, fitted with a drain, of course. In many parts of the world the outhouse or public privy are still the rule, but in most developed nations the trusty flush toilet bowl is the device found in almost all bathrooms. Toilet bowls are made of white glazed stoneware, glazed porcelain, or vitreous china, with or without a reservoir. A toilet with a reservoir employs a float to shut off the entering water when the reservoir is filled. Toilets without reservoirs draw their water directly from the water-supply pipes, and can be flushed again and again without waiting for the reservoir to fill up—an advantage that has made this kind of toilet unpopular among water-supply officials in some cities. Although the overhead reservoir has virtually disappeared in new American homes, we still call the handle on a modern toilet a "chain" in memory of its dangling predecessor.

Among the many names now applied to the toilet, *pissoir* and *crapper* are probably considered two of the more vulgar. Actually, *pissoir* is the accepted term for the enclosed public urinals that still appear on the sidewalks of Paris and other French cities. And the term *crapper* is derived, in the most curiously coincidental linking of an inventor with his invention, from Thomas Crapper, a 19th-century English sanitary engineer.

At the tender age of 11, Crapper left his home in Thorne, Yorkshire, and walked 165 miles to London, where he began work as a plumber's assistant. In 1861, he founded his own sanitation business. On the strength of a number of Crapper's inventions, the firm was soon installing the world's most advanced W.C.'s in English homes.

In 1889, D.T. Bostel of Brighton invented the washdown water closet, the basic prototype of the modern toilet.

317

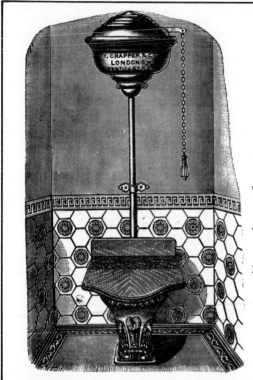

CRAPPER'S

Improved

Registered Ornamental

Flush-down W.C.

With New Design Cast-iron Syphon Water
Waste Preventer.

No 518.

Improved Ornamental Flush-down W.C. Basin
(Registered No. 145,823), Polished Maho-
gany Seat with flap, New Pattern 3-gallon
Cast-iron Syphon Cistern (Rd. No. 149,284),
Brass Flushing Pipe and Clips, and Pendant
Pull, complete as shown £6 15 0

The original crapper.

Crapper's major innovation was a mechanism that shut off the flow of clean water when the reservoir was filled. Previously, the supply of clean water had to be turned on and off by the user, and many fastidious Victorians preferred to leave the water running continually to assure cleanliness.

In Crapper's W.C., the user pulled the chain to raise a plate inside the reservoir that propelled water up a tube and into the pipe leading to the bowl. As the water level in the reservoir went down, a float sank until it opened the attached intake valve. The same float closed the valve when the reservoir was filled again. Since

the clean water valve could not open unless the chain was pulled, the saving of water with Crapper's W.C. was considerable.

The ingenious sanitary engineer advertised his product as "Crapper's Valveless Waste Preventer—Certain Flush with Easy Pull," although individual models later took on such names as Deluge, Cascade, and Niagara. In the 1880s, Crapper's firm installed the sanitary facilities in Queen Victoria's Sandringham House—including 30 toilets and a bathroom with side-by-side sinks

labelled *Head & Face, Hands,* and *Teeth.* Expensive cedar wood was used for the toilet seats, since the wood, in the words of a Crapper official, "has the advantage of being warm . . . and subtlety aromatic."

The term *crapper,* little used in England, was introduced to the American idiom by GI's returning from World War I who found Thomas Crapper's name emblazoned on many English toilets. To those who remain skeptical, we might point out that the firm of "Thomas Crapper & Co., Merchants of Sanitary Equipment," has achieved four royal warrants, and operates "By Appointment to Her Majesty the Queen."

TOMATOES

The tomato is now such an integral part of many southern European cuisines, especially Italian and Spanish, that you'd surely surmise that the plant is a native of Mediterranean parts. But spaghetti sauce and Spanish omelette notwithstanding, the tomato was unknown in Europe until the 16th century—the fruit is actually indigenous to South and Central America.

Spanish explorers in the New World found the Mayans cultivating a plant they called *tomatl*, and brought back some seeds to Europe for experimentation. Tomatoes, it was found, would grow well in Iberia. At first, the Spanish didn't quite know what to do with them—the tomato was considered too tart to be enjoyed as a fruit. But an adventurous chef at the Spanish court combined tomatoes with olive oil and onions for Europe's first tomato sauce, creating a culinary sensation at the royal dinner table.

The English were at first skeptical of the new fruit—or is it a vegetable? A Briton named Gerard tasted the tomato during a visit to Spain in the 1590s and remained unimpressed. "In Spain and those hot regions," he wrote, "they eat the Apples of Love prepared and boiled with pepper, salt, and oyle; but they yield very little nourishment to the body . . .

Likewise, they eat the Apples with oyle, vinegre, and pepper mixed together for sauce to their meat, even as we in these cold countries doe Mustard."

Well, it seems that the mustard-catsup controversey has rather ancient roots. Gerard brought some tomato seeds back to England for his garden, but found the plant "of ranke and stinking savour."

"Apples of Love?" Yes, that's what the tomato was called for hundreds of years after its introduction in Europe. The origin of the term is uncertain, but one doubtful tale suggests that Sir Walter Raleigh dubbed it thus when he presented a tomato plant to Queen Elizabeth and affectionately told her his gift was an "apple of love." Another story has it that love apple, or *pomme d'amour* in French, is derived from the Italian *pomo di mori*—"apple of the Moors," since Italians at the time called the Spanish *Mori*. And claims have been heard for the erstwhile belief that tomatoes, along with vanilla, cocoa, and many other New World novelties, were aphrodisiacs.

The French were introduced to the tomato via Spain, but the *pomme d'amour* didn't enter the classic cuisine until the 19th century, when Empress Eugenie brought Spanish dishes to the French court. In Italy, meanwhile, the plant made its first appearance around 1544, and quickly became a popular farm product in the southern regions.

Italy now produces some three-and-a-half million tons of tomatoes annually for home consumption and export throughout the world. Spain, Portugal, and Greece have become major exporters of the tomato as well.

Oddly enough, even while the tomato was being widely cultivated and eaten in southern Europe, many people in England and northern Europe considered the raw fruit poisonous until the early 19th century, and cultivated the tomato chiefly as a decorative plant. Though the tomato is a New World native, most Americans shied away from the presumably poisonous plant until Robert Gibbon Johnson stood on the steps of the Salem, New Jersey courthouse in 1830, and dared to eat a raw red tomato. Onlookers were horrified, and fully expected Johnson to die before the next morning!

Johnson did not, of course, suffer death by tomato; and by

1860, the plant was accepted by most Americans as versatile, delicious—and safe. By 1900, the tomato was a major farm crop in the United States. Today, tomato production tops the 40-million bushel mark each year. But that's not enough for the American appetite—another three or four million bushels are imported each year from Mexico and Europe.

The tomato is vine-ripened in warmer climes, but grown almost exclusively in hothouses in England, northern Europe, and some parts of the United States. The plant requires strong, steady sunshine. Hothouse tomatoes are usually picked when fully grown—but still green—and placed in cartons for the ride to market. Many American carton tomatoes are sprayed with dye to provide them with a "real" tomato color; but these carton tomatoes are, not surprisingly, far inferior to the vine-ripened variety in both flavor and nutritive value.

The "love apple" has become one of our most versatile plant foods, eaten raw, pickled, cooked, or pureed, and made into soups, sauces, pastes, preserves, juices, and dehydrated flakes. Tomato juice—the major weapon in the arsenal of many anti-hangover potions—was virtually unknown in America until 1929, when the first 230,000 cases were canned. Today, we gulp down some 35 million cases of juice each year.

And let's not forget catsup. The ubiquitous red condiment reportededly was based on an Oriental invention, called "kay-chup" in Malay, and was enjoyed in England for some 100 years before becoming popular in the United States. Some dictionaries, incidentally, will accept not only "catsup" and "ketchup," but "catchup" as well. The H.J. Heinz Company of Pittsburgh, packers of pickles and horse-radish, began marketing their catsup in 1876. The Heinz name soon became virtually synonymous with the condiment—despite a reputed 56 other varieties of product.

There is no standard formula for ketchup, but most are made from various combinations of tomato pulp, sugar, salt, vinegar, spices, and sometimes, mustard. The U.S. Food and Drug Administration merely stipulates what optional ingredients may be added, and the maximum amounts of sugar and preservatives allowed.

The largest tomato on record, a proud 1974 product of the British Isles, tipped the scales at a whopping four-and-a-half pounds—that's a lot of catsup!

Let's settle once and for all that oft-echoed query: is the tomato a fruit or a vegetable? The question is difficult to answer. Botanically, the tomato is a fruit, the seed-bearing berry of the *Lycopersicon esculentum*. But in the United States, the tomato is classified as a vegetable for trade purposes, since it is most often eaten *with* the meal, rather than *after* it. In short, the "fruit" is used as a "vegetable." But to further cloud the issue, a U.S. ruling dating from 1893 defines the tomato as a fruit when it is eaten out of the hand or as an appetizer. Legally, then, the tomato in the juice you sip before dinner is a fruit, and the tomato in the salad that follows is a vegetable!

And one more thing: do you say "tom-A-to" or "tom-AH-to?"

Though the tomato is a New World native, most Americans shied away from the presumably poisonous plant until Robert Gibbon Johnson stood on the steps of the Salem, New Jersey courthouse in 1830, and dared to eat a raw red tomato. Onlookers were horrified, and fully expected Johnson to die before the next morning.

320

Toothpaste

Americans presently consume over one billion tubes of toothpaste each year, each tube a product of the very latest refinements in modern dental science. Yet caries, or tooth decay, is by far the most common disease in the United States today, afflicting about 90 percent of all people. Ancient peoples had neither effective toothbrushes nor toothpastes of any seeming worth, but we have no proof that they suffered from tooth decay any more than people do today!

Equally puzzling, many people who never put a brush to their teeth, go through life without a single cavity, while others who brush regularly spend considerable time in the dentist's chair. Diet certainly has an effect on dental health, for people sharing certain cuisines are conspicuously free from tooth decay. But the precise nature of tooth decay—and the way to prevent it—remain largely a mystery.

The science of decay prevention is relatively new. Early dentistry was entirely corrective—decayed teeth that became too painful to bear were unceremoniously removed with forceps, twine, or whatever else was handy. Medicinal remedies were often tried first, but most were of questionable value. One ancient remedy for toothache was to eat a mouse! Only since 1910 have dentists largely turned their attention to preventive dentistry, treating the teeth *before* they begin to decay.

The first tooth-cleaning device was undoubtedly the toothpick. Gold toothpicks dating from around 3500 B.C. have been found among ancient ruins in Mesopotamia, many of them encased in skillfully decorated gold boxes. It's doubtful that many people could have availed themselves of such luxury. The Greeks and Romans may have employed a brush or toothpick for cleaning their teeth, but a finger or a sponge were more the rule—perhaps dabbed in *dentifricium*, aromatic tooth powder. In India, sixth-century physician Susruta advised that "a man should leave his bed early in the morning and brush his teeth," promising that cleaning "removed bad smells from the mouth," and promoted "cheerfulness of mind."

Until modern times, two varieties of toothbrush were employed, the *fiber-pencil* and the *bristle-brush*. The *fiber-pencil* consisted of pieces of root or twig attached to the end of a thin handle, similar in design to the brush used for oil painting. Though the wood must have offered a rather rough brush, the substances most commonly used contain some of the very chemicals used in modern toothpastes. A fiber-pencil brush called a *misrak* was popular for a long time among Arabs, and Mohammed himself used the *misrak* as a religious symbol. Ancient Brahmins of India, who brushed their teeth with cherry wood while facing the sun, also considered the act of brushing to have religious significance. Natives of Ceylon, meanwhile, placed their pearly-whites on an altar when they had fallen out, beseeching the gods to spare those remaining—a custom not unlike the Western rite of placing a child's lost tooth under a pillow for the "tooth fairy."

In the *bristle-brush*, the toothbrush we're most familiar with, the fibers are attached at a right angle to the handle. In addition to cleaning food particles from between the teeth, a bristle-brush massages the gums. More teeth are lost to poor gums than to tooth decay.

By the 18th century, silk floss, the bristle-brush, and the fiber-pencil were all in use in Europe. The first toothbrush with synthetic bristles appeared in 1938, dubbed Dr. West's Miracle Tuft Toothbrush. The latest brushes on the market are equipped with two sets of bristles, one to remove food particles, and the other specially designed to massage the gums.

The earliest dentifrices used in conjunction with a toothbrush were made from natural oils, plant extracts, honey, or a wide range of herbal ingredients. While substances such as charcoal, chalk, baking soda, and pumice were genuinely effective, there

321

may seem to be a touch of superstition associated with the use of "crab's eye" and "dragon's blood"—but both are curious names for plant extracts!

Late in the 19th century, American commercial dentifrices began to include heavy flavoring ingredients to overcome the often bitter, astringent taste of most tooth powders or pastes. But the "active" ingredients remained, as bizarre as hart's horn, cuttlefish bone, oyster shell, and myrrh. Most dentifrices were sold in the form of powder, which could then be mixed with honey to form a paste. One dentifrice advertised in the 1870s, billed as "Magic Tooth Paste," contained marble dust, pumice powder, rose-pink, and attar of roses. The paste was suggested as a "favorite nostrum for rapidly cleaning and whitening the teeth," though it was admittedly "one not adapted for free or frequent use."

Nineteenth-century mouthwashes were hardly less drastic— straight cologne was a favorite. Today, commercial mouthwash is basically an American phenomenon. So too, it seems, is an abundance of dentists. The United States can now boast over 125,000 registered dentists, more than any other country on earth—but two out of three Americans rarely or never call on their services.

During the 1880s, an American doctor named Willoughby Miller proved that caries was due in part to bacteria in the mouth. These microorganisms produce a substance known as dental

Gum-tinted toothpaste, manufactured in France, tints the gums pink, supposedly making the teeth look whiter by comparison.

plaque, which combines with carbohydrates to form organic acids. The acids then dissolve the calcium salts that make up most of the tooth.

Certain chemicals will retard the growth of oral bacteria or blunt their effects on the teeth, and these chemicals form the active ingredients in the toothpaste commonly used today. Most dentifrices contain an abrasive such as chalk or alumina; glycerine, which retains moisture and so improves taste; a gum to serve as a binder; and small amounts of detergent and flavoring. The formulas for commercial toothpastes are constantly changing, but the trusty collapsible toothpaste tube has been a familiar sight on the bathroom sink since early this century.

Within the last 40 years, scientists have learned that fluoride ions in water are especially effective in reducing caries. Most toothpastes now feature a fluoride compound as the chief preventer of decay. Fluoride was even administered for a time in the drinking water of some American communities.

Despite the recent advances in dental hygiene, tooth decay remains a problem, perhaps as serious as ever. The best advice a dental specialist can offer against tooth decay is still to brush and floss the teeth regularly, avoid sweets, and visit a dentist frequently. If all else fails, you might try a dentifrice, imported from France, that tints the gums pink to make the teeth look whiter by comparison!

TULIPS

To many minds, the tulip and the windmill are virtually synonymous with the Netherlands. Most historians would agree that the windmill in Europe made its first appearance in the Low Countries, sometime before the 12th century. But you may be surprised to learn that the tulip is not a native of Holland, and was totally unknown in that country until the 16th century.

The colorful, cup-shaped flower, long popular among gardeners, is actually a native of the western Mediterranean and the steppes of Central Asia, and some species can be found growing wild in northern Africa, southern Europe, and in Japan.

The empire of the Ottoman Turks once included much of the tulip's natural habitat, and it was through Turkey that most tulips reached western Europe and the Netherlands.

The Turks prized the tulip, and were cultivating that flower on a large scale by the mid-16th century when the Austrian ambassador to the Turkish empire brought some tulip bulbs from Constantinople to his garden in Vienna. From Austria, the flower found its way to the Low Countries. In 1562, the first large shipment of Turkish tulips

reached Antwerp, then part of the Dutch nation.

The tulip quickly became a favorite among European gardeners and the Netherlands soon took the lead in producing prized specimens.

In the 1630s, a rage of tulip speculation, called tulipomania, gripped much of Holland, and farmers rich and poor began speculating in the tulip trade. Single bulbs of prized varieties sold for as much as $1,000—one particular bulb for $4,000, a small fortune at the time. Alas, the tulip rage tapered off within a few years, leaving thousands of Dutchmen penniless. The economic scars of the tulipomania were felt in Holland for decades.

This cross-section of the tulip graced an 18th-century botanical guide.

323

Still, the Dutch continued to raise their favorite flower. Today, the Netherlands remains the chief source of tulip bulbs for much of the world, with millions cultivated each year. The total value of Dutch horticulture approaches a quarter-billion dollars annually!

Tulips are also grown on a large scale in Belgium, the Channel Islands, and in parts of England, Ireland, and the United States.

The Turks, meanwhile, endured a period of tulipomania all their own. During the 12 years between the defeat of the Empire by Austria and Venice in 1718 and the revolution of 1730, the cultivation of tulip gardens became a craze in Constantinople.

The origins of most modern tulip varieties are untraceable, due to frequent hybridization and the plant's peculiar power of variation. Tulips grown from a single parent flower can change so greatly over the course of two or three generations that the relationship between the later specimens and their parents can be scarcely recognizable. It is this property—and not hybridization—that produces the prized variegated tulip.

New tulip varieties are raised from seeds. They produce flowers after about seven years of meticulous cultivation. At that stage, all tulips have but one color throughout. After the poorer specimens are weeded out, the good plants are saved as "breeder" tulips. A breeder tulip and its offspring may then grow for years without producing anything but flowers of the same hue.

But then, suddenly and unpredictably, some of the flowers "break," producing flowers with variegated colors. The so-called "rectified" tulip is then graded according to its coloring. If it is yellow, with purple or red markings, it is called a *bizarre*. If it is white with purple markings, it is called a *bybloemen*. If it is white with rose markings, it is called a *rose*.

Most tulips are raised from the shoots of a parent plant, not from seed. A shoot will begin producing flowers of its own in about three years. Most bulbs require a period of darkness and a thorough winter chill to bloom in spring; thus, many commercially grown tulips are produced in darkened bulb cellars. If you plant tulips in your garden, you can expect most species to bear blossoms for several seasons.

Among the many thousands of tulip varieties, we might mention the colorfully named *Rising Sun, White Hawk, Couleur de Cardinal, Pride of Haarlem,* and *Prince of Austria.*

But the tulip tree is not related to the tulip. It owes its name to its tulip-like green-yellow flowers. This tree is also known as the canary whitewood in England and the yellow poplar in the United States. Tulipwood, a white or yellow wood prized by cabinet makers, is, as you might expect, not a product of the tulip, but rather of the tulip tree.

Tulips have been the subject of at least two popular songs: *Tiptoe Through the Tulips,* and *When I Wore a Tulip, and You Wore a Big Red Rose.*

The word *tulip* has a rather odd origin. When the tulip was introduced to Europe, many gardeners saw a resemblance between the flower's shape and Turkish headwear, and they dubbed the flower *tulipan,* from *tulbend,* a Turkish word for "turban." From *tulipan* came the French word *tulipe* and the English word *tulip.* There is, as you can see, only a whimsical connection between *tulips* and *two lips.*

Photo courtesy of Consulate General of the Netherlands.

324

Vinegar

In many minds, the word "bacteria" suggests the scourge of disease, the threat of sinister microorganisms lying in wait for us and the plants and animals we rely on. But only a small percentage of all bacteria are in any way harmful to man. A great number are not only useful, but essential.

Without nitrogen-fixing bacteria in the soil, plant life would be impossible. Bacteria and other microorganisms aid in the digestive processes of most animals, including man, and play a vital part in the manufacture of cheese, the leavening of dough for baking, and the production of alcohol. Bacteria are also responsible for one of man's oldest and most useful culinary substances: vinegar.

Oddly enough, vinegar is both a product of bacterial life, and an inhibitor of bacterial growth. The specific bacteria that play a role in the production of vinegar are called *acetobacters*. In the presence of oxygen, these microorganisms convert alcohol into acetic acid, which can kill or limit the growth of other bacteria. When the strength of an acetic acid solution reaches a certain level, no bacteria, including the acetobacters themselves, can grow. Foods kept in an acetic acid solution will remain free of bacterial contamination for as long as the acid solution remains potent.

Vinegar is simply a dilute solution of acetic acid. The strength of the solution is usually between four and 12 percent, depending on the type of vinegar and its intended use. Household vinegar is low in acetic acid; vinegar used for pickling is usually of higher grain. *Grain* is the term used to measure the strength of vinegars: 10 grains are equal to one percent acid; thus "40 grain" vinegar is a four percent solution of acetic acid.

Vinegar can be manufactured from any saccharine, or sugar-containing, substance capable of converting to alcohol. Fruit juices that produce wine can also be used to produce vinegar, as can grains that are used to make beer and whiskey.

The process that turns this saccharine substance into vinegar consists of two chemical reactions. In the first, yeasts act upon sugar in the fruit or grain product and convert it into alcohol and carbon dioxide. In the second, acetobacters convert this alcohol along with oxygen into acetic acid and water—in other words, into vinegar. In most vinegar production, already fermented fruit juice or fruit mash is placed in an aerated container with a small quantity of bacteria, which convert the fermented material into an acetic acid solution.

Vinegar is used today as a food flavoring and a household cleaner, but by far its most important historical role lies in its use as a food preservative. Before refrigeration and chemical preservatives were developed, man had to rely on salting, drying, and pickling to keep food edible for any length of time. The most important pickling solution has always been vinegar.

Alcohol was the first pure organic compound made by man, and acetic acid produced by the natural souring of wine was man's first acid. The origin of vinegar's use is remote, but pickled meats and vegetables were important items in the diets of many ancient civilizations. Vinegar was mentioned in the Bible, and widely used among early peoples as a food, a preservative, and a medicine.

To the ancient Egyptians, Greeks, and Romans, vinegar was the only acid substance known. In the fourth century B.C., the Greek philosopher Theophrastus gave directions for the preparation of pigments from vinegar and lead, while the physician Hippocrates prescribed vinegar as a medicine. In the Roman Petronius' *Satyricon*, a character

A vinegar seller of old London, as depicted in a 19th-century publication.

who scratches his leg reaches for vinegar the way we might reach for a bottle of iodine.

In earlier times, most vinegar was produced from wine. The English word "vinegar," in fact, is derived from the French words *vin*, "wine," and *aigre*, "sour." France has long been noted for its fine vinegars, which have been exported since at least the 16th century. Frenchman Louis Pasteur used vinegar to a great extent in demonstrating the existence of bacteria.

There are two basic ways to manufacture vinegar: the slow barrel process and the quick generator process. The older slow barrel process is now used only for household production, while the quick generator process is used exclusively for commercial production.

In the *slow generator process*, a mixture of fermented matter—wine, fruit juice, mash, or whatever—is placed in a large aerated cask. The substance containing the acetobacters, called "mother of vinegar," is then added. Fermentation continues for about three to six months, when the vinegar is drawn off via a spigot at the bottom of the cask.

In the past 200 years, discoveries by a Dutchman named Boerhaave and another scientist named J.S. Schutzenbach determined that the rate of vinegar production will be greatly increased if both the surface area of the fermented matter and its oxygen supply are increased. The modern *quick generator process* is a result of these findings.

In this process, a tall vat or "generator" is packed with corncobs, pumice, coke, beechwood shavings, or other suitable materials, which are then covered with the bacteria-laden mother of vinegar. Alcohol trickles into the generator through the top, and comes in contact with the bacteria, in the presence of oxygen provided by air currents rising from the bottom of the vat. Thus more of the alcohol is exposed to bacteria and air at the same time, and vinegar production that once required months now requires as little as eight to 10 days.

The flavor of the vinegar produced by any process is determined by the kind of fermented materials used. In the United States, cider vinegar made from apples and apple cider is the favorite, while in France wine vinegar made from wine or grapes remains the most popular. Vinegar has also been made from fruits such as oranges and pineapples, and—believe it or not—from honey.

White vinegar, also called distilled vinegar, is a relatively tasteless substance made directly from a dilute alcohol solution. So-called wood vinegar is merely a dilute solution of acetic acid, and owes its name to the former practice of distilling acetic acid from wood. Some of the vinegars sold for household use are actually combinations of two or more kinds of vinegar, and many are flavored by the addition of spices such as garlic or tarragon.

The English favor malt vinegar, made from mixtures of barley, oats, and other grains. Malt vinegar is stronger than cider or wine vinegar, and is often used in food preservation. The first vinegar to be used in England, it originally was produced as a way of disposing of soured beer and ale.

Fortunately, most vinegar today has a less glorious origin.

Violins

An old vaudeville joke tells of a society hostess who thought it would be the height of elegance to play a few violin solos after a posh dinner. Accordingly, she had chairs set up in the living room, and invited the guests to be seated for her recital.

She began playing unevenly, and grew steadily worse. As the guests fidgeted, one music lover turned to his neighbor and politely asked: "What do you think of her execution?"

The second man replied instantly: "I'm in favor of it."

Probably no musician has been more ridiculed than the unskilled violinist, for there are few sounds more ear-piercingly offensive than the squeal of a bow scraping across the strings of an ill-played violin. But there are also few sounds more beautiful and evocative than the music of that same instrument in the hands of a master. That potential for lyric beauty has made the violin, though only a few centuries old, the most important instrument in Western orchestral music—and the violin virtuoso, along with the master pianist, the most admired of all concert soloists.

String instruments in general, including the ancient lyre and lute, originated in Asia. The bow, from Persia, was applied to early string instruments by the Arabs to produce the forbears of the modern violin family. In Europe, medieval bowed instruments included the *vielle*, with four fingered strings and a drone string, and the *rebec*, which probably had two or three strings. Of

Five-stringed waisted fiddle.

CXXII *Instrumento Indiano*

Ancient Hindu violin.

Some Stradivari violins have been valued at over $450,000.

these, not a single specimen survives. Both instruments were small, and rested on the shoulder when played.

The *viol*, which developed from these medieval fiddles, was the principal bowed instrument that was played from the 15th century until the 17th century. Normally, the viol had six strings,

and a fingerboard with frets, like the guitar. The body sloped down obliquely from the neck, and bore sound holes in the shape of the letter *c*. The instrument was held downward on, or between, the legs when played.

In its earliest use, the viol doubled vocal parts, for through the Middle Ages vocal music had been more important than instrumental music. The viol family included three instruments, one for each of the three voice parts: a treble viol, a tenor, and a bass—and later, a double bass. Eventually, composers began to write instrumental pieces for the viol trio and the solo viol.

But the viol had a weak, delicate tone. Gradually, it was altered to increase its resonance, becoming lighter, with more lightly strung strings. The treble viol evolved into the violin, while the tenor viol became the viola. The new instruments featured fretless fingerboards, and four strings like the medieval fiddles, with sound holes in the shape of an *f* rather than a *c*. But the bass viol, or *viola da gamba*, survived into the 18th century, until supplanted by the cello. The double bass viol, or *violone*, is the ancestor of the modern double bass.

The viola was the first of the new instruments to emerge, taking its name directly from the viol. The word *violin* is a diminutive form of *viola*. The cello was originally called the *violoncello*, which literally means "little violone' or "little big viol."

The violin family began to emerge around 1600, and superceded the viol during the 17th century. By 1750, the violin's form was fixed, and it has undergone only minor changes since then. The neck was made longer to increase the violin's range, and alterations were made to give the instrument a stronger tone suitable for playing in large concert halls. The violin eventually found its way back to Asia, and is now commonly used to play folk music in many nations.

The string quartet, the showpiece of the violin family, is an outgrowth of the old chamber ensemble. Until the 18th century,

LXIX. *Violino Turchesco*

Ancient Turkish violin.

this chamber group consisted of two violins along with a harpsichord and bass to play the *basso continuo,* or figured bass. But the harpsichord was an unwieldy instrument for traveling musicians or street performers. So the keyboard was replaced with the viola. By 1750, the cello had replaced the bass, and the string quartet was as it is today: two violins, a viola, and a cello.

By that time, the orchestra had still not reached its modern form. Though the Greeks were familiar with many instruments from the ancient world, they rarely used these instruments together. In medieval times, only

329

Sordino, an old type of fiddle.

The violin, though only a few centuries old, is the most important instrument in Western orchestral music.

vocal music was notated; and it's not until the 15th century that we find the earliest surviving piece of instrumental music. By the end of the next century, there was still no "orchestra" as we know it, but merely a collection of instruments—harpsichord, lutes, viols, flutes, trumpets, and drums, for instance—used in concert with lit-

tle regard for balance or grouping.

The earliest music written for an instrumental group similar to the modern orchestra was Monteverdi's opera *Orfeo*, premiered in 1607. Monteverdi was the first composer to realize that a large string section was necessary to give the ensemble a balanced tone. The viol family or the newly developed violin was adopted for the orchestral string section, and all other unbowed stringed instruments were rejected, except the harp. Initially a back-up ensemble for vocal music, the orchestra gradually assumed an existence of its own, and composers began to write music for the unaccompanied orchestra.

The orchestra remained an aristocratic luxury until later that century, when orchestral music was first performed in theaters—and many German nobles boasted private orchestras well into the 18th century. In 1626, Louis XIII established a renowned orchestral group called "The Twenty-four Strings of the King," which featured, not surprisingly, 24 stringed instruments, plus horns.

A Bach piece, written about a century later, called for an orchestra of four trumpets, two flutes, five oboes, first and second violins, violas, cellos, and drums, plus an organ and four voices. Later, composers such as Haydn and Mozart helped shape a new orchestra, with clarinets, bassoons, French horns, and double basses. The modern orchestra usually contains a string section of 18 first violins, 16 second violins, 12 violas, 10 cellos, eight double basses, and two harps; a percussion section; a woodwind section with three flutes, clarinets, oboes, and bassoons, plus a double bassoon, piccolo, English horn, and bass clarinet; and a brass section with four trumpets and trombones, six French horns, and a tuba.

The violin, now the most important single instrument in the orchestra, is also regarded by many as the most beautiful, versatile, and expressive of all musical instruments. Some may opt for the piano, but when it comes

Viola da Gamba, made in Hamburg in 1691.

to ease of transport, the violin has it all over its keyboard cousin. A violin is on the average just 23 inches from end to end, with a body 14 inches long, a neck with a fretless fingerboard, and four strings, tuned in fifths: g, d, a, e. The horsehair bow is pulled

across the strings, whose vibrations are carried by the bridge through the body, where they resonate.

The viola, tuned a fifth lower than the violin, is usually 26 inches long. In the orchestra, the viola initially doubled the cello part, until composers such as Mozart and Haydn gave the instrument independence. But solo viola pieces are rare. Bartok

331

did write a viola concerto, and Hindemith wrote a number of viola sonatas.

Similarly, the earliest cellos were used to reinforce the bass lines. But the cello took on an identity of its own during the 18th century, when it supplanted the viola de gamba. The instrument is generally 48 inches long, tuned an octave and a fifth lower than the violin. Unlike the viola, the cello is often featured as a solo instrument. Bach wrote six suites for an unaccompanied cello, and Beethoven wrote five sonatas for cello and piano.

Violin cello.

The double bass is about 72 inches from end to end, and is tuned two octaves and a third lower than the violin. The instrument originally had three strings, but it now has four, and sometimes five strings. One double bass constructed in the 19th century, called the octobass, stood more than 10 feet tall, and was played with foot levers!

At the other end of the scale, so to speak, we find a tiny violin of recent vintage, completely functional, that measured just two inches from end to end!

To the list of peculiar stringed instruments we might add the *violinista*, a sort of automated violin found in penny arcades in the 1920s. The machine was about three feet long and two feet high, and was electrically operated by air flowing through the perforations of a music roll. Then there was the *pantaleon*, the largest stringed instrument ever constructed for a single player, with 276 strings stretched over a soundboard 11 feet long. Built by an Englishman in the 1760s, the instrument was played with wooden mallets, like a xylophone.

These instruments may have been novel, but far more valuable are the simple violins produced by the greatest violin craftsmen, most of whom flourished in northern Italy between 1600 and 1750. All other musical instruments have reached the peak of their perfection during our century, but the greatest violins were undoubtedly produced during this earlier period.

Antonio and Geronimo Amati of Cremona were two of the early master violin makers who helped shape the instrument. Ge-

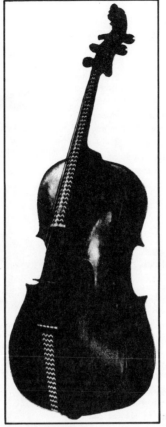

Bass viol (1662).

ronimo's son Nicholas Amati made further improvements on violin construction, but it was Nicholas' star pupil, Antonio Stradivari, who settled the design of the violin and constructed its finest specimens—though some violinists prefer the instruments of Giuseppe Guarnieri, another Cremona master of the time.

No one is quite sure what gave Stadivari's violins their exquisite tone. Some people have attributed their characteristic sound to the physical properties of the wood, or to the special pitch that Stradivari derived from the sap of trees then growing in

Italy. Others credit his varnish, whose formula has never been discovered. But basically the "secret of Stradivari" is as much a mystery today as it was more than 250 years ago.

Stradivari fashioned about 700 violins, plus scores of violas and cellos; 540 of his violins still exist. One of these instruments, made in 1716, recently sold at auction for $250,000, and other Stradivari violins have been valued at over $450,000!

Among those who have profited most by the work of Stradivari and other violin makers are the great concert violinists, such as Austrian Fritz Kreisler, who reputedly earned more than three million dollars during his career. Another violinist who was amply repaid for his hours of practice was Nicolo Paganini, an eccentric 19th-century master considered by some the greatest violinist of all time. To demonstrate his virtuosity, Paganini occasionally played instruments with just one or two strings, or deliberately played with frayed strings so that when one broke, he could bedazzle his audience by continuing to play with three strings!

Among the most determined violinists, we must certainly mention Otto Funk, who at age 62 walked from New York to San Francisco, playing his violin continually.

But among the most fortunate violinists, we must point to Alexander Schneider, who once left his violin—a Guarnieri valued at over $200,000—in a New York City taxicab. The violin was found by the cab's next passengers, who happened to be sympathetic musicians, and returned it to its thankful owner!

Weasels

Should we see some small animal running in the woods, we might guess that it was a woodchuck or a skunk, or perhaps a raccoon. Most of us do not know that there are many, many small animals which, because of their size, look alike, but which are, each one of them, a distinct species. Here are some beasties you are likely to confuse:

PARADOXURUS *Also known as the palm civet, this cat-sized Asian native feeds on fruit and vegetation as well as small animals.*

ZIBETH *A close Asian relative of the civet.*

RACCOON *A strictly nocturnal, omnivorous creature common in North America. Before eating anything, the raccoon first washes its food in the nearest available water.*

ERMINE *Some ermines are brown in summer and white in winter. All are sought for their luxurious fur.*

SKUNK *This fearless American native is most noted for the fetid-smelling secretion it squirts to ward off would-be attackers. Skunks prefer insects, but also eat small rodents, frogs, and eggs.*

WOODCHUCK *This burrowing North American native is also known as the ground hog and American marmot. The woodchuck feeds mainly on grass and other vegetation.*

POLECAT *Americans use the word "polecat" to refer to the skunk, but in Europe, the polecat is a bloodthirsty, ferretlike night hunter.*

RATEL *A clumsy-looking native of Africa and India that is often called the honey badger. Ratels live in pairs, hunting small rodents, birds, and insects.*

MONGOOSE *A small Indian native long used to control rodents. The mongoose is noted for its ability to battle the feared cobra.*

MINK *A small, slim carnivore prized for its fur. The mink has partly webbed feet, and spends much of its time in the water.*

POTOMOGALE *An arboreal native of the Americas.*

335

COATI *Also known as the coatimundi, this American tree-dweller is sometimes tamed as a pet.*

ZORIL *This African native closely resembles the skunk in both appearance and odor.*

WOLVERINE *Also known as the glutton due to its voracious eating habits. The cunning, stealthy wolverine lives chiefly in the colder regions of North America.*

MANGUE *Also known as the kusimansel, the mangue is a native of West Africa. This dark-brown coated, burrowing animal is closey allied to the mongoose.*

CIVET *A catlike carnivore from Africa and Asia, the civet is noted for a musky secretion used to make perfume.*

336

BADGER *A sharp-clawed burrower found in many northern climes, and is the namesake of the state of Wisconsin.*

GENET *The spotted, catlike genet hunts along stream banks in Africa, Europe, and the Near East.*

SABLE *This Siberian native is famous for its fur.*

MARTEN *There are a number of marten species, including the sable. Many live in trees. The fisher is a large marten.*

GLUTTON *A carnivorous mammal named for its gluttonous habits. A relative of the marten and the sable, the glutton is about two-and-a-half feet long and lives in Northern Europe and in Asia.*

TAYRA *An otter-sized, long-tailed South American native often confused with the grison.*

WEASEL *A courageous hunter, the weasel can pursue its prey up a tree or in water. Some weasels turn white in winter.*

FERRET *The ferret is actually a domesticated breed of the polecat, used since ancient Roman times to hunt rabbits and to "ferret out" rats from their holes.*

CACOMISTLE *A raccoonlike native of the United States and Mexico.*

Wild Dogs

The dog has been domesticated by man for so long, and today is such a tame, obedient member of the family, that it's easy to forget that the dog was once a wild animal.

Man began his long and happy relationship with the canine well before recorded history began. Most likely, jackals and primitive dogs, originally independent hunters and scavengers, found it advantageous to follow nomadic human hunters for the bones and food scraps left behind when they broke camp. Gradually, prehistoric man came to realize that the presence of these beasts surrounding the camp at night could benefit him, since the howling canines would warn of the approach of deadly predators.

As the hunter went out of his way to feed his watchdogs, the more dependent upon him they became. Slowly, dog and man began to join forces in hunting, the dog contributing his scent to flushing out game, and man returning the favor by providing dog with a steady diet of meat.

But wild members of the dog family still remain on earth. There follow some of the strange ones of the *Canus familiaris* species.

BRAZILIAN BUSH DOG *This wild creature belongs to a different genus than the dog proper, with one less lower molar than the family pooch.*

COYOTE *The coyote, or prairie wolf, can be found from Alaska to Central America, resting in its burrow by day, hunting and howling by night. The coyote favors small rodents, and eats a good deal of vegetable matter, but his appetite for domestic poultry has made him a menace in many Western states.*

SIBERIAN WILD DOG *A relative of the husky, this undomesticated dog lives in the frozen, forest-covered wilds of northern U.S.S.R.*

340

JACKAL *Found in Africa, Asia, and parts of Europe, the jackal is not strictly a scavenger. Jackals hunt at night, either alone or in packs, and a group can bring down prey as large as an antelope. When fresh meat is scarce, they feed on carrion, sometimes following a lion or tiger to finish off an animal the cat has killed and left partially uneaten.*

CAPE HUNTING DOG *An African doglike animal resembling a hyena, which hunts its prey in packs.*

DINGO *Also called the war rigal, the dingo is the native wild dog of Australia. Dingoes have interbred with domestic dogs brought by settlers to Australia, and few pure-bred dingoes remain in some areas. But in other regions, the rapid spread of the rabbit, which provides these wild dogs with a staple food supply, has led to a large population of dingoes whose predatory habits threaten sheep farmers.*

Wind

And t'is an ill wind that blows no good. This is certainly true for artists, who discover all kinds of possibilities in depicting the winds.

Here are drawings in varied styles and moods, each a remarkable conception.

A drawing from Judge *shows effects of the wind on a flapper of the 1920s*

"Wind in the Trees," a drawing by a Russian artist which appeared in Art of the Book, *published in Moscow in 1971*

A drawing depicting the awful blasts of England as they appeared to an English cartoonist in Punch

A concept of the winds drawn by Dorothy Braby, circa 1950, New York

A drawing by the great satirist, Grandville, which first appeared in Un Autre Monde, *published in Paris in 1844.*

The Comic Almanac *was published by Chato & Windus of London during the 1850s. This is a drawing which appeared in that notable magazine.*

Women's Apparel

Oh, my goodness gracious! What they used to wear!

Today, some of these things seem absolutely absurd, as probably our vestments of today will appear to be 100 years from now.

Here are a few of the eccentricities of a former age.

In days when it was extremely stylish for a gal to have a very thin waist, the shirtwaist came into vogue.

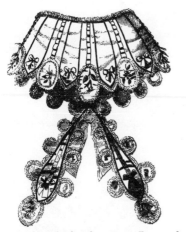

This is a fichu, a kind of decorative collar, as advertised in the London News *of the 19th century.*

Back a hundred years or so, bonnets were the rage.

Here are some very stylish hats of the 1890s.